At a Bend in the River

The History of Spread Oaks Ranch

in

Matagorda County

R.K. Sawyer

At a Bend in the River

The History of Spread Oaks Ranch

in

Matagorda County

R.K. Sawyer

www.nuecespress.com

Published in the United States of America by NUECES PRESS
www.nuecespres.com

Copyright 2023 © R.K. Sawyer, Jim Moloney and Nueces Press

ISBN 978-1-7339524-6-0

Library of Congress Control Number 2023914137

10 9 8 7 6 5 4 3 2 1

Printed and bound in the United States of America.

Sawyer, R.K. AT A BEND IN THE RIVER

Includes index.

1. Spread Oaks Ranch — History.
2. Matagorda County — History.
3. Colorado River — History.

For a complete list of Nueces Press titles please see www.nuecespress.com.

Cover design by Jeff Chilcoat.

Foreword

The owners and staff of Spread Oaks Ranch never set out to research and write a history book. It evolved initially from, of all things, debates over the ranch's landforms. The first were about the origin of the linear canals that crisscrossed the property. One popular version was that they were dug by hand, the work force composed of Chinese immigrants. But such a mammoth undertaking by a labor force of any nationality seemed far-fetched, particularly one that left no trail of its comings or goings in the county or, for that matter, the state. An equally implausible theory was that the waterways were excavated for river steamships to by-pass the log jam that clogged the Colorado River, closing it to boat traffic for nearly a century. Both legends were intriguing, but wrong.

Then there was Jennings Creek. Or lake. Or both. The morphology of the Jennings waterway appeared to alternate between the hand of nature and the hand of man. We knew it was a natural creek or lake, but its modern extent had changed markedly from hundred-year-old maps. We still wonder about its history, but we've answered a lot of questions.

Jennings Creek also opened the door to the ranch's early landowners. That first research foray revealed that the creek was named for Jacob Jennings, who arrived in Texas in 1821 as one of Stephen F. Austin's first colonists. That discovery led to other names, and it began to unveil a surprising number of early ranch deed holders who had connections to many of Texas history's best-known events. Some fought in the Texas Revolution and others the Mexican American War. One landowner held a place of prominence during the era of the great cowboys and cattlemen. Others tamed a wild land for the coming of a new crop to Texas – rice. I didn't expect these connections. The more I followed the chain of titles, the more interesting the story became.

The Wylie family of Spread Oaks Ranch is composed of energy investor Forrest Wylie, Audrey Wylie, daughter Jesse and her husband Carter Fields, and Forrest's wife Oxana Beliaeva and their son Oscar. That the Spread Oaks family underwrote and supported such a project as this reveals their passion for the land and commitment to its place in Matagorda County history. The world outside its boundaries is moving faster. Urban and industrial development have overtaken other places that also once had a deep connection to Texas history. The Spread Oaks Wylie family has ensured that, for at least one piece of geography, its legend and lore will endure.

Acknowledgements

Newspapers were the daily diary of Texas, and anyone who has spent hours staring through the optics of a microfilm reader can appreciate the benefit of digitized papers. Hundreds of newspapers were scanned for this project, and several people were involved in the effort. The writer is indebted to the Matagator Foundation for funding this project, Barbara Smith and Jennifer Bishop of the Matagorda County Museum and Samantha Denbow of the Bay City Library for its organization, and Ana Krahmer of the University of North Texas for spearheading the work. Newspapers that were digitized for this book reside with the Portal to Texas History.

Assistance with research material was provided by Michael Bailey of the Brazoria County Museum, Jennifer Bishop from the Matagorda County Museum, and Susan Chandler, Director of Nesbitt Memorial Library.

A special thanks to John Dickerson, who allowed me access to his personal library, and for the hours we talked about Matagorda County history. Gary McGee and Larry Ripper reviewed the work on the *Kate Ward* and Colorado River steamboat traffic during the mid 1800s. Doug Huebner taught me how a rice field was prepared and planted a hundred years ago, and that section is better from his input. Legal counselor Robert Riddle provided interpretation of court documents and cases. Will Kearncy kindly proofed a couple of sections.

Several people shared stories of their or their family's experiences on Spread Oaks Ranch, and their words gave life and color to the sentences. The author is indebted to Evan, Neal, and Lynn Watkins, the keepers of the Watkins family lore. Sculptor Danny Stephens told the story of Tommy LeTulle's famous statue. Danny Hemphill, Danny Savage, and Manuel Briones, who lived and worked cattle on the property, also provided valuable input.

Spread Oaks Ranch produces an unparalleled palette for photographers, and the ranch has had some good ones. Les Tompkins, Shannon Tompkins, Karen Sachar, Jerzy Trybek, Kayla Lambert, Nate Skinner, and Susan Ebert have each contributed their images to this book.

The author's knowledge of Matagorda County was greatly assisted by the compilation titled *Historic Matagorda County*. Published in 1986 by the Matagorda County Historical Commission, under the direction of the late Mary B. Ingram, the pages in its three volumes were invaluable.

Jim Moloney, owner of Nueces Press, provided a comprehensive critique. It took a month to implement his suggestions. It was time very well spent.

Introduction

There are two Colorado Rivers in North America – one west of the Rocky Mountains, and the other originating in the red siliciclastic rocks of the Llano Estacada of the Texas High Plains, then bending around the Balcones Escarpment white limestone country before meandering across unconsolidated sediments of the lowland plains. It is this river that splits Matagorda County's Bay Prairie down the center, passing through Spread Oaks Ranch and, after a journey of some 600 miles, makes its way to Matagorda Bay and the Gulf of Mexico.

The river width through the prairie varies from 200 to 400 feet and in places, the adjacent terrain falls dramatically 40 feet or more along erosional escarpments, called cutback banks. In other river bends, the topography rolls gently to the stream by way of dazzling white sand deposits that make up the river's point bars. Everywhere the river cuts the same walls of sediment that it once deposited, exposing in each parallel bed of sand, silt, and mud, a history of floods, droughts, and changes within its course. If only those layers could speak.

The river and creek banks were lined with miles of dense canebrake colonies that towered to heights of 25 feet. Their dominant flora, *Arundinaria gigantea* – giant river cane – flourished beneath a canopy of trees and included a cherry laurel dubbed the wild peach tree. Their association gave rise to the colonial name "peach and cane land" for this part of Matagorda. Beyond the river, in the higher elevations, canebrakes yielded to a community with more switchgrass, Eastern gamagrass, Florida paspalum, little bluestem Indiangrass, Maximillian sunflower, and bundle-flower – the Texas tallgrass prairie.

For thousands of years no human witnessed the annual rhythm of the changing of seasons. Spring brought out the best in the land, as native grasses changed from winter browns to shades of green. Trails within the grasslands became active – some little more than burrows, while others showed signs of large animal passages. Wildflowers covered parts of the prairie, their purple, red, white, blue, and yellow colors supporting butterflies that flashed with fluttering blots of orange, purple, green, and black. Uncountable clusters of monarchs covered tree branches along the river during migrations to and from the Mexican Sierra Madres.

The thickets were the domain of the songbirds, and along the course of the river were ceaseless flights of ibis, egrets, herons, and the distinctive pink of the roseate spoonbill. Below them, at the water's surface, thick yellow pollen masked eyes on the waterline belonging to alligators, bullfrogs, turtles, and snakes. Spring could be loud between the cacophony of songbirds, the shrieks of nightjars and big birds of prey, and the shrilling of the frogs high in the trees.

The spring bounty became more subdued during the heat of summer, the movements of most life restricted to dawn, sunset, and darkness of night. At times, the only perceptible movement was a haze of newly hatched insects, or of the sky as pastels of blue changed into pink or deep orange, or of the clouds – wispy cirrus before a warm front and withering and swelling cumulus during high pressure that turned black before a summer rain. Sometimes those rains brought lightning that illuminated the night sky, and the crack of thunder as a bolt splintered the highest tree of an oak motte, the remnants of its blackened trunk creating more space for the next seedling to grow.

Then came fall and winter, the sky changing to a deep cerulean hue after the first norther. With it, overhead, came waves of wintering waterfowl on their annual journey to Matagorda Bay – whooping and sandhill cranes; two species of swans; Canada, white-fronted, snow, and occasional blue geese; dozens of puddle and diving ducks, and countless shorebirds. Birds of prey trailed the big flocks southward. Kestrels and merlins were the earliest arrivals, then red-tailed, Coopers, and sharp-shinned hawks, and eagles – mostly the American bald, but sometimes the big golden. After a hard norther, flocks of passenger pigeons abandoned their Hill Country roosts, streaming south in countless millions to Matagorda's oak mottes, feeding on the bitter mast of first-year acorns with such voracity that they broke tree limbs.

From the 1500s to the 1700s, Karankawa Indians roamed the land that would become Matagorda County. The first European footprints were those of the Spaniards during the 16th century, a time when caravels, galleons, and brigantines carried the adventurous to the New World in pursuit of land and riches. Governor Narváez led the inaugural journey, embarking in 1527 with 600 soldiers and settlers in quest of gold and glory. A year into their ocean voyage, Narváez's lieutenant Álvar Núñez Cabeza de Vaca and a greatly diminished number of the original crew would wash ashore on the Gulf Coast. The onerous inland expedition of de Vaca – lasting some eight years and covering 2,400 miles – provided the first written account of the Lone Star State's aboriginal inhabitants, geomorphology, botany, and biology.

It was 127 years later Frenchman René Robert Cavelier, Sieur de La Salle claimed the same land for France. The Matagorda Bay that La Salle described in 1685 was "not cheering, with its barren plains, its reedy marshes, its interminable oyster-beds, and broad flats of mud bare at low tide." La Salle constructed a provisional fort on Matagorda Island before moving inland to Garcitas Creek. His bold journey was as arduous as de Vaca's before him. Disease, hunger, murders within the party – including that of La Salle – and incessant attacks by the Karankawa whittled away at the remaining Frenchmen, a few of whom made their way to French Canada, while others remained among the native population.

From these early accounts, we get a sense of a pristine but formidable land. It was the Spanish who named Matagorda County the land of "thick brush," a reference to its impenetrable canebrakes. Explorers and settlers who journeyed into the canebrakes sometimes never came out. They got lost, wandering in circles until they died from hunger, thirst, or went crazy. Canebrakes also sheltered the apex predators – panthers, red wolves, black bears, and canebrake rattlesnakes, and though they weren't always seen, they were nearly always sensed. Sometimes they were heard – mostly the wolves and panthers – and the sounds sent a chill up the spine of all but the most unflinching. The high ground was the domain of the plain's bison, their backs all that was visible in the tall prairie grasses as they grazed. Later, wild Spanish mustangs and longhorn cattle would share the same territory.

This was how the first of the settlers saw Bay Prairie. To them, it represented not so much natural magnificence as it did opportunity. Canebrakes could be burned, and the rich soils used to grow crops. Bison and longhorns could be killed for hides and meat. Rivers would be tamed for transportation, trees felled for lumber, and wild game harvested for sustenance. They would make the most of it.

Compared to so much of American history, momentous events on the Texas timeline seem implausible, measured in lengths of time of only a few years, sometimes in just months. From a Spanish to a Mexican colony then to the Republic of Texas in under 15 years, and a state in the Union a decade later. In just 15 more years it was a Confederate State, with a return to the US in another 10 years. In total, six wildly dissimilar governments in less than 50 years. When history is made with rapidity it is also made with intensity. And conflict. Texas history is the story of struggles between colonists and Native Americans, Texians and Mexicans, North against South, and White against Black. But always, it was Texian against nature – diseases, floods, droughts, and hurricanes chief among a hauntingly long list.

The story of early Matagorda County and the future Spread Oaks Ranch mirrors Texas, the drama played on a smaller stage. The southern portion of the ranch, for instance, changed hands four times in 30 years, its diverse ownership a result of untimely death, murder, and indebtedness. The northern part of the ranch has an equally colorful past.

It was on the land that is Spread Oaks Ranch that the first of the Austin Old 300 colonists put down roots and built a log cabin in 1821. Called Jennings Camp, the structure provided respite for the earliest of the Austin's settlers who put down stakes in Mexican Texas. Fourteen years later, the Texian volunteers who made-up Stephen F. Austin's ragtag army camped beside Jennings Creek before marching to Gonzales and the first battle of the Texas Revolution. The same campsite was occupied just 15 months later by General Santa Anna's troops.

A litany of landowners played parts in the Texas Revolution. Others became famous cattlemen of the day, pasturing herds of longhorn on the land before driving them north over America's great cattle trails. When rice came to Texas, the ranch was home to one of the state's most ambitious early irrigation schemes. Their work transformed the natural landscape, and the face of modern Spread Oaks Ranch reflects their hand today. In many ways, to tell the story of Spread Oaks Ranch is to tell the story of Texas.

The term *Bend in the River* is used throughout the text. It is a general term that refers to a portion of the Colorado River, mostly on its west side, that encompasses Spread Oaks Ranch and the surrounding area. Its use is simply to help define the geography for the reader as the subject matter moves from a Texas scale to a county scale, and finally to a local scale. Really, the Bend in the River naming convention covers a corridor of about a dozen meanders in the river, extending approximately from about the Matagorda-Wharton county line south to about today's Highway 35 for about eight miles.

The term *Bay Prairie* is also used. This phrase came into use during the mid 1830s and was coincident with the coastal plain from Galveston Bay to the Lavaca River. By the late 1800s historians refined its geographic extent, limiting Bay Prairie mostly to between the Brazos River and the Tres Palacios Creek. Modern Bay City is situated, approximately, at its center. The map at the end of this piece illustrates and describes some of the key geographic nomenclature.

The story of Spread Oaks Ranch is divided into two parallel themes. Section 1 is a history of the people that owned land at the Bend in the River and future Spread Oaks Ranch. Section 2 contains accounts of related historical topics, its themes selected primarily because Bend in the River denizens had a role in them. Or, looking at it another way, they were events that had an impact on the Bend in the River and its landowners. This is the basis for the selection of the historical chapters, and they include early Texas settlement, the Texas War for Independence, the Colorado River log raft, Matagorda's cattlemen and cowboys, and the early rice and irrigation industry. In the historical chapters there is very little original research, and certainly no ground-breaking revelations. It's storytelling. It's still fascinating.

Accounts of the Bend in the River landowners is also storytelling, but it does break new ground. One of the things that made this part of the research so enjoyable was how often the Spread Oaks Ranch owners were integral to, or a part of, the greater Texas story.

Historical research has changed over the years. The basis for much of our current Lone Star State knowledge comes from the men and women who translated original documents from Spanish and uncovered dusty, esoteric manuscripts from equally obscure archives. Using multiple, hard-earned sources, they pieced together and published accounts that were usually rigorously peer reviewed. It was good work and an unparalleled contribution to who we were – and are.

Increasingly, historical topics have been made available on the internet. It is a luxury. The power and rapidity of searching a subject across multiple platforms allowed the writer to uncover details that, before, were buried too deeply to access easily. The weakness in modern methods is the danger of drawing conclusions that lack depth or an interpretation of an event that is simply inaccurate. I tried very hard to avoid these pitfalls.

Note: Present county boundaries and names shown for geographic reference

Spread Oaks Ranch is located in Matagorda County just north of Markham and Bay City, and about 30 miles north of the Gulf of Mexico. It is part of the broad geographic designation of Bay Prairie on the Texas central coastal plain. The name Bend in the River is used to describe the west bank of the Colorado River from about where Markham is situated, then north to the Matagorda-County line. Spread Oaks Ranch lies within this corridor. The ranch is approximately 5,500 acres with over five miles of Colorado River frontage. Owned by the Wylie family, it is a working cattle and farming operation.

Table of Contents

SECTION 1

Landowners of the Bend in the River

CHAPTER 1
Landowners of the Bend in the River

1820s to 1860s

The practice of populating "vacant land" between New Spain and the western edge of the United States with "foreigners" – anyone not of Castilian blood – originated with the Spanish, who used unpopulated and inexpensive land as a lure to settle their untamed frontier. After gaining independence in 1821, Mexico continued to permit colonization in the Texas frontier for reasons not dissimilar to those of Spain – its defense and for potential economic gain.

Like Spain, the Mexican army after independence was stretched too thin to attend to Texas. The list of threats to Mexico, both real and imagined, included the rumored return of the Spanish military to reclaim its former territory, continued United States expansion, and persistent mayhem at the hands of Native Americans intent on driving usurpers from their ancestral lands. The government's reasoning was that its colonists, with a vested interest in protecting their property, would also have an inherent interest in its defense.

The other settlement incentive was monetary. The northern frontier was rich in natural resources, rivers and deep-water bays that could facilitate maritime trade with the United States and Europe, and arable soil along the coastal plain. Development of these assets, in addition to producing a prosperous economy, could provide a well needed tax base to Mexico's treasury.

Mexico initially opened colonization to settlers from Mexico, the United States, and Europe. The task of managing the enterprise was given to empresarios, or immigration agents, as contractors to Mexico's national government and its confederation of states. Colonization laws mandated settlement of a quota of families and unmarried men within an allotted time frame. Empresarios were obliged to establish one or more towns, schools, and a Catholic Church within each grant. They were also responsible for raising and leading a local militia, the title of colonel inferred upon them by the legislature. They appointed surveyors and shared responsibilities with a government commissioner to issue land titles, administer the settler's oath of allegiance, prepare records, and collect fees. After fulfillment of the contract terms, the empresario's financial reward was earned through land grants and sales, and service fees.

Mexico entertained many empresario aspirants and spurned most. Of the contracts that were approved, the honor of inking their names on the face of the Mexican Texas map was no guarantee of success. Some who failed were inept, a few deceitful. Of those who tried but couldn't meet the contract terms, much of the blame lay on Mexico. The National Colonization Law of April 6, 1830, for example, transferred its colonization authority from Mexico City to Saltillo, and applicants who had been waiting for approval from the central government – some for several years – had to shift their allegiances to Saltillo. Less than two years later the holdings of many sanctioned ventures were eroded by Mexico's Law of April 28, 1832, that permitted only Mexican companies to settle untitled lands.[1] More insidious was the Law of April 6, 1834, that banned Anglo-American immigration altogether.

Artfully drawn and colored land grant boundaries on 1830s maps might give the impression that there was proficiency, or even consistency, to the Texas contract process (Fig. 1). In that, the maps would be misleading. Stephen F. Austin's First Colony, which became the largest Anglo-American settlement in Mexican Texas, was no exception to the challenges of Texas colonization.

First Colony. Stephen F. Austin was Mexico's first empresario and its most influential foreign ambassador for 14 tumultuous years. Austin's original contract, called First Colony, extended from the Lavaca River on the southwest to the San Jacinto River on the northeast. Bounded by the coast and to the north by the El Camino de Real, it encompassed the fertile floodplains of the lower Brazos and Colorado rivers valleys. Here Austin was given the authority to settle 300 families – later dubbed the 'Old 300' – with the first 40 arriving in 1821. Austin chose a site on the Brazos River for the town of San Felipe de Austin as the colony's administrative headquarters. He would be a busy man, not just promoting and settling the new colony, but as its government commissioner, a responsibility he shared with Baron de Bastrop and, later, Gaspar Flores. Austin was also the appointed civil chief, or judicial officer, the head of the local militia, and a commandant of the federal military department.[2]

Austin described the challenges of his empresario duties to Mexico's consul in New Orleans, James Waller Breedlove, in 1829. He commented that "not one person in the settlement could correctly translate any law or order of the government." He complained about finances – most of the settlers, he wrote, "were unable to pay anything" and "in order to keep all afloat I did exact prompt payment from those who were able to make it, and out of the money thus raised I paid the way of the poor who were unable to pay anything."[3] He described toiling under a government often "unsettled and shaken by frequent political revolutions and changes of systems, policy and officers." Other of Austin's words portended the future. Among his colonists, he wrote, were "frontier men" who "had never known restraint." It was these unrestrained men who would one day follow him in the Texian's 1835 fight for independence.

None of Austin's other land dealings were as successful as First Colony. There was a failed colonization partnership with English soldier of fortune Arthur Goodall Wavell. Another was his successful acquisition of the controversial Leftwich, or Robertson's Colony, but that earned him the lasting enmity of powerful detractors. The ambitious Austin was never immune to using his influence to further his ambitions. One example was his attempt to monopolize all settlement activities in Texas in partnership with politically connected entrepreneur Erasmo Seguín. As other applicants in 1824 were lining up for contracts in Mexico City, Austin circulated a proposal to officials that, had he been successful, would have made him the sole foreign empresario in Texas.[4]

Bend in the River. The Bend in the River was part of Stephen F. Austin's First Colony. The deeds encompassed by the present Spread Oaks Ranch boundaries were signed by Stephan F. Austin and, representing Mexico, Gaspar Flores, or more properly Gaspar Flores de Abrego. Flores was the Béxar land commissioner who recorded many of the documents for Austin's original 300 and later switched allegiances during the Texas Revolution. A believer of the federalist principles of the 1824 Mexican Constitution, he became an enemy of the state when he formally denounced President Santa Anna at the onset of hostilities in 1835. Refusing to surrender the official documents of his office to Mexico, he was branded a traitor with a price on his head. After donating all his goods and cattle to the Texians who would remain in Béxar – the Alamo – to face Santa Anna's army, Flores sought safety in East Texas in the exodus known as the Runaway Scrape. He might have returned a hero after the Battle of San Jacinto but died of a fever along the route at age 55.[5]

The first sanctioned Bend in the River headright was its southern portion (Fig. 2), pledged to Mississippi riverman Captain Jacob Jennings, from Sicily Island, Louisiana (Figs. 3 & 4). Jennings arrived on the *Lively* in 1821 and settled on a creek that flowed into the Colorado River, renamed Jennings Creek in his honor after he died in 1822.

The Southern Survey at the Bend in the River

Jacob Jennings. The air as it hung over the banks of the Mississippi River reeked of man, beast, lumber, leather, hemp rope, cotton sails, and all manner of agricultural goods, and it carried the sound of longshoremen shouting in a mixture of French, English, Spanish, and local dialects. From their French Quarter levee vantage point above the wharves, Stephen F. Austin and business partner Joseph H. Hawkins viewed a forest of masts, their timber rising from the decks of sailing crafts of all shapes and sizes as draymen ferried goods to and from the docks, the planking bowing under the weight of their carts, mules, and horses. The two men eyed the scene anxiously, hoping for any sign of the schooner they recently purchased, the *Lively*, on its return from refitting in Bayou St. John.

Few others at the landing during the fall of 1821 took any notice of the ship as the bar pilot pointed her upriver into the current, then broadside to her mooring. As far as seagoing vessels went, the two-masted *Lively* was small, weighing just 30 tons, and otherwise unremarkable.[6] She was probably a retired privateer, originally built for speed and nimbleness. She would be more sluggish now, burdened with the weight of a floor and sleeping berths constructed above the freight hold. Although the role of the *Lively* was to change from high seas plunder to a manifest of human cargo, she was about to sail into history as the vessel that delivered the first Anglo settlers to Texas.

Spain approved Moses Austin's scheme to recruit Anglo-Americans to settle Spanish Texas in the spring of 1821. Austin, however, died from pneumonia a few months later and the enterprise fell to his son, Stephen F. Austin. With financial backing from lawyer Joseph H. Hawkins, Austin was in New Orleans that fall to organize the maiden voyage of colonists and provisions to the Texas frontier. One group would travel by sea, and Austin would lead another expedition on the El Camino Real from Natchitoches to Goliad, then to the Colorado River mouth to meet the *Lively*. Austin was carrying a heavy burden – he had to convince Mexico, freshly independent from Spain, to honor its predecessor's immigration agreement. When the first waves of emigrants left the United States for the Province of Texas by land and sea, they had absolutely no guarantees.

The passengers and crew preparing to board the *Lively* were a mix of colonists, adventurers, and opportunists. Some had accompanied Austin on earlier Texas reconnaissance journeys, others were enlisted in New Orleans during the weeks the boat was overhauled, and still others learned of Texas settlement prospects from advertisements, circulars, or newspapers, the latter inspired by Austin's words of a land in which "the gold and silver mines are getting into more extensive operation, and money is becoming more abundant" and "the restrictive system heretofore pursued in regard to foreigners has been suspended by the most liberal encouragement."[7]

Almost as soon as the *Lively* passed through the channel to the open Gulf she encountered a gale. Wind whistled through the rigging, wood groaned as the vessel rose and fell with each mountainous swell. When the storm diminished the captain made a brief landing at Galveston Bay. For most of the passengers now scattering on the shoreline, it was their first look at Texas, and it brought a reality to whatever vision they may have had of the place. The initial foraging party navigated unbroken head-high prairie grasses that, after five or six miles, transitioned to timber. They found drinking water in a hole in a buffalo path. Kentucky rifles procured two wild turkeys, a "mule-eared rabbit," and a bear, the meat field dressed and hauled back to the *Lively* before it set out again and into the open Gulf for the Colorado River.

When the *Lively* set anchor in January 1822 at the mouth of the Brazos River – not the Colorado, as intended – she was not the first seafaring vessel to land at the wrong river. With passes that snaked through low-lying, fringing marshes, Gulf Coast waterways had a way of eluding mariners as far back as the 1500s. Ship's clerk W.S. Lewis, who later chronicled the trip, put the blame of the *Lively's* cartographic oversight on the captain, a man he grew to disdain during the journey. Lewis knew him only as Captain Cannon, a man he described as about 50 years old, "quite fleshy, fond of his toddy, and quite on the lethargic order." The choice of "Yankee miscreant" Captain Cannon to command the expedition, Lewis continued, was "a most unfortunate circumstance for the expedition and particularly for the poor devils of immigrants."[8] But as the travelers spilled from the schooner and stumbled ashore, they had no idea they weren't on the Colorado.

Among the approximately two dozen men who embarked on the *Lively* now surveying the Brazos River scene was Jacob Jennings, a veteran Mississippi riverman with roots in Sicily Island, Louisiana. W.S. Lewis did not believe Jennings was on Austin's list of colonists and pondered why "old men" such as Jennings, "should take an interest in the success of such an expedition if it were not for pecuniary interests." In this, he was wrong. Austin had pledged Jennings a headright for services he was to render to the fledgling colony. Jennings did indeed have an important role but, like so many Texas figures, he played it for only a very short time.

Jennings headed a small party to explore upriver in the *Lively's* yawl while the others made a crude camp. Situated adjacent to a salt marsh stretching "as far as the eye could see," its horizon was animated by a swirling mass of ducks and geese that, after a single rifle discharge, were "made so very wild in one day that it was impossible to get in killing distance of them." The river mouth was stacked, in places, with chest-high driftwood. Some of it would be useful, such as plow stocks and handles, wheel spokes, pieces of wooden chairs, vessel spars, and even old canoes and pirogues. With no known nearby settlements, the origin of the objects of civilization were puzzling. They may have been from shipwrecks and transported by the Gulf's longshore current, or possibly originated from Spanish activity along the overland El Camino Real route and deposited downriver.

The colonists settled in a second Brazos River camp as they awaited Jennings's return and the expected news of Austin's arrival by land. Trees were felled to construct small boats, and hunting parties spread out along the canebrakes and stands of pecan and hackberry trees. After a "prairie hawk" found its way into a pot of soup, their makeshift camp bore the name "Camp Hawk." As the days passed, steel-barreled rifles found their mark on several deer and turkeys, an otter, a few bears and buffalo, and a panther they called a "Mexican tiger." W.S. Lewis wrote derisively of life at Camp Hawk, including a reference to its occupants who kept "others awake at night with kinds of most obscene brothel songs and stories and yarns to match."

Captain Jennings only rarely visited the second encampment, having determined the error in the *Lively's* landing after his first trip upriver. Relocating his ship mates to the Colorado via a land crossing from the Brazos, they settled in an oak motte at the juncture of the west bank of the Colorado and a creek that would soon bear his name. Jennings, John Hannah, Israel Massey, and Phillip Dimmitt constructed a log cabin at the site to store the remaining supplies brought by the *Lively*.[9] Other settlers who arrived in 1822 on the *Only Son, Good Intent*, and *John Motley* headed upriver from the coast to the newly named Jennings Camp, storing more provisions before some made their way to San Felipe and other points.

To this wave of immigrants, outposts carved from the Colorado River bottoms like Jennings Camp must have seemed like a godsend after the hardships of their maritime voyages. During efforts to shuttle settlers between New Orleans and First Colony, two early passages ended in shipwrecks on Galveston Island. One was the foundering of the *Lively* on its second voyage, its passengers rescued by the schooner *John Motley*.[10] Provisions ran short on most of the excursions and many "suffered much for want of water." As well, "there was much sickness among the new arrivals," including a Mrs. Nelson who died at sea from "the consumption." Many of the settlers who arrived at Jennings Camp after their landing remained for several weeks to even months as they awaited news of their land applications, the site providing a source of fresh water, abundant game, and a place to grow small plots of corn.

After the initial *Lively* landing, other settlers built a crude fort at the mouth of the Colorado River to store incoming supplies destined for the new settlement. Here, four men assigned as guards were killed by Karankawa, and much of the cargo and the colonist's personal property was either stolen or destroyed. Families camping in the proximity of the raid quickly moved up to Jennings Camp.[11] Supplies that had been stored at Jennings before the attack would prove critical until other goods arrived.

Captain Jennings died in 1822, the details of his passing and place of burial unrecorded. Only a few families remained at Jennings Camp by 1823, and settlers upriver were anxious to retrieve its remaining stores. Austin placed these under the jurisdiction of Littleberry Hawkins,[12] who dispatched John Hanna to collect the "wares and merchandise" from Jennings Camp. Hanna also gathered Jennings' personal belongings and those of "poor Harrison," a reference to Thomas Harrison who died about the same time as Jennings. When Hanna returned upriver, he carried the last vestiges of Mississippi riverman Jacob Jennings – $150 cash, his rifle, and any clothing "that was worth anything."[13]

Hanna evidently disappeared with the Jennings Camp inventory. In a letter to Stephen F. Austin, Hawkins charged that he never received payment for any of its articles or stores. Further, he wrote, Hanna owed him for the failings of their "Mule and Horse business" in which Hawkins advanced monies for the purchase of 260 horses, 75 mules, "4 Jacks and 6 jinney's." In desperation, he advised Austin that "after all my toils and privation and separation from my family fifteen months I have been swindled out of all that I sent out of the country."[14]

By 1824 Jennings Camp was abandoned. The name continued to appear for several more years, but only as a geographic marker. The last reference to a cabin on Jennings Creek was in the summer of 1824, when depravations by the Karankawa reached a boiling point. Austin determined to put an end to it, leading an expedition of some 40 to 50 men from San Felipe. During their march south, they crossed the Colorado River near Eagle Lake, then proceeded down the west side of the river to Jennings Camp before abandoning the effort at the Lavaca River mouth. Although the Indians slipped away, the expedition succeeded in opening a road through a wilderness of "dense thickets and canebrakes." As for Jennings Camp, they reported that all that remained was a cabin "surrounded by implements and provisions scattered by thieves." And two barrels of whiskey.[15]

Jared Cable. A year after Jennings died, the Jennings League, or Survey, was transferred to Jared Cable. Cable was Stephen F. Austin's forwarding agent in Natchitoches, Louisiana, but for reasons unknown, he never took claim of the land. (Fig. 5) Austin later wrote that Cable "abandoned the country and forfeited his right because of not having complied with the provisions of the law." His wording suggests that Cable may have visited Texas but returned to the United States. In 1827 the Jennings headright passed to Hosea H. League, and League had every intention in settling it.[16]

Hosea League. Hosea H. League was born in 1790, and by the 1810s made his home in the southern Appalachians of northwest Tennessee near the Kentucky border. He married Jennette Horton in 1812, and with his brother-in-law William D. Horton immigrated to Texas in 1826. League petitioned for a headright in Austin's Colony, and as married man qualified for a *sitio de ganado mayor*, defined as 4,428 acres. He was granted the Jennings tract on the west bank of the Colorado River, its third owner in just five years. The League contract was officially inked in 1827 and signed by Stephen F. Austin and Gaspar Flores, or more properly Gaspar Flores de Abrego (Fig. 6).

League was a 37-year-old lawyer when he took possession of "my league at Ginnings [*sic*] old camp"[17] in the spring of 1827. He celebrated his fortune according to the custom of the day, in which he "shouted aloud, pulled up grass, threw stones, planted stakes, and performed the other ceremonies."[18] That year he built a large plantation home on the lower third of the grant.

League made a name for himself in a very short time. He was a founder of the port town of Matagorda and was its elected president with town secretary Ira Ingram and treasurer Seth Ingram. League and the Ingram brothers soon divided their time between Matagorda and San Felipe. In the latter town they operated a mercantile business, and League opened a law practice with East Texas empresario and future interim Republic of Texas president David G. Burnett. League next successfully petitioned to become empresario of the Texas Association's Leftwich Colony, located north of the El Camino Real and between the Colorado and Brazos rivers.[19]

Virginian Robert Leftwich abandoned his bankrupt mercantile business in Tennessee and travelled to Mexico City in 1822. Now in his fifties, he would make a fresh start representing Nashville investors who called themselves the

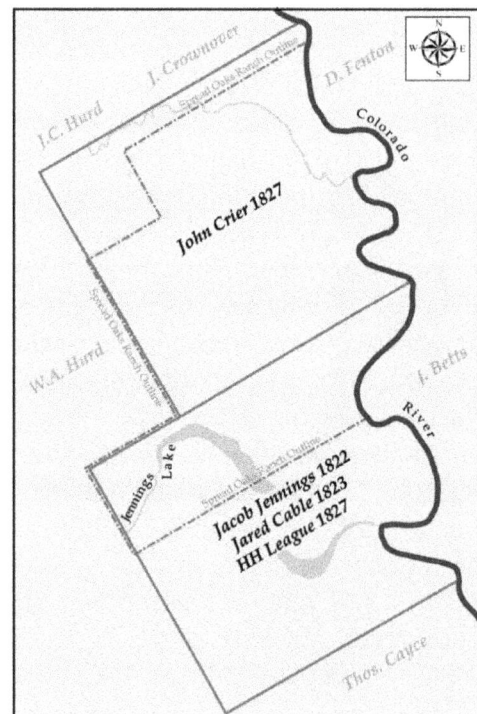

Texas Association, later the Nashville Company. Leftwich lingered in Mexico City for nearly three years awaiting government approval of his land venture before he followed the shifting land prize to new administrative offices in Saltillo.

Leftwich's Colony was finally sanctioned in 1825, but in its documents, Leftwich omitted the Texas Association moniker and designated himself the sole contractor.[20] His oversight would have profound implications. The next year he was fired, replaced by Benjamin Foster, who was appointed to correct the contract documents. The amendment, however, required government approval in Saltillo, and despite Foster's request for Stephen F. Austin to "facilitate his undertaking," Saltillo did not consent to Foster or the Texas Association as legitimate agents.[21]

Next to lobby for Austin's support was Hosea H. League. League may have just immigrated to Texas, but he was rapidly proving himself in civil affairs. The new Texas Association agent made his first excursion to Leftwich Colony in September of 1826. Writing of his travels, he advised that after a month "our company is nearly all sick," and League himself was "crippled by a fall from a horse from which I have suffered much and not yet recovered."[22]

During the summer of 1827, the Texas Association implored Austin to support League's empresario bid and pursue "an additional memorial to [the] government in their behalf." Austin was successful, and by October both League and the Association were free to "attend to advancement of the colony."[23] By now, the original 74 shareholders in the struggling venture had grown to 592, its investors including future Republic of Texas general and president, Sam Houston.[24]

By 1829, the ambitious League was appointed a *regidor* in the San Felipe Ayuntamiento. It would be the beginning of two very troubled years. The *ayuntamiento* was still smarting from criticism, levelled by the Coahuila y Texas legislature, that it was not meeting its administrative obligations (see Figure 2 for the geography of the Mexican states of Coahuila and Texas). Part of its failing was due to lack of finances, and League was charged with raising funds. He decided on a municipal tax, a topic that outraged the colonists who trusted they were exempt from taxation under Mexico's settlement terms. They took their fury out on League. Nestor Clay – later a member of the Second Convention of April 1833 and an author of the proposed Texas Constitution – was the principal in one altercation.[25] Clay railed against League, announcing he would raise an armed force "of the best men in the country" to oppose the tax and told League to pay the tariffs himself, adding "if you report us in a state of rebellion, we will take no other notice of you than to tar and feather you."[26]

Equally offensive was the passage of a League-backed 'vagrant law' to control "rioting, drunkenness, and fighting." Under the previous *ayuntamiento*, San Felipe town had a reputation for the "morality of a grog shop or common brothel, rather than [a reputation] in law or the offices of justice." *Regido*r League's circular pronouncing the vagrant law and its penalties created more animosity. Stephen F. Austin anticipated the backlash, describing the colonist's actions as the "great mass of depravity which revolts from restraint or legal control."[27]

League took the insults and abuse personally, and that winter resigned his office. The conflicts and "the violence of feeling against me," he wrote, makes it "impossible that my health can ever be restored under my present state of depressed and mortified feelings." He planned a trip to New Orleans to recover his strength yet was optimistic that one day he "may be useful to the public in some other way."[28]

League's time in New Orleans was short, returning to his *regidor* duties in San Felipe in the winter of 1830. That year the *ayuntamiento* passed a recommendation to survey the "Brazoria to La Baca Road" (Fig. 7) that was to pass through League's "Jennyngs [*sic*] Camp league." League requested authority to site a ferry at the Colorado River on his headright. Although both measures were approved, League never got to operate his ferry. He was in prison.[29]

In April 1830, the San Felipe Ayuntamiento counted the 'ayes' in a poll for the appointment of John G. Holtham as official translator and secretary. Only one 'nay' vote was cast, that of first *regidor* Hosea H. League. The impetuous Holtham was appointed but then resigned after four months. Two months later, a drunken Holtham wandered into Ira Ingram's yard and after words, "was ejected by him." Holtham challenged Ingram to a duel that Ingram declined. His honor at stake, Holtham posted a memorandum on the door of the *alcade's* office denouncing Ingram "as a coward, a rascal, and a man without honor."[30]

It wasn't the first time Holtham blasphemed a foe. Years earlier he addressed "the people of Texas" in a handbill denouncing a Mr. John Cook, thought by those who knew as him as "a temperate, sober, genteel man." Holtham's circulars, however, portrayed him "as a swindler, etc.," and "some blows passed between them and they parted on bad terms."[31]

This time, the outcome of Holtham's temper would be different. As he posted his slanderous bills around the town, Ira's brother Seth confronted him, demanding he remove them. When he didn't, Holtham got his highly anticipated duel, although with Seth, not Ira. When the black smoke at the end of Seth Ingram's gun barrel cleared, John G. Holtham writhed mortally wounded on the ground, "a pistol ball passing through his body."[32]

The historical record is silent on how League came to be implicated in the shooting. Allegedly, he was at the scene and armed,[33] but he wasn't the man who pulled the trigger. He spent 16 months in irons because of it. Most historians infer that *Regidor* League was so unpopular in San Felipe that his enemies at last found a way to punish him. Stephen F. Austin seemed to agree. "Public opinion is very much excited against League," he wrote, "there is a furious excitement all over colony against him."[34]

There is also the question of the time that passed between the smoking gun and League's eventual freedom – three years. Perhaps the deferral was because Mexico had never granted Texas the authority for a trial by jury. The matter was also complicated because defendant League was also the judicial chief who would have weighed on its judgement. For part of those three years, League and Seth Ingram were confined to a makeshift San Felipe jail and chained to a wall. They were released after nearly a year and a half, then rearrested, and finally liberated in 1833.

When their records were cleared, Seth Ingram regained his vocation and reputation. He returned to surveying, was named to the Matagorda Committee of Safety and Correspondence in the months before the Texas Revolution and was later a land agent and justice of the peace. He died in 1857 of "consumption" and was buried in Matagorda beside his brother Ira.

League never really recovered. Immediately after his arrest, he wrote Austin that "among the evils that result to me from my confinement, my pecuniary affairs are by no means the least. I have not the power to prosecute my rights or to repel their invasion." He added that "my ruin is inevitable unless I can dispose of so much of my property as will pay off all demands against me be them just or unjust." The property he determined to sell was his "league of land at Jennings camp"[35] (Fig. 8).

The outcome was that League deeded the top two thirds of his grant in 1833 to Thomas Cayce, and the bottom third, that included the League family's plantation home, sold to Elisha Flack.[36] League and his wife relocated to the banks of Buffalo Bayou. He still evidently had supporters, as delegates to the 1835 Consultation, the second government of Texas hastily formed during the Texas Revolution, appointed him first judge for the Harrisburg jurisdiction. The next year he was nominated as election judge to select delegates for the Washington-on-the-Brazos Convention of 1836.[37]

As League observed the new Texas government proceedings in 1835 and 1836, he must have been keenly aware of a bitter irony – his failed stewardship as empresario of the Texas Association's Leftwich Colony was at least part of the reason that Stephen F. Austin was given no substantial seat in the Republic of Texas administration.

Likely preoccupied with civil and judicial affairs as San Felipe *Ayuntamiento*, Hosea League neglected to comply with the terms of the Texas Association contract. Three years lapsed without any new settlement. After he was arrested for murder in 1830, he received a visit from Texas Association and Nashville Company investor Sterling C. Robertson. Chained to the walls of the makeshift jail, League gave his signature to papers conceding power of attorney to new empresario Robertson.[38]

Robertson also failed to meet the colonization terms, and when he did, Austin pounced. He and Samuel Williams successfully petitioned for the grant, renaming it their Upper Colony. But the back and forth between Robertson and Austin over title made Austin bitter enemies of Robertson and his supporters, who slandered him as "corrupt and tyrannical" and a man who operated with "treachery and malice."[39] Austin wrote Williams that "I am of the opinion that the upper colony will totally ruin me."[40] Politically, at least, it did – he did not receive enough support for the governorship of the Provisional Government and was passed over in 1836 as president of the Republic of Texas (see Section 2, titled *From Spain to Mexico*).

Hosea H. League died in May 1837, just four months after 43-year-old Stephen F. Austin succumbed to pneumonia.

Thomas Cayce. They marched hurriedly, traversing from north to south over the divide between the Coosa and Tallapoosa rivers along the eastern edge of Mississippi Territory. It was Creek Indian land, with Georgia to the east and the freshly chartered state of Tennessee to the north. Beneath their feet was the soil of the southern Appalachian Mountains foothills, the rolling terrain incised by deep rivers along wide floodplains punctuated by rapids formed over shallow gravel bars derived from the adjacent mountain belt. Dense stands of hardwoods covered the highlands, following the slope down to the river's edge, their branches bare in the January cold.

America's War of 1812 was justified as retaliation for British damages against the young nation's maritime trade rights. But no opposing red coats could be seen as some 900 Tennessee volunteers trailed Andrew Jackson deep into Creek Indian territory. What motivated the soldiers during that winter of 1814 was bloodlust, their goal to avenge the massacre of some 250 settlers by Creek 'Red Stick' warriors five months earlier at Fort Mims on the Alabama River. Far from the front, there were others gathered in smoky political backrooms with an entirely different agenda – they were eager to lay claim to Creek land. Both groups were to get what they wanted.

There were some well-known future Texans among the Tennesseans in the Creek War campaign, including Sam Houston and David Crockett. Among them was a 19-year-old soldier named Thomas Dodson Cayce, who served under Col. Nicholas T. Perkins and Capt. Mathew Patterson in the 1st Regiment West Tennessee Mounted Volunteers.[41] Cayce participated in two of the fiercest skirmishes in the war, known to history as the battles of Emuckfau and Enotochopco Creek.

At Emuckfau Creek, the Red Sticks converged on the left and rear flanks of Jackson's camp in the pre-dawn darkness of January 22, 1814. Repulsed, the Creeks returned after daybreak and made a second attack on the right and left wings. Jackson's lines held but, with as many as 100 of his 900-man army killed or wounded, he retreated towards the stockade at Fort Strother.[42]

Two days later, the Creeks struck again as Jackson's retreating army crossed Enotochopco Creek. Their thrust overwhelmed the Volunteer rear guard and when it fell, soldiers on the flanks either followed the fleeing rear or rejoined the fight by filling the gaping hole at the center. Kentucky rifles were useless in the ensuing hand to hand melee, the Red Stick warriors wielding primitive instruments of destruction – buffalo jawbone or stone war clubs, spears – some with solid blades and others with sharpened tines, tomahawks and knives fitted with honed quartz blades or forged metal affixed by rawhide to wood or bone handles. It was a battle that could have gone either way, but the rallying Tennessee Volunteers took the field, leaving behind a trail of the dead as the Creeks withdrew.

During the Enotochopco Creek battle, future Bend in the River citizen Thomas Cayce was assigned to Col. Nicholas Perkins' regiment. Perkins was ordered to hold the right flank, but he was not giving any commands as he and his troops scattered. After the campaign Perkins was court-martialed for cowardice, disobedience of orders, and abandonment of his post, although he was later acquitted. During the melee Cayce had a choice to make – follow the right flank's flight or stand and fight. Cayce after the war was honorably discharged with the rank of sergeant, an outcome that suggests Cayce must have been among the warriors who fought and saved the beleaguered rear guard.[43]

That summer Jackson returned to the Coosa and Tallapoosa rivers, this time with a force of 5,000 men. When they returned victorious, the British had lost the Creek as a key ally and 23 million acres of Creek lands were annexed to America's coffers. Sargent Cayce's ambitions after the war were less lofty. When he returned home to Davidson County he took a bride, 20-year-old Hannah Elizabeth Stanley. Fifteen years later, 35-year-old Thomas, his wife, four sons, and one daughter boarded a Memphis riverboat to New Orleans then took passage on a schooner bound for Texas.

The Thomas Cayce family landed at Velasco at the mouth of the Brazos River in December 1829. By April he secured a league of land in Austin's First Colony on the Colorado River in Matagorda County, located south of and adjacent to H.H. League's Survey. Cayce divided his time between the Colorado River, where his slaves broke the

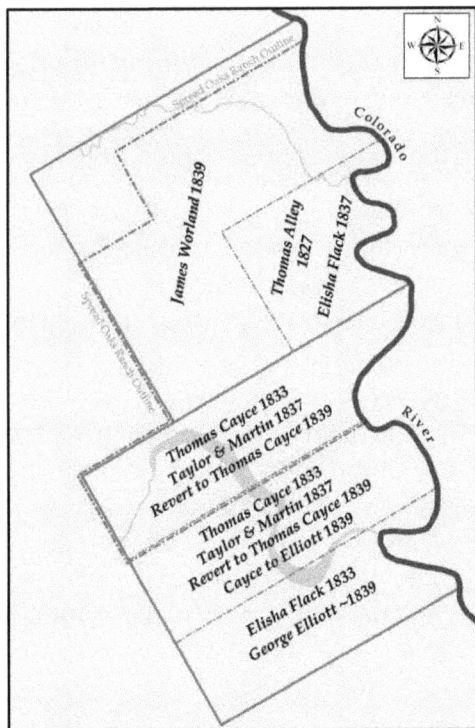

Spread Oaks Ranch Outline

Colorado

James Worland 1839

Thomas Alley 1827

Elisha Flack 1837

River

Thomas Cayce 1833
Taylor & Martin 1837
Taylor to Thomas Cayce 1839
Revert to Thomas Cayce

Thomas Cayce 1833
Taylor & Martin 1837
Taylor to Thomas Cayce 1839
Revert to Thomas Cayce
Cayce to Elliott 1839

Elisha Flack 1833
George Elliott ~1839

prairie to grow sugar cane and cotton, and San Felipe, where he was named a *regidor* to the San Felipe de Austin Ayuntamiento.[44] He began investing in land, and in 1833 signed a promissory note to Jeanette Horton League for the upper two thirds of the H.H. League Survey. The deed encompassed the original League Ferry (Fig. 9), and with it, planter and public servant Thomas Cayce added ferryman and public house proprietor to his list of enterprises.

Before the early 1830s, the ebb and flow of goods between Austin's Colony and the western frontier mainly followed the established El Camino Real de los Tejas or the Atascocita-La Bahía routes to the north (Fig. 7). Now, the recently surveyed Bay Prairie Road traversing the lower coastal plain became an important artery. Traffic passing over the new overland route, and keel boats and steamers that ran upstream from Matagorda town to San Felipe, called at Cayce's Ferry for supplies, a place to eat and sleep, and to bring or hear the latest news.

Eyeing nothing in the future that might limit his growing Bend in the River prosperity, Cayce launched a scheme to establish the town of Augusta at Jennings Creek (Fig. 10). Among Augusta's advantages, he extolled prospective buyers in 1834, was its location on the "great trading thoroughfare" – the 'Brazoria to La Baca Road' or Bay Prairie Road – as well as its timber, an "inexhaustible supply of excellent water," and soil "equal to any in the country for gardening."[45] The venture, however, failed to attract the anticipated "enterprising portions of the community" or its "speculators and adventurers." They were preoccupied with war rumblings.

Business was brisk, but tense, at Cayce's crossing in the summer of 1835 as the threat of war put more riders, couriers, and government officials on the move. Following Stephen F. Austin's call to arms, circulated during September, the ferrymen were barely able to keep up with the flow of Texian volunteers to enlistment camps at "James Kerr's on La Baca" and "League's old place on the Colorado." Some camped at Cayce's, where they signed their enlistment papers before a march to Gonzales and the first battle in the Texas War for Independence. Throughout 1835 and early 1836, Cayce's crossing was used by most of the Matagorda and Brazoria area soldiers (see Section 2, *Early Texas Settlement* and *The Battle for a New Republic*).

The next year the crossing saw even more traffic, but no one was paying any ferry tolls. The first wave of travelers was part of the Runaway Scrape, the Texians who were fleeing the approaching Mexican army. Most were fearful, many were sick, and as they slogged along, they left a trail of abandoned belongings, and often their dead, in a desperate bid to reach Louisiana or Galveston. Throughout 1835, with the Cayce men in the field, it was Hannah that kept the ferry and public house in operation. Now Hannah, daughter Mary Ann, and the Cayce slaves and servants joined the flood of Texian families as they poured east. The second wave of travelers that arrived at the banks of the Colorado River weren't paying any tolls, either. They were part of Santa Anna's army.

Eyeing the crossing at Cayce's Ferry from the prairie on the west bank of the Colorado River, General José de Urrea's scouts chose the crossing for their planned subjugation of Matagorda and towns further east. No one was left to witness what must have been a spectacular sight a few days later as Urrea's army, consisting of his original force of nearly 600 cavalrymen and infantries joined by another 700 men from the San Luis and Jiménez battalions, stretched entirely across the horizon on the banks of the Colorado River.[46]

Theirs was an army with blood on their hands. These were the men who, in the past weeks, annihilated Volunteer Army commander Francis W. Johnson's detachment at San Patricio, Coahuila empresario Dr. James Grant's command at Agua Dulce Creek, and slaughtered Captain Amon B. King's men after they surrendered at the Refugio mission. Most recently, they butchered 344 of Fannin and Ward's men outside the walls of the Goliad La Bahía presidio (see Section 2, titled *The Battle for a New Republic*).

According to historian Gregg J. Dimmick, Mexican troops crossed the Colorado at Cayce's ferry three times in April. General Urrea's contingency used the route twice during early April. After Santa Anna's defeat at San Jacinto, General Vincente Filisola intended to follow Urrea's route, sending a detachment under Colonel D. Francisco Garay with 130 infantrymen and cavalry, and 20 "artisans, carpenters, and canoeists to fortify the crossing."[47] Filisola chose a northern route, instead, but the Tres Villas Battalion of nearly 200 infantrymen – the last of the Mexican army – crossed at the Bend in the River during late April.

The Cayce's returned after the war to find their homestead and public house still standing, but little else. The Texian volunteers had earlier taken their cattle, horses, oxen, and mules, exhausted their supplies of salt, sugar, molasses, winter provisions, and dismantled their outbuildings and fencing for firewood. What the Texians didn't consume, the Mexicans destroyed.

The story is told how Hannah, before fleeing east, "had one of the slaves plough three deep furrows in the garden" to bury her set of fine China "which she then covered, raked the ground carefully and sowed mustard thickly over the area. The piano, cookstove and other household furniture she could only leave to their fate." The Mexican armies were not kind to her possessions. Of the China, "the mustard bed had been uprooted and only one or two dishes remained unbroken." The household furniture ruined, and the piano was found with its wires torn out and the legs cut off. Legend has it that the piano wood was used to construct a livestock watering trough, and it lasted half a century.[48]

The Cayce men had left their Bend in the River property to its fate at the outbreak of the war. Thomas Dodson Cayce and two of his sons, George Washington and Shadrack, spent part of the conflict together in Captain Thomas Stewart's company of Matagorda Volunteers.[49] Sixteen-year-old Shadrack was an early volunteer, enlisting in the fall of 1835 and seeing action at first Goliad. Next, he threaded a path between scouts, spies, foraging parties, and enemy detachments to haul armaments to Béxar. He narrowly avoided Fannin's fate at second Goliad, sidestepping the carnage and joining General Houston on the Colorado River before the Texian army's retreat. Although eager to join the Battle of San Jacinto, Houston sent him back from the front lines because of his "young age."

Cayce probably rued the day he came to operate the ferryboat. Between the Texian volunteers, the Runaway Scrape, and the Mexican army, the war cost him financially and crushed his livelihood. He later received some monies from the Texas claims and accounts court, his petition "praying remuneration for diverse things furnished the Government," and "his sufferings and losses at the hands of the Texan army."[50] But at war's end, he was a man in debt.

Thomas Cayce borrowed heavily to finance his land speculation and was hounded by creditors from 1837 until the day he died. In addition to his Colorado River holdings, Cayce had signed notes for land in the towns of Matagorda, Columbia, Quintana, and unimproved in Fort Bend and Brazoria County. Undeterred by the failure of the moribund Augusta townsite venture, he also partnered in a second town, Preston, with son Shadrach and son-in-law Daniel Davis Baker, husband of his oldest daughter, Mary Ann.[51]

Cayce sold the top two thirds of the League sitio, or survey, in 1837 to John B. Taylor and George W. Martin for the remarkably unrealistic sum of $30,000. When they defaulted a year later, the land reverted to Cayce. Cayce, however, needed cash more than land. In 1838 he was in arrears for $2,260 to financiers Charles Howard and A.B. Fleury, and the brokers seized Cayce's Hosea League holdings for public sale (Figs. 11 & and 12). Cayce settled by forfeiting half his original headright south of League's grant.[52] He also owed money to creditors Hinton Curtis, Samuel Thompson & Co., and A.G. Kellogg, and in 1839 the Matagorda County sheriff seized the remainder of his original Bend in the River grant.[53] Cayce deferred part of the liability by selling the middle third of the League headright to George Elliott.[54] With Elliott's signature, the troubled ferry crossing would have its fourth owner in just five years.

The Cayce family abandoned the Bend in the River shortly after the war, moving to the town of Columbia and overseeing Cedar Grove cotton plantation in Brazoria County near Cedar Lake.[55] Creditors, however, followed him there, and by 1840 he advertised his Cedar Grove holdings for sale. In his announcement, Cayce defended the validity of his title, unleashing on the "unprincipled villains" and "vindictive enemies" who questioned his integrity and caused him "embarrassment."[56] But his antagonists had a point. In one questionable 1834 transaction, Cayce bought a league and half in Fort Bend County but, 13 years later, had still "not paid one dollar of the purchase money." He did, however, sell the land during that time – twice. A judgement was brought against him charging the conveyances without title as fraudulent, and the Fort Bend County sheriff was enlisted to haul him to court.[57]

Cayce lost his remaining Bend in the River land in 1845 after John S. Royall filed suit in the Brazoria County court for a loan of $595.72. Royall sought the upper third of League's grant as payment for the uncollected balance, and although the court agreed, each time the Brazoria County sheriff attempted to collect he reported back "no property found." It wasn't until 1853 that Matagorda County Sheriff George Boyer finally succeeded in serving papers. The property was to be sold at public auction and – either by coincidence or convenience – the highest bidder was John S. Royall, who offered pennies on the acre. Boyer handed him the deed in exchange for $147.60.[58]

Finances aside, Thomas Cayce and his extended family were important period players. Thomas Dodson Cayce fought in the War of 1812 and Texas War for Independence. As a public servant, he served as *regidor* in Austin's Colony, a Matagorda County representative to the Texas Republic government in 1836 (Fig. 13), and a member of the committee to solicit candidates to hold Republic offices in 1838.[59] Keenly aware of the importance of river commerce to Texas, Cayce was an original shareholder in the Caney Navigation

Company, founded in 1837,[60] and that year Sam Houston and senate president Mirabeau Lamar named him a principal in the Colorado Navigation Company.[61] Cayce died in 1856 and is buried in an unmarked grave at Columbia Cemetery.[62]

Cayce's Sons. Son Shadrach Cayce, who fought in the Texas War for Independence alongside his father and brother George Washington, relocated to Preston after the war and maintained a plantation in Wharton County. George Washington Cayce died early.

George Washington Cayce was in San Antonio on a spring day in 1840 with plans to marry, arriving just the day before. The weather was pleasant, and in the town's courtyard and Main Plaza, he watched as the Anglos and Mexicans seemed to mix easily with the Penateka Comanche women and children. In the adjacent flat-roofed, stone courthouse, most of the tribe's chiefs were in a parlay with Republic President Mirabeau Lamar's mediators. The temperament inside the room was tense, negotiations for the return of Penateka Comanche hostages nearing a breaking point. The Texans unwisely decided to hold the tribal delegates until the captive issue was resolved, and when soldiers entered the building, the courthouse erupted in a hail of arrows and bullets.

George was standing by the front courthouse door as the Comanche's bolted for the courtyard. Texas Regulars fired a volley into the crowd that cut down Comanche and Texans alike. It was called the Council House Fight, and when the smoke cleared, over 30 Comanche chiefs and warriors were killed and more than 30 taken prisoners. Ten Texans were wounded, and one Mexican and six Texans were killed. One of those was Cayce, who died instantly.[63]

Of the children born to Hannah and Thomas after they settled in Texas, son Augustus never reached adulthood. Kicked by a horse, the eleven-year-old boy "lingered in intense agony a few days, and was relieved by death."[64] Son Henry Petty Cayce had a long life with a colorful resume. As a 16-year-old boy he served in three War of Independence campaigns. Coincidentally, at the Siege of Béxar, one of his commanding officers was Captain Phillip Dimmit, the colonist who first settled at Jennings Creek in 1821 on the Bend in the River land that his father, 12 years later, came to own.

Henry Petty later fought in the two Mexican invasions of Texas, both of which resulted in the capture of San Antonio, during March and September of 1842. In the latter campaign, led by Mexican general Adrián Woll, Cayce's military career intertwined with another citizen of the Bend in the River, Andrew Neill. Neill was the commanding officer of a detachment of Permanent Volunteers stationed at Cayce's Ferry – on the land his family had owned – from 1836 to 1837 (Fig. 14). Neill during the 1840s was practicing law and was at the San Antonio courthouse when Woll's troops seized the town. Henry Petty was with the Matagorda Volunteers that stormed their position, but Neill had already been taken prisoner and marched to Mexico. He escaped that December.[65] Henry Petty also fought in the Mexican American War under General Zachary Taylor, and from 1861 to 1865 was a Lieutenant Colonel in the 13th Infantry Regiment of the Confederate Army stationed between Matagorda and Galveston.[66]

Henry Petty returned from the Civil War in debt. His San Bernard River estate near Columbia, with its two-story home, with separate kitchens, smokehouse, gin house and press, corn cribs, "and six good houses for laborers" – no longer called slave quarters – as well as his crops and farming tools, were advertised for sale in 1865.[67] He practiced law in Wharton County, then in 1873 determined to resettle his extended family to the north, on the Edwards Plateau. In another link to the Bend in the River, the land he chose was in empresario Hosea H. League's former Leftwich's grant. He never made it, however, dying in route in 1875.[68]

Remarkably, the Bend in the River location of the original Cayce Ferry and its public house are lost to history (Fig. 15). There are no traces of the structures, perhaps claimed by course changes of the Colorado River. At some point after 1839, George Elliott moved the ferry a few miles downstream. Lost as well are any remnants of the volunteer camp where the Texian militia first mustered in late September 1835 in response to Stephen F. Austin's circular calling for "every man in Texas" to take up arms and "take to the field at once." Those volunteers later marched from "League's old place on the Colorado" and "James Kerr's on La Baca," to Gonzales and the skirmish that effectively marked the beginning of the Texas Revolution.[69]

John S. Royall. John Shelton Royall was the son of Virginia and Alabama plantation owner Richard Royster Royall. Father Richard had recognized opportunity in Texas earlier than most, purchasing two Spanish land grants near Nacogdoches during the late 1810s and early 1820s. In 1824, he wrote Stephen F. Austin querying him about the validity of the Spanish titles after Mexican independence,[70] and informed Austin that he and associate Dr. Charles Douglas intended to visit Texas the next year.

Austin corresponded regularly with Richard Royall and Douglas before their journey. Doctor Douglas posed questions to him on such things as the Texas climate, flooding, soil, disease, and religion. The latter subject troubled the doctor. He feared the absence of religious liberty not for himself, but for "our females, whose influence we must submit to in everything relating to social and domestic happiness or be deprived of the pleasures for all other earthly enjoyments."[71] Royall was not concerned about female gratification – he was more worried about laws prohibiting slavery, and postponed committing to Texas because of it.

Richard Royall's slavery concerns were soon placated, and in 1830 he left Alabama for Texas accompanied by his son William, age five, and two-year-old John Shelton Royall. Father and sons journeyed by wagon, living on the open prairie with "18 or 20 negroes" and remained long enough that they "made a crop."[72] Richard Royall returned to Alabama to settle his affairs after choosing a headright in Austin's Colony, but he changed his mind about the site, deciding instead on DeWitt's Colony. When he vacillated a third time, Austin intervened, advising Royall that he "was too particular" and to "finish the thing at once."[73]

Captain Cannon, who had piloted the *Lively* to Austin's Colony with its first settlers a decade earlier, was at the helm of the *Emblem* as it passed Matagorda Peninsula and through the narrow inlet to Lavaca Bay. The year was 1832, and among his passengers were the Royall family, their household goods, livestock, and about 20 slaves. Once ashore, draymen ferried them north to their homestead on the Karankawa Creek at the southern end of the original Matagorda Municipality.[74] Royall soon relocated his family closer to the town of Matagorda to practice law. He traded heavily in land (Fig. 16), eventually owning thousands of acres between Matagorda Bay and Caney Creek.

Richard Royall is best known to Texas history for his role in early Texas government and the Revolution (see Section 2, titled *From Spain to Mexico*). He represented Matagorda in the 1833 Convention and as chairman of the Matagorda Committee of Public Safety and Correspondence. He was unanimously elected president of Texas's first organized government, the Permanent Council, in 1835 (Fig. 18),[75] and was also elected to the

15

Consultation, its second governing body. He did not serve for long. Voting improprieties instigated by parties loyal to Ira Ingram permitted the committee to seat, instead, popular future Texas Secretary of the Navy S. Rhodes Fisher.[76] Richard Royall did not fight the political shenanigans – he mounted his horse and went to war.

For most of the winter of 1836, Royall was in the field with Thomas McCoy's Company of Mounted Riflemen. That summer, at the end of hostilities, he formed a 100-man ranger company, authorized by Republic President David Burnett to round up wild cattle between the Nueces and the Rio Grande to supply the army.[77] The large sum of monies he loaned to the Texas government during the war was eventually paid in land covering 36 counties.[78]

After the war the Royall family resided on a plantation near Caney Creek (Fig. 19), where family matron Ann Underwood Royall died in 1836. Forty-two-year-old Richard Royall died four years later. In the last year of his life, Richard Royall married 21-year-old Elizabeth Ann Love from New York. His sons William and John relocated to Matagorda County after their stepmother married Matagorda lawyer James Denison, in 1848. John Shelton Royall resided under the Denison roof in Matagorda from 1848 until the mid 1850s. Although John listed his occupation in the 1850 Federal Census as "none,"[79] the 21-year-old with no occupation had plans. He intended to follow the lure of gold to California, and one of his first orders of business before travelling was to collect a debt from Thomas Cayce.

The finances of War of 1812 hero and Texian patriot Thomas Cayce were crumbling after the Texas Revolution, and it would cost him all his land holdings along the Bend in the River. One of his debts was to John S. Royall for $595.72. How Cayce came to owe 17-year-old Royall this substantial sum could only be explained if Cayce had earlier borrowed the money from his father, Richard Royall. There is little doubt that John S. received solid counsel about recovery from his land title-savvy stepfather, James Dennison. In 1845, John Royall filed suit in the Brazoria District County court, seeking the upper third of Cayce's Hosea H. League holdings as payment.[80]

Although the judgement found in his favor, it remained unsatisfied for the next seven years. Each time either Brazoria or Matagorda sheriffs attempted to serve Cayce papers, they reported back "no property found."[81] It wasn't until 1853 that sheriff George Boyer seized the property and auctioned it, without appraisal, to the highest bidder. The sheriff, who "cried the same in a loud voice...for a reasonable time" at the courthouse door sold, or "knocked down," the tract to John Royall for 10 cents an acre.[82]

It is unlikely that John Royall spent much of his adult life on the Bend in the River – gold fever had struck. By 1857 he was in Tuolumne County California, operating a gold mining company and "quartz mill."[83] In 1867 he discovered a rich coal

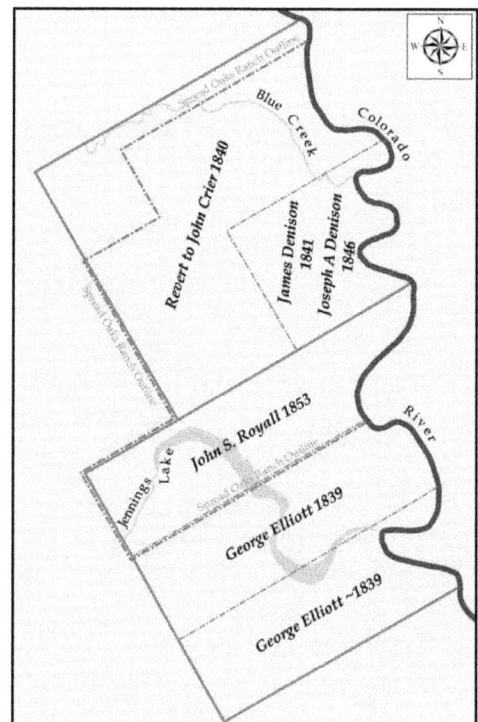

16

deposit in the San Joaquin Valley, and by the 1870s founded other mines in Lower Lake and Mariposa.[84]

John S. Royall spent over 20 years in the mining business. His was an occupation ruled by "mining camp law" and enforced by vigilantes in which "claim jumpers were shot or hung on the spot, but murderers were given a trial."[85] One of those given a trial was a man named Ivey, and he was hung in 1879. Ivey was found guilty of striking Royall in the back of the head with a pickax at one his mines in Mariposa, and the blow killed him instantly.[86] Two years earlier, in 1877, Royall had sold his Matagorda holdings to another absentee landowner, Californian Andrew Olcese.[87]

The Northern Survey at the Bend in the River

John Crier (also spelled Cryer). John Crier was born in 1790 in Spanish Florida. His father, Morgan Crier, had been a volunteer in Thomas Sumter's South Carolina regiment during the American Revolutionary War.[88] Between 1792 and 1804 the Morgan family resided in Louisiana, Georgia, South Carolina, and by 1820 in Hempstead County, Arkansas, where John Crier's wife Cynthia died. The 24-year-old widower packed up his son Andrew, daughter Telitha, and five slaves, relocating to Texas in 1826. He received a 4,428-acre *sitio*, the term used for Spanish land measures, the next year. The land he chose was on the west bank of the Colorado River, adjacent to Hosea League's Survey. Crier did not remain long in Matagorda, resettling in Colorado County, later part of Fayette County, on Ross's Prairie.

The trail of John Crier, either by design or coincidence, is hard to follow. As a young man he relocated frequently, and he went by different names. Most often he was John Crier or Jack Cryer, but both his given and surnames were often interchanged. Sometimes he gave his name as Cryor. The name challenge was made still harder because he couldn't write – he signed his documents with an 'X,' a mark often so illegible that the deed recorder in at least one land transaction referenced his signature as "being a scrawl." Even his death was uncertain – some references show him killed by Comanches in the 1840s and another that had him murdered at 100 years old. The reality was that John Crier died peacefully in 1856.[89]

Crier was a man known as much for his resolve as for "his deplorable habitat of profane swearing." Crier and his slaves first broke the virgin Ross Prairie soil to farm cotton (Fig. 19) and tobacco. A profitable planter, he continued to increase his slave holdings. Although details are scarce, criminal charges were once brought against him by the State of Texas for abusing a slave.[90]

At least some of Crier's income came from smuggling tobacco into Mexico. Tobacco importation from Texas carried a duty, and the surest way to profit from a good crop was to sneak it across the border. Pioneer Noah Smithwick related the story of a smuggling journey with Crier in which they faced the rigors of flooding rains, swollen rivers, a diet of horse meat, and near arrests by – and payoffs to – Mexican officials as they hauled contraband through the border country.[91] On this adventure, profit became less of a motive than survival.

Another source of income was from land sales. Almost as soon as Crier was deeded his Bend in the River property, he began selling, bartering, and mortgaging parcels. The first year he acquired the land he ceded a quarter of his league to Thomas Alley for $295. Alley paid in full at the time of sale. The deed, consummated by Austin land judge Robert Peebles, was not recorded until 1834 because, curiously, Crier had gifted the same quarter league to his children Andrew and Telitha three years earlier.[92] In 1839, Seth Ingram witnessed Crier's signing of the remainder of his 3,311 acres to James Worland for the remarkable price of $7,473. Crier held the Worland mortgage and received the parcel back after Worland's death in 1840.[93]

Crier would sell the land again. In 1849, he gifted a quarter league along with "one negro named Frances" to his daughter, Telitha Crier Grover. The documents were signed with his mark, his customary 'X (Fig. 20).'[94] Crier next resold another quarter league to Galveston resident Jacob L. Briggs in 1855. William J. Jones had to swear that Crier signed the Briggs instrument in his presence, but Crier did not actually appear at the sale.[95] Somehow, Crier managed his land transactions without paying all or some of its taxes – by 1830 he owed $35.91 in back taxes on his Colorado River holdings and remained delinquent a decade later.

During the early days of the Texas Revolution, Crier enlisted in the volunteer army. His name is best known, however, for his role as war-time host to Sam Houston at his plantation house on the east bank of the Colorado River south of the Burnham's Ferry crossing. Houston had taken command of the regular army at Gonzalez just days after the Alamo fell but was now retreating from the tentacles of the approaching Mexican Army. Crier received his esteemed but hurried guest two days before he moved his small force south to Beason's Ferry. Here, he received reinforcements and initially determined to meet the Mexican forces.[96] (see Section 2, titled *The Battle for a New Republic*).

Instead, Houston fell back to the San Jacinto River. Crier's son Andrew joined Houston on his withdrawal, and during the battle at San Jacinto, was with army surgeon general Dr. William P. Smith, tending to Texian soldiers ill with the measles.[97] Andrew, who desperately wanted to be a part of the fight, instead "had the misfortune to be selected as camp guard at Harrisburg."[98] He finally got his chance to fight in 1846 during the Mexican American War, enlisting in Capt. Caleb C. Herbert's Colorado County Mounted Rifle Company and Captain Price's Texas Mounted Volunteers with postings in Monterey, Point Isabel, and Goliad.[99]

Frontiersman John Crier died in 1856 when he was 66 years old, having outlived his second wife, Polly, by three years. By then, he had sold all his Bend in the River holdings. His land to in northern Colorado County became part of the city of Fayetteville.

Thomas Alley. Thomas Alley was the third landowner at the Bend in the River. Like John Crier, Alley was a little hard to track down. In his case, it was because there were two Alley families in frontier Texas, and both had notable roles in its early history. Alley family contributions are not referenced as often as they should, perhaps because researchers wrestled with the challenge of deciphering which family was which. The two extended Alley families not only lived and died at about the same time, but they mostly shared the same names. In total there were three Thomas Alleys, three Williams, and two Johns – not including their offspring, often also with identical given names. Middle names or initials could have been helpful but in most cases those, too, were alike. The family patrons even married sisters, Catherine and Mary Baker.

The first Alleys to immigrate to Texas was the Thomas Valentine Alley Sr. family. Thomas Sr. and his wife Catherine Cynthia Baker were born in Missouri, their sons including Abraham, Thomas Valentine, Jr., William A. Alley, John Caswell, and Rawson

Ross by senior's first wife. The Alleys were acquainted with Stephen F. Austin in Missouri and joined him in his Texas settlement venture. Rawson Alley, the first from the family to emigrate, settled on a league and a half of land in Colorado County in 1821. Rawson's half-brothers John and Thomas moved to Texas a year later. John was killed by Karankawa Indians near the mouth of Skull Creek in 1823, and three years later Thomas drowned in the Brazos River during a skirmish with Waco and Tawakoni Indians. The longest surviving brother, William, founded Alleyton on the Colorado River before the Civil War.[100]

The patron of the second Alley family to settle in Texas was William A. Alley Sr. Born in 1778, William Sr. and his wife Mary Baker raised three sons, John C., Thomas Valentine, and William A. Alley Jr. Like the Colorado County Alleys, they hailed from Missouri. Arriving in Texas in 1826, the William Sr. family located on a land grant they received in the Matagorda Municipality – present-day Jackson County. William Sr. seems to have been killed in an Indian attack the same year.[101]

Thomas and William were granted a second league of land on the San Bernard River in Brazoria County, and Thomas, either by barter or to pay debts, came to own a quarter of John Crier's Bend in the River league in Matagorda County in 1827.[102]

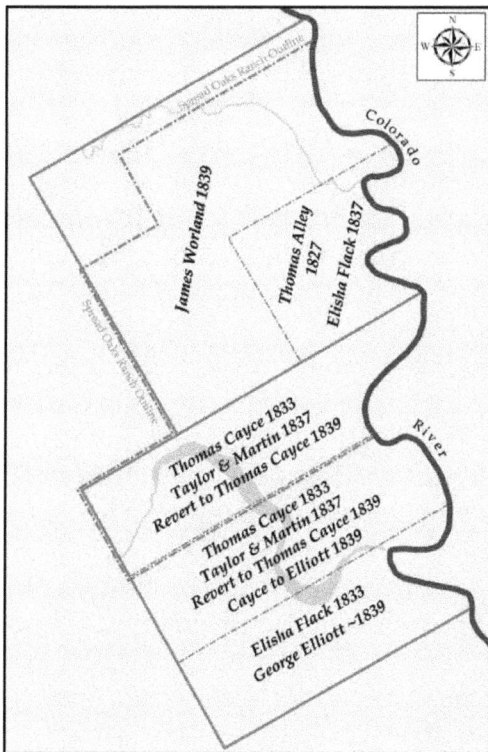

John and William were farmers and raised stock before the Texas War for Independence. Thomas preferred the adventures of military life and by 1829, the *ayuntamiento* of the Austin district elected him a lieutenant in the First Company of the Austin Battalion, a civil militia under Colonel Stephen F. Austin sanctioned for the defense of the province and its settlers.[103]

William, John, and Thomas Alley were at William Millican's gin house on the Lavaca River on that hot day in July 1835 when the assembly unanimously and boldly declared against Santa Anna in a document known as the Navidad Resolutions.[104] All three brothers swore an oath that they were prepared to take up arms. That autumn, they got their chance (see Section 2, titled *From Spain to Mexico*).

The brothers Alley participated in most of the 1835 campaigns of the Texas Revolution. Captain Thomas Alley raised a militia called the Minute Men of Lavaca and, with a company of 31 men, was one of the first to reach the action at Gonzales in October (Fig. 21).[105] The brothers were at La Bahía – the first battle of Goliad – where recently promoted Captain John Alley commanded 111 men from Victoria with Ben F. Smith.[106] They were also at Béxar throughout the two-month siege during the winter of 1835, and John led a company under Ben Milam during heated first days of fighting.[107]

In November, John Alley was appointed to General Austin's headquarters staff. He left the field on December 6, 1835, to organize the local militia in the southwestern part of the Matagorda Municipality. In February he served as a judge at the election of delegates to the Convention of 1836. John's 31-year-old wife died the next year and he returned to his native Missouri. His "handsomely situated" two-thirds of a league on the Navidad River was advertised for sale in 1838.[108]

Brother William was still in Jackson County in 1860, the census that year listing his age as 58 and his occupation as farmer. His net worth, listed at $7,820, dropped to just $2,000 after the Civil War. William abandoned farming to become a retail merchant.[109]

Thomas Alley sold his Bend in the River quarter Crier league to Elisha Flack in 1837. The next year he prepared his will, (Fig. 22) and in 1839 died "without wife or issue."[110]

Elisha M. Flack. Elisha M. Flack came to Texas in 1830 and died early. In a span of just seven years, he served in the Texas Revolution and amassed thousands of acres of land in Matagorda and Brazoria counties. Part of his holdings included two tracts at the Bend in the River – the lower third of Hosea League's Survey and the Thomas Alley tract on the Crier Survey. Deeds and probate documents tell few tales, but in this case, they don't hide that the Elisha Flack story is the tale of a love triangle, an early demise, uncertain business dealings, and years of litigation amongst powerful period players.

Elisha Flack was born in 1799 in North Carolina, marrying Ann Boon in 1821 and relocating to Kentucky. Flack was a widower when he came to Texas in 1830. He received a land grant from Stephen F. Austin in Brazoria County and purchased the Hosea League homestead on a third of his league in 1833.[111] His Army of Texas military record is not easily deciphered, but he was probably in Captain Jacob Eberly's Company commanded by General Thomas Rusk.

Flack's cause of death is unknown, but within six months after returning from the war (Fig. 23), the 38-year-old penned his last will and testament. Beginning with the words "it is appointed for all men to die," he proceeded to grant half of his estate to his 18-year-old Kentucky fiancée America Patton. The remainder was willed to his Kentucky brothers Andrew B. and Thomas Pinkney. Eliza Jane Flack, his sister in Kentucky, would claim any of his properties remaining in the United States.[112]

Elisha Flack died in October 1837 near Bell's Landing on the Brazos River at the home of farmer Morgan Rector. Rector immediately applied to the Brazoria County probate court as Flacks' estate administrator claiming that, on his deathbed, Flack changed his will and deeded all his possessions to his daughter who, he asserted, was Flack's fiancée. If Rector's version was verity, then previous bride-to-be America Patton had been replaced by a new love interest.

The appraisal of Flack's estate was assigned by the probate court to Brazoria County resident William Burrell Aldridge, who dutifully prepared a detailed inventory listing of Flack's possessions (Fig. 24), including the Thomas Alley deed, appraised at $2,200. But, after witnessing the appraisal, Aldridge – not petitioner Morgan Rector – was named by the court named as estate administrator.[113] While Aldridge was settling Flack's estate, he married America Patton – the love interest originally named in Flack's will as his rightful heir.

Estate administrator Aldridge began selling assets to settle claims, including a mandated "public sale" of Flack's League land holdings, approved by the court to settle a $1,000 judgment brought by H.H. League's widow. But in the interim, before any other properties were disposed, the probate judge instructed Aldridge to sell Flack's Thomas Alley tract on the basis that "there is a mortgage to secure the purchase money" (Fig. 25).

There was no mention of who bought the land, or how much was paid. This would be revealed later, a little further down the title chain.

Flack had purchased the Alley quarter league in early 1837 – the year that he died – for $4,000, a figure substantially more than the land was worth. On the same day he signed the deed, he also signed a mortgage to secure payment of the debt, issuing Thomas Alley a promissory note for $1,466.50 with $800 payable in 90 days and the $600 balance "to be paid in groceries and farming utensils at Marion."[114] Flack paid on the note but died still owing $700.[115]

In 1842, the estate of Thomas Alley sued Flack's heirs and administrator William B. Aldridge for the amount due on the note and mortgage. When the Flack heirs did not appear in court, a default judgment was rendered for the balance. County sheriff R.J. Calder was ordered to sell the land. But Calder was aware that the probate court had, in 1841, already sold the land to Matagorda lawyer James Denison. The inconvenience was overlooked, it seems, as Denison again took a second but evidently new deed in 1843.[116]

Denison got a very good deal. According to court records, Flack's initial $4,000 investment was still valued in 1840 at $2,200. Yet the sworn appraisers hired by Sheriff Calder in the 1843 judicial foreclosure assessed the land at just 30 cents per acre, or $332.10. Denison's discounted payment was made to Thomas Alley heir William Alley.[117]

The historical record after Flack's death leaves many questions. The first is Rector's assertion that Flack had a deathbed change of heart – and change of will. Another is why the court appointed Aldridge as estate administrator rather than Morgan Rector. Then there is the question of Aldridge's marriage to America Patton. At best, Aldridge's was a conflict of interest, and it's an intriguing point because if Rector had prevailed, the future Mrs. Aldridge would have lost her Flack inheritance. Lastly was how James Denison was deeded the land twice, in 1841 and 1843.

The players in the Flack estate debacle seem to have flawless records, at least on the surface. There was nothing to suggest that Morgan Rector, for example, was anything other than a man of high moral character. Rector was born in 1778 in Virginia, then moved to Tennessee where he married and started a family. The Rector's next moved to Alabama, arriving in Texas by way of a Mississippi River flatboat to New Orleans where they boarded the schooner *Emblem*. The *Emblem*, under the command of Captain Cannon landed at the head of Lavaca Bay in the spring of 1831. Onboard was another passenger who would contribute to early Texas history – Richard R. Royal.[118]

After they made port, Rector and his 12 children traveled upriver to join 20 Methodist families from northern Alabama that settled on the Navidad River. Knowing they were "entering a foreign land where Protestantism was not tolerated," the community practiced their religion devoutly, but quietly, and were said to have "exerted a wholesome moral and religious influence" as "pioneers in the moral wilderness of [Texas]." The Rector's did not remain for long. Two weeks after landfall, son Joseph was struck dead by lightning. The grieving family packed up again and moved to Brazoria County. It was on Rector's Brazoria farm outside of Columbia that Elisha Flack went to die, apparently in the companionship of the woman he intended to marry. Morgan Rector later organized the first Methodist church at Columbia before moving to San Saba in 1848. Morgan died in his bed in 1866, an open bible on his chest.[119]

William B. Aldridge was to business what Rector was to piety. Aldridge was born in 1810 in Virginia before settling in Texas in the early 1830s. At about the time of the Flack estate dissolution he bought two substantial properties: a cotton plantation between Linnville Bayou and the San Bernard River in 1841[120] and a graceful two-story house in East Columbia. The timing of his financial good fortune is doubtless coincidence, as during this period he was named as an agent on numerous estate foreclosures other than Flack's. Aldridge was a respected icon in the community and, although he did not practice law, was commonly addressed as "Esquire Aldridge." His letters pertaining to the Revolution and plantation life in Brazoria County reside today in the Dolph Briscoe Center for American History.

As for James Denison, he had been in Texas only three years when he signed the first Flack deed. He was a prominent attorney in Matagorda and later San Antonio, served in the Texas Legislature, and was named an associate justice to the Supreme Court of Texas after the Civil War. He was likely guilty of nothing more than recognizing a good land opportunity when he saw it.

The outcome of Elisha Flack's estate generated a lot of smoke, but no gun. Perhaps the record is reflective more of frontier law than the result of a calculated effort to defraud Flacks' heirs. Or not. But in a land and a time where the most egregious infractions were usually resolved by a bullet, the Flack finale was remarkably tame.

James Worland. Texas was far from tamed in the years between its War for Independence and the Civil War, but the resume of many of the men who would relocate to the Lone Star State was evolving. They were no longer always colonists, pioneers, or veterans of any American or Republic of Texas war. The first of the new breed of Texan who came to own parts of the Bend in the River was merchant James Worland.

James H. Worland left very little of his life story behind when he died in 1840 at the age of 26. He had arrived in Matagorda about 1836, which gave him only four years to make his mark. Worland was 23 years old when he opened a mercantile business in the town of Matagorda, first promoting his "new store" in 1837 (Fig. 26 & 27). His was a quickly prosperous enterprise that carried a "beautiful and general assortment of staple and fancy goods," along with clothing, hardware, saddles, bridles, glassware, China, and other staples "required by the settler" but priced at "the most favourable terms."[121] Within a year, Worland added cotton trading and shipping to his company resume.

The list of goods that Jas. H. Worland & Co. advertised in Matagorda newspapers provides a glimpse of the times. Staples included spices, candies, tea, tobacco, soap, bacon sold by the cask, sacks of salt, molasses, and several different fortified liquors such as Madeira, "Cherry Bounce," peach brandy, and ports. Some of the items he carried would be hard to find today, such as baskets of "sweet oil," sperm oil measured in units of "tierces," "Pilot Bread," and "kitts" mackerel (Fig. 28).

In 1838 Worland took a respite from his business and travelled to New Orleans (Fig. 29). On his return he was named to Matagorda's first chamber of commerce, its formation approved by the Texas Senate and House of Representatives in a goal to "diminish litigation and to establish uniform and equitable charges."[122] In 1839, Worland purchased John Crier's original league in Matagorda County except for the 1,117 acres previously transferred to Thomas Alley. He committed to pay $7,473 on a three-year note held by Crier. The deed was witnessed by Seth Ingram, the man who fired the fatal bullet into John G. Holtham with alleged accomplice H.H. League.[123]

Fever came to Matagorda late in the summer of 1840. It didn't have a name – it could have been yellow, or bilious, or congestive. Matagorda's Dr. A.M. Levy announced that he was close to understanding its origin, reporting his theory in 1838 that fevers were linked to "great exposure by bathing in the noon-day sun." For prevention, he advised "careful avoidance of the immoderate heat of the meridian sun, a prudent use of animal food, and abstinence from spiritous drinks."[124]

Evidently not enough people heeded the advice. Two years later fever killed a number of Matagorda County residents, including 26-year-old James H. Worland, who succumbed in September. He was among the first interned at the newly established Christ Episcopal Church but was soon joined by others who died from "the fever," two of consumption, and another who was shot.[125]

Worland died without a will and with a debt of $12,700.[126] His estate was administered by his brother Charles R. Worland, who was permitted to sell the holdings through the county probate court. The auction took place in Matagorda town in 1841 and the highest bidder was John Crier, who received his Matagorda land back.[127] He would sell it again.

James H. Denison. Born in 1812 in Bethel, Vermont to Dr. Joseph Adam and Rachel Denison, James H. Denison was one of nine children. As a 26-year-old bachelor lawyer, he set sail for Texas in 1838 on the schooner *Maria*, landing in the town of Matagorda where he started a law practice with Henry Brewster (Fig. 30). Denison remained in Matagorda throughout the 1840s and represented the town as city alderman for several terms.[128] During the 1842 Texas raids by Mexican generals Ráfael Vásquez and Adrián Woll, Denison served as a private in Colonel Clark L. Owen's Regiment of Albert C. Horton's Volunteer Company. In 1848 he married 33-year-old Elizabeth Ann Love Royall, the widow of Texas pioneer Richard R. Royall.[129]

Lawyer Denison purchased the Flack quarter of John Crier's League from the Matagorda probate court in 1841 and took a second deed on the land in 1843, paying just 30 cents per acre, or $332.10, for land appraised at $2,200.[130] Keenly aware of the title inconsistencies, Denison did not record the deed until 1845.[131] Eight months later he gifted half his interest to his father, Joseph A. Denison Sr., and the other half to William G. Ewing, holding both the title and the mortgage.[132] There is no evidence Denison spent much time at the Bend in River.

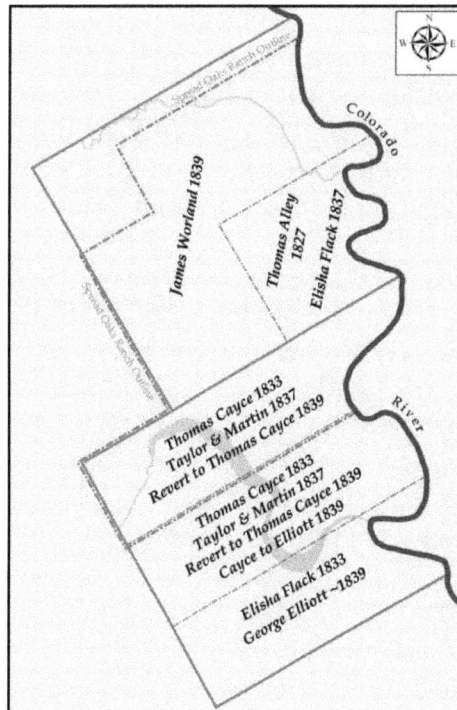

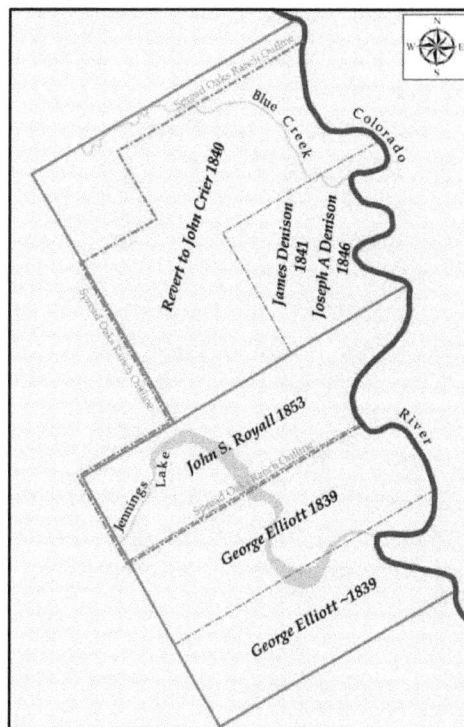

By 1850 the Denison family had residences in both Matagorda and San Antonio, and in the federal census that year, James Denison was listed as the head of a Matagorda household that included his wife, her brother Thomas whose occupation was recorded as a cooper, and her mother Julia Love. Virginia and John Shelton Royster, two of Richard Royster's children by his first wife, were also listed. John was 21, owned five slaves, and reported his occupation as "none." The first of James and Elizabeth's three children, Alice, was born in 1849. Daughter Mary Chase was born in 1851 but died the next year. Son Joseph Adam Denison born in 1856.[133]

Transfer of land titles from Mexico to the Republic of Texas was anything other than orderly, and attorney Denison dedicated his practice to the topic. By 1847 he represented clients in the "prosecution or defense of land suits in district court" in Victoria, Goliad, Refugio, Bexar, Comal, Guadalupe counties.[134] He formed several San Antonio law partnerships, including Denison & Lytle and Denison & Pryor, advertising their expertise in "any business relating to lands" and trying cases in district, federal, and the Texas Supreme Court in Austin.[135]

In one of his most cited litigations, he represented former empresario James Power of the Power and Hewetson Colony in a bid to restore legal title to some 30 leagues of lands issued them by the Coahuila y Texas legislature. The suit pitted Denison and his client against the Republic of Texas, whose courts had ruled the land titles invalid. Denison had a lot at stake – if successful, he would gain an eighth interest in all of Power's claims, making him a substantial Texas landholder. He lost.[136]

In May 1861, as Texas prepared for the Civil War, Denison enlisted in the Bexar County Alamo Rifles under Captain John A. Wilcox.[137] Likely he never served, as he continued his San Antonio Presa Street law practice during 1864 and 1865.[138] More importantly, after his nomination as associate justice of the Texas Supreme Court in 1870, he swore in his oath of office that he never took up arms against the United States.[139]

Denison accepted his supreme court appointment in a state badly divided. Tentacles of the Northern military occupation reached deep into Southern government and politics, the period euphemistically termed Reconstruction. On one side were those who remained loyal to the rebel cause, disparaging Reconstruction as a collection of "negroes, non-resident carpet-baggers, military adventurers, camp-followers, and soldiers of fortune" that "destroyed the liberties of the people."[140]

On the other side was the US Army, its leadership determined to eviscerate the old political order. The military took a hard stance against the former Confederate States, "spurred to severity," and one of the issues was the federal government's establishment of the Freedmen's Bureau. Established in part to assimilate former slaves into society and encourage political participation, it was anathema to everything Southern, and "met in Texas with arson, murder, mayhem, and a pointed lack of relief from a judiciary largely stocked with former rebels."[141]

For a decade, turmoil roiled the Lone Star State political structure. The Texas governorship, for example, was an office so volatile that, in the seven years between 1863 and 1870, it was occupied by six different leaders with almost as many disparate loyalties – Confederate, Union, and military. The same revolving door applied to the Texas Supreme Court. From 1863 to 1870, the chief justice position was filled by no less than five barristers. One chief justice and four associate justices of the constitutionally elected court were ejected as "impediments to reconstruction," replaced in 1867 with a military appointed court by Major General Philip Sheridan, commander of the Texas and Louisiana military district. Detractors labeled the move a "culminating act of a despotic regime" that resulted in encumbering the court with "foreign scalawags."[142]

The Supreme Court fellows during Reconstruction were caught in a political whirlpool, and it took a toll. Chief Justice Royal T. Wheeler suffered from "melancholia and remorse from the consciousness of having espoused the wrong side of the secession issue" and ended "his life by his own hands."[143] Associate Justice Colbert Caldwell, a Sheridan appointee, also had a troubled tenure. A moderate on the issue of negro suffrage, his position was deplored by hardline rebels who accused him of "moral corruption and mental imbecility."[144] At one point, they tried to kill him. Even the Unionist rank and file never trusted Caldwell, citing that he was a former slave owner.[145] James Denison accepted General Joseph J. Reynolds' appointment after Caldwell was removed by order of the military commandant of the Texas district.[146]

Associate Justice Denison served for only seven months, the court undergoing another upheaval in July 1870. He died in San Antonio three years later. As for his Bend in the River land, Denison had disposed of his remaining 543 acres almost 20 years earlier, in 1854.

William G. Ewing and Juliette C. Watts Fretwell. William Gibson Ewing was born in Northern Ireland in 1818, immigrating with his sister Juliette Constance to Linnville on Lavaca Bay in 1839. Within a year, Ewing opened a commission and warehouse business in the port town, and Juliet married port customs collector Major Hugh Oran Watts. Then came the Comanches.

Hugh and Juliette Watts were one of two families with Bend in the River land whose lives were forever changed by hostilities involving Comanche Indians. George Washington Cayce was the first, mistakenly shot and killed by Texas Regulars who opened fire on after negotiations with the Comanche failed at the Council House in San Antonio. Only one Comanche chief survived the Council House fight, chief Buffalo Hump. Now he, with some 1,000 Peneteka warriors and their families, was making a retaliatory raid through the Guadalupe River floodplain on a looting, burning, and killing spree.

They first appeared on the outskirts of Victoria, killing several residents along the route and collecting a herd of some 1,500 horses. William G. Ewing was headed to Victoria at the same moment as the Comanche. As he rode the through the night, he passed their campfires but assumed that the conflagrations were those of Mexican traders. Then he came upon the empty wagon of a man the Indians killed only hours before, and it wasn't until he reached Victoria that he realized how narrowly he avoided a similar fate.[147] Ewing's thoughts turned to his sister and her husband of just 21 days, customs collector Major Hugh Oran Watts, in Linnville.

Buffalo Hump and his followers surprised Linnville village on August 8, able to make their approach because the townspeople did not expect "that a body of Indians would venture so low down the country, and supposed they were Mexican traders with a large caravan."[148] As mounted warriors circled the buildings and dashed down dirt streets, they produced a fearsome spectacle on horses adorned with colored ribbons, their riders bearing headwear of pelts and skins adorned with buffalo horns, antlers, and beaks, claws, and feathers from eagles, hawks, and owls. Then there were the terrifying sounds of war whoops, yells, wolf-like howls, and screams.

The invaders made for their enemy with unparalleled fury but were quickly distracted by the opportunity for plunder. Homes, stables, and warehouses were pillaged and burned. Hats and umbrellas from John Linn's warehouse were looted, and "these the Indians made free with, and went dashing about the blazing village, amid their screeching squaws and little Injuns like demons in a drunken [celebration]."[149] Feather beds were tied to their horses and dragged through the dusty streets, the attackers entertained by the sight of feathers floating in the wind. Cattle were driven into pens and "burned or cut to pieces with their knives and lances."[150]

Linnville's panicked citizens hurried to the bay, taking shelter aboard an assortment of ships moored off the shoreline.[151] Juliette and her husband were among them, until she remembered her gold watch. Although versions differ, in one telling, she and the Major waded back ashore through the throng headed to the bay, past the raider's intent on their plunder, to retrieve the gold piece. From their maritime galleries, the townspeople watched in horror as the newlyweds were intercepted. Major Watts was cut down and scalped while he was still alive. Juliette, a slave, and child were captured.[152]

The raiding party gathered their pack animals, booty, and captives and headed north to make camp, their retreat dogged by militia, Texas Rangers, and the Texas Regular Army. The Texans made a decisive move a hundred miles north of Linnville along a tributary of the San Marcos River known as Plum Creek. Saddled with more than 2,000 horses and mules, Buffalo Hump attempted to protect his main force with a delaying tactic at his rear.

The rear stand was inspiring sight, described by one soldier as "wild and fantastic" as they "stood in battle array." Horse and riders were "decorated most profusely, with all the beauty and horror of their wild taste combined. Red ribbons streamed out from their horses' tails as they swept around us, riding fast." Some sported attire from their Linnville looting, such as the "huge warrior, who wore a stovepipe hat," and another wearing a silk top hat, leather gloves, and "a fine pigeon-tailed coat" with shiny brass buttons – fastened up backwards – who paraded on the field with an open umbrella.[153]

The dramatic rear feint failed. Convinced his medicine would protect him from enemy volleys, one of the revered chiefs paraded recklessly in front of the Texan line. Lucy Turk, the granddaughter of a Texas soldier, wrote that "the old chief kept daring all of them. He kept circling all around. He was decorated all over in ribbons made of calico, feathers in his hair. He was riding a big paint horse and he kept daring them all, until Grandpa Smothers shot him off of his horse."[154] Mourning the chief's loss, the Comanche gave the Texans the edge. They first charged headlong into the rear line, then swept up and along the flanks in a decisive route.

Accompanying the Texan troops were family members of the hostages, intent on their return. The Comanche were notoriously cruel to their captives, and Buffalo Hump's raid was no exception. Victoria citizen Cyrus Crosby, whose wife Nancy Darst Crosby and infant daughter Mary were taken on the road between Victoria and Linnville, is said to have reached his wife as she was lay dying, a lance through her heart.[155] Mary had been dispatched earlier, her little corpse tossed along the roadside.[156]

As the Comanche broke ranks in the teeth of the Texas charge, an Indian boy fired an arrow into Juliette Ewing Watts. Only a steel enforced corset prevented her from a mortal wound. Baptist minister Rev. Z. N. Morrell reported that, when he came upon her, she was found "with an arrow in her chest furiously trying to remove it herself." [157] By some accounts, William Ewing had ridden with the Texas soldiers to rescue his sister, and later accompanied her back to the ruins of Linnville.

In the days following the Linnville raid and Battle of Plum Creek, Texas was rife with stories. There was little truth to most of them. The *Brazos Courier* promulgated that that the raid was the work of 2,500 Mexicans and Cherokees, not Comanche. After Linnville was sacked, the raiders were alleged to have marched and pillaged Texana before taking possession "of all of the West." The anxious editor furthered that, with the Republic at stake, all good citizens were urged to immediately rendezvous at "Casey's [Cayce] old ferry" on the Colorado River and prepare the "line of march for the scene of the war."[158]

Captain William H. Watts, brother of the slain Major H.O. Watts, later published a version of the Linnville events in the *Austin City Gazette*. His intent, he wrote, was only to correct "rumors and various accounts," but mostly, it seemed, he wanted to rewrite the narrative of his brother's demise. In his version, the Watts's never foolishly waded back to shore to retrieve any keepsake items. Instead, "being in the lowest house," the newlyweds simply did not hear the invaders and "could not make their escape."[159]

After Linnville burned (Fig. 31), brother and sister relocated to the town of Port Lavaca. William mortgaged 555 acres of the southeast corner of the original Crier league from James Denison in early 1846 but died just months later. Juliette buried her brother next to her late husband, the two men sharing a headstone and a loving epithet written by sister and wife.

William Ewing's will, prepared and executed by George Peacock and James Denison, left his estate to his sister. It was a large amount of property that included the Bend in the River Denison tract, although the deed wasn't recorded for another 12 years, in 1854.[160] By then, the former Mrs. Juliette Constance Watts had become Mrs. Juliette Stanton, then finally Mrs. Juliette Fretwell.

Juliette married James M. Stanton in 1842 and the couple opened the first hotel in Port Lavaca, the Stanton House. The marriage ended five years later, allegedly because of Mr. Stanton's infidelity. Theirs was the first registered divorce in the new State of Texas. Juliette ran the former Stanton House, renamed the San Antonio House, with third husband Dr. Richard Fretwell. They remained married until her death in 1878.[161]

Jacob Briggs. Galveston merchant Jacob Lawrence Briggs bought a quarter league of from John Crier in 1855 after James Worland's demise. Galveston and Colorado County lawyer William J. Jones swore Crier signed the Briggs instrument in his presence – with his customary 'X' since he could not write – but the absentee Crier did not actually appear at the sale.[162] It was the last parcel the old frontiersman, who died the following year, would sell. The Briggs purchase is curious because he was not a planter and had no ties to Matagorda County. He only held the Crier title for a year.

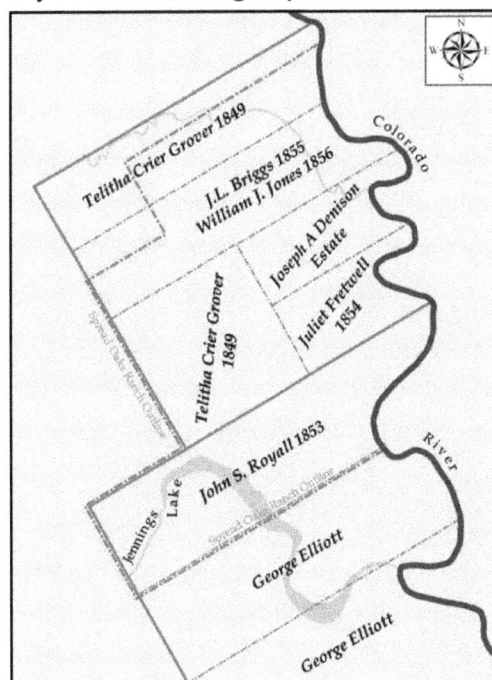

Jacob Lawrence Briggs was born in 1813 and came to Texas in 1843 from his native New York by way of Ohio. In the 1850 Federal census, the 36-year-old Briggs was married to Vermont native Marcia Garfield and had three sons, two who born in Ohio, and a third son born in Galveston. After the death of his first wife in 1850, he married Mary L. Quigg. According to the 1870 Federal Census, their union produced three daughters, Fanny, Mary, and Kate. In census language of the day, no one in the family was recorded as "deaf and dumb, blind, insane, or idiotic."[163]

Briggs owned a forwarding and commission business with warehouses at the port of Galveston and formed the Briggs & Yard "Clothing Emporium and Gentlemen's Furnishing Goods" on Temont St.[164] Merchant Briggs took an active civic interest in his adopted city. He was a founding father of the first Methodist Church in Galveston,[165] a city alderman, and established the first fire department of Galveston. Called the Galveston Hook and Ladder Company No. 1, in its 1847 by-laws he felt he needed to explain the importance of the venture, writing of "the great utility to be derived from well-regulated hook and ladder companies in times of fire."[166] Later, he was an incorporator of the Fireman's Insurance Company of Galveston. In the 1850s Briggs was president of the Scott and Graham Club, established "to aid in the election of the Whig candidates to the presidency and vice-presidency."[167]

Briggs supported the South during the Civil War, but like many former Confederate soldiers, he never discussed his secessionist sentiments or war record. After making himself "liable to heavy pains and penalties" for his role in the rebellion, he was given an executive pardon by President Andrew Johnson (Fig. 32).[168] Then, like many Texans, he focused almost entirely on rebuilding his fortunes after the War.

Briggs had been a director of the Galveston and Brazos Canal and Navigation Company from its inception, the company operating the 14-mile-long Brazos Canal connecting west Galveston Bay to the Brazos River, an important artery for Galveston commerce that delivered goods to the coast via steamboats and sailing vessels without passing through Houston. Briggs was also the vice-president and one of the originators of the Galveston, Houston & Henderson Railroad, a 50-mile track connecting Galveston to Houston.[169]

The 120-foot steamship SS *Varuna* of the Mallory Line sailed from Galveston on October 1, 1870, headed for New York with 335 bales of cotton, 9 bales of wool, 2,178 hides, and 450 barrels of tallow.[170] There was nothing remarkable about her run, the ship's helmsman Captain Joseph Spencer having made the voyage between the two port cities twice a month for over a year (Fig. 33). Readied for her return voyage, the vessel advertised for passengers and freight, setting sail for Galveston on October 15 (Fig. 34). Onboard were 36 travelers, mostly Galveston residents spending the summer in New England to avoid the pestilence of the Oleander City's yellow fever and malaria season.[171]

The *Varuna* was expected in Galveston towards the end of October, but by early November "grave fears" were entertained that the vessel had been lost.[172] She was. On October 20, the ship broke up off Florida's Jupiter inlet during a gale. Some of the crew succeeded in making the coast in a small tender, but the captain, other officers, and every passenger – some 48 people total – were drowned. Their bodies were never recovered. Many of Galveston's most prominent citizens were among the dead, the entire city of Galveston "plunged in grief" and draped in black mourning flags after the disaster.[173] Listed among the *Varuna's* passengers was Jacob L. Briggs.

A year later, I.L. Briggs conveyed his brother's Crier land to William J. Jones. Jacob's wife Mary settled the remainder of his estate in 1872.[174]

William Jefferson Jones. William Jones was born in the Rappahannock Valley of Virginia in 1810. He graduated from the University of Virginia with a law degree law at 19, and just two years later became the youngest man to practice law before the US Supreme Court. He left Virginia first for Charleston, then Baltimore, Washington D.C., and Mobile Alabama. Throughout his travels, he fostered acquaintances that would help him throughout his career, among them future US President James Monroe in Virginia, banker Nicholas Biddle, South Carolina Governor James Hamilton, and future Republic of Texas president Mirabeau Lamar during his stay in Alabama.[175]

In 1837 Jones put down roots in Galveston and was immediately appointed as pay master to the army by outgoing Texas Republic president Sam Houston. During the winter of 1838, newly elected Republic of Texas president Lamar signed an act to raise a ranger company and regiment "for the further protection of the frontier against the Comanche and other Indians." Jones was appointed to the rank of major and headed west.[176]

President Lamar's western frontier shifted east in the summer of 1839 when he resolved to remove the Cherokee from East Texas by negotiation, compensation, or force. Early parleys with Cherokee Chief Bowles were initially favorable, but as time passed the Texans believed he was stalling and preparing for war. Roughly 800 Cherokees and 500 Texans engaged in several battles along the upper reaches of the Neches River. Colonel Edward Burleson had command of the Texas Regular Army and Major William J. Jones led the Volunteers. The Cherokee abandoned the field after Chief Bowles "was shot in the back, near the spine, with a musket ball and three buckshot. He breathed a short while only after his fall."[177]

The mission successfully cleared East Texas of the Cherokee, but commander Jones would forever dwell on his misgivings. In what was certainly a minority view at the time, he viewed the Native American's expulsion with "shades of sorrow," believing that most of the tribe had been manipulated by "Mexican emissaries on the one hand, mischievous Indians on the other and the grasping desire of unprincipled land grabbers for their territory."[178]

Jones returned to Galveston where he was appointed judge of the Second Judicial District and elected to the first Republic of Texas Supreme Court as an associate judge in 1840. He briefly moved to Palacios, in Matagorda County, where he married Princeton New Jersey native Elizabeth Giberson.[179] Capitalizing on irregularities in the transfer of land titles from Coahuila y Texas to the Texas Republic, Jones began acquiring large tracts of real estate. He and his family of 11 children divided their time mostly between plantations in Colorado County and near Virginia Point along the west side of Galveston Bay.[180]

Although he probably did not spend much time there, one of the properties he purchased was John Crier's southwest quarter league from Jacob Briggs. Jones held the land for the next 25 years, from 1856 to 1881. Whatever plans he might have had for his Matagorda County holdings were interrupted by the Civil War. His war time record is not well documented, but it is known that during 1863 Jones was a First Lieutenant in Lt. Col. Griffin's C Company. He was cited for bravery in repulsing two Union boats that came ashore at Sabine Pass in April of that year.[181]

William Jefferson Jones was also a planter and slave owner (Fig. 35). After the Civil War, he studied horticulture. Although he experimented with various vegetables, fruits, and native and imported grasses to improve hay yields, his passion was improving cotton varieties. He had grown cotton since the early 1850s, his only hiatus during the Civil War when he donated his Virginia Point crops to "invalids of the hospital here" for them to "manage for their own use and behoof."[182]

As an early authority on the cultivation of Sea Island Cotton, planter Jones advised that it prospers under a "saline influence" that gives it its "softness and length and strength of fiber which cause it to be so highly prized."[183] He studied pesticides, proving a theory that the destructive cotton worm could be eradicated by "poisonous remedies" – notably arsenic – in experiments with the carcinogen labeled with such innocuous names as "Pure Paris Green," "the Cotton Worm Destroyer," and "London Purple."[184]

His scope of horticultural knowledge was so widely celebrated that he was appointed by the Department of Agriculture as a "cotton worm" observer in the late 1870s.[185] He saw and promoted the economic benefit of machine ginning and the baling of seed cotton. Jones's foray into diseases was less memorable, as he curiously linked detrital cotton to malaria outbreaks, commenting that "it is well known that the surplus cotton seed is generally thrown out from the gin-house and permitted to decay and to breed malaria."[186]

Jones during his later life was a staunch supporter of the southeast Texas railroad industry and advocated improvement of deepwater portage in Galveston Bay. In the 1880s, he convinced the Texas House of Representatives to pass a bill relinquishing the state's title to Galveston Bay's "submerged grounds" to support his scheme to dredge waterways and expand shipping.[187]

William Jones died peacefully at his Galveston home in 1897, his death "painless and like a child going to sleep."[188] His wife Elizabeth died in 1903, the newspapers of the day carrying the news with headlines such as "Mrs. Elizabeth G. Jones Expired Last Night" and "the Passing of an Old Citizen."[189]

Epilogue. Many of those who came to Texas were single men with wanderlust or who were seeking a second chance. Of the latter, some left the States because they were unable to regain their financial footing after bankruptcy, or relocated after their spouses died, and a surprising number came to avoid charges for murder. Families emigrated as well, intent on land opportunities not possible north of the Texas border. Regardless of their motives, their success was anything but guaranteed. Texas was not just a foreign country – it was a foreign land. What the settlers didn't know about Texas would test them, and even come to hurt them.

Each of the Texas ecoregions presented unique challenges, and the crescent shaped lowlands of the coastal plains fringing the Gulf of Mexico were no exception. Although the region provided planters with rich alluvial soils and transportation access via innumerable waterways connected to the Gulf, it was prone to river floods and tropical cyclones, a long list of diseases, and a name not yet familiar to them – the Karankawa.

The Karankawa. The domain of the Karankawa was mainly the Texas Coastal Plain. They were nomadic, eating only what they could find, catch or kill. Each of the five Karankawa subgroups was loosely governed by a civil and a war chief. Karankawa's worshiped two Gods and assigned mystical properties to such things in the natural world as the moon and the setting sun. Their canoes were crude but their bows, strung with deer sinew, were remarkably refined. Women were assigned mostly camp duties and were treated as property, to be freely swapped for a horse or glass beads. Karankawa men were tall, often over six feet, their bodies heavily tattooed with lower lip and nipple piercings of cane and reeds.[190]

Their culture would put them at odds with the mores of White settlement, including their appearance, non-Christian rituals, extreme torture of captives, and the practice of eating the heart of a dead warrior for courage or their brains for wisdom.[191] When they stole sheep and cattle, or viciously attacked and murdered Austin's settlers, it ensured that the Karankawa's time in Anglo Texas would be short. For his part, Stephen F. Austin had no thought of compromise from the beginning. One side was going to lose – it was the Karankawa, and they lost quickly.

The first killings credited to Karankawa in what would be Matagorda County occurred in 1822, when four Anglo scouts disappeared at the mouth of the Colorado River. The remainder of the travelling party sought shelter upriver on Jennings Creek. In 1826 a band swept into Live Oak Bayou, attacking two settler families, the Cavanah and Flowers. Polly Flowers was scalped, and Mrs. Cavanah and her three daughters butchered. Another daughter with an arrow in her back, along with Mrs. Flowers daughter, survived.[192]

After the Cavanah and Flowers killings, some Bay Prairie colonists abandoned the country. Settlers from the more densely settled Canebrake Creek preferred to fight. Under the command of renowned adventurer and frontiersman Captain A.C. Buckner, some 60 Texans pursued the Karankawa's, killing several in two skirmishes. They tracked the band to the Colorado River, killing most, then followed the survivors along the coast and exterminated the remainder. When the battles ended over 40 warriors, women, and children were killed.[193]

The next year Stephen Austin represented the Mexican government in negotiating a treaty with the Karankawa that ceded the colonists all lands east of the Lavaca River. It was broken when the Indians destroyed the fort at the site of that would become the town of Matagorda. Again, the colonists drove them west. There were no Karankawa depravations in what would become Matagorda County after 1830. Compared to the Comanche, whose reign was mostly north of the coastal plain, the number of colonists killed by the Karankawa was small. But it was enough that, by 1840, Anglo persecution ensured that only a small number remained in Texas, and those mostly south of the San Antonio River.[194]

Quiet Killers. Early Texas was often promoted as a "healthful place" with a "salubrious climate." The reality was different. Summer heat and humidity was stupefying, and winter's brutal blue northers killed crops, livestock, and not uncommonly, colonists. In summer and early fall coastal Texas's humid air could be thick with biting gnats, deer flies, greenhead horseflies, and mosquito swarms sometimes so impenetrable the sun appeared to be in eclipse. Texas land and water could be alive with alligators, rattlesnakes, cotton-mouths or water moccasins, copperheads, and coral snakes.

Colonists died from wounds that wouldn't heal. They drowned in all kinds of ways – on ships at sea, on boats in the passes and bays, on rivers they tried to cross on horseback during times of flood or not. For women, the biggest killer was childbirth, followed by burns as they tended the cooking hearth in long, flowing garments of the day. Mostly, whether man, woman, or child, they died of diseases.

Diseases came with less fury than the Karankawa but took a far greater toll. The litany of infections including pneumonia, "flux," consumption, meningitis, fevers, both "yellow congestive and bilious," smallpox, diphtheria, scarlet fever, Asiatic cholera, malaria, typhoid, and tuberculosis. Usually, they were clueless as to the cause, conjecturing the loss with descriptions such as "she was subject to spasms, and died in one," or died of a "fever from exposure to the sun" or "from a polpus in the nose."[195]

In the cholera epidemic that struck the Coastal Prairie in 1833, 43,000 Texians were stricken and 18,000 died.[196] Much like the Santa Anna's thrust into Texas and the Runaway Scrape that turned settlements into ghost towns three years later, entire communities were abandoned as families fled the scourge. It is not known how many died in the town Matagorda, only that the cholera outbreak "swept off numbers of the settlers." Malaria also killed at regular intervals, but the summer and fall outbreak in 1843 was said to be the worst in Matagorda's short history.

Yellow fever epidemics were probably the most dreaded of the diseases, the most substantial outbreak occurring in 1862. D.E.E. Braman chronicled the epidemic, reporting that of the 150 "white inhabitants" of Matagorda town, 88 caught the fever and 45 died. Of the 50 slaves in the town, "some were very sick, but none of them died."[197] There weren't enough healthy residents of either color to properly bury the town's dead. The epidemic was described in the *Gonzales Inquirer* that October with "the yellow fever still prevails in Matagorda. There were four deaths on Thursday night. The people of the town are moving their goods, furniture, etc., to the country as fast as they can in fear of an attack. The town is defenseless."[198]

West Indian Cyclones. Nearly as deadly as epidemics were hurricanes, but they did not come as silently. Matagorda suffered two major hurricanes in its formative years, one in 1837 and another in 1854. Before they were known as hurricanes, they were called tempests or cyclones. The Republic of Texas was barely a year-old when, sailing under the flag of the Union Jack, the British brig *Racer* set anchor in the Brazos River in April 1837. The ship's arrival was met with much trepidation as memories of the War of 1812 lingered, although the *Houston Telegraph and Texas Register* reassured readers the brig had no warlike intentions, only to "investigate the civil and political condition of the country." *Racer* would make headlines again a few months later as the name of the first hurricane to hit the Republic of Texas.

Hurricane of 1837. "Racer's Storm," as it would be dubbed, was spawned in the Caribbean and crossed the Yucatan Peninsula where, on September 29, the H.M.S. *Racer* sailed into its wrath. Despite a length of over 100 feet and a 33-foot width, the vessel was twice "blown flat on its beam ends." Fatigued sails and running rigging failed, then both the main and fore masts. Three sailors and a child were killed onboard. The storm next crossed the Gulf of Campeche then tracked along the Texas Gulf Coast.[199]

Loss of life in sparsely settled coastal Texas was minor, the brunt of the storm affecting mainly mariners. In Matagorda, a Galveston-bound ship moored at Decrow's Point was blown offshore and the entire crew was lost. A four-foot storm tide surge damaged wharfs and buildings in the town of Matagorda, but there was no loss of life on the mainland. Racer's Storm made landfall again at Grand Chenier, Louisiana, then crossed the southern United States, returning to sea off the southern North Carolina coast. On its way the storm would kill again, and among the dead were those in a fleet of schooners and brigs bound for Texas.[200]

Mariner Richard Grimes left port on the Connecticut River that fall bound for Austin's Colony, his schooner *Henry* loaded with all his earthly possessions. In New York he rendezvoused with another 26 sailing ships, mostly merchants eager to trade with the new Republic. After a stay in Havana, the fleet sailed into the jaws of Racer's Storm off the Alabama Coast. Captain Grimes remained at the helm for three days surviving on only "coffee and whiskey" as the ship negotiated masthead-high swells. All 26 of the other ships were lost at sea. Grimes came to settle at Bay Prairie along the Tres Palacios River and raise a family. With his son William Bradford, he built one of Matagorda County's first promising cattle operations.[201]

Hurricane of 1854. The first sense of danger was the large, rolling swells that broke on the outer bar. Then a strong wind began to churn the Gulf and Matagorda Bay. The next morning the full wrath of the September 17, 1854, storm came ashore on Matagorda Peninsula, crossed the Bay, and made landfall near Matagorda town. Like Racer's Storm, the list of dead was longer for mariners than for mainland residents. One casualty was the first steamboat to negotiate the Colorado River and pass future Spread Oaks Ranch, the *Kate Ward*, that wrecked near the mouth of the Colorado River, killing eleven seamen. Elijah Decrow's schooner *Tom Payne* sank in Matagorda Bay with a loss of its crew and captain. All hands were lost when another schooner was blown to sea at Pass Cavallo, and a third that capsized at anchor and was spotted bottom-up in the giant breakers on the outside bar.[202]

At the peak of the storm, Bay and Gulf waters converged on Matagorda Peninsula, the churning mass of water reaching ten feet above sea level in places. Only the ribs of the highest sand dunes protruded above the sea, and they saved many from perishing. Decrow's resident James Green hauled his eight children by buggy up the beach, and to prevent them from blowing away, he buried the youngsters in hastily dug holes in the dunes. When the family crawled from the sand and returned to Decrow's, every structure in town was either leveled or washed into the sea. The Green's walked inland for 30 miles, carrying every remaining thing they owned in a single sack.[203]

Nearly all the buildings in the town of Matagorda were demolished, including a livery stable that disintegrated with such fury that it killed every horse. Only three houses "escaped prostration or unroofing." Four people lost their lives. One witness to the storm's rage wrote that houses were seen "crashing and breaking up, their materials flying through the air, women and children screaming and running wither they knew not." Upriver, the storm uprooted an immense number of trees, the roads along the Colorado River remaining impassable for weeks. Much of the cotton and corn crops in the storm's path were destroyed, as well as hundreds of acres of sugar cane that were blown flat to the ground "so late in the season that it will be unable to right itself."[204]

Texian colonists fought nature, native Americans, Mexican armies, and within themselves for the place they called Texas. They thrived, but it was an uncertain journey. In a span of just thirty-six years Texas flew four flags. One as a Mexican territory, another as a Republic, and then in 1845 as part of the United States. The fourth flag was a Confederate one, and it would cost her dearly.

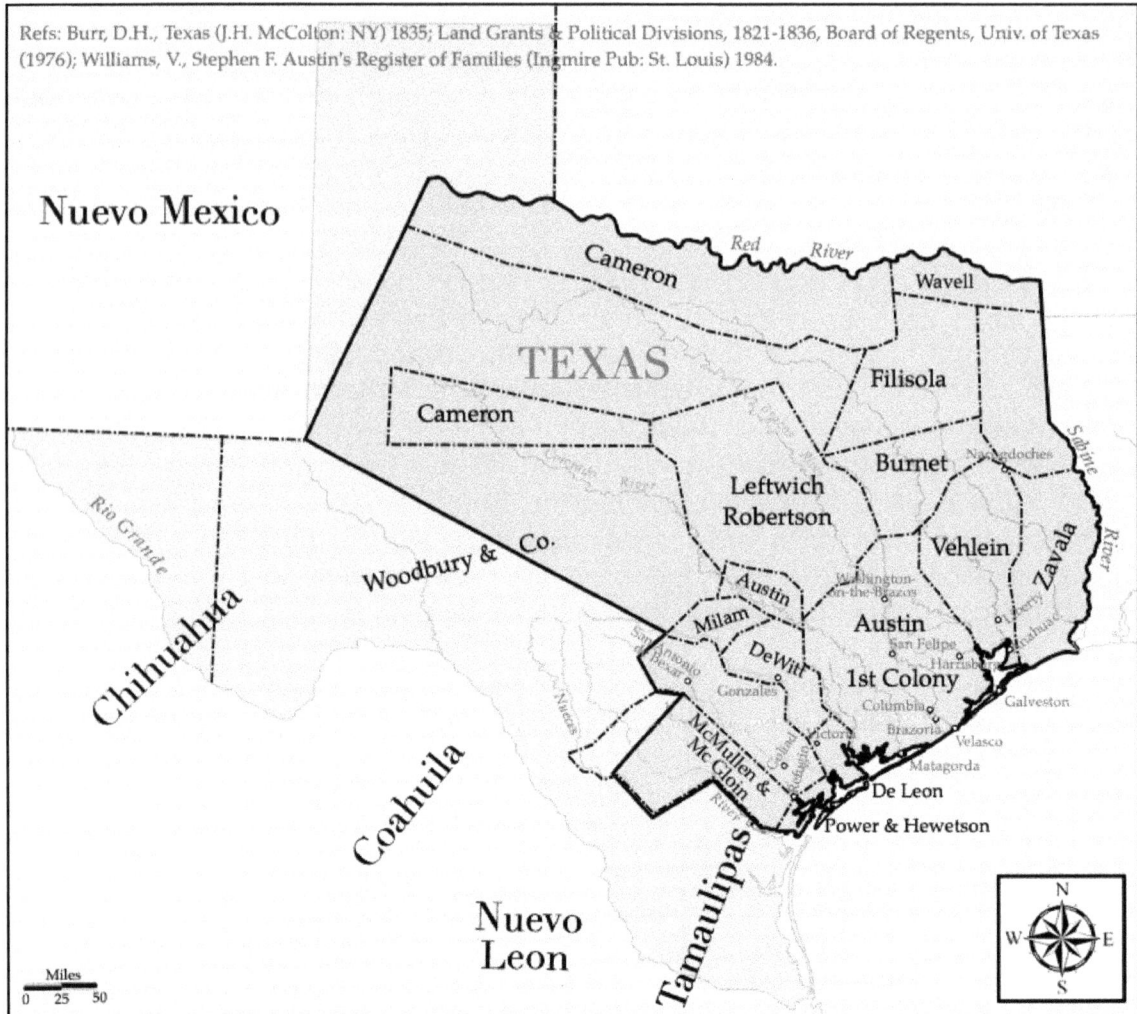

Fig. 1. The original extent of Mexican Texas was much different from the present, extending south to only as far as the Nueces River. Of the many colonies and grants ceded by Mexico to empresario aspirants, only a few were successful. The 1824 *Federal Constitution of the United Mexican States* followed the Spanish model that organized Mexico into states and departments that were headed by a provisional chief who oversaw municipalities governed by an *ayuntamiento*, a council consisting of an *alcalde* (chairman), *regidores* (councilmen), and *síndico procuradors* (jurisprudence).

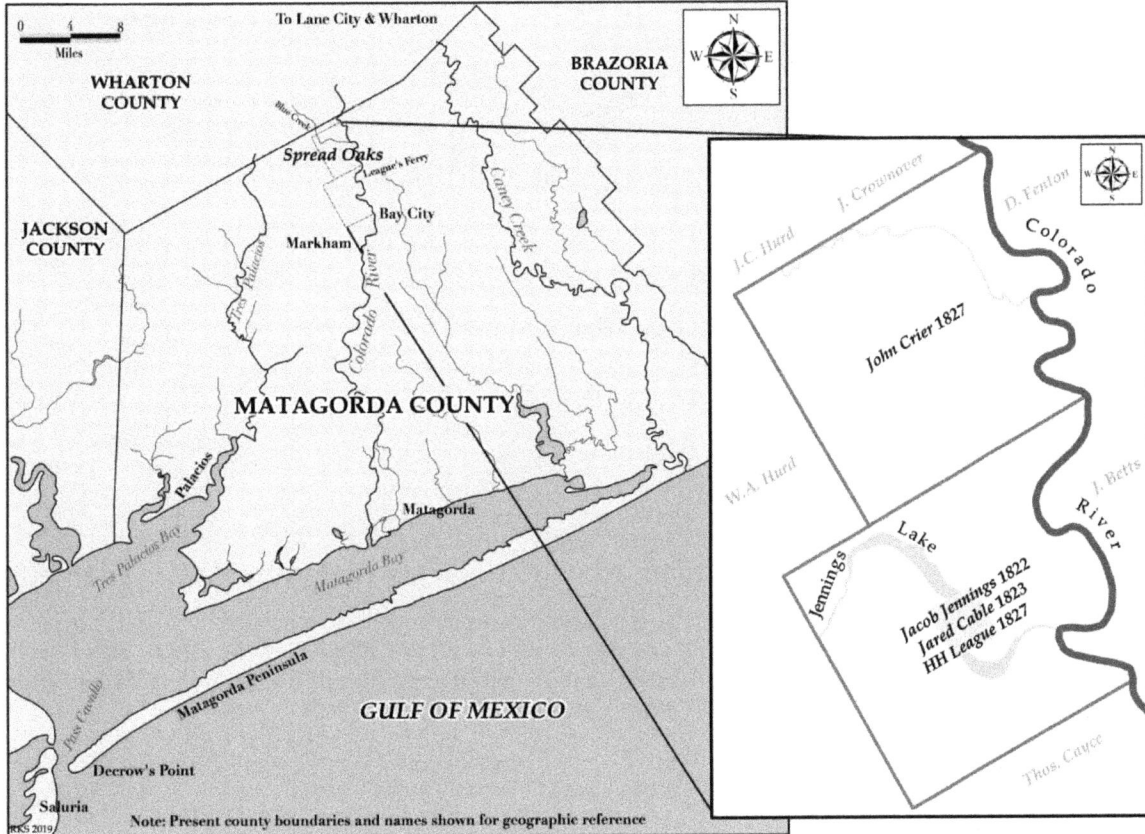

Fig. 2. Area map with inset of the original grantees of the H.H. League *sitio*, or survey, and the location of John Crier's *sitio*. The term *sitio* was abandoned after Texas land was no longer administered by Mexico, but it remains in original documents from the period.

JOHN, keel boat, of New Orleans. Built on Ohio River, 1815. 29 8/95 tons; 95.10 ft. x 12 ft. x 2.4 ft. One deck, one mast, stem and square stern the same.

Enrolled No. 26, March 13, 1818. *Owners*: James Barnett, New Orleans. *Master*: Jacob Jennings.

ARKANSAW, steamboat, of New Orleans. Built in Tennessee, 1820. 51 tons; 95 ft. 10 in x 14 ft. 6 in. x 3 ft. 10 in. One deck, no masts, square stern, hurricane house on deck.

Enrolled No. 101, Sept. 23, 1820. *Owners*: Jacob Jennings, Garret Jordan, Henry Young, Oliver Jones, New Orleans. *Master*: Jacob Jennings.

Figs. 3 & 4. Before he came to Texas 1821, Jacob Jennings was a Mississippi River pilot. Modified from *Ship Registers and Enrollments of New Orleans, Louisiana*, Survey of Federal Archives in Louisiana, v.1, 1804-1820, p. 73. 9, Hill Memorial Library: Louisiana.

Natchitoches 14th Oct. 1823

Dr Sir,

I have not complied with the certificate which you gave me when in Natchitoches last, to settle on your grant of land am in hopes it will make no great difference if I should come on in two or three months from this date, by Mr McWilliams I send you a file of news papers which I have procured on purpose for your perusal, of the latest dates, we have no news more than you will find in those papers, I am

J. Cable

To Col. S.F. Austin Brazos

Fig. 5. A year after Jennings died, the Jennings Survey was transferred to Jared Cable, Stephen F. Austin's forwarding agent in Natchitoches, Louisiana. Cable, however, never took claim of the land. Modified from Eugene Barker, ed., *Annual Report of the American Historical Association for the Year 1919: The Austin Papers*, (Washington, D.C.: Government Printing Office, 1924), v. 1, 1, p. 699.

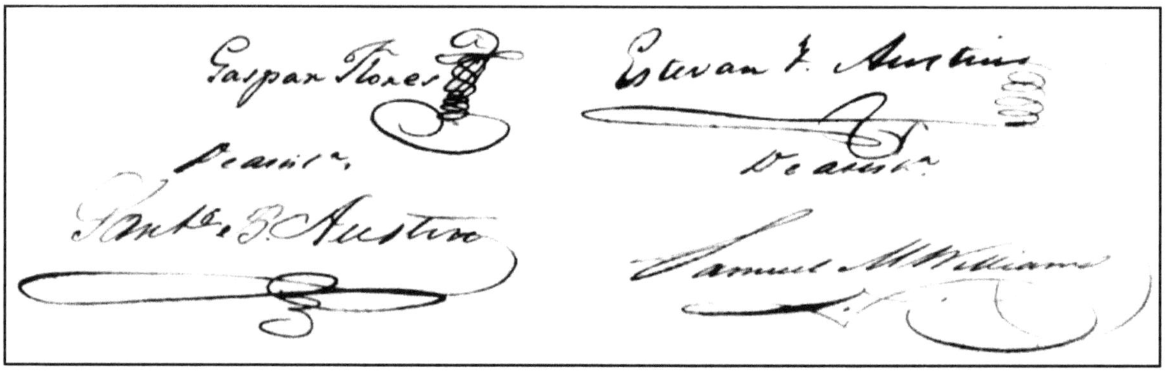

Fig. 6. Signature on the League title of Béxar land commissioner Gaspar Flores, who recorded deeds for Austin's original 300 after Baron de Bastrop died. A loyal federalist, he later had a role in the Texas Revolution, denouncing dictatorial President Santa Anna and resigning his position in 1835. Matagorda County Deed v. 162, p. 567-8, dated May 25, 1827.

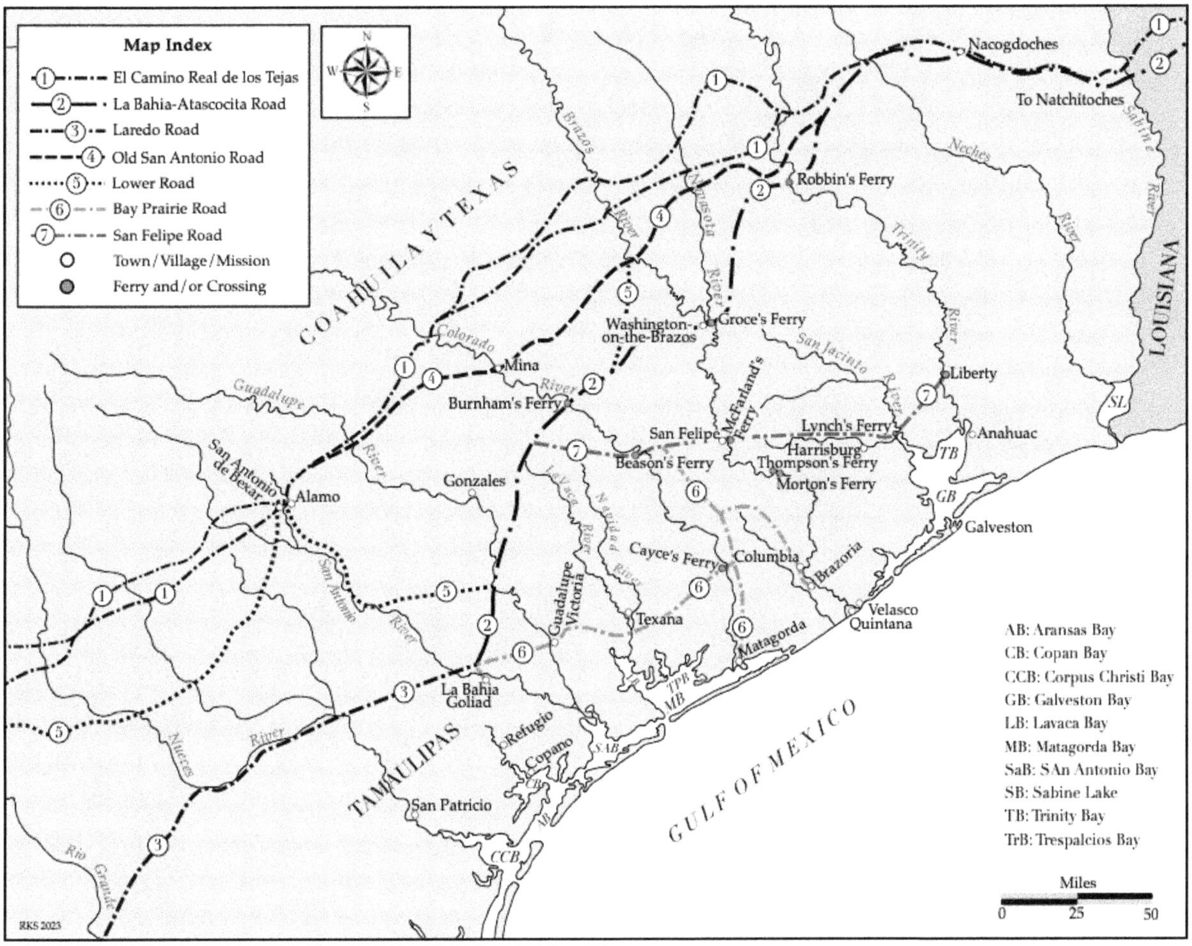

Fig 7. Map showing some of the major roads and ferries of early Texas. Various references, incl. *Texas 1820-1836*, Plate 105, credited to Carlos E. Castaneda, courtesy Michael Bailey, Brazoria County Museum; El Camino Real de los Tejas NHT (Sante Fe: National Park Service) http:/txu-plmaps-oclc-89397661-el-camino-real-de-los-tejas-map.

Colonel Stephen F. Austin

Dear Sir,

My wife will start tomorrow morning to remove to Jennings camp. It is unnecessary for me to attempt a description of her deplorable situation and feelings, of my own I have not sufficient use of my faculties to address you as I would wish, but I call upon your humanity and merciful feelings to come down and see and have an interview with Mrs. League with before she starts and also with myself.

H.H. League
Nov. 13th, 1830

Fig. 8. Letter from H.H. League to Stephen F. Austin, Nov.13, 1830, writing of his discouragement as he prepared to leave his Colorado River land and home. Modified from Eugene Barker, ed., *Annual Report of the American Historical Association for the Year 1919: The Austin Papers* (Washington D.C.: Govt. Printing Office, 1924) v.1, part 2, p. 537.

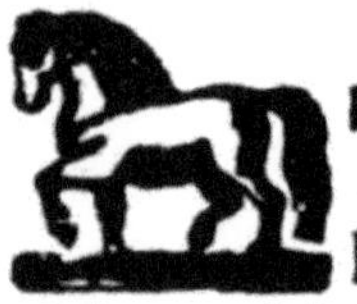

ESTRAY NOTICE.

TAKEN up by Henry Williams near League Ferry, a Bay Spanish MARE, with one hind and one fore foot white, and a small star on the forehead, branded A S. Appraised at $40.

THOMAS HARVEY,
Clerk pro tem. C. C. M.

Matagorda, April 18, 1838. 36—3t

Fig. 9. Cayce's Ferry was still known in Bay Prairie as League's Ferry long after it changed ownership. *Matagorda Bulletin*, April 25, 1838, Univ. of North Texas Libraries, The Portal to Texas History, https://texashistory.unt.edu/ark:/67531/ metapth80348/m1/1/.

TOWN OF

AUGUSTA.

THE most valuable portion of the league of land granted to H. H. League, and situate on the Colorado river about twenty five miles above Matagorda, is appropriated by the undersigned and present owner, as the scite of this town. The locality and other advantages of this point on the river, for the establishment of a town, have induced the proprietor to appropriate several hundred acres for the accommodation of the public. The situation is contiguous to timber suitable for building, and has an unobstructed navigation to the lumber region above; it has an inexhaustible supply of excellent water, and the soil is equal to any in the country for gardening. The place has been settled for many years, and has been found as healthy as any on the river. It is on the great trading thoroughfare to the Interior of the country, and will be found a more eligible position than any other in American Texas, for concentrating the trade, and supplying the markets of the interior. As such, therefore, its peculiar position recommends it to the notice of the steady and enterprising portion of the community, and invites the attention of speculators & adventurers.

TERMS—A sale of lots will be opened at the dwelling house of the proprietor, on Wednesday the 24th of December next, and closed on the 29th of the same month. A credit of one, two and three years will be given to purchasers; requiring notes bearing eight per cent interest for the amount, retaining a lien on the property sold, till final payment.

THOMAS CAYCE.

Augusta, Nov. 10, 1834.

Fig. 10. Thomas Cayce's dream of establishing the town of Augusta were dashed by the Texas War for Independence. *Texas Republican*, Dec. 13, 1834, Univ. of North Texas Libraries, The Portal to Texas History, https://texashistory.unt.edu/ark:/ 67531/metapth80250 /m1/2/.

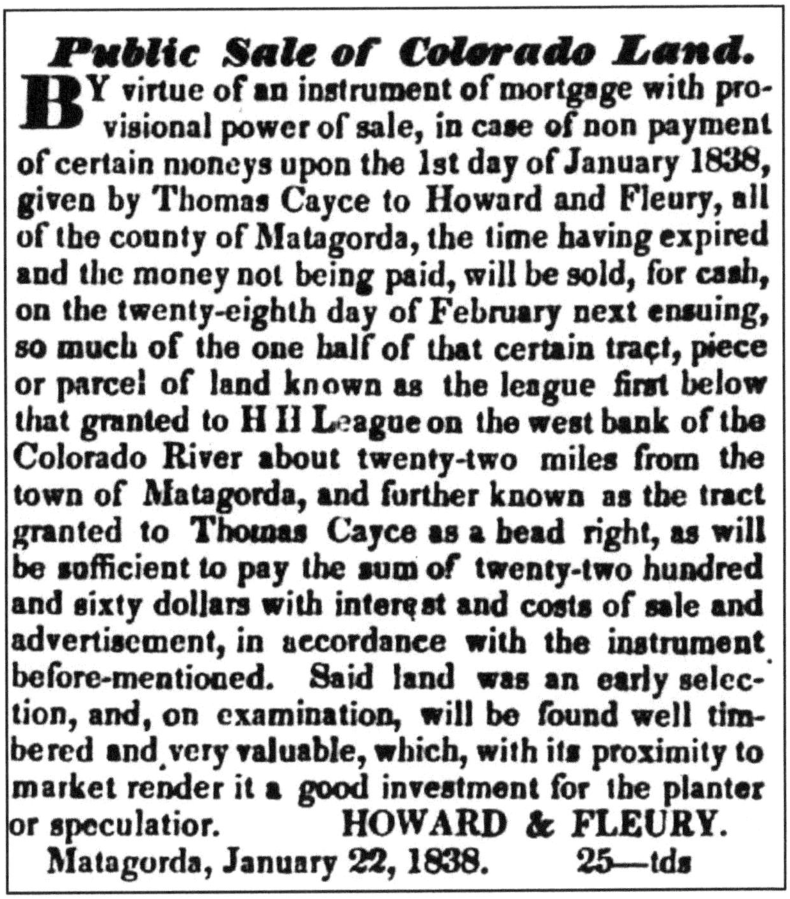

Public Sale of Colorado Land.

BY virtue of an instrument of mortgage with provisional power of sale, in case of non payment of certain moneys upon the 1st day of January 1838, given by Thomas Cayce to Howard and Fleury, all of the county of Matagorda, the time having expired and the money not being paid, will be sold, for cash, on the twenty-eighth day of February next ensuing, so much of the one half of that certain tract, piece or parcel of land known as the league first below that granted to H H League on the west bank of the Colorado River about twenty-two miles from the town of Matagorda, and further known as the tract granted to Thomas Cayce as a head right, as will be sufficient to pay the sum of twenty-two hundred and sixty dollars with interest and costs of sale and advertisement, in accordance with the instrument before-mentioned. Said land was an early selection, and, on examination, will be found well timbered and very valuable, which, with its proximity to market render it a good investment for the planter or speculatior.   HOWARD & FLEURY.
Matagorda, January 22, 1838.   25—tds

Fig. 11. Financiers Charles Howard and A.B. Fleury seized Cayce's Hosea League holdings for public sale in 1838. *Matagorda Bulletin*, Jan. 24, 1838, Univ. of North Texas Libraries, The Portal to Texas History, https://texashistory.unt.edu /ark:/67531/ metapth80339/m1/2/.

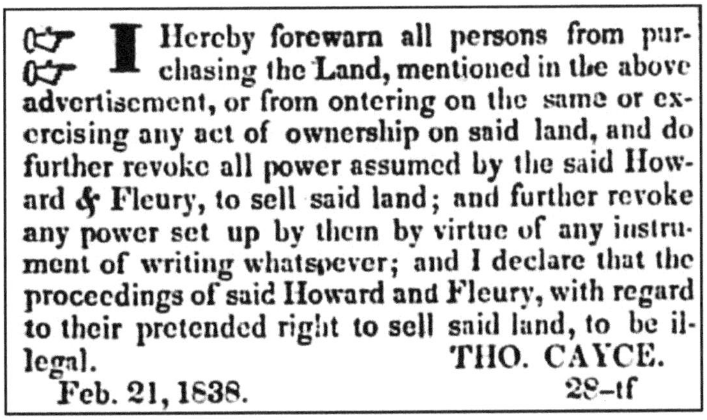

I Hereby forewarn all persons from purchasing the Land, mentioned in the above advertisement, or from entering on the same or exercising any act of ownership on said land, and do further revoke all power assumed by the said Howard & Fleury, to sell said land; and further revoke any power set up by them by virtue of any instrument of writing whatsoever; and I declare that the proceedings of said Howard and Fleury, with regard to their pretended right to sell said land, to be illegal.   THO. CAYCE.
Feb. 21, 1838.   28–tf

Fig. 12. Thomas Cayce's published response to the "illegal" seizure of his holdings. *Matagorda Bulletin*, Feb. 28, 1838, Univ. of North Texas Libraries, The Portal to Texas History, https:// Texashistory.unt.edu/ark:/67531/metapth80343/m1/1/.

TELEGRAPH.

COLUMBIA, TUESDAY, AUGUST 23, 1836.

We have been requested to announce the following citizens as Candidates at the ensuing election, under the new Constitution.

STEPHEN F. AUSTIN, *for President*,
SAM. HOUSTON, " "
HENRY SMITH, " "
M. B. LAMAR, *for Vice President*.
WALTER C. WHITE, *Senator for the County of Brazoria*.
WM. H. WHARTON, " " " "
P. R. SPLANE, " " " "
BRANCH T. ARCHER, *Representative for* " "
WM. H. JACK, " " "
JOHN A. WHARTON, " " "
J. Æ. PHELPS, " " "
WM. H. PATTON, " " "
M. C. PATTON, " " "
A. SOMMERVILL, *Senator for the District of Austin and Colorado*.
MOSELEY BAKER, *Representative for the County of Austin*.
JESSE H. CARTWRIGHT, *Representative for Harrisburgh County*.
DANIEL PERRY, " " " "
ROBERT WILSON, *Senator for the District of Harrisburgh and Liberty*.
A. B. HARDIN, " " " "
E. T. BRANCH, *Representative for the County of Liberty*.
D. D. D. BAKER, *Representative for the County of Matagorda*.
THOMAS CAYCE, " " "
GEORGE SUTHERLAND, *Senator for the District of Matagorda, Victoria and Jackson*.

Fig. 13. When he was nominated as a candidate for Matagorda County Representative in 1836, Thomas Cayce was in good political company – S.F. Austin, Sam Houston, and Henry Smith were vying for Republic president, and M.B. Lamar for vice president. *Telegraph and Texas Register*, Aug. 23, 1836.

To Captain Neill Commanding at Casey's Ferry

Sir: you are desired to hand over the property of Fuldon B. Turner and let him pass also with the carbine in addition to what he before had.

I send two letters to your care which I wish sent on to their address with greatest expedition and any word that you can send to the people in Bay Prairie to forward Beeves to the army. I wish it done speedily. I will pay them in cows and calves in sixty days! If there can be no other cattle furnished, let the public cattle be sent.

General Huston is out hunting his horse, or he would give you this order. The weather is so bad that it has detained us until now. In a few minutes we will set out for camp. No news from camp at this time.

Sam Houston

Fig. 14. Letter from Republic of Texas president Sam Houston to Andrew Neill, the commanding officer of a detachment of Permanent Volunteers stationed at Cayce's ferry – known briefly as Colorado Station – from 1836 to 1837. Neill in 1842 was taken prisoner by Adrián Woll's and marched to Mexico. Modified from A.W. Williams and E.C. Barker, ed., *The Writings of Sam Houston*, v. II July 1814-March 31, 1842 (Austin: Univ. Texas Press, 1938) p. 61.

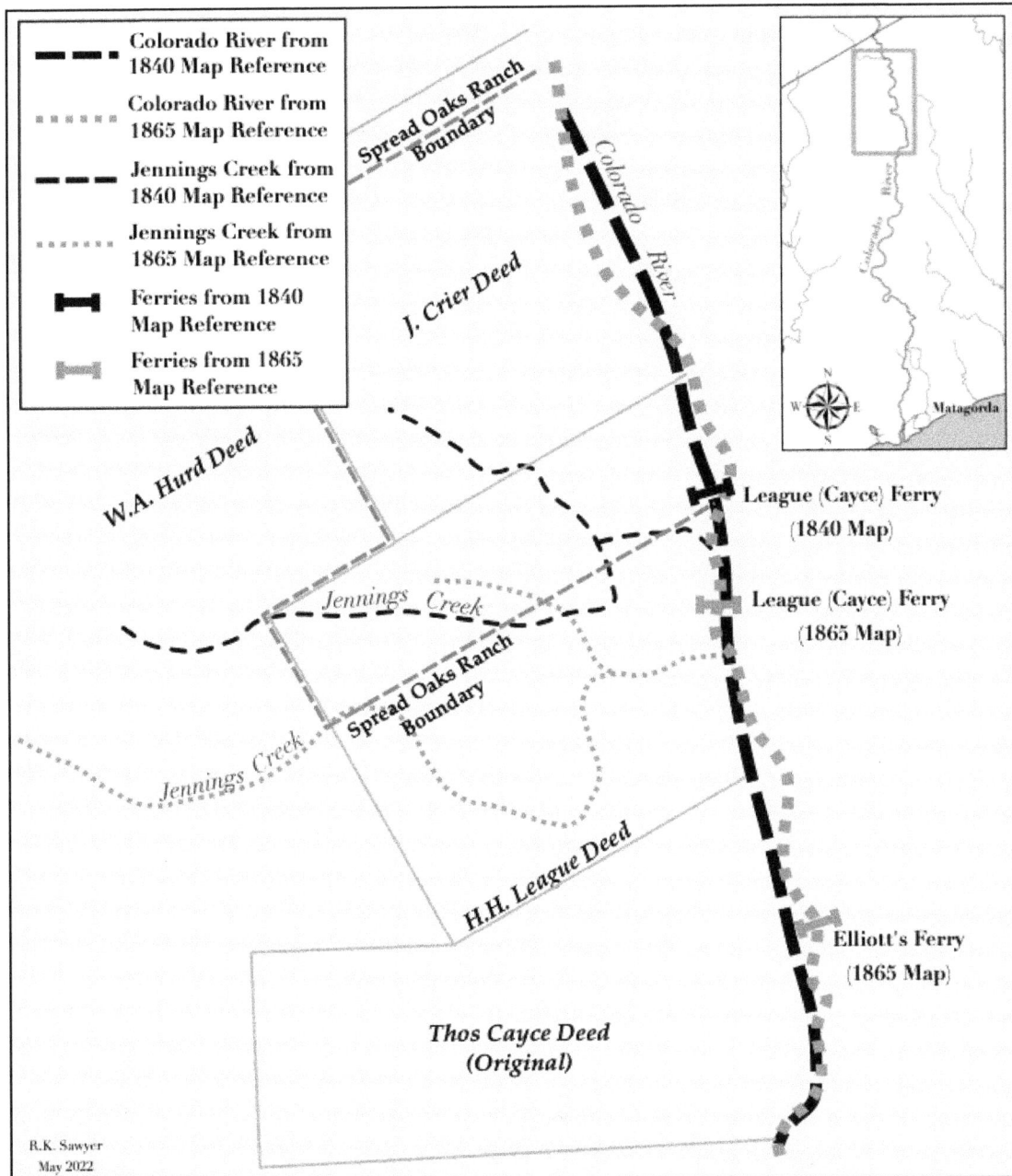

Fig. 15. Part of the reason the League-Cayce ferry location is unknown may be that no one knows exactly where to look. There are about a half dozen maps from the era with references to the ferry, and most show a different Jennings Creek configuration and even location. End member examples are shown on the figure, but they are just two of several. Most maps are more consistent with the 1865 morphology.

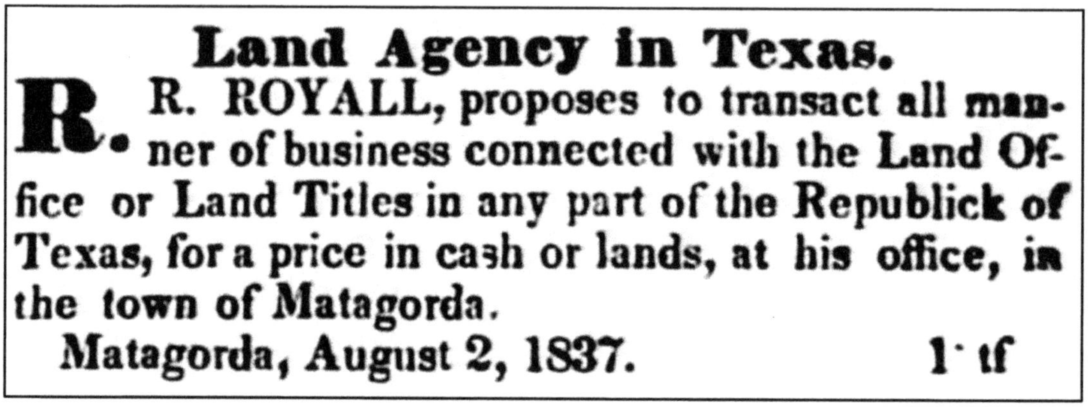

Land Agency in Texas.

R. R. ROYALL, proposes to transact all manner of business connected with the Land Office or Land Titles in any part of the Republick of Texas, for a price in cash or lands, at his office, in the town of Matagorda.

Matagorda, August 2, 1837. 1·tf

Fig. 16. Advertisement for Richard Royall's land agency business. *Matagorda Bulletin*, Nov. 8, 1837, Univ. of North Texas Libraries, The Portal to Texas History, https://texashistory.unt.edu/ark:/67531/metapth80329/m1/4/.

To all to whom these may come

The bearer Mr Erasmus Smith is on his way to camp with a tired horse—we wish to forward him by all means in our power as we think he may be very importantly usefull

And we therefore request that any citizen will do his best to assist him to camp with a horse.

(Signed) R.R. Royall.
President.
of Committee

San Felipe
Oct 15. 1835

Fig. 17. Transcript of letter from R.R. Royall, Oct. 15, 1835, to the Permanent Council. In his short tenure as its president, Richard R. Royall sent voluminous dispatches covering subjects such as the movement of army volunteers and supplies, the new postal system, and the closing of land offices. This letter, with original spelling preserved, references Erastus 'Deaf' Smith, who became one of the more trusted scouts of the Texas Revolution. Modified from Austin Papers: Series III, 1835, *Digital Austin Letters*, http://digitalaustinpapers.org/.

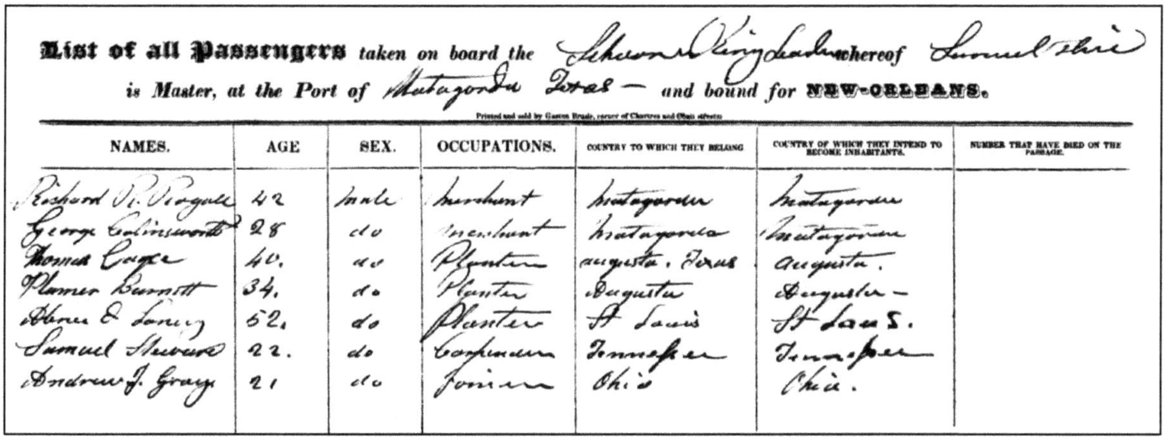

List of all Passengers taken on board the Schooner King whereof Samuel is Master, at the Port of Matagorda Texas — and bound for NEW-ORLEANS.

NAMES.	AGE	SEX.	OCCUPATIONS.	COUNTRY TO WHICH THEY BELONG	COUNTRY OF WHICH THEY INTEND TO BECOME INHABITANTS.	NUMBER THAT HAVE DIED ON THE PASSAGE.
Richard R. Royall	42	male	merchant	Matagorda	Matagorda	
George Collinsworth	28	do	merchant	Matagorda	Matagorda	
Thomas Cayce	40.	do	Planter	augusta, Texas	augusta.	
Plamer Barnett	34.	do	Planter	Augusta	Augusta —	
Abner E. Lacey	52.	do	Planter	St Louis	St Louis.	
Samuel Stewart	22.	do	Carpenter	Tennessee	Tennessee	
Andrew J. Gray	21	do	Joiner	Ohio	Ohio.	

Fig. 18. After Richard Royall moved to Caney Creek, he sailed on a schooner bound for New Orleans, along with some good company – Colorado River and war veteran Thomas Cayce, who listed his residence as Augusta town, and George Collinsworth, who fought at the Battle of Velasco and first Goliad. Passenger Lists, 1813-1963, Ancestry.com, https://www.ancestry.com/discoveryui-content/view/403159:748.

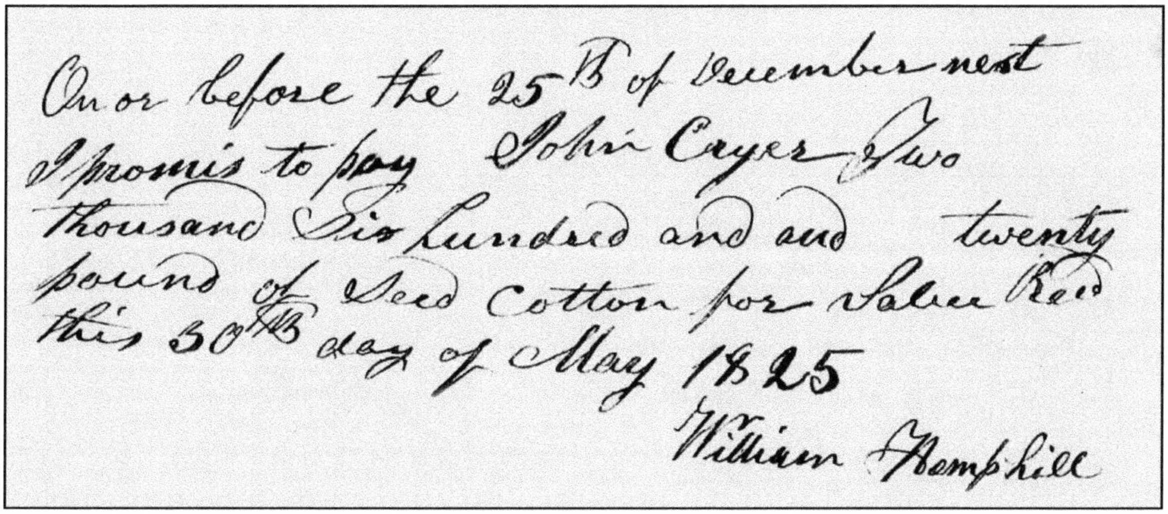

On or before the 25th of December next I promise to pay John Cryer Two thousand Six hundred and one twenty pound of Seed Cotton for Value Rec'd this 30th day of May 1825

William Hemphill

Fig. 19. An 1825 John Crier cotton promissory note. Collection of Bob Parker, Ancestry.com, https://www.ancestry.com/mediauiviewer/tree/87337187/person/ 445553 46014/media/f7d329e5-10ff-4055-992b 169a3c56243e.

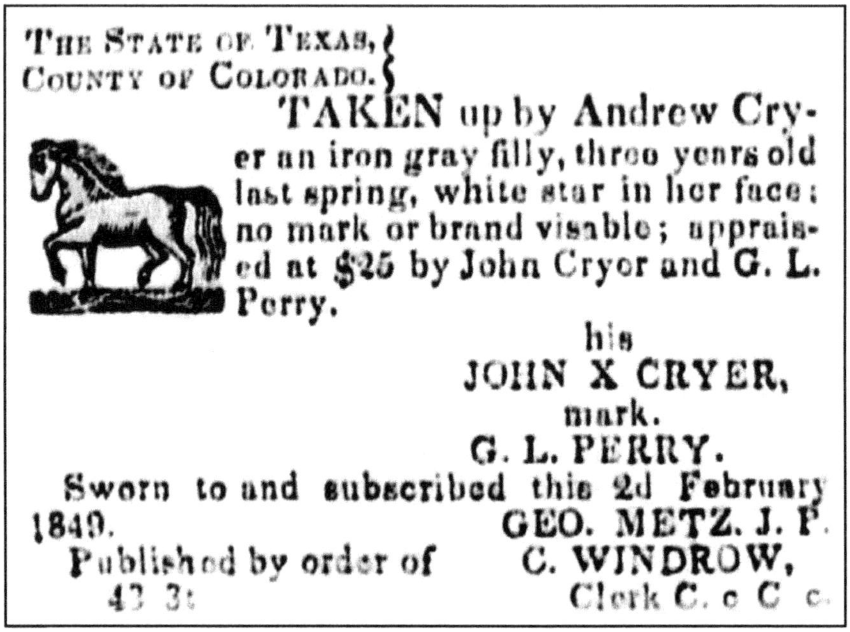

THE STATE OF TEXAS,
COUNTY OF COLORADO.

TAKEN up by Andrew Cryer an iron gray filly, three years old last spring, white star in her face; no mark or brand visable; appraised at $25 by John Cryor and G. L. Perry.

his
JOHN X CRYER,
mark.
G. L. PERRY.

Sworn to and subscribed this 2d February 1849. GEO. METZ. J. P.

Published by order of C. WINDROW,
43 3t Clerk C. c C c.

Fig. 20. A lost horse advertised in 1849 with its $25 appraisal certified by John Crier, who affixed his customary 'X' mark for his signature. *Texian Advocate*, March 2, 1849.

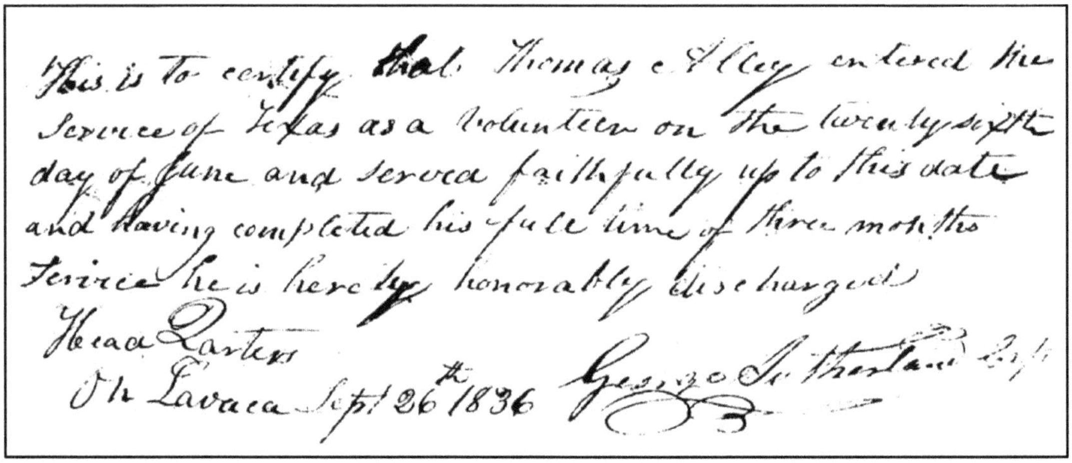

This is to certify that Thomas Alley entered the Service of Texas as a Volunteer on the twenty sixth day of June and served faithfully up to this date and having completed his full time of three months Service he is hereby honorably discharged

Head Quarters
On Lavaca Sept 26th 1836 George Sutherland

Fig. 21. Thomas Alley discharge from volunteer service during the months after the Battle of San Jacinto. *This is to certify that Thomas Alley entered the service of Texas as a volunteer on the twenty sixth day of June and served faithfully up to this date and completed his full time of three months service he is hereby honorably discharged.* Signed at Headquarters "on the Lavaca," September 26, 1836, by Captain George Sutherland. *Texas Adjutant Records*, Texas State Library and Archives Commission, https://www.tsl.texas.gov/apps/arc/service/viewdetails/329.

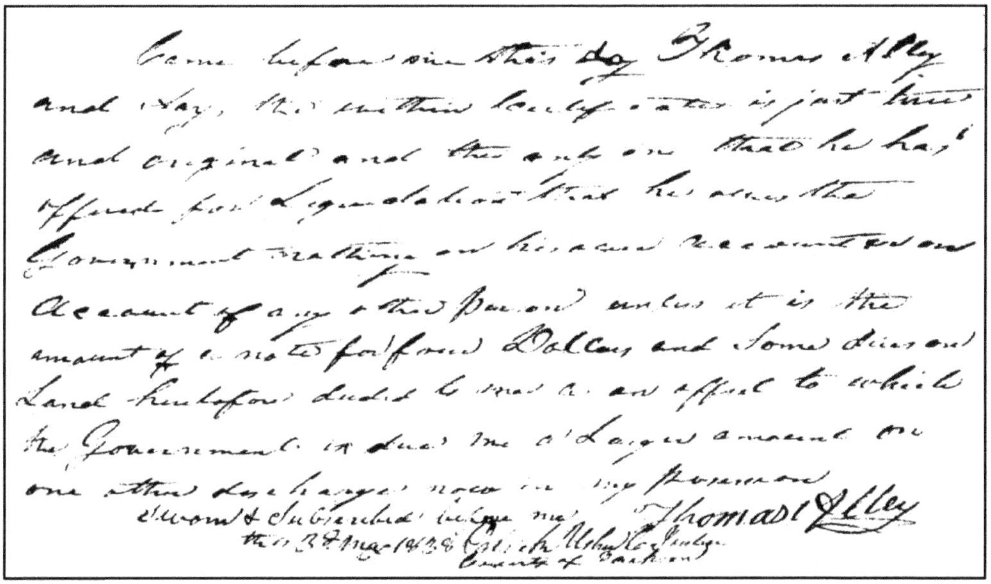

Fig. 22. Thomas Alley Last Will and Testament: *Came before me this day Thomas Alley and say, this written certificate is just, true and original and the only one that he has offered for liquidation that he owes the Government nothing on his (illegible) account of any other person unless it is the amount of a note for four dollars and [Matagorda surveyor Thomas] Tome dies on Land heretofore deeded to me as an affect [sic] of which the Government is due me a larger amount on one other discharge now in my possession. Sworn and before me 3rd May 1838.* Thomas Alley Papers, from *Texas Adjutant Records*, Texas State Library and Archives Commission: https://www.tsl.texas.gov/apps/arc/service/viewdetails/329.

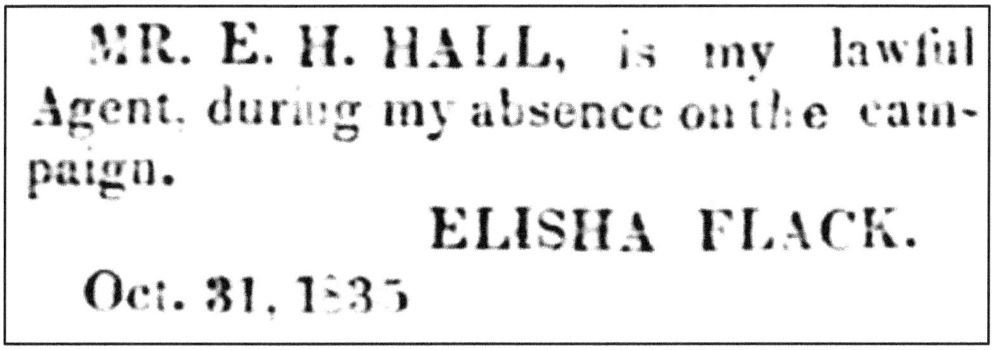

MR. E. H. HALL, is my lawful Agent, during my absence on the campaign.

ELISHA FLACK.

Oct. 31, 1835

Fig. 23. Elisha Flack's agent assignment before the fall 1835 "campaign" of the Texas Revolution. His agent, E.H. Hall, operated a tavern and stable in Marion (East Columbia) and evidently borrowed the purchase money from Elisha Flack. *Texas Republican*, Nov. 14, 1835, Univ. of North Texas Libraries, The Portal to Texas History, https://texashistory.unt.edu/ark:/67531/metapth80278/m1/3/.

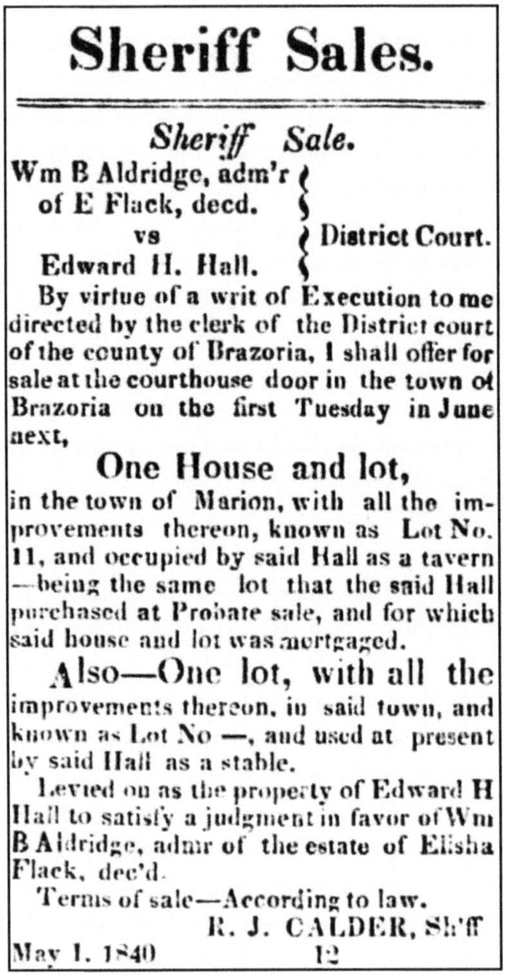

Sheriff Sales.

Sheriff Sale.

Wm B Aldridge, adm'r of E Flack, decd. vs Edward H. Hall. } District Court.

By virtue of a writ of Execution to me directed by the clerk of the District court of the county of Brazoria, I shall offer for sale at the courthouse door in the town of Brazoria on the first Tuesday in June next,

One House and lot,

in the town of Marion, with all the improvements thereon, known as Lot No. 11, and occupied by said Hall as a tavern—being the same lot that the said Hall purchased at Probate sale, and for which said house and lot was mortgaged.

Also—One lot, with all the improvements thereon, in said town, and known as Lot No —, and used at present by said Hall as a stable.

Levied on as the property of Edward H Hall to satisfy a judgment in favor of Wm B Aldridge, adm'r of the estate of Elisha Flack, dec'd.

Terms of sale—According to law.

R. J. CALDER, Sh'ff

May 1. 1840 12

Fig. 24. William B. Aldridge's notice of sale on Brazoria County properties foreclosed during his handling of the Flack estate. *Brazos Courier*, May 5, 1840, Univ. of North Texas Libraries, The Portal to Texas History, https://Texashistory.unt.edu/ark: /67531/metapth80157/m1/3/.

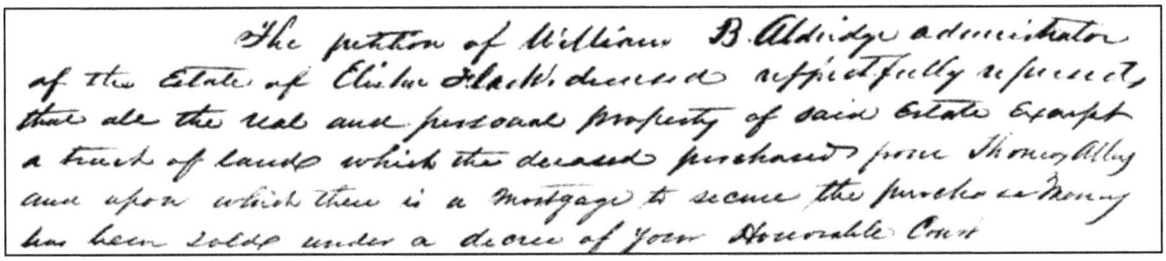

The petition of William B. Aldridge administrator
of the Estate of Elisha Flack deceased respectfully represents
that all the real and personal property of said Estate Except
a tract of land which the deceased purchased from Thomas Alley
and upon which there is a mortgage to secure the purchase money
has been sold under a decree of your Honorable Court

Fig. 25. Probate court document of Flack's assets and claims from 1840 showing that "*The petition of William B. Aldridge administrator of the estate of Elisha Flack deceased respectfully represents that all the real and personal property of said estate except a tract of land which the deceased purchased from Thomas Alley and upon which is a mortgage to secure the purchase money has been sold under a decree of your Honorable Court*." Flack probate records, courtesy Michael Bailey, Brazoria County Museum.

New Store

HATS, Boots, Shoes, Russet Brogans, &c., by the Package or Dozen.—A General Stock of Hard-ware, Queeus-ware, Cut-Glass Decanters, Pitchers, Tumblers, and a few choice setts of Moracian, Guilt, plain & common China

J. H. WORLAND & cO.

Matagorda, December 12, 1837.   19—tf

JAS. H. WORLAND & CO.,

MATAGORDA,

ARE now opening a beautiful and general Assortment of *Staple and Fancy GOODS:* also, a choice lot of *ready made Cltohing,* embracing each and every article in that line, and of every quality. Likewise a large and general assortment of *Hardware, &c.,—Hats, Boots, Shoes, Saddles, Bridles, Queens-ware, Glass-ware, and China.*

JAS. H. WORLAND & CO.,

HAVING located themselves permanently at Matagorda, intend keeping a *general assortment of* GOODS of every description, usually required by the Settler, all of which will be sold on the most favourable terms.

Matagorda, Dec. 13, 1837.   19—tf.

Figs. 26 & 27. Top: announcement for James Worland' new store in the town of Matagorda (*Matagorda Bulletin*, Feb. 14, 1838), and his line of goods, both "staple and fancy" (Bottom), (*Matagorda Bulletin*, June 28, 1838). Univ. of North Texas Libraries, The Portal to Texas History.

JAS. H. WORLAND & Co. have just received from New Orleans, per schr. Louisiana, the following articles, which they offer for sale on the most reasonable terms:

60 barrels Flour	30 brls Pilot Bread
15 tierces Rice	12 qr. casks Madiera
20 sacks Coffee	20 boxes Starch
20 boxes Spm. Candles	20 do 6-lb. caddies Tea
15 barrels Loaf Sugar	10 baskets Sweet Oil
10 do Port Wine	10 boxes Sweet Choco-
10 ½-do Madeira	late
20 do M. Whiskey	6 boxes Vermicelli
15 do domestic Gin	3 sacks Black Pepper
10 do Brandy	10 boxes Cayenne
10 do Peach ditto	30 baskets Champaign
6 pipes Holland Gin	10 kitts Mackerel
10 ½-do Cognac Brandy	20 boxes Lemon Syrup
20 boxes Claret	15 cks. London Porter
30 boxes Cordials	10 boxes Tobacco,
40 M Spanish Cigars	chewing & smoking
20 boxes best Tobacco	20 dozen Pickles
4 tierces Sperm Oil	5 boxes Lead
30 kegs Nails	5 do. Fancy Soap
30 boxes Tea	25 boxes Sarsaparilla.
20 dozen Brooms	and Ginger Syrup
60 boxes Champaign	20 gross Merry Andrew
40 do. Brandy Fruits,	and Highlander
Cherries, Bitters	Cards
20 sacks Pepper, All-	10 bx. Raspberry Syrup
spice, &c. &c.	15 do Assorted ditto
30 sacks Salt	6 nests Tubs
30 dozen bottles Mus-	20 barrels Molasses
tard	30 boxes Soap
10 brls Cherry Bounce	10 casks Bacon

Matagorda, Sep. 26, 1839.

Fig. 28. The list of goods that Jas. H. Worland & Co. advertised provides a glimpse of the times. Pilot bread was a dense bread or cracker nearly impervious to spoilage, cherry bounce a brandy and cherry mixture with cinnamon and nutmeg, the tierce was a 42-gallon cask or barrel, sweet oil was likely olive oil, and "kitts" mackerel was probably a reference to a mackerel that originated in the Caribbean Islands. *Colorado Gazette and Advertiser*, Nov. 9, 1839.

List of all **Passengers** taken on board the *Sch* *Henry* whereof *H W Clark* is Master, at the Port of *Matagorda* and bound for New-Orleans.

NAMES.	AGE.	SEX.	OCCUPATION.	COUNTRY TO WHICH THEY BELONG	COUNTRY OF WHICH THEY INTEND TO BECOME INHABITANTS	NUMBER THAT HAVE DIED ON THE PASSAGE
W. G. Ewing	21	Male	Merchant	United States	New Orleans	
J H Worland	23	"	"	"	"	Texas
Mrs Trunelly	25	Female		Texas	Matagorda	
J V Belknap	22	Male	Merchant	"	"	"
F J Trippard	20	"	Printer	"	"	"
Danl L Applick	25	"	Mechanic	United States	"	"
— James	25	"	"	"	"	"

Fig. 29. James H. Worland was listed on an 1838 passenger list aboard the Schooner *Henry*, sailing from the Port of Matagorda to New Orleans. William G. Ewing, who came to own part of Crier tract in 1846, was also listed on the manifest. Note the right column header provides a tally for those who died at sea. *Passenger Lists of Vessels Arriving at New Orleans, Louisiana, 1820-1902*; The National Archives at Washington, D.C.; Washington, D.C., NAI no. *2824927, Records of the Immigration and Naturalization Service*; Record Group no. 85.

LAW NOTICE.

HENRY P. BREWSTER & JAMES DENISON Attorneys and Counsellors at Law, have associated themselves in partnership (under the name of DENISON & BREWSTER) in the practice of the law, and will attend to business in all the courts of the Republic.

Office at Matagorda, on the Bluff.
May 7, 1841.—tf

Fig. 30. Notice of the James Denison Henry Brewster law partnership, 1841. *Colorado Gazette and Advertiser*, May 28, 1842, Univ. North Texas Libraries, The Portal to Texas History, https://texashistory.unt.edu/ark:/67531/metapth80356/m1/3/.

W. G. EWING respectfully informs his friends and the public that notwithstanding his late severe loss by the entire destruction of his property by the Indians at Linnville, he is yet determined to rebuild immediately at the same place, and again commence the *Forwarding and Commission Business*, and solicits a share of public patronage.   Linnville, Sept. 6—6m

Fig. 31. W.G. Ewing reopened his warehouse and commission business in Port Lavaca after the 1840 Linnville Raid. *Texas Sentinel*, March 18, 1841, Univ. of North Texas Libraries, The Portal to Texas History, https://texashistory.unt.edu/ark:/67531/metapth80050/m1/4/.

ANDREW JOHNSON,

PRESIDENT OF THE UNITED STATES OF AMERICA,

To all to whom these presents shall come, Greeting:

Whereas, *Jacob L. Briggs* *of Galveston Texas* by taking part in the late rebellion against the Government of the United States, has made himself liable to heavy pains and penalties;

And whereas, the circumstances of his case render him a proper object of Executive clemency:

Now, therefore, be it known, That I, **ANDREW JOHNSON**, President of the United States of America, in consideration of the premises, divers other good and sufficient reasons me thereunto moving, do hereby grant to the said *Jacob L. Briggs* a full pardon and amnesty for all offences by him committed, arising from participation, direct or implied, in the said rebellion, conditioned as follows:

1st. This pardon to be of no effect until the said *Jacob L. Briggs* shall take the oath prescribed in the Proclamation of the President, dated May 29th, 1865.

2d. To be void and of no effect if the said *Jacob L. Briggs* shall hereafter, at any time, acquire any property whatever in slaves, or make use of slave labor.

3d. That the said *Jacob L. Briggs* first pay all costs which may have accrued in any proceedings instituted or pending against his person or property before the date of the acceptance of this warrant.

4th. That the said *Jacob L. Briggs* shall not, by virtue of this warrant, claim any property or the proceeds of any property that has been sold by the order, judgment, or decree of a court under the confiscation laws of the United States

5th. That the said *Jacob L. Briggs* shall notify the Secretary of State, in writing, that he has received and accepted the foregoing pardon.

In testimony whereof, I have hereunto signed my name and caused the Seal of the United States to be affixed.

Done at the CITY OF WASHINGTON, this *Eleventh* day of *February* A. D. 186*6* and of the Independence of the United States the *Ninetieth*

L.S.

By the President:

Andrew Johnson

W Hunter Acting Secretary of State.

Fig. 32. Confederate soldier Jacob Briggs' letter of amnesty from President Andrew Johnson. *US Pardons Under Amnesty Proclamations*, v. 17, Sept. 1865 to Aug. 1866, Ancestry.com, https://www.ancestry.com/imageviewer/collections/5256/images/40466_1521003240_0514-00266?pId=7276.

GALVESTON AND NEW YORK.

REGULAR WEEKLY STEAMSHIP LINE.

Consisting of the following named steamers:

ARIADNE, Capt Eldridge.
GEN. SEDGWICK, Capt. Gates.
VIRGINIA, Capt. Kennedy.
WILMINGTON, Capt. Cole.
VARUNA, Capt. Spencer
GULF STREAM, Capt. McCreary.

One of the above named steamers will leave New York for Galveston regularly every SATURDAY, and Galveston for New York every SATURDAY, or sooner if full.

S. S. VARUNA, Capt. Spencer,
Will leave for New York on TUESDAY July 19.

For freight or passage, apply to
T. H. McMAHAN & CO.,
Galveston Agents.
C. H. MALLORY & CO.,
sep16d1y 153 Maiden Lane. N. Y., Agents

Fig. 33. Schedule sailing of the *S.S. Varuna*, 1870, that ran a regular line between New York and Galveston. *Galveston Flakes Daily Bulletin*, July 17, 1870.

TEXAS LINE OF GALVESTON STEAMERS, DIRECT.— The A1 steamship VARUNA, Captain Spencer, at pier 20 East river, will sail when full.
A mail bag will be made up for this ship at this office.
All goods for Houston or the interior will be forwarded by our agents, Messrs. T. McMahon & Co., free of charge.
For freight or passage apply to
C. H. MALLORY & CO., 153 Maiden lane.

Fig. 34. The *Varuna* advertisement for passengers and freight on the eve of her final voyage. Of the 48 passengers and crew who were killed when the ship was lost at sea, 36 were from Galveston. *New York Herald*, Oct. 14, 1870.

$150 REWARD

RANAWAY from the plantation of the Subscriber, (living on the Brazos River, in the lower edge of Fort Bend county,) three negro men of the following description, viz: One a tall and very black fellow—wears a very heavy head of hair, generally platted on the side of his head—rather knock-kneed, quick spoken, and with considerable blarney about him. His name is Harmon; about 30 years of age; pretends to be a preacher; is a cooper by trade, and was brought to this State by Col Turner, who is settled near Columbus, on the Colorado River, and sold by him to Judge W. J. Jones. The second is a very tall, slim fellow, very black, with but one eye, he usually stands very straight, is slow spoken, has the most of his front teeth out, and is about 45 years of age. The other is a boy I raised; about 18 years old, copper colored, rather slim, with rather a cast-down look, and speaks low. I will pay the above reward for the apprehension of the above negroes, or fifty dollars each delivered at my plantation, or lodged in some safe jail, so that I can get them. They stole three horses which they rode off—one a bay, one a brown, and one a sorrel; for the delivery of the horses I will pay $10 each.   J. D. WATERS.

June 25th, 1853.   50t6.

Fig. 35. Reference to a runaway slave owned by William Jones in the early 1850s. The language used was consistent for descriptions of slaves during the era. *Texas Monument,* Aug. 17, 1853.

CHAPTER 2

Landowners of the Bend in the River

1870s to 1900s

At first, the hero of the Battle of San Jacinto tried to ignore it, hopeful that the clamor of secession would go away. In his heart, he knew better. Sam Houston had been reelected as governor (Fig. 1), and the fading warrior wasn't surprised when the separatist leaders went around him, the Texas delegates of the Secession Convention voting 166 to eight to join the Confederate States of America in February of 1861. Vilified in the press, Houston (Fig. 2) retired in Huntsville and died three years later.

Texas formally surrendered on June 2, 1865, almost three months after General Robert E. Lee at Appomattox. For the next five years, the Lone Star State was not a state in any nation, but a territory occupied by the Federal Government, the period euphemistically referred to as Reconstruction. Like most of the South, the Civil War came at a great cost to Matagorda. Before the war, the net worth of its plantation owners was strongly tied to the value and productivity of their slaves. The human indifference, but economic importance, of slavery was succinctly described by one planter, with: "the time has been when the farmer would kill and wear out one negro to buy another, but it is not so now. Negroes are too high in proportion to the price of cotton, and it behooves them to make them last as long as possible."[1]

Cotton production was another leading source of income to Bay Prairie plantation owners. But agricultural profit, including lesser volumes of corn and sugar cane, was realized only because of cheap labor. Black smoke covered the prairie as slaves torched native prairie grasses to plant cotton in early spring. Next, they plowed the ground while others poked a stick into the fresh earth to plant one or two seeds of *Gossypium barbadense* – Petit Gulf cotton. For the next several months the crop was weeded by hand until, during the hottest part of the Texas summer, it matured. When it did, slaves were sent into the field with a jute or canvas sack that they dragged beside them on the ground while they picked the bolls. The worth of a slave was measured by the number of pounds they could produce in a day, including separating the seeds from the fiber.

The loss of Matagorda's leading pre-war commodities – slaves and cotton – crippled plantation owners. Smaller Matagorda County landowners typically owned less than a dozen slaves, but larger holdings had as many as a hundred. At the start of the Civil War, Matagorda's slaves numbered 2,365 with a net worth estimated at $1,130,300 – nearly $500 per person. When President Lincoln penned the 1862 Emancipation Proclamation, his words erased over a million dollars of net worth – more than $33 million in today's dollars – from the ledgers of Matagorda planters. Its effect on their agricultural interests was immediate. In 1859, for example, Texas produced 431,645 bales of cotton. A decade after Appomattox, the state produced less than 1,000 bales.[2]

It took time after the Civil War for the Matagorda economy to find its footing. Bend in the River settlement had dwindled, the land held primarily as an investment or, in some cases, squatters or renters who eked out a small living from crops. There were no Bend in the River land transactions between the years leading up to the Civil War and the late 1870s. Hosea H. League and Thomas Cayce were both deceased, their land titles having already passed to buyers outside of their families. John Crier had died, his remaining holdings transferred to heirs Andrew and Telitha Grover. For one reason or another, every pre-Civil War landowner sold or forfeited their holdings within a decade or so after its conclusion.

Texas business visionaries recognized that the coastal prairie, with its largely undeveloped acres of stirrup high rangeland grasses, could be a force in the economics of the post-war order. They would raise cattle, and those grasses presented an endless grazing resource (see Section 2, titled *Matagorda Cattle & Cowboys*). Bend in the River land, between the mid-1870s and the 1890s, was at the center of a land speculation boom, the catalyst a rush to control pasture. There were three main players who dominated the land grab on the west side of the Colorado River – Abel Head "Shanghai" Pierce (Fig. 3), his brother Jonathan E. Pierce, and William Cheever Braman.

A.H. Pierce busily amassed tens of thousands of acres from his new Pierce Ranch headquarters on the Colorado River near Wharton. His name was signed on but a few of the Bend in the River deeds, the signers instead mostly his cronies who were involved in various Pierce partnerships. They included Jonathan E. Pierce, William C. Braman, whose father, D.E.E. Braman, facilitated Pierce's unravelling of complicated title ownership, and the Texas Land & Cattle Company. Pierce owned a 1/6 interest in the company with its principals, Augustus and Herman Kountze.

Regardless of the name on the deed, the Bend in the River was best known as "Pierce pastures lands" or "Pierce Range," and later, "the Braman pasture." A.H. Pierce left little doubt that, even if his name did not appear on the title, he controlled it. The exception was Andrew Olcese, who acquired title to the John Royal tract on the League Survey.

The Southern Survey at the Bend in the River

The southern two thirds of the original League Survey passed from Thomas Cayce to George Elliott in 1839. Elliott and his family took over operation of the original League and Cayce Ferry, its location moved at some point to the south of the earlier crossing. Still critical as a transportation artery, the ferry was the site of a Confederate camp during the Civil War, and by 1869 the town of Red Bluff was established at the ferry landing.[3] By the early 1880s, the ferry location was passed to William Cheever Braman, although the William Elliott family continued to run until at least 1900.[4] The northern third of the League Survey was owned by John S. Royall until 1877, when he deeded his acreage to Californian Andrew Olcese.

The Andrew Olcese Family. The 1,476 acres that made up the northern third of the League Survey, part of present day Spread Oaks Ranch, was deeded by John S. Royall to Andrew Olcese in November 1877 for $150. Both were residing in Mariposa County, California. The deed instrument that was recorded in California misspelled Olcese's name as Olase, and the county incorrectly identified as Mariford.[5] Olcese had no need for land in Texas, and it is likely the deal was made for cash or barter related to Royall's mining business. Olcese had never seen the property before he became its owner.

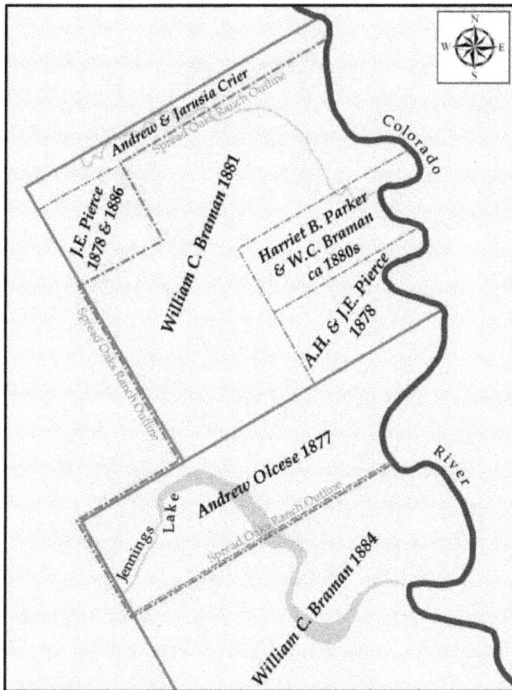

Andrew Olcese Sr. was born in 1830 in the coastal limestone highlands of the Liguria region of Italy, in 1830. He emigrated to the United States and followed the lure of California gold in the early 1850s, marrying Margherita Camiccione in Mariposa in 1858. Olcese preferred the mercantile business to the rigor of panning for gold, and after opening his first store owner in central California, the Olcese & Garibaldi firm opened branches throughout the San Joaquin Valley.[6]

After Andrew Sr. died in 1893 in Oakland, Almeda County, daughter Margaret Olcese became the heir and family executor of the Matagorda Bend in the River land. Margaret was as much an absentee landowner as her father, but she and the next heirs held the property during three important economic times – cattle, rice, and oil.

The Northern Survey at the Bend in the River

Through their inheritance, John Crier's two children, Andrew and Telitha Grover, were the second generation of Crier's to own Bend in the River land. By the 1870s, Telitha's husband, B.F. Grover, and Andrew's children and spouses held title to different pieces but for short durations, the names including Mittie Crier Reed and her husband E.F. Reed, and S. and T.F. Magness, and Amanda Sachtleben. Between 1880 and 1892, the John Crier heirs had liquidated all the old pioneer's Matagorda County holdings, their tracts folded – directly or indirectly – into the Pierce brother's land empire.

The Pierce Brothers. It had been over 20 years since the last recorded title change on the Crier Survey when Matagorda tax collector Frank Rugeley seized 120 acres from its "unknown owners" in 1878. Located on Blue Creek, the land had passed to Crier son-in-law B.H. Grover, who evidently failed to render its tax payments. The tract was sold at auction and J.E. Pierce's $10.15, or eight cents an acre, was the highest bid. The same year, Rugely appropriated the 555-acre Julia C. and J.R. Fretwell tract (Fig. 4). It sold "within hours" at public auction to Jonathan E. Pierce, for $138.87. The deed was recorded with his brother, Abel H. Pierce, as an equal owner.[7] Two years later the new tax assessor, I.W. Mathews, provided Pierce with another opportunity for 22 acres of the Crier tract for $37.46 owed in Grover's unpaid taxes.[8]

J.E. Pierce's fourth and final Bend in the River acquisition was his purchase of 140 acres from Crier heir Amanda Sachtleben.[9] Initially purchased in 1885 for $150 by county clerk John L. Croom (Fig. 4), who was also a "leading Wharton lawyer and prominent dealer in real estate," it was another year before J.E. Pierce could resolve title. When he did, it cost him $420. Lawyer Croom, who made a considerable profit, was often chided by the Pierce brothers for thwarting their purchases and by demanding "extra legal fees and agent commissions" for "confused titles."[10]

The 221-acre northernmost tract of the Crier Survey traded hands three times in 1892. Although the Texas Land & Cattle Company (TL&CC) had been paying taxes on the acreage since 1888, it wasn't until 1892 that D.E.E. Braman was able to acquire title for his client. Jarusia and Andrew Crier Jr. sold it to John Matula in 1892 for $442, and Matula turned it for $475 to F.C. McReynolds the same year. McReynolds, a director of the Kountze brother's TL&CC, then transferred title to Augustus Kountze. A.H. Pierce owned a 1/6 interest in the TL&CC venture, and with the transfer, all but 555 acres of the Crier Survey was effectively controlled by loyalists to the Pierce dynasty.[11]

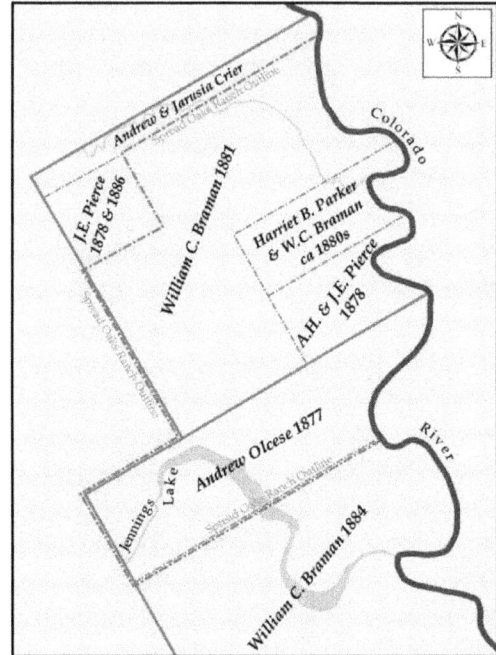

A.H. "Shanghai" Pierce. The theme of Abel Head "Shanghai" Pierce's copious storytelling was nearly always Abel Head "Shanghai" Pierce and, because "you could hear [him] in a quiet conversation seven or eight blocks," his orations were hard to ignore.[12] A.H.'s yarns ranged from vulgar to insightful, and they were as popular around the campfire as with newspapermen in his later years. A vein of truth usually lay somewhere in his words, although his versions were nearly always revisionist. The quest for verity confounded historians – then and now. A.H. Pierce was nothing if not a man of contradictions, and he preferred it that way.

He came from Rhode Island as a stowaway on a New England schooner bound for Texas, making landfall at Port Lavaca during the 1853 yellow fever epidemic. Before wrangling and trail drives, he first worked as a rail splitter and bronc-buster. A.H. Pierce had been in Texas barely a year when he made his first visit to the town of Matagorda. The future Cattle King of America crossed the Colorado River at Elliot's Ferry on the H.H. League Survey, near the southern boundary of what is now Spread Oaks Ranch. Neither he nor anyone else would fathom that in the not-so-distant future this land would be his land.

Pierce accumulated his wealth in the years after the Civil War, and he made it fast. He built a cattle empire from cows he got fairly and perhaps as many not so honorably. He built a land empire of hundreds of thousands of acres the same way he did his cattle. Abel Head Pierce was tough enough to flourish on the cattle trail, yet insightful enough to foster relationships with lawyers, investors, bankers, and politicians. His toughness and shrewdness were by no means unique traits, but in A.H. Pierce they were used with remarkable effectiveness.

Abel "Shanghai" Pierce put his first cattleman's stake in the ground in 1852, when the 20-year-old Yankee was hired by William Bradford Grimes at the WBG Ranch on the Tres Palacios River. Rather than cash, A.H. Pierce negotiated his $200 yearly pay in cattle he would register under his freshly recorded BU brand. For a year, Pierce toiled for the promise of 28 cows and 28 calves as his reward. Instead, A.H. claimed that Grimes cut him

56

"four old cows and three scrawny calves, the poor old shelly bellies and swaybacks fit for nothing." During their first winter they were unable "to lift themselves from the bogs [and] died mostly moaning for help." By spring, all that remained to carry Pierce's BU brand were "three motherless spindle-legged dogies."[13] Like all things Pierce, there is probably some truth in his version of the event, although Grimes almost certainly would have remembered it differently.

A.H. learned his lesson. Although the next year he doubled the amount of cattle he branded for Grimes, he carried two branding irons. One was his own, and he once said that "I'm damned glad [Grimes] didn't ask me whose branding iron I used this year."[14]

For the remainder of the 1850s, A.H. mavericked on the open range and often returned to WBG Ranch where he was promoted to "boss beef driver."[15] The man who eventually drove longhorns to every northern shipping point made his first overland drive east, to New Orleans, in the mid 1850s.[16] A.H. proved his mettle in his chosen vocation on that journey. He made his employer a solid profit and relished the drover's life with its river crossing challenges and the rigors of mud-filled trails traversing the Louisiana swamp.

Younger brother Jonathan, who had remained at the family farm in Rhode Island, came south in 1860 and was hired by the Grimes operation as ranch bookkeeper. The brother's tenure was interrupted by the Civil War, and both joined the First Texas Cavalry. Private A.H. Pierce was immediately named its "Regimental Butcher."[17]

A.H.'s return from the war coincided with the onset of his famous feud with William Bradford Grimes. The two men would not only part ways but developed a lasting enmity. In Pierce's version, he visited his former boss to claim $500 owed him in backpay. Grimes, however, paid him in worthless Confederate script. This may have been true, but it is just as likely that the split resulted from Grimes' objection to Pierce marrying his daughter, Fannie Charlotte.[18]

Between 1857 and 1860, Fannie Grimes's letters were replete with references to the man she called Abel, and the two were often seen socially, and at church, and spent holidays together. Although there were few prospective suitors in rural Matagorda County "equal to her station," her protective father would not allow her to "settle for [any] overconfident, uneducated, and immoral men." That included A.H. Pierce. Regardless of whether the catalyst for the grudge was money or unrequited love, A.H. swore revenge on his former mentor. He would get it.[19]

During his cattle shipping trips to the Indianola docks, Pierce frequented Sullivan's General Mercantile Store (Fig. 5) and became a trusted acquaintance of its owner, Daniel Sullivan. Although he had nothing as collateral, the Irishman loaned Pierce the money to buy his first cattle and land.[20] With his brother Jonathan, A.H. founded the 'A.H. & J.E. Pierce Stock Raisers and Cattle Dealers,' in 1865 (Fig. 6) and made their headquarters on 11 acres purchased on the Tres Palacios River, naming it the Rancho Grande Ranch.[21]

With no export beef market immediately after the war, the Pierce brothers resorted to killing cattle for the tallow and hide market. But A.H. was looking to the future, burning the BU and AP brands onto the flanks of a growing number of cattle and buying beeves with gold coin. In a formerly Confederate state reeling from a post-war currency crisis, the lure of gold loomed large, and the Pierce camp quickly attracted an assortment of cow hands, described as a collection of blacks, Mexicans, and a few white men – some hardened from war, while others were "mere boys cheating their teens." Twenty-seven-year-old

Wiley M. Kuykendall, who had made his first Kansas trail drive as a barefoot, 12-year-old orphan in the 1850s, would become the Pierce trail boss.[22]

The First Family. The Pierce family was growing along with the brother's cash flow and the size of their herds. A.H. had married Frances E. Lacy during the fall of 1865, and gave birth to their first child Mary Frances, or Mamie, in 1867. By his own admission, the absentee Pierce shared his bride's bed for only four nights during their first year of marriage.[23]

Jonathan married Nancy Deborah Lacy – the sister of A.H.'s wife Fannie – and settled at the Rancho Grande headquarters in 1866. In contrast to his brother, J.E. preferred companionship with his wife to time in the saddle. He remarked that his "young wife" made him "take a bath every night," and convinced him to end his customary consumption of three daily pints of whiskey, a habit not beneficial to his health or "morals of temper."[24] As for the saddle, there was no one who could ever even remember seeing him in one.

A.H. And J.E.'s sister Susan came south in 1867, investing in land and building her own small cattle herd. Susan married Pierce foreman Wiley M. Kuykendall (Fig. 7) in 1869, her husband described as a man with a passion for just three things in life – "Susan, liquor, and longhorns" – and the pair settled near Rancho Grande.[25]

Becoming Big Business. In an early Pierce brother's transaction, A.H. purchased a herd on consignment with funds provided by J.M. Foster and brothers James and Joseph Collins. A.H. successfully drove it overland from John Wood's pastures at St. Mary's, on Copano Bay, to New Orleans, and pocketed a remarkable $1,400 in profit. Next, he was employed as the western cattle purchasing agent for Galveston Bay cattlemen and shippers Samuel William Allen and Thomas Jefferson Poole for their company Allen & Poole.[26]

The shipping firm Allen & Pierce evolved from the Samuel Allen and Thomas Poole partnership. At first, mostly AP brand cattle thundered down the wooden chute of the Indianola wharf to Allen & Pierce steamships bound for Cuba, New Orleans, and Pensacola. After a landing was constructed closer to Rancho Grande at Palacios Point, cattle were packed into waiting steamers as quickly as they could be delivered, their numbers reaching as many as 25,000 a year. A.H. sold his Allen & Pierce interest in 1869, and this time, A.H. wasn't paid in "shelly bellies, swaybacks, or Confederate bills."[27]

A seismic shift was felt in the Texas cattle industry in the late 1860s after Jesse Chisholm staked out an overland route to Kansas railroads to deliver cattle to growing northern and eastern meat markets. A.H. Pierce was one of the first to drive his longhorns over it. His first drive up the Chisolm was to Abilene, moving 2,500 head with 20 cowboys under the supervision of trail boss of Wiley M. Kuykendall. It took four months.[28]

Pierce herds were driven north for the next 15 years. In the early days he drove the herds himself, then began taking a stagecoach to meet the drive at the end of the line. In addition to Kuykendall, as business grew Pierce added other trusted trail bosses, including Tom Nye, Pierce nephew A.P. Borden, and Asa Dowdy, the latter affectionately described by Pierce as the only man he knew who was "a good deal more windier than I am." Kentuckian Tom Hamilton was hired in the later 1870s to oversee Pierce's cattle as they were fattened on northern pastures in Indian Territory.[29]

Not Without Controversy. A.H. Pierce played by the rules of the day. The herds he came to own were composed of legitimate unmarked "slicks" claimed with the branding iron, and others acquired by the "running iron" used to change an existing brand to AP or BU. The horses he stocked for roundups and drives were often "wet ponies," stolen from

Mexico. A.H. had a reputation for culling the best beeves from a herd before sale or sneaking "little yearlings" into a herd sold as marketable steers. At least once, he received an advance payment to deliver a herd that, near its destination, somehow found its way back to the Pierce Range – only to be sold again.[30]

A.H. boasted of one of his trades as the "time we robbed the Sante Fe [Railroad]." A great many cattle had died in route to market, and rather than suffer the loss, one of his hands "tied their heads up to make them stand." The ruse allowed him to get paid for a "lot of dead cattle." While most herds pointed north experienced losses – sometimes substantial – it was "well known" that the size of Pierce herds "increased amazingly." "I had to rustle," Pierce once admitted, and "I could not be very religious about the trades I made."[31]

About the only way to best A.H. Pierce in a deal was at the end of the barrel of loaded gun. Not just the threat of shooting him – that was never good enough, as he always talked his way out of those scrapes. One cowboy "borrowed" 300 steers to finish a shipment to Missouri with a promise to replace them. When A.H. went to collect, the debtor's hand reached for his pistol. Pierce sensibly replied that he didn't need those steers, and narrowly avoided becoming another notch etched in outlaw John Wesley Hardin's ivory pistol grip.[32]

Farmer's milk cows were sometimes gathered into a herd during A.H.'s round ups. Only staring into the barrels of a shotgun or Winchester rifle caused him to reconsider their ownership, and in one confrontation, Pierce told the fuming farmer to take his cow, then added: "cows have been here before you and I came, and they will be here after both of us are gone. But remember, son, there will never be another Shanghai Pierce."[33]

Another side to the Cattle King was the vigilante Pierce. Cattlemen like A.H. lived by the code of the open range, making their own laws and delivering "their own form of prairie justice." If word circulated about rustler activities, respectable Matagorda cattlemen put their differences aside long enough to form vigilante committees. Dozens of armed area men joined these pursuits, and A.H. Pierce was evidently at the head of more than a few.

One tale involved Captain Leander H. McNelly of the frontier law force, the Texas Rangers. Rushing to prevent the "Pierce boys" from hanging a suspected cattle thief, McNelly offered to exchange his neck for the intended victim's. A.H. Pierce stood down.[34] Another was a group of cattle thieves caught with 450 hides that carried the Pierce brand, the perpetrators lynched by a mob as soon as they were captured.[35]

There is the often-told account of four men, including Ed Lunn and John M. Smith, who were hung from the limb of an oak tree during the summer of 1870. By most accounts, A.H. was at the head of the posse who nudged their horses from under them. The hanging would have been overlooked had not one of the Lunn brothers, Wilburn W., escaped capture.[36] Wilburn was the only hanging witness, and although he was talking, he wasn't saying enough to indict A.H. It was enough, however, for the prosecution to schedule Pierce to testify as a witness in Lunn's trial for stealing cattle hides.[37]

The summer and fall of 1870 were troubling for A.H. Pierce. His son Abel, born in July of 1870, died five weeks later. His wife Fannie died in December. For a while afterwards, A.H. rode the prairie alone with just his Winchester for company. Now, with the added uncertainty of the Lunn and Smith hangings, and a $200 bond posted for him to appear in a Matagorda courtroom, the widower took a hiatus from Texas. After a sale of cattle worth $110,000 to Allen & Poole, he headed to Kansas City.[38]

Pierce began to remake himself in Kansas City. He would always answer to the sobriquet Shanghai but began calling himself Colonel. His quest for respectability was a bumpy road. It was Colonel Pierce who established relationships with leading lawyers and bankers during his months in Kansas City. But it was Shanghai who reverted to his old ways when he crossed a Kansas City banking firm that had crossed him, and it cost him thousands of dollars in lawsuits.

A.H. returned to Texas in 1871. He spent part of the next three years at Rancho Grande and part of the time on cattle drives. He continued to build associations with area cattlemen, such as B.Q. Ward and W.H. Kyle, that allowed him to expand his holdings from the Brazos River west to the Guadalupe River. Of the 70,000 branded cattle in Matagorda County by 1871, A.H. and J.E. Pierce were credited with 35,000. Former employer William Bradford Grimes, once the largest stockholder in the county, could count only 7,000.[39]

Partnering was one thing, but the Shanghai in A.H. Pierce was in a hurry. It was during the 1870s that he solidified his reputation for the fearless, ruthless – and effective – methods he used to build his land and cattle empire. The land part of his enterprise was visionary. Cattle in the southwest had always ranged on open land, and it was almost unheard of to own it. A.H. started his massive land grab either because he – again – saw the future or, in his preferred version, to exact revenge against his competitors. The outcome was two range wars with W.B. Grimes and Robert E. 'Bob' Stafford.

Shanghai's Range Wars. A.H. Pierce's first expansion encompassed range land on all sides of W.B. Grimes, his gradual squeeze known as the "Shanghai circle." "I bought the land right out from under the hooves of Grimes cattle," he later quipped. But initially, it was Grimes who nearly put Pierce out to pasture.[40]

Grimes adopted some of Pierce's own tactics when he went toe to toe with him in the early 1870s. Although he had always ascribed to the free range as opposed to owning large tracts, Grimes purchased 3,000 acres of pasture claimed by Pierce. Other stockmen, as intent on surviving the Pierce expansion as Grimes, joined him and grew their combined holdings to over 10,000 acres. Then, they constructed a six-and-a-half-mile wooden plank fence from the Colorado River to Palacios Creek. A.H. was fenced out of his pastures and could only watch as the opposing partnership's 20,000 cattle grazed it clean.

Complaining of the "cruel and reckless disregard of my rights," Pierce hired attorney D.E.E. Braman to file suit. Braman found an obliging judge three counties away who, although he didn't rule in the plaintiff's favor, granted a temporary injunction. A.H. seized his window of opportunity, directing Tom Nye and his cowboys to sweep the cattle from within the Grimes enclosure. Grimes lost 11,000 head and was done in Matagorda County.[41]

In the late 1870s, A.H. took a page from Grimes's book and built his own plank fence, this time to squeeze the holdings of nemesis Bob Stafford. The barrier, skirting the A.H. and J.E. Pierce and Pierce-Ward pastures, extended from Lavaca Bay to the Navidad River. Pierce's cowboys then drove out every longhorn that didn't carry a Pierce or Ward brand. It didn't stop there. The *Colorado Citizen*, on August 9, 1877, printed a threat proclaiming that Bob Stafford and his associates would "never raise any moor [sic] cattle in the State of Texas," and was signed by the "comitee [sic] of 25 Navidad."[42] The document has always been credited to A.H.'s hand, to which Stafford responded by pronouncing his "resolve to shoot Mr. Pierce on sight." He tried, and nearly succeeded.[43]

Colonel Pierce's Range Wars. It could be said that it was Shanghai Pierce whose overt, often merciless maneuverings expanded his business interests in the 1870s. His business dealings during the 1880s, however, were less the old Shanghai and more the evolving

Colonel Pierce. The methods were still ruthless, but the hammer was wielded more often by lawyers, politicians, and increasingly in a courtroom rather than from a saddle.

It was Colonel Pierce who built a partnership with the New York based Kountze Brothers, who were investing large sums in Texas railroad certificates, land, cattle, and timber. Brothers Augustus and Herman offered A.H. the cash to buy 200,000 acres of prime Colorado River grazing land and 12,000 cattle to stock it. For his part, Pierce was to supervise the selection of both to earn a 1/6 working interest in the enterprise, registered as the Texas Land and Cattle Company (TL&CC). Herman Kountze and A.H. inspected thousands of prospective grazing acres together. Some of the TL&CC acquisitions were original Mexican land grants, and others were Republic of Texas veteran bonus land. A.H., however, made sure that quite a bit of it was also Bob Stafford grazing land.[44]

Pierce formed another large land partnership with San Antonio banker Danny Sullivan, nephew of Indianola merchant Daniel Sullivan who loaned the Pierce brothers their initial seed money 20 years earlier. Banker Sullivan put up 25% of the initial funding and A.H. was trusted with the selection and purchase of 55,000 acres in Matagorda and Wharton counties, and the cattle to stock it. Two years later, in 1884, the Pierce-Sullivan Land and Cattle Company was chartered with a capital stock of $1,000,000 that, Danny Sullivan cynically said, was raised from "unsophisticated Yankees and English lords."[45]

Still Not Without Controversy. During Pierce's 1880s expansion, the landowners and cattle raisers who lost to him weren't as big as Grimes and Stafford. They were mostly small operators, vulnerable because no laws protected them from the "Big Pasture Men." One politician even promised Pierce that, if the legislature ever passed any laws unfavorable to him, they would "never be enforced on this section." Small landowners had no recourse when A.H. neglected to pay rent for running his cattle on their land or pay for grazing rights. If he met resistance, he resorted to purchasing tax titles then "turned his cattle onto it and grazed it clean." One who was caught in the Shanghai circle was told "if you don't like what I've done I know of no law prohibiting you from moving your land from my pasture."[46]

Stockmen large and small saw their cattle swept into Pierce herds, on instructions such as "turn out all you can find" and "say nothing about it."[47] Some landowners lost their homes. One was the McMann family, who resided on a log house on Blue Creek at the Bend in the River. A.H. allegedly ordered the Matagorda County sheriff to "come down and put them out of the house." He did. When the sheriff departed, however, they moved back in.[48] Not all were as fortunate. It was A.H. who told the story of a "squatter" who built a house on his land. He was shot dead by the man hired to remove him, and it cost Pierce "five hundred dollars to clear him."

When a non-enclosure law was finally approved by the Texas legislature in 1884, some of the aggrieved got justice. The legal reclamations were always, however, minor. During this period A.H. was only indicted twice in Matagorda County court, once for the theft of a single cow from his own sister Susan and brother-in-law Wiley Kuykendall, and another time for counter branding a single yearling. Both times he was found not guilty.[49]

Wire Pastures. Barbed wire salesman and showman John Gates had an idea. Texans were still reluctant to trust their herds to new-fangled barbed wire, and he lacked the patience to watch competitors increase their hold on his sales territory. Gates chose the Market Square in San Antonio to hold a much-publicized demonstration of the effectiveness of barbed wire in 1876. One who saw the show that year was A.H. Pierce. He immediately began fencing his immense holdings, and the Kountze brothers did the same. By the early 1880s, Pierce and his partnerships had as much as 400,000 acres behind wire. The Yankee who had come to Texas to build his fortune from the open range was now closing it off.

Barbed wire didn't come to Matagorda, or anywhere else in cattle country, peacefully. As fast as the Big Pasture men could stretch it, fence cutters removed it. In 1883, crews cut every strand of barbed wire on every cedar fence post surrounding nine miles of A.H.'s pastures. They did the same at the Kountze's K and KO ranches. Pierce "at once commenced putting up more wire," but feared "there is every prospect of that being severed the same way." For a long time, they were.[50]

Big Business and a New Ranch. The volume of cattle that A.H. Pierce owned and drove to market was among the largest in the state by the late 1870s, and Western newspapers begam following his every transaction. Between June and December 1880, he grossed $272,000 in sales. With cattle valued at about $16 per head that fall, Pierce and his cowboys must have driven about 17,000 longhorns over those six months. In 1885, A.H. used the proceeds of one $90,000 sale to buy 20,000 yearlings for $4.50 a head. So many Pierce cattle were now making their way west, north, and east that the standard names used for any Texas steer became "Pierce sea lions" or "Shanghai Pierce coasters."[51]

Some of A.H.'s large beef contracts were with the US government. Pierce, when he banished himself to Kansas City during 1870 and 1871, was in the right place at the right time. A government official in the city was seeking to contract 1,000 head for "Indian Territory," and Pierce immediately found the steers to fill it. For the remainder of his cattle trading days, he negotiated agreements in the ever-changing landscape of Indian Territory between Texas and Kansas. Twenty years after his original sale of 1,000 head he was shipping 10,000 a year to "Indian Territory."[52]

A.H. was far more ambitious than the home-loving Jonathan, and the entrepreneurial Pierce began drifting away from his brother. After A.H. remarried in October 1875 to Hattie James, the daughter of Galveston merchant A.F. James, A.H. moved the center of his operation further north, on the west side of the Colorado River, There he built his new wife the kind of home they both thought she deserved. Called "BU headquarters" or "Pierce's Ranch," construction began on a fine two-story ranch house, an office, blacksmith shop, barns, and tenant houses.

The Right Railroad in the Right Place. New railroad lines had been coming to cattle country as quickly as barbed wire. In contrast to the days of a continuous drive across an unbroken landscape from Matagorda to Kansas, A.H. and other cattlemen were increasingly sending their cattle north with shorter drives to, or between, expanding railroad shipping points. Most of A.H. Pierce's cattle sales by the 1880s reflected the changes coming to transportation in the West. A sale of 3,500 head in 1886 reached Henrietta, northwest of Dallas, on the Fort Worth & Denver City Railway before they were unloaded and trailed north. It was the same with a $72,000 sale of 4,000 head that sold in Kansas for $18 per head.[53]

In 1883, Pierce got his own railroad. Three years earlier, Giuseppe "Joseph" Telferner, best-known for his success in constructing railroads in South American, announced his intention to invest in a 100-mile track from Richmond to Victoria. The venture, called the New York, Texas, and Mexican Railroad (NYT&MR), would pass through grazing land between Pierce's Ranch and the Kountze Brothers TL&CC KO Ranch. For Cattle King Pierce, the NYT&MR that would pass by his doorstep was a godsend.

In 1881, surveyors and "600 Italian laborers" descended on the prairie, completing the NYT&MR line in 1883. Railroad principals Joseph Telfener, D.E. Hungerford, and J.W. Mackay named depots along its route after themselves, adding Telfener's daughter Inez Lolita and Hungerford's daughters Louise and Edna. A.H. dictated station names on his property, selecting the names Pierce, Shanghai, and in a nod to his nephew, the Borden depot (Fig. 10). The man who once spent weeks on trail drives was now building cattle pens along the new rail route. A year later he shipped his Wharton and Matagorda herds north and east exclusively in stock cars ordered a hundred at a time.[54]

A.H. Pierce prided himself with his attention to financial details large and small, and the rail company that now crossed his land was not immune to his unsparing financial needling. He quibbled over lumber costs to improve landings and buildings, rental prices for stock cars, and always over shipping rates. He filed claims each time a cow or steer was maimed or killed by a train. He even sent a bill for a horse that broke its neck when a ranch cowboy lost a bet that he could ride faster than the NYT&MR locomotive.[55]

Indian Territory. Like most "Big Pasture Men," A.H. had long fattened his cattle on "free" Indian land as he moved his stock to Midwest markets, and wintered herds in designated areas to circumvent Kansas quarantine laws. But fickle government Indian resettlement policies, expansion of Anglo settlement, and friction between competing cattle syndicates and Native American tribes were creating a landscape increasingly difficult for southern cattlemen like Pierce to navigate.

To cattle interests, one of the most important areas, but also the most contentious, was the Cherokee Outlet. Located along the southern border of Kansas, the Cherokee Outlet took on an enormous significance after Kansas imposed its 1873 quarantine restriction on southern cattle. A.H. leased tens of thousands of Cherokee Outlet acres in two tracts. One, called the New York Cattle Company pasture, was leased to the Kountze interests and located adjacent to the Texas Cattle Trail along the Canadian River. Another Kountze piece, contracted to the Texas Land & Cattle Company, was along the Dodge City and Red River trails. With another business partner, G.W. Miller, he also had access to 60,000 acres in Miller's Salt Fork and Deer Creek leases, situated between a northern branch of the Chisolm Trail and, to the east, the Arkansas City Road.[56]

The rapidly deteriorating conditions in the Cherokee Outlet put Pierce's lease holdings at risk. Most insidious were the "Boomers," the land grab squatters whose claims were accompanied by the burning of ranch buildings, cattle killing, fence cutting, and the torching of grazing land. Another hurdle was the Kansas cattlemen who formed the Cherokee Strip Association and ultimately controlled six million acres of the Cherokee Outlet. The association was successful in blocking southern access with armed fence riders that began turning away Texas herds with impunity.[57]

The way A.H. Pierce played his hand to protect his interests was a reflection of how far he had advanced from his Shanghai Pierce roots to the more upright Colonel Pierce. Twenty years earlier, Shanghai probably would have gone north to confront each contest with his usual ruthless resolve. Colonel Pierce, however, was in a position – and in a stage in his life where, instead, he could leverage political connections in Washington. Pierce appealed to congressman William Henry Crain to explore what he called "the trail matter" with the US Interior Secretary and War Departments. Crain agreed but named his price – $8,000.

Thanking A.H. for his "kind and prompt response to my [financial] appeal," Crain wrote that "Prejudices against the drovers is very strong, owing to complaints from the Indians, from settlers, and from parties interested in keeping Texas cattle from the market." Then he forwarded the latest Interior and the War department policies. It was not the news A.H. hoped for. The "trail" was no longer "intended for fattening purposes, but simply as a highway," and each drover was now limited to "just ten days' time in Indian Territory." No longer would he, or other cattlemen, be able increase his margins by fattening cattle before their sale, or time their delivery to market to match optimal pricing peaks. More importantly, he wouldn't be able to circumvent Kansas quarantine restrictions.[58]

Congressman Crain thought, however, that Pierce and other cattlemen might prevail if they engaged the bureaucracy. Meet with "a few prominent stock raisers," he wrote, and "agree upon a route" drawn on "a nice map" showing the proposed trails "by red or blue lines." The illustration was evidently critical, as the land agent's office only map was one "cut out of some Kansas or Colorado stock journal." Crain also recommended filing an application with the appropriate "office" – assuming the politico with the applicable approval authority could ever be found.

It is not known if Pierce submitted "a nice map," but he turned to the congressman again, this time to determine the legality of a Chickasaw tribe demand that cattlemen pay a "grass tax" of 15 cents on every head crossing their land. Crain relayed that the Commissioner of Indian Affairs ruled the tax unconstitutional only if the drove was passing through, but legal if they were held "for fattening purposes." Then Crain wrote Pierce to wire him another $500.[59]

Between quarantine regulations that closed Missouri and Kansas to Texas cattle, barbed wire, settlement, and the spreading web of railroads linking cattle raisers directly to the nation's markets, the heyday of the cattle drives had passed by the mid 1880s. Perhaps its final nail was in 1890, when the original "Government Lands" and the western part of "Indian Territory" became the Oklahoma Territory. Colonel A.H. Pierce was one of the first to hear the news when Congressman Crain forwarded a copy of an order, signed by the President of the United States and the Secretary of the Interior, directing the removal of all cattle from "the Cherokee Strip or Outlet."[60]

The Pierce-Kountze Split. Wholesale cattle prices headed lower in the mid 1880s to mid 1890s and, combined with their loss of some 2,000 "Little Eastern Swamp Angels" during the 1886 and 1888 freezes, the Kountze brothers started to thin their K and KO herds. In one of the largest single cattle trades ever made, the Kountze's sold 10,000 steers at $17.75 a head.[61]

Pierce had charge of the shipping from Pierce Station to Missouri, but the herd he delivered was short 2,700 head. The conveyance was also plagued by delays, inflated railroad delivery charges, and a commission fee that A.H. unexpectedly added to the Kountze's invoice. Pierce then called in his 1/6 interest in the Texas Land & Cattle Company. The relationship was strained, but it passed the breaking point when A.H. quietly filed on "vacant" land within the Kountze's K and KO ranches. The result "a serious row" with the New Yorkers, and it was the end of the Kountze-Pierce enterprise.[62]

In 1894, Herman and Luther Kountze announced their intention to divide and sell the K and KO Ranches for "colonization," and to market their remaining 25,000 cattle. Of the

300,000 acres they had accumulated in Wharton County in 1893, more than half had been sold five years later. Their widows and heirs later dispensed of the remainder.[63]

The Last Decade. By the mid-1890s, A.H. Pierce's net worth was estimated at $2.9 million, and he owned 182,000 acres of land and 43,000 head of cattle. The estimate, promulgated in the *Galveston Tribune*, was probably low.[64] Throughout the 1890s, the Colonel continued to make huge cattle trades. The 1890s also brought a conclusion to the long-standing Bob Stafford feud, the dissolution of A.H. & J.E. Pierce Stock Raisers and Cattle Dealers, a feud with Danny Sullivan, a potentially fatal finish to Pierce's dealings with G.W. Miller, and the rise and fall of banker Colonel A. H. Pierce.

More Big Sales. In 1891, A.H. purchased nearly 12,000 cattle for two shipments, and in one deal, sold 8,000 4-year-old "sea lion steers" at $14 a head to the "Arizona Armours."[65] He added another $200,000 worth of cattle to his balance sheet when he was named as receiver for the Campbell Commission Company of Kansas City and Chicago, a deal that cost him his business association with G.W. Miller.[66] A.H., who in 1884 had ordered NYT&MR rail cars by the hundred to handle his spring shipping needs, was now requesting their delivery to Pierce Station by the thousands.[67]

The Bob Stafford Finale. Pierce received a telegram from A.P. Borden, in July 1890, with news that his nemesis, cattle and businessman Bob Stafford, and his brother John, were gunned down in the streets of Columbus. The killing was related to another long-standing feud unrelated to Pierce, but the trigger men, Columbus City Marshall Larkin S. Hope and his brother Marion H. Hope, penned a letter to A.H. that linked him to the killings. "Dear Sir," it read, "I have understood from some of my friends that you would let us have a thousand dollars to help us out of our trouble in the Stafford killing."[68]

The Hope brother's correspondence was followed by a subpoena from the Colorado County sheriff to appear as a witness on their behalf. In a move not unlike his timely departure 20 years earlier after the Lunn hangings, A.H. decided to leave Texas for a few months. This time he did not go to Kansas City. Instead, he chose Europe.[69]

A.H. & J.E. Pierce Stock Raisers and Cattle Dealers. A.H. acquired J.E.'s Pierce-Sullivan Pasture & Cattle Company stock when the Pierce brothers amicably dissolved their 20-year partnership in late 1894. In exchange. J.E. took title to land to lands near the Tres Palacios. Ownership of properties close to Pierce Ranch headquarters were transferred to A.H. and his daughter Mamie Pierce, now Mamie Withers, who succeeded Jonathan as director during the company reorganization.

The G.W. Miller Partnership. The firm of Miller and English, formed in the early 1880s, supplied provisions to cattlemen during their drives and traded in cattle. Owner G.W. Miller was involved with A.H. Pierce in several cattle ventures over a seven-year period. In one sale to Miller, in typical Pierce fashion, A.H. Borden was instructed to cull all the top animals before delivery. In his telegram to Borden, he wrote: "ship out all the Little Eastern Texas Devills [sic]. Say nothing about it, as Miller will not take them if he knew any of the tops had been taken out." The Cattle King then cautioned to show Miller the herd "in the evening," or "very early in the morning" as they would "look better" that time of day.[70]

Miller adopted similar tactics in some of his transactions with Pierce. He was once intercepted removing an entire BU herd from a Pierce pasture without consent. Another time, he emptied a neighboring pasture that belonged to a widow. Miller sent the aggrieved woman a note telling her that Pierce would make a settlement. A.H. knew nothing about it.[71]

The partnership may or may not have survived the small spats, but it shattered in 1895. Miller was in debt to the Campbell Commission Company, which in turn was in debt to the International Bank of St. Louis. None of the players had a strong hand to play in negotiations with Pierce and his attorney son-in-law, Henry Withers, who were contracted by the Campbell Company to deliver 159 stock cars of Miller owned cattle from Pierce Station to Kansas City. The agreement favored A.H. Pierce first, Campbell second, and if there was any money left, the proceeds would go to Miller.[72]

While the controversial cattle were in route, Pierce was served a court order demanding seizure of the shipment. The Campbell Commission Company had gone into receivership, and the St. Louis bank responded by suing Miller for his debt. The Campbell principals quickly transferred ownership of the shipment to Pierce in a deal that gave him clear title to a $200,000 windfall.[73]

George Miller was livid. He would shoot the bank principals, he warned, then shifted his target to the Campbell Commission Company, and finally to A.H. Pierce. As the cattle were nearing their destination, Miller bounded up the steps to Pierce's Pullman car steps to make good on his threat, but he was met with a shotgun blast. It missed him – probably deliberately – but it sent him scurrying away. Miller returned to Pierce's car, this time armed with two Winchesters, and shouted a challenge to Pierce. A.H. was not on the train.[74]

The End of Pierce-Sullivan Pasture & Cattle. In the middle 1890s, Danny Sullivan told A.H. he was through with the Pierce-Sullivan partnership. A.H. did some fast arithmetic, and conveyed that, together, they held about 8,000 to 10,000 head, worth about $80,000. He offered Sullivan $20,000 for his quarter interest. Sullivan hesitated, and while he pondered, A.H. set a trap.[75]

At the January 1895 Pierce-Sullivan Land & Cattle Company stockholder and director's meeting, held in San Antonio, its president and majority stockholder – A.H. Pierce – was strategically absent. The proceedings seemed to be business as usual until his lawyers announced a resolution to transfer future meetings from the board room "to the pasture of said company in Matagorda County." Then they moved that the "officers of the corporation shall receive no salary, except the president and superintendent." Shouts of "fraud!" echoed through the room, but the Pierce majority votes carried the amendments.[76]

Before the first meeting in the pasture was held, Sullivan directed his secretary Herman Brendel to study the company bookkeeping. When Brendel visited Pierce, he learned the company had no bank account – all transactions went, instead, through Pierce's personal accounts. Brendel was denied access to the company sales ledgers, with A.H. explaining "I am the best cow man in the state today. I see no way of arriving at the number sold except to take my word for it" and "the price they sold for." Brendel returned to San Antonio from his failed mission, announcing to Sullivan that "Mr. Pierce is a dangerous man."[77]

Sullivan then proposed to sell his interest at cost plus 8% interest per annum, to which Pierce replied, "I hardly deem an answer necessary." Sullivan settled for $50,000, but then had a change of heart. He filed a suit in US Circuit Court in 1898 alleging that A.H. had designedly and fraudulently robbed him in the sale and wanted a reinstatement of $250,000 in company stock.[78]

The hearing took place in Galveston, and Pierce's nemesis G.W. Miller was one of the first to take the stand. His testimony might have been damming, but a Pierce attorney deftly submitted a copy of a criminal conviction against Miller. The charge was small – for the theft of a single cow in Indian Territory – but the result was not. As a felon, Miller's testimony was inadmissible.[79]

A.H. Pierce on the stand was, not surprisingly, colorful. To George Washington Miller's testimony, he responded that "He is not only the biggest liar [in America] but also the biggest thief and a son of a bitch." Pierce's counsel admonished him to stop cursing, and he apologetically addressed the judge. "I did a considerable cursing this morning," he acknowledged. "I call it cussin' [but my counsel] Mr. Proctor calls it profane language. I was not aware I was cussin.' I had cause, I admit. Still, using cuss words don't do any good. I wish to withdraw my profanity [and] I will try to keep from doing it again."[80]

Cussin' Shanghai Pierce won the case. Sullivan appealed the decision and lost again. In the first trial, over 10,000 sheets of manuscript covering months of depositions were taken by the court's "expert stenographers." The appeal transcript, compiled in the US Circuit Court of Appeals in New Orleans, consisted of 2,700 pages and weighed nearly a hundred pounds. It was thought to be the largest document ever recorded by the court.[81]

Pierce the Banker. A.H. added the appellate 'banker' to an already diverse resume when he purchased the Weekes-McCarthy & Company bank in 1899 (Fig. 9). The Galveston bank originated in 1894 through a combination of the failed Island City Savings Bank and the more prosperous American National Bank. American National was financially sound in part because of the acumen of its stockholders, and in part because Weekes, its president, and McCarthy, the cashier, were up-and-coming county politicians who directed public money to the institution. Political opponents, however, demanded the pair give up one or the other. A.H., who recognized the benefit of politically connected bankers, bought out the shareholders.[82] A convoluted railroad scheme and a hurricane would quickly break the bank.

When Matagorda County rice farmers planted their first 600 acres in the spring of 1900, area farmers and businessmen anticipated the beginning of an important new industry. More than a few eyebrows were raised, however, by the hurried announcement that a "syndicate of experienced rice growers" intended to expand that first crop to 25,000 acres. Rather than an ambitious agricultural scheme the move was, instead, a railroad subterfuge. A.H. Pierce's sale of the land to Houston attorney Jonathan Lane was, in reality, for a proposed Gulf, Colorado & Sante Fe Railroad (GC&SF) route connecting Eagle Lake and Bay City.[83]

To A.H. Pierce, Lane's scheme would provide him with another railroad across his holdings, but more importantly, the opportunity to relocate the Wharton County seat to Pierce Station. In anticipation of the occasion, A.H. surveyed 160 acres of the Pierce Townsite. He laid out its streets, and set aside land for a public square, courthouse, and cemetery. A church was built, a two-story grocery store, and a grand three-story, 22-room hotel.[84]

Pierce's goal was further emboldened by a proposal from railroad promoter Uriah Lott, who had announced a new rail line from San Antonio to Victoria, and connecting the coastal town of Alligator Head to Alvin on Galveston Bay. Called the Tampico, San Antonio & Galveston Railroad (TSA&G), its route would also pass through Wharton

County. Between Lott's TSA&G and Lane's GC&SF, Pierce was convinced that one or the other of the railroaders would lay tracks to Pierce Station.[85]

Behind the curtain, A.H.'s banking partners Weekes and McCarthy poured $555,000 of bank money into the stock of GC&SF subsidiary Gulf & Interstate Railway (G&IR), a bold move give that Weekes was also the railroad's president and McCarthy a member of the board. The G&IR owned a track between the Sabine River and Port Bolivar, and the two bankers were making a terrific gamble that, whichever of the TSA&G and GC&SF won the contest, the winner would eventually connect to the G&IR.[86]

The next move on the railroad chessboard was Lane's, who received a $50,000 bonus from Wharton to run the line through that town then south to Bay City. A.H. Pierce's railroad dreams and his town of Pierce Station were dashed. The deal was made as part of the GC&SF-affiliate Cane Belt Railroad, and Lane was named its president. Then Lott, who had planned to join the GC&SF from the onset, entirely avoided the G&IR and its Weeks-McCarthy monopoly on the port facilities at Bolivar.[87]

The failed venture landed Pierce and his Weekes-McCarthy Company Bank in the hole for $710,000, and Pierce decided to liquidate. In Chris Emmett's analysis, A.H. struggled admirably to settle with creditors and depositors. A little of the old Shanghai came out during the challenging financial time, however, as he spluttered about some of the more intransigent players. Of one, he said, "I see no way to get rid of the old cuss but to pay him and trust the good Lord will bless him and strike him with lightning." Of a second, A.H. anticipated that "he be removed from earth to heaven which would be very beneficial to us."[88]

On September 16, the Texas Upper Coast bore the fury of the great hurricane of 1900. Galveston experienced the worst of the tempest, but few inland towns, farms, and ranches – including those in Matagorda and Wharton counties – were spared. In a letter to G.G. Williams of the Chemical National Bank in New York, A.H. acknowledged the large numbers of Galveston people "gone from this world." Then he wrote of his ranches and the destruction to houses, barns, and feed houses laid "flat to the ground." His "very nice little church" was in disarray, and dozens of windmills were down. As for his troubled G&IR, he advised that miles of track were wrecked, and cars were "blown from the track and five engines turned bottoms up."

A.H. expressed concern that, because of the storm, "at least 100 German and Bohemian farmers to whom I have sold land" were now unable to pay their notes, but he would be "lenient." Evidently, he was. To still other financially strapped mortgage holders, he uncharacteristically forgave payments for a year, suggesting they use the money, instead, to "fix up their houses" and "make a crop." Even more out of character, and although he was bleeding money, Colonel Pierce wrote an $80,000 check for "the relief of Wharton County people."[89] Then, he offered a $20,000 bonus to the builders of the Cane Belt – the railroad that by-passed him in favor of Wharton – if the line reached Bay City by July 1, 1901. His estate paid the bonus when the tracks were completed with six hours to spare.[90]

On Christmas night, 1900, Colonel Abel Head "Shanghai" Pierce ate his holiday turkey and oyster, went to bed and died.

A.H. Pierce Revisited. Whether he told the stories himself or they were related by others, the image of A.H. Pierce is not a simple one. He did business with many but trusted few. He made bitter, lasting enemies of those who were barriers to his ambitions, and just as many from his business partners. A.H. often fretted more over pennies than the details of his larger transactions. Sometimes his dealings were carefully planned and executed; other times they were rash or impetuous. Both styles made him money, and both lost him money. The man who came to own a bank and deal professionally with its creditors was the same man who, in a rage, shot holes through the doors of another bank after robbers made off with his gold from a cattle sale.[91]

A.H. was visionary. He saw future trends in cattle and land and was an early proponent of Brahman stock (Fig. 10) for its potential to repel ticks that caused "Texas fever." He saw barbed wire and railroads that began to dissect the open range as more of an opportunity than a threat and embraced them both. As a long-standing member and contributor to the State Cattlemen's Association, he worked with legislators to gain favorable positions on topics important to the day, such as penalties for theft and fraud, regulations covering branding, quarantines, and railroad issues, and the instigation of "a system of sanitary laws" to protect cattle from contagious diseases.

His wit was dry, and he used it often. At the 1897 Cattlemen's Convention, for example, A.H. received a standing ovation when he announced he would pay the dues of every member in Wharton County. Later, the cash-strapped organization realized there was only one other member in the county.[92]

A.H. was inspired by the statues he saw during his 1890 Europe trip and decided to construct a monument to himself. German-born sculptor Frank Teich was given instruction to build it "higher than any statue of a Confederate general." Undeterred by the San Antonio sculptor's price of $2,250, plus materials, the 30-foot granite and marble edifice were completed the next year. It arrived at El Campo on the Southern Pacific, and with block and tackle, was moved to a waiting wagon hitched to six oxen. From there, the monument was erected at the Demings Bridge cemetery, near the place where the Rhode Island stowaway got his start as a cattleman. Not just any cattleman, but the King.[93]

After A.H. Pierce died in 1900, his married daughter Mamie P. Withers and A.P. Borden were named as trustees to his holdings, their tenure lasting from 1902 until 1929.

Jonathan E. Pierce. As the bookkeeper for the Abel and J.E. Pierce partnership, Jonathan Pierce's (Fig. 11) name was on all the brother's Bend in the River land deeds. There is no indication he ever spent time there, preferring the Rancho Grande homestead on the Tres Palacios River. In contrast, brother Abel knew the land well. He not only regularly traversed the Bend in the River countryside working cattle between Rancho Grande and the Kountze K and KO Ranches, but he also settled at Pierce Ranch on the west bank of the Colorado River 13 miles north of the Bend in the River.

J.E. told an interviewer of the *St. Louis Globe Democrat* in 1898 that, when he left Rhode Island for Texas, he had only "some knowledge of carpentering, blacksmithing, and plumbing." From that meager beginning, the writer estimated that the 58-year-old had built an empire of 200,000 acres and 30,000 head of cattle in partnership with his brother.

While A.H. was the better-known cattleman, J.E. founded various cattle ventures in partnerships outside of his holdings with A.H., and for a time owned a herd that carried the Ace of Clubs brand.[94] J.E.'s legacy lives on as a Matagorda County philanthropist and businessman. He donated land for the building of the New York, Texas & Mexican Railroad that extended from Wharton to points throughout the county. The town that sprouted next to the tracks in 1903 was initially named "Thank God" until J.E. was convinced the name Blessing was more suitable. J.E. also constructed the Blessing Hotel and partnered with his son to open the Blessing State Bank (Fig. 12).[95]

Always fascinated with horticulture, J.E. Pierce was an early proponent for the introduction of rose hedges as an alternative to fencing. Originating in China, the nearly impenetrable, thorny bush, according to Pierce, would "prove a blessing to the cattlemen of Texas." His experimental hedge at Rancho Grande covered 37 miles, he said, and it was "planted to keep out horse thieves and other depredators," adding that "the thief who will penetrate a rose bush hedge is hardly fit for business after the trip."[96] J.E. intended to cultivate more, and so were other stockmen. Called McCartney or Cherokee rose, it has today covered half a million acres of the tallgrass prairie and is considered high on the list of noxious invasive species.

Sam Watkins. For reasons unknown, the Pierce brothers sold the 555-acre Julia C. and J.R. Fretwell tract to Sam Watkins for $276.75 in 1882. They made a good profit on their initial $138.87 investment, but the sale, witnessed and executed by Pierce confidant and Matagorda County notary William C. Braman, was probably more about strategy than profit. Sam Watkins was just the kind of man that the Pierce's could trust to guard a piece of what was then a remote portion of their far-flung empire.[97]

In the 40 or so years between settlement as part of the Mexican Texas land grants and the end of the Civil War, the duration of most Bend in the River landowners on their property was remarkably short. Only Hosea H. League and Thomas Cayce attempted to build a life on the land, and they quickly failed for various but justifiable reasons. All other deed holders either died, relocated, or were little more than absentee landowners. The Watkins' were not only the first family to thrive at the Bend in the River after the Texas Revolution, they did so for three generations.

The originators of the Matagorda Watkins were John Dill and Susan Favor, who were born in North Carolina and Georgia, respectively. They married in 1831, the union producing six children born between 1834 and 1845. The family moved from Alabama to Texas in 1850 and settled for at least part of the time in Matagorda County between 1854 and 1858.[98] The Matagorda location is uncertain, but it may have been on Blue Creek at the Bend in the River – various references allude to it, and vintage maps often show two Watkins Lake's – one where Blue Creek emptied into the Colorado River, thought to be their earliest homestead, and another, to the south, on the land the family owned after the 1880s.[99]

John and Susan resided in Dallas for a few years, where Susan died in 1861.[100] Widower John is difficult to trace after relocating to Dallas, but his oldest son, Alabama born Samuel Ward Watkins, returned to Matagorda County about 1860. At the onset of the Civil War, he enlisted as a private in Company H of the Bates Regiment of Texas Volunteers Cavalry and was honorably discharged from Gibbon's Texas Battery in 1865.[101] Three years after the war ended, Samuel married Alabama native Irene Clementine McGehee.

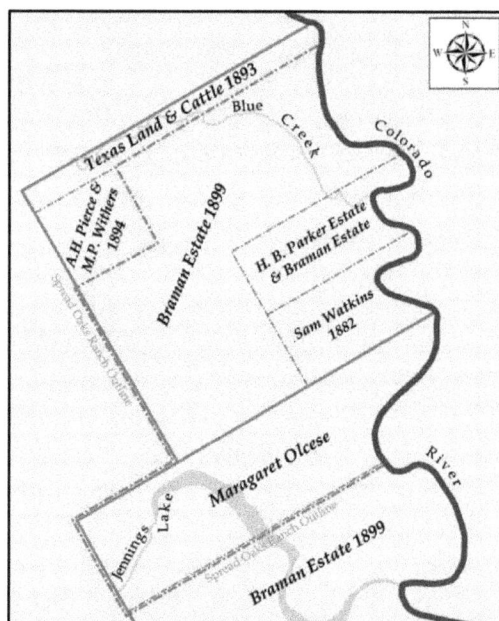

According to the 1880 Federal census, Samuel Watkins was 43-years old, married, and a farmer, with four sons and a daughter.[102] Between 1880 and 1881, he constructed a log cabin on the shore of the second water body that carried the name Watkins Lake, this one approximately 50-acres and situated north of Elliott's Ferry. Sam and Irene called their 555 acres on the banks of the Colorado River "Old Hog Ranch," and they signed the deed in 1882. With no roads, travel to and from the Watkins homestead in the "isolated district known as 'up on Blue Creek'" was mostly by boat or the ferry. During wet years, months might pass before the family could hitch up their wagon and mules and travel the 16 miles to Deming's Bridge, the nearest town before Bay City was founded, to procure supplies, groceries and mail.[103]

Samuel Ward Watkins was well-liked in the Bay Prairie community. County newspapers, which regularly chronicled his personal or business trips in the 1890s to Bay City, Matagorda, El Campo, or Wharton, affectionately dubbed him "Uncle Samuel." They rarely bothered to print his last name – everyone in the community knew who he was. In addition to an outgoing personality, Watkins was an enthusiastic host, and for many years sponsored seasonal socials, dances, and picnics at the Old Hog Ranch, the local papers printing the dates and directives such as "everybody and their basket is invited." At his 1899 picnic Watkins even constructed "a platform for dancing."[104] Revelers reached the inaccessible Bend in the River location by the ferry.

Of Samuel Ward and Irene Clementine's seven offspring who were born on the Blue Creek ranch, three died between the ages of six and 13. Son Evan, born in 1870, and Samuel Jr., who was born in 1873, would live or spend part of each year at the Bend in the River for nearly half a century. They married sisters – Evan wed Frances Harris, and Samuel married Jessie Harris, rearing some 19 children between them. As the family grew, they built a second home on the banks of Watkins Lake next to the original family cabin, raising cattle, horses, and hogs, and growing rice. They sold summer vegetables, the catfish they netted, and ducks they shot during winter as Bay City grew after the mid-1890s.

William Cheever Braman. William Cheever Braman put his name on everything that the Pierce brothers didn't. John Crier's daughter Telitha and husband B.F. Grover sold their 1,107-acre holdings in 1880 for $400 to Chauncey Southwick of Spanish Camp, Wharton County, who sold it months later to Braman for $971.35. The same year, 1881, Braman purchased the 1,107-acre William Jones tract for $553.50, then the 140-acre inheritance of Mittie Reed, daughter of Andrew Crier, for $140. Jonathan E. Pierce sold Braman another 92 acres from his Crier tract holdings. In 1882, I.S. "Samie" Magness, a daughter of Andrew Crier, transferred her 140-acre inheritance to brother-in-law E.F. Reed for $125 who in turn sold it to Braman just a month later for a $15 profit.

These land purchases were only a part of the 9,436 acres W.C. Braman amassed along the west side of the Colorado River in the 1880s. His would have been a continuous, nearly 8-mile swath covering most of the original League and Crier surveys were it not for the Olcese tract at the top of the original League Survey and a partial interest in 555 acres acres claimed by Harriet B. Parker.[105]

Braman was the son of Massachusetts native Don Egbert Erastus Braman. Father D.E.E. first came to Texas a volunteer in Albert Sidney Johnston's New Orleans and Texas Volunteers in 1836. Returning to Texas in 1837, he applied for a title to land in Matagorda County, settling in the town of Matagorda and acquiring properties on Matagorda Peninsula. Braman served as the port of Matagorda customs officer for a year, was appointed clerk of the First Judicial District Court in 1847, and in 1853 admitted to the bar (Fig. 13). After the Civil War, D.E.E. was a mayor of Matagorda, appointed a town and county judge, and continued buying and selling property.[106]

D.E.E. Braman is best known for his 1857 *Information About Texas*, its publication intended for emigrants to the state. The ambitious work included chapters with descriptions of each Texas county, stock raising, crops, schools, taxation, laws and court, various land documents, and a section that curiously combined sheep raising with honeybees. Chapters incorporated his opinions on soils, climate, health, disease, religion, family, and a wide range of other topics. For the rest of his life, his expertise was sought on each Texas drought, flood, epidemic, or any other issue of the day, and his views were dutifully published in state newspapers.[107]

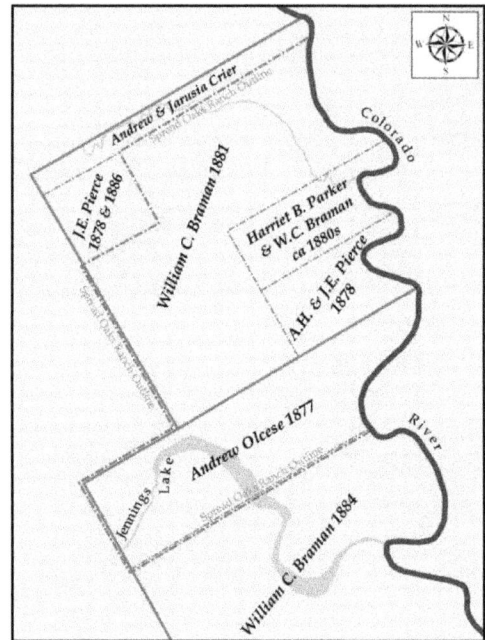

Braman married Mary Elizabeth Burkhart, the daughter of George and Catherine Dorothy Robideaux Burkhart, both natives of Philadelphia, in 1841. Son W.C. Braman, born in 1855, was one of ten surviving children. For most of his life, W.C. lived in Matagorda with his parents and usually half a dozen brothers and sisters – some, like W.C., remaining there well into their adulthood. He left Texas for his education, attending the eminent Phillips Academy in Andover, Massachusetts, and graduated in 1875. Of its 30 students in the 1873 junior class, all but W.C. were from the north – who was the single Southerner in a New England institution just eight years after the close of the Civil War.[108]

After graduation, W.C. returned to Matagorda and was appointed District Clerk for Matagorda County in 1877, replacing the wayward Elias Baxter, who was "absent from the County for some time and his whereabouts unknown." W.C. studied law, despite his father's advice that any person seeking "peace, prosperity, and health, [should] avoid lawyers, doctors, and quack medicines, and all other unseemly monsters," and was named Matagorda County attorney in 1888.[109]

W.C. joined his father in his land business during the late 1870s and early 1890s, the pair making acquisitions for their own holdings and for Bay Prairie clients such as the Pierce brothers. It was during the A.H. Pierce land grabs that D.E.E. and son took title to nearly 9,500 acres along west side of the Colorado River, the acreage including 3,121 acres on the Crier Survey.

D.E.E. moved his family to Victoria in 1887, and W.C. relocated to the city from Matagorda in 1895. Unmarried and childless, he was "a very frail man" and not in good health. During the latter part of his short life, he "suffered for years from an abscess in his side, caused by necrosis of a rib." Forty-four-year-old W.C. Braman died in the summer of 1899, just a year after his father succumbed to "la grippe."[110]

When W.C. died in 1899, his 9,436 acres passed to brother Daniel Hawes Braman and three sisters, Mary Elizabeth, Nancy Hawes, and Julia Hawes. On tax records it was called the W.C. Braman Estate, but to anyone from the area, those lands were known as Mary E.

Braman's. Just a year after W.C. died, Mary E. was at the helm when the irrigation and rice industry rose to prominence in Matagorda County. A.P. Borden was initially credited with leasing all Mary E.'s expansive acreage for rice cultivation,[111] but that was not true. It is more likely that he acted as a mentor, at first, until Mary E. developed into one of the most knowledgeable, if not shrewdest, landlords in the region.

The Harriet Parker Enigma. Harriet B. Parker's name was on 555 acres of the Denison tract before 1895, and was a resident of Jefferson County, Alabama, when she died in 1896. Nothing else is known about Parker. At first the writer linked her to Matagorda's Henry Parker. Henry Parker was an Old 300 granted a headright in 1833, the land located four miles west of the League Survey on the Tres Palacios River at the crossing of the "La Vaca & Brazoria Road."[112] But the Henry Parker trail soon fizzled – leaving "the who of Mrs. Parker and the why she came to own Texas land" – as stubbornly unknown entities.

Part of the 1,100-acre Denison tract shows clear title to the Fretwell-Pierce-Watkins chain, but there is a gap in the record for the adjacent upper 555 acres. Harriet B. Parker was paying taxes on it by at least 1895, and after her 1896 passing, her heirs alternately rendered taxes on both the full interest and a two-third interest until 1903. Between 1904 and 1907 no taxes were paid. Then, in 1908, the lawyer handling the Parker estate, R.H. Kerr, paid on a two-third interest, and niece Emma J. Beasely a one-third interest.[113]

One of the ironies in a story replete with ironies is that, in the execution of the provisions of the disposal of the land, the probate judge of Matagorda County Court ruled that Harriet Parker had only an undivided one-third interest in the 555-acre tract. Yet Mrs. Parker had been paying the full tax value on 555 acres for years. Now, evidently, her heirs learned she did not own the other two thirds. Who did? The answer seems to be William Cheever Braman. Although no deed between Denison and Braman or Parker either survives or was ever recorded, 1907 court documents ascribe Mary E. Braman as its owner.[114] By inference, her brother William C. Braman probably absorbed the tract during his collection of Bend in the River acreage in the early 1880s.

Rightful title to the original 555-acre Crier-Thomas Alley tract was contested fiercely between the late 1890s and 1907. The first legal action was a 1901 suit in trespass to title by heirs to the Elisha M. Flack estate against Mary E. Braman and others. The "others" were Franklin P. Dawson, Harriett B. Dawson, Emma J. Beasely, and R.H. Kerr. Harriet and Emma were Harriet Parker nieces, and Kerr was her legal counsel. The Flack heirs lost, filing an appeal that was heard in 1907. They lost again.

When the Flack versus Braman et al. petition was tried in the Supreme Court of Civil Appeals of Texas on March 13, 1907, it exposed many of the weaknesses and intrigue of early Texas land ownership. According to attorney Robert Riddle, it was a precedent setting appellate court case, cited eight times between 1908 and 1948, involving the topics of issues of notice, probate, policy, uncertain legal system at the time, adverse possession of land, statute of limitations, and burdens of proof on appeal.

The plaintiffs claimed superior title under Thomas Alley, contesting two main points arising from the Matagorda County sheriff's 1843 default judgement seizure of the Alley land for non-payment of taxes and its sale to James Denison. In one argument, the plaintiff's deemed the seizure invalid because they, as heirs, had not been notified of its foreclosure. The court, however, maintained that in 1843 Texas had no laws protecting heirs of a deceased mortgager, rationalizing the legal oversight as a result of a Texas judicial system too occupied "in the arduous labor of establishing a government and formulating a system of laws."[115]

The court also overruled the plaintiff's second position that, when the sheriff's deed was executed, the Flack estate was still in probate and that execution on the judgement should have been made through a probate court. The court agreed in principle but found the Alley transfer lacking specific language stating that the "note was given for the purchase money of the land."[116]

Attorneys representing Mary E. Braman and the heirs to Harriet Parker's estate cited that the defendants had not claimed, used, or occupied the land for 60 years, and that the Braman's could legally claim adverse possession because A.H. Pierce and W.C. Braman had fenced more than 10,000 acres of the original League and Crier surveys. Although their enclosure encircled lands belonging to "various parties," Braman's actual possession, they argued, took precedent over earlier titles. Per their interpretation of the complex terms of Texas' fencing laws, the defense pleaded possession under both the five- and ten-year statutes, citing the testimony of a G.C. Gifford, who claimed he was in possession "for the owners" from 1887 to 1897.[117]

The specifics of how Gifford could claim he was in possession of the disputed tract was not entered into the legal proceedings. The best explanation is that he pastured cattle on the contested land. G.C. Gifford was George Chester Pierce Gifford Sr. Born in New Bedford, Massachusetts, in 1852, Gifford was a ncphew of A.H. Pierce and came to Texas as a 19-year-old to join his uncle as a cowboy. In the 1880 Federal Census, he listed his occupation as "stock driver," was unmarried, and lived in Jackson County. For the next 15 years, he pastured his growing herds in three counties. There is little doubt that some of Gifford's grazing grounds covered Braman land and the challenged Flack acreage.

Gifford abandoned the cattle business after large losses during the freeze of 1895. He moved to Wharton, where he started Gifford Mercantile Company (Fig. 14). The former Pierce cowhand did well for himself – he was president of the Wharton Bank and Trust Co. and the G.C. Gifford Bank, and a director of People's Oil and Cotton Company. Gifford invested heavily in land and had a founding role in the town of the Glen Flora. He was shot to death in downtown Wharton by an aggrieved business associate in 1915.[118]

Legal contests for the Parker tract ended after the 1907 Flack heir's appeal. In 1911 Thomas J. Poole Sr. and Jr. of the Poole Cattle Company were paying taxes on a two-third interest of the 555 acres, presumably purchased from Mary E. Braham, and the estate of Emma J. Beasely sold Harriet Parker's remaining one-third interest in 1919.

Epilogue. The defining event that shaped Matagorda County during the 1870s to 1890s was the aftermath of the Civil War. It took decades to rebuild Matagorda's economy, social, and political structure. Nature still intruded with its epidemics, and the county suffered two hurricanes. Cattle were a shining star in the financial landscape, and advancements in farming technology were beginning to ease the toil of its labor and increase its yields. Except for cotton. In 1900, the boll weevil invaded the cotton fields of Texas, and farmers could do nothing but watch as brown lesions first appeared on acres of buds, then collapse as the larva evolved into a beetle that fed on the tissue of both bolls and leaves. Matagorda County in 1900 produced only a hundred bales.

The Civil War. Between the Indian frontier and long simmering uneasiness with Mexico, the Federal Government had maintained a strong presence in Texas long before the Civil War. It set the stage for the first action of the conflict when former Indian fighter

General Earl Van Dorn marched from the hastily formed Texas Confederate headquarters in Indianola to the US Department of Texas offices in San Antonio. Here, a greatly outnumbered Major General David Twiggs was forced to hand over all United States government property. Trudging south to board ships and return to Washington, the Union soldiers got only as far as Saluria before Van Dorn made them the first Texas prisoners of war.[119]

Matagorda County men, like most in Texas, served in major battles throughout the southern theatre. The war did come to the coast, but not with the fury of the fields and forests of Virginia, Pennsylvania, or Maryland. In the first years of the conflict, forts were constructed at the mouth of Caney Creek and two at Pass Cavallo, the latter including Fort Esperanza at Saluria and Decrow's battery on Matagorda Peninsula. Built from logs, shell, and sand, they were never a high Confederate priority. In fact, few soldiers had any interest in serving on the coast – out of 304 West Point graduates in 1861, only one volunteered to go south.

The Confederates surrendered Fort Esperanza in November 1863, unable to withstand a Federal bombardment from sea and an overland force under Major General Banks. The Caney Creek fort fared better, holding off a substantial attempt to land federal forces in 1864.[120]

The largest loss of life in Matagorda during the war was not from combat. On New Year's Eve 1863, Union gunboats landed on Matagorda Peninsula. Although gale force winds churned the bay water and protected shorelines were covered in ice, when Confederate Captain Edward S. Rugely asked for volunteers, every man in his regiment stepped forward to resist the landing. Forty-five men set sail in borrowed boats, 22 of whom drowned or died from exposure when one capsized. Their bodies were picked up the next day along the bayshore, brought to the Colorado House, and buried in a common grave.[121]

Matagordians had another role in the War Between the States – smuggling cotton to Mexico to sell to English buyers. Because most of the ports along the Texas coast were occupied by the Union, cotton was covertly freighted by ox teams overland to Brownsville and by Southern blockade runners in swift sloops that sailed from Caney Creek and Matagorda town, usually at night. Blockade runners returned the same way they came, carrying cash, other times gold, and much of the time rifles, percussion caps, and ammunition. Merchants in the town of Matagorda who received the supplies devised ingenious ways to get them the Confederate Army.[122]

Texas formally surrendered on June 2, 1865, almost three months after General Robert E. Lee at Appomattox. For the next five years the Lone Star State was not a state in any nation, instead a territory occupied by the Federal Government. While the population of Texas increased markedly in the 1870s, Matagorda County lagged. Its problem was largely its economy. With little infrastructure, shipping mostly passed by its port towns. Agriculture was slow to rebound. Cattle were the only shining star in an otherwise bleak financial landscape.

Despite the economic distress, the thing that stuck deepest in Matagorda craws was the Reconstruction. In addition to Federal troops, for the first two years of Reconstruction the town was occupied by a regiment of "negroes," a command structure entirely at odds with the social fabric of pre-war Matagorda. Too, Reconstruction gave Matagorda's people of color and former slaves – Freedmen – their first taste of liberty, as well as the opportunity to wield a wholly new political prestige as they aligned with the Unionists, both black and white, to remake the social and political order of Matagorda.[123] On paper, Reconstruction ended when Texas was readmitted to the Union in 1870. The reality was different. The carpetbaggers, with black support, dominated county political offices into the 1880s.

One place the old order reasserted itself was in the labor system. The Freedmen's Bureau, the detested vehicle designed to transition emancipated slaves to the free labor system, was eviscerated by the fact they didn't own any land. Agrarian labor fell to sharecroppers, tenant farmers, and to a cunning alternative to slave labor – the prison farm work force. In many cases the new labor system was little better than old one.[124]

The party of Lincoln was slow to erode. By the mid-1890s, Democrats took back nearly every Matagorda County political office.[125] They were to hold them for a very long time.

Return of the Tempests. Until September 16, 1875, the human toll from hurricanes in Texas was limited to mainly mariners. That was about to change. Indianola, the pearl of the central coast, was hardest hit. Located on the west side of Matagorda Bay, the storm swept 15 feet of bay water over the town. Winds reached a hundred miles per hour before the weather station anemometer blew apart. Three-fourths of the buildings in Indianola disintegrated, and of some 2,000 residents, 150 perished, their bodies littering the bay shore for 20 miles.[126]

In Matagorda County, residents in the towns of Saluria and Decrow's Point at Pass Cavallo endured seething breakers as a raging Gulf of Mexico overtook the barrier islands. On the eastern edge of Matagorda Island, only one house remained standing in Saluria. Initial reports were that "the men are all drowned at Saluria," but that was an exaggeration. Of about 43 residents, between 18 and 30 were drowned, including all but one of its bar pilots.[127]

Dr. John H. Leake, summoned to Saluria to attend to a Mrs. John Nicholls who succumbed to a dose of "fly plaster instead of blue mass," drowned when the Nicholls' house was pounded from its foundation and washed to sea. John Nicholls, who refused to leave his sick wife's bedside, drowned with his wife and child. Son Henry and house guest Olivia Decrow floated off on the roof, clinging to a wooden gutter until they reached the branches of a cedar tree. They were rescued the next morning.[128]

At Decrow's Point on Matagorda Peninsula, the Thomas Decrow family tried to ride out the tempest in his two-story home. He and four family members died. Daughter Cordelia and son Thomas W. survived and were reunited with Olivia after her ordeal at Saluria. The three remaining Decrow children moved inland.[129]

Further down the Peninsula, James Hutching watched his entire family drown, including all his children. Found floating on a log but refusing assistance, rescuers presumed he had gone crazy from his loss. William Mitchell's household drowned along with their house guest Lizzie Raymond. The John Frederick Vogg family boarded a sloop and sailed for the mainland, but it flipped on its side and drowned their daughter, Mary Ann. They moved to the mainland after they buried her.[130]

Maritime losses were high. The schooner *Witch of the Wave* was lost at sea before it reached Galveston. In Pass Cavallo, the schooner *Rescue* was wrecked, a Captain Smith drowned. A man named Maddox floated in Matagorda Bay for three days on driftwood. Between Saluria and Decrow's Point, the hurricane destroyed the West and East Shoal screw-pile lighthouses, built to mark the channel leading into Matagorda Bay at Pass Cavallo, and drowned its four light keepers.

Citizens in the town of Matagorda fared better. There was no loss of life, although substantial damage was done to buildings by wind and water. Agricultural interests in the county suffered, particularly husbandry – over 15,000 cattle and 18,000 sheep were killed.

Matagorda Bay suffered an equally devasting hurricane eleven years later. It sounded the death knoll for Indianola. Likely Saluria and Decrow's Point would have suffered a similar fate, but after the 1875 storm both settlements were entirely abandoned. There was no loss of life in Matagorda County during the 1886 storm. Buildings lost a few roofs, and other than damage to wooden structures along the waterfront, the only thing Matagorda town suffered was an infestation of rattlesnakes.[131]

God First. One thing that allowed Texian settlers to soldier through adversity was a belief in God. They never doubted their fate was in his hands. If they were to survive a tempest, sickness, or a battle, it was only because the outcome was ordained by God. If they didn't, a better life awaited them in Heaven.

Protestantism was illegal in Mexican Texas, and non-Catholics were forced to hide Protestant beliefs. After 1836, travelling ministers started to visit the new Republic of Texas. The Reverend Caleb Ives put down stakes in Matagorda town in 1838, establishing the first Episcopal parish in Texas in 1939. Unable to raise funds for a proper building, he had one shipped by sea from New York. Methodism came to Matagorda the same year, its church building destroyed during the 1854 hurricane. The first Baptist church in the county was a log structure erected on Tres Palacios Creek in 1852. J.E. Pierce and wife Nannie Lacy donated the funds to construct a building in 1893, and its cemetery at Deming's Bridge was renamed Hawley's Cemetery in 1898.[132]

With few churches and a widely dispersed population, the gospel in the mid 1800s was often delivered at camp meetings that were as religiously significant as they were important community social events. Word spread whenever travelling minsters and other laymen passed through the area. The community contributed a cow, vegetables and fruit from their fields, and families pitched tents.[133] The words of the preachers were delivered with fervor and attentively absorbed by the congregation, despite fidgeting children and old men who snored.

The family bible was sacrosanct. It not only carried the doctrine that guided them through their lives, but it was where they recorded their marriages, births, and expirations. When the Robert Moore home was destroyed during the 1875 Indianola storm, the family searched the wreckage until they found their most prized possession – their Bible. Ruined, they tore out the page with family history. When it dried, the widow and daughter added the drowning of Robert Moore to the page.[134]

Bay City. Denver mining magnate Colonel David Swickhimer travelled south each winter to duck hunt in Matagorda County during the late 1880s. His was a long journey, requiring train connections to reach Wharton, then horse and wagon to Bay Prairie. Tiring of the ardours of tent camps, he determined to build a town near his hunting grounds. Swickhimer and his partners formed the Bay City Town Company, purchasing 640 acres of cattle pasture in 1894 east of the Colorado River, and began promoting the new town in newspapers across the United States.[135]

Part of their development strategy included a petition to move the county seat from Matagorda to the new town. It was county politics at its best. Supporters argued for the location change because of Matagorda's susceptibility to hurricanes, citing destruction of the courthouse during the 1854 storm and damage to it again in the 1875 storm. The reality, however, was financial, and founding Bay City businessmen played hardball. The "remote" Matagorda location "blights every prospect for progress and posterity," they informed voters. The Bay City Town Company even promised to pay for a new courthouse. It was a "grand victory" for Bay City in the 1894 county election when Matagorda lost its seat by a vote of 778 to 141. With their seemingly last vestige of political prominence slipping away, the town petitioned to hold another election the next year. They lost again.[136]

When Bay City completed its new courthouse in 1896, the sheriff travelled south by horseback to take possession of the old Matagorda courthouse. By 1900 the population of the new county seat swelled to a thousand residents, but people began moving away from Matagorda town, its property values dropping to a record low.[137]

CAMPAIGN
CHRONICLE.
EXTRA.
E. W. CAVE, Editor.
NACOGDOCHES,
Monday July 4, 1859.

Independent Ticket.
FOR GOVERNOR:
GEN. SAM HOUSTON.
FOR LT. GOVERNOR.
EDWARD CLARK,
OF HARRISON COUNTY.

GEN. HOUSTON
ON
TEXAS FRONTIER
PROTECTION.
BE NOT DECEIVED BY GARBLED EXTRACTS FROM HIS SPEECHES!
HEAR THE FACTS!

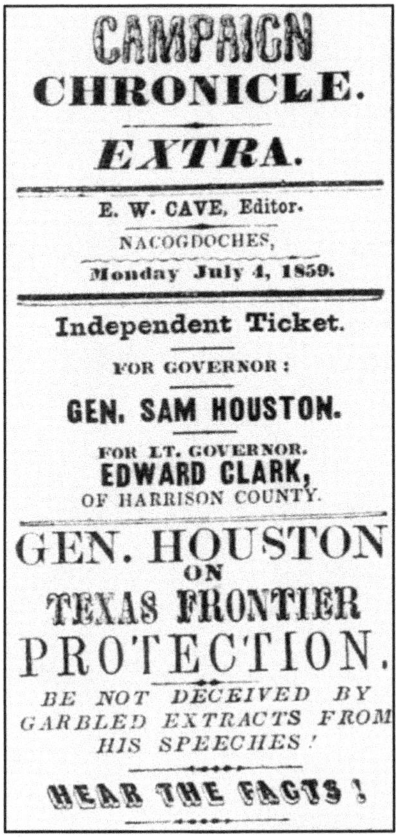

Fig. 1. A Sam Houston political notice from his 1859 run for governor. Note the line "Be not deceived by garbled extracts from his speeches!" Although Houston was elected, he was removed from office because of his loyalty to the Union. *The Campaign Chronicle*, July 5, 1859. Portal to Texas History, https://Texas history.unt.edu/ark:/67531/metapth713316 /m1/2/.

Fig. 2. Sam Houston, ca. 1848-50, by photographer Mathew B. Brady. Library of Congress Prints and Photographs Division, Washington, D.C. 20540 USA, no. 2004663991.

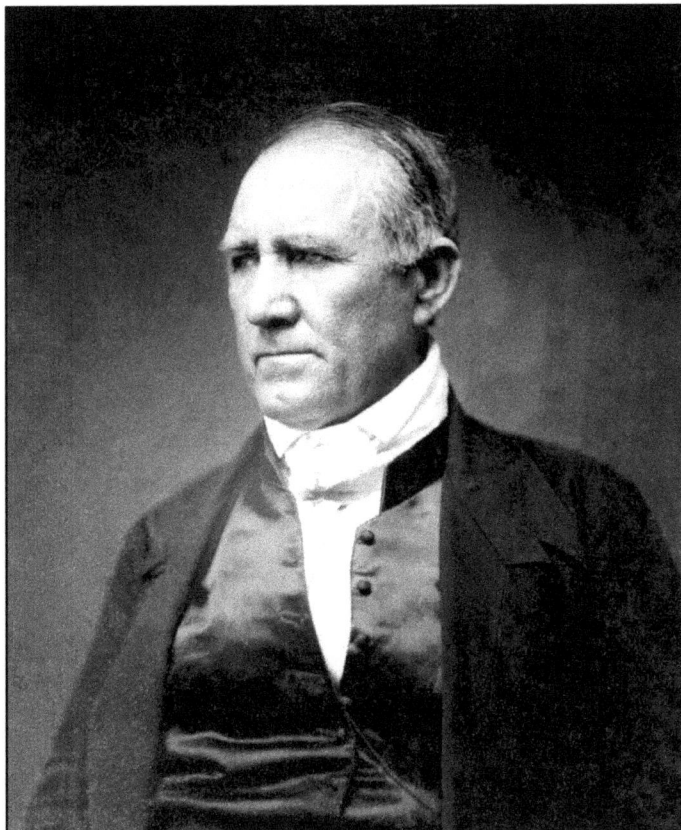

Fig. 3. Abel Head "Shanghai" Pierce, ca. late 1870 to early 80s. Courtesy Matagorda Museum, File No. 17.1984.12.10 CP.17.

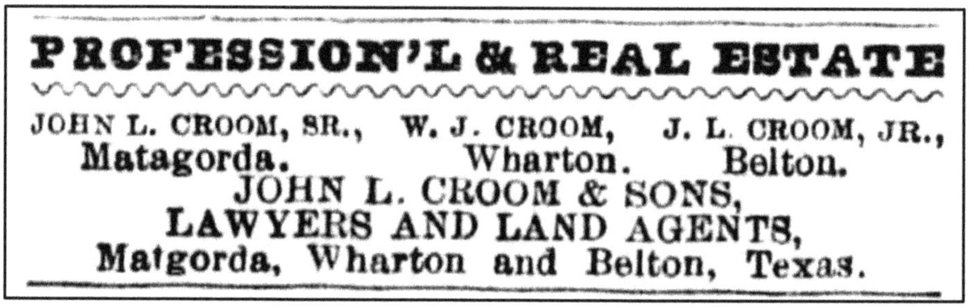

PROFESSION'L & REAL ESTATE

JOHN L. CROOM, SR.,   W. J. CROOM,   J. L. CROOM, JR.,
Matagorda.   Wharton.   Belton.
JOHN L. CROOM & SONS,
LAWYERS AND LAND AGENTS,
Matgorda, Wharton and Belton, Texas.

Fig. 4. Lawyer John L. Croom and his sons were sometimes allies and sometimes foes in the Pierce brother's land purchases. *Galveston Daily News*, October 19, 1885, The Portal to Texas History, University of North Texas Libraries, https://texashistory.unt.edu/ark:/67531/metapth463268/.

DANIEL SULLIVAN,

WHOLESALE AND RETAIL GROCER,

CORNER OF MAIN AND FANNIN STREETS

INDIANOLA,................Texas.

HAS on hand and is contantly receiving a fresh supply of Corn, Flour, Coffee, Tea, Sugar, Lard, Hams, Bacon, Whiskey, Brandy, Gin, Soap, starch, Candles, all of which will be sold cheap, for cash. Aug. 11, '60—ly.

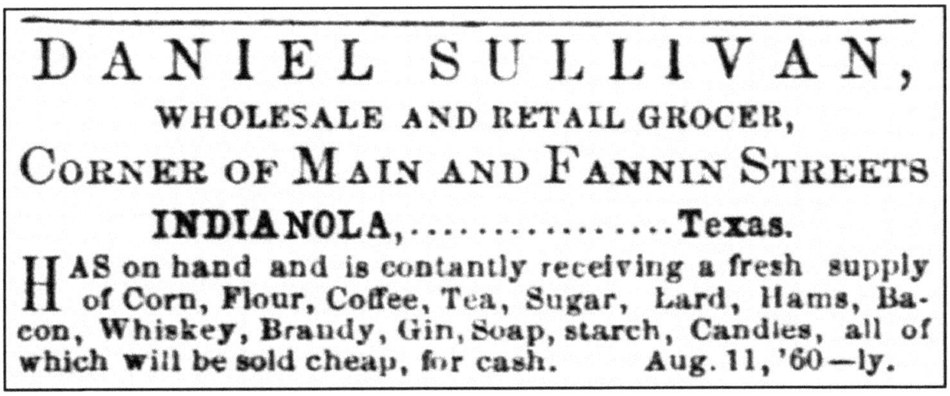

Fig. 5. With business booming in Indianola, merchant Danny Sullivan loaned A.H. Pierce some of his seed money. His son, also named Danny was involved in various Pierce partnerships. *Indianola Courier*, Nov. 24, 1860, The Portal to Texas History, Univ. of North Texas Libraries, https://texashistory.unt.edu/ark:/67531/metapth739638/m1/.

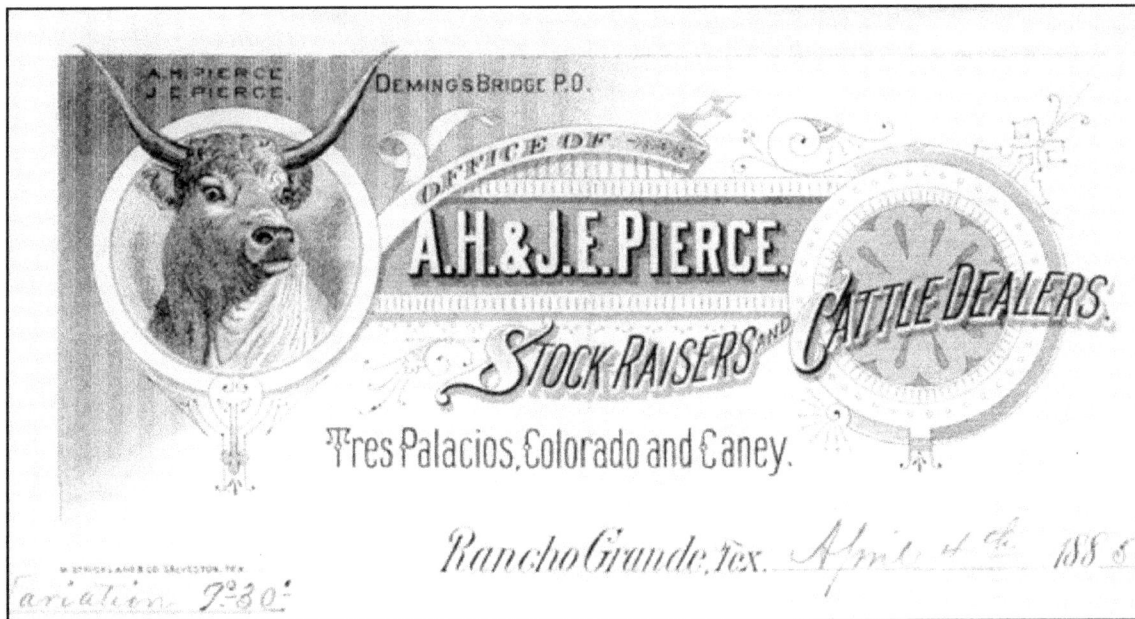

Fig. 6. Letterhead of the Pierce brother's cattle business before A.H. relocated to Pierce Ranch, near Wharton. Courtesy of the Texas General Land Office, https://s3.glo.texas.gov/glo/history/archives/map-store/zoomer.cfm?z=https://s3.glo.texas.gov/ncu/SCANDOCS/archives_web files/arcmaps/ZoomWork/8/8348.

Fig. 7. Cattleman Wylie M. Kuykendall, ca 1885. Kuykendall was a Pierce foreman and married A.H. Pierce's sister Susan in 1869. Courtesy Matagorda Museum, File No. 1989.09.10BK.12.

Fig. 8. No railroads connected Bay City to Wharton until 1901. Other than horseback, the only way to travel was by stagecoach, which delivered its passengers to Pierce Ranch railroad depots after 1883. *Matagorda County Tribune*, September 23, 1899, The Portal to Texas History, Univ. of North Texas Libraries, https://texashistory.unt.edu/ark:/67531/metapth1346130/.

Bay City & Pierce.
Mail Hack Line
——(o)——
Hack leaves Bay City at 6:00 every morning except Sunday, connects with both trains at Pierce and returns same day.
GOOD COVERED HACK.
Passengers wishing to go will leave word at the Post Office.
WM. DOUGLAS, Proprietor.

N. WEEKES. ED. McCARTHY, A. H. PIERCE.
Weekes, McCarthy & Co.,
BANKERS,
Successors to American National Bank
OF GALVESTON, TEXAS,
Foreign and Domestic Exchange bought and sold. Cable and telegraphic transfers made. Credits furnished.
Accounts Solicited.

Fig. 9. Posting for A.H. Pierce's new Weekes Bank partnership. *Galveston Tribune*, October 96, The Portal to Texas History, Univ. of North Texas Libraries, https://texashistory.unt.edu/ark:/metapth1281753/.

Fig. 10. The A.H. Pierce legacy – barbed wire fences, longhorns, and Brahman cattle. Photo is of Pierce Ranch, 1915. Courtesy Matagorda Museum, File No. 1989.09.100.1.

Fig. 11. Jonathan Edward Pierce was the bookkeeper for the *A.H. & J.E. Pierce Stock Raisers and Cattle Dealers* partnership and a founder of the town of Blessing. Ancestry.com, https://www.ancestry.com/media-ui viewer/collection/1030/tree/14163533/person/27017 9058222/media/6f63cbdf-8fc2-4999-b2ea-768c2 e17b002.

A.B. Pierce, Pres. J.E. Pierce, V.-Pres. Chas. E. Duller, Cashier.

BLESSING STATE BANK

Capital, $25,000.00

Learn To Do Banking

No matter how small your business may be.

Have a Bank Account

Small accounts as well as large ones are welcome here. You do not need to wait until your business has assumed great proportions before opening an account.

Do It TODAY

Fig. 12. J.E. Pierce donated land for the New York, Texas and Mexican Railway and built the Blessing railroad depot, Blessing Hotel, and partnered with his son to A.B. Pierce in the Blessing State Bank. *Matagorda County Tribune*, Sept. 23, 1899, The Portal to Texas History, Univ. of North Texas Libraries, https://texas history.unt.edu/ark:/67531/metapth1346130/.

D. E. E. Braman,

ATTORNEY & COUNSELLOR AT LAW,

MATAGORDA, TEXAS.

Fig. 13. Braman was the port of Matagorda customs officer, clerk of the First Judicial District Court in 1847, and in 1853 admitted to the bar. After the Civil War, D.E.E. was a mayor of Matagorda, appointed a town and county judge. *Matagorda Gazette*, April 11, 1860.

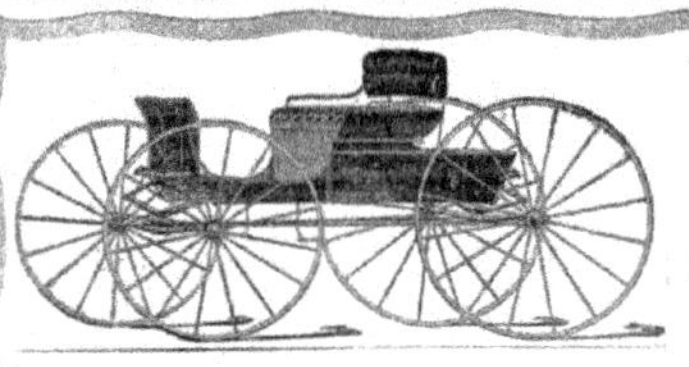

Three Carloads of Wagons---

Old Hickory, New Harrison,

Linstroth and Florence.

One Carload Buggies.

Carts and Hacks Just Received.

Sash, Doors, Blinds, Cisterns, Brick, Lime, Cement, Shelf and Heavy Hardware, Pipe and Fittings,

Rubber Hose, Barb Wire, Nails, Poultry Netting, Blacksmiths' Supplies. Blacksmith Coal, Charcoal, Paints, Oils and Glass. If you want a Hack Buggy or Waggon or set of Harness I can save you money; this is not idle talk. I can and will do just what I claim. I can make it to your interest to get my prices on above lines.

YELLOW PINE AND CYPRESS LUMBER.

G. C. GIFFORD,

MILAM ST. - - - WHARTON, TEX.

Fig. 14. Former Pierce cowboy turned Wharton businessman, G.C. Gifford, pastured cattle on the future Spread Oaks Ranch in the late 1800s. *Bay City Breeze*, Aug. 21, 1897, The Portal to Texas History, Univ. of North Texas Libraries, https://texashistory.unt.edu/ark:/67531/metapth1329935 /manifest/.

CHAPTER 3

Landowners of the Bend in the River

1900s to 1930s

Rice, after 1900, was as economically important to the Bay Prairie region as cattle had been from the 1870s to the early 1900s. For men with land, or money, or with nothing more than ambition, rice and rice irrigation represented an unprecedented financial opportunity. They would seize it. Situated adjacent to the Colorado River and dissected by waterways such as Blue Creek and Jennings Creek, the Bend in the River was central to Bay Prairie's rice boom. Every land transaction between 1910 and 1930 on the future Spread Oaks Ranch was precipitated by the rice industry – in part for growing it, but mostly for irrigation. The Bend in the River would see the construction of large reservoirs and a behemoth network of canals extending from the Colorado River for miles in every direction across the prairie.

The names of Victor LeTulle, Ross Sterling, A.J. Harty and the companies they owned were to dominate Bay Prairie and Matagorda County irrigation. Irrigation was big business, but its players held the center stage for just a short while, their drama entirely played out by the early 1930s (see Section 2, titled *Matagorda Rice*).

The Irrigators. The irrigators came to own much of present day Spread Oaks Ranch between 1918 and 1927, holding title to over 2,250 acres that encompassed the Olcese, Watkins, and Parker-Poole tracts. They also owned a 7,040-foot easement parallel to the river on the Braman Estate, and controlled portions of the 18-mile Blue Creek canal network that, in part, covered the northernmost 221-acres of the Crier Survey.

The irrigators held plenty of deeds, but never lived on the Bend in the River. At least one of them, A.J. Harty, probably knew the land better than anyone before or after him.

A.J. Harty. Andrew James 'A.J.' Harty arrived in Texas about 1900, hanging his shingle as a contractor first in Houston and then Bay City. It was A.J. Harty's name most frequently associated with the design and construction of Matagorda County canals, levees, reservoirs, and pumping plants. He was a mechanical genius credited with originating the Colorado River gravity pumps, and even held a patent for an "apparatus for grinding cultivator disks."[138] Although he came to own irrigation land, irrigation companies, properties, and a bank, he was a man most comfortable in the field fiddling with equipment and operating the machinery that defined the earth moving industry of the early 1900s.

Harty's first mention in Matagorda business circles was in 1910 as a foreman with the Security Canal Company. A year later he was named a principal in the W.C. Moore-Cortes Canal Company.[139] Harty was an early director of the Rice Growers Association, the organization chartered in 1909 in partnership with the Farmers' Rice Selling Corporation to control rice prices, but "not come in in contact with the Federal anti-trust statute."[140]

Harty gained a stellar reputation quickly. He was portrayed in a 1910 court case as an expert "thoroughly familiar with conditions of the Colorado River at all times during the past 10 years." After planters faced years of drought in the 1910s, a Matagorda County newspaper editorial opined that Matagorda fared better than other parts of Texas only because of the irrigation and "constructive genius" of "the far-sighted wizard and miracle worker of Texas, A.J. Harty." Twenty years later he was still lauded, an area newsman writing "there is no man, probably in the state, who understands the idiosyncrasies of the Colorado River as does A. J. Harty."[141]

After 1913, Harty's name was inseparable from V.L. LeTulle's. Both were commissioners of Matagorda County Drainage District No.1 for over a decade. In 1914, Harty was Markham Irrigation Company's (MIC) general manager, and after 1917, Victor LeTulle was its president.[142] Harty purchased the Gulf Coast Irrigation Company for $150,000 in 1920 and sold the enterprise three years later to V.L. LeTulle, who designated him its vice president and general manager (Fig. 1). He was also the owner and president of First National Bank in Bay City until 1921, and remained a director under its new owner, V.L. LeTulle.[143]

Harty's 1918 to 1919 purchases of the Olcese, Parker-Poole, and Watkins tracts were linked to MIC's plan to convert the west side of Colorado River into a complex of four reservoirs covering 3,500-acres (Section 2, *Matagorda Rice,* Fig. 15). The basins would be charged from canals connected to the river, and a network of laterals would move irrigation water to area rice farmers. Harty designed it all.

MIC was reorganized in 1927 with Victor L. LeTulle and A.J. Harty its owners, along with LeTulle family members Louis and Sam LeTulle. Two years later, in October 1929, V.L. filed suit against his own company. When the Matagorda County District Court found in his favor, MIC's holdings were seized, its assets liquidated at auction. The company that was worth $3.5 million just four years earlier sold to the highest bidder, V.L. LeTulle, for $40,000. A.J. Harty was not part of LeTulle's new organization, or any LeTulle venture afterwards.[144]

The historical record is mostly silent on A.J. Harty after LeTulle's windfall. Nephew Tommy LeTulle wrote that Harty was bankrupt by the late 1920s. V.L. LeTulle, he said, loaned him $30,000, then foreclosed on the last of his irrigation holdings around 1930. After that, the name A.J. Harty faded from county newspapers, and he evidently never again returned to the irrigation business. Among the last references to Harty was in 1932 as the co-owner of a barbeque restaurant called *The Rendezvous* (Fig. 2). It closed a year later.[145]

Victor Lawrence LeTulle. V.L. LeTulle's father was born in West Virginia, coming to Texas in the mid 1850s and settling in Colorado County. The family migrated to Caney Creek in 1888, where the 24-year-old helped run a general store and farm cotton. It was during this time that he acquired an injury that caused him to walk with a noticeable limp for the remainder of his life. In V.L.'s no doubt preferred version, a cotton gin flywheel "came off its shaft and struck him in his shin," the broken limb never setting properly. In another, less circulated version, V.L. was shot off his horse during an argument with his brother, John James.[146]

V.L. had his hand in a variety of ventures during the late 1890s. He flirted briefly with politics as a Matagorda County delegate to the Democratic National Convention in 1896 and 1900. He raised cattle that he sold and shipped by rail. The family was already successful cotton farmers, but after 1895, V.L. turned to convict labor. The next year, he supervised the planting of 500 acres, and it was one of the largest crops ever produced in the county. When the boll weevil infestation caused a decline in cotton yields around the turn of the century V.L., like many area farmers, looked to rice.[147]

V.L. moved to Bay City in 1900, and a year later opened LeTulle Mercantile Company of Bay City with $25,000 of capital stock (Fig. 3). Catering to the needs of the new, booming rice business, he ordered and sold so many plows, harnesses, saddles, rice binders, and threshers that the railroad built a spur to the side door of his store. He poured his enormous energy into another venture as a principal in the Bay Prairie Irrigation Company, the company in its first-year planting 23,000 acres of rice near Lane City.[148]

Businessman V.L. was described by his nephew as a man with "a mind like rapier [who] enjoyed an encounter as much as an Irishman enjoys a fight." Evidently one of his preferred money-making tools was a loan followed by an early call, and then a foreclosure. The long list of failed irrigation companies that V.L. consolidated into his Markham Irrigation Company (MIC) was perhaps, in some instances, not a coincidence. Even his flagship MIC found its way into receivership, although he ended up as its sole owner, purchasing its assets for just pennies on the dollar.[149]

One of the few deals in which he was bested was his "transfer" of his last irrigation company, Gulf Coast Irrigation, to the Interstate Public Services Company. V.L. maintained it was not a sale, but a reorganization. When the IRS piled up penalties and interest on the unpaid taxes from his "reorganization," V.L. reluctantly paid out $110,234, then sued the government for a refund. He lost, the US Supreme Court unanimously disagreeing with his interpretation.[150]

History would come to show that VL. LeTulle was as fierce as was benevolent. He shot and killed Wiley Henry in an argument over cotton on the Caney Creek Plantation in 1898, the shooting ruled self-defense. The next year, he was arrested for manslaughter, and in another indictment that year, V.L. was charged with another murder. Both cases were later dropped.[151]

The compassionate side of V.L. LeTulle is what most Bay City citizens prefer to remember. Among a lengthy legacy of philanthropy was the 25-acre LeTulle Park he gifted to Bay City in 1933, the sanctuary of the First Baptist Church that he built as a memorial to his first wife, Sallie Bell, and his purchase of the Bay City Gas Company that he presented to the town. The Buckner Orphan Home in Dallas received a $30,000 gift in 1931 and the entirety of his 8,400-acre "LeTulle River Farm" near Bay City. He gave a $200,000 gift to Houston Memorial Hospital in 1943 and provided a $100,000 donation to build the Battleship Texas. According to nephew Tommy LeTulle, he "sent young people to college, and crippled children to Shriner Hospital."[152] Victor L. LeTulle died in 1944 at age 79.

Ross Sterling. Ross Shaw Sterling was born in 1875 near Anahuac, in Chambers County. He left home at the age of 21 and, in 1903, followed the lure of oil to Sour Lake, north of Beaumont. Here he opened a feed store and invested small sums in oil wells that grew quickly into the ownership of banks and more wells. By 1910 he and Walter Fondren Sr. organized the Humble Oil Company, the parent company of the Humble Oil Corporation and Exxon Corporation.[153]

Sterling invested his oil largess in a wide range of projects and companies, his business acumen earning him the sobriquet "captain of finance." He bought real estate and railroads, including ownership of the Dayton-Goose Creek Railway Company. He purchased the *Houston Dispatch* and the *Houston Post* newspapers that he merged under the umbrella of the Houston Printing Company. No expense was spared in his construction of the swank, art deco 21-story Sterling Building in Houston.[154]

It was during this period of frenzied expansion that Sterling cast his eye to irrigation, becoming a majority stockholder in V.L. LeTulle's Markham Irrigation Company (MIC) in 1923. MIC's reign over Bay Prairie rice irrigation was a contentious one, and Sterling opted out in 1927 (see Section 2, titled *Matagorda Rice*).

Ross Sterling redirected his diverse interests to yet another new endeavor in 1928 as chairman of the Texas Highway Commission under Governor Dan Moody.[155] While in Austin he got a taste for politics, casting his eye towards the governor's seat. It was the dawn of the Depression when Sterling made his run for governor, and although he defeated Miriam 'Ma' Ferguson, his timing couldn't have been worse. Money was pouring out of state coffers at a rate faster than it was coming in. He attempted to pass legislation to prop up oil and cotton prices, but they were overturned by federal and state courts. His term lasted only two years, from 1931 to 1933, when Miriam Ferguson thwarted his reelection bid. Governor Sterling filed suit over the run-off election results, citing 20,000 illegal votes in 130 counties.[156] He lost.

He was about to lose again. While Sterling occupied the governor's mansion, the Depression was eroding his business holdings. Sterling, who owed over $1.6 million on his Sterling Building skyscraper to millionaire Jim 'Silver Dollar' West Jr. and his West Securities Company, pledged 2,088 shares of his Houston Printing Company to secure a $250,000 loan.[157] When West and his legal counsel decided in 1931 to cash in his chips, it started a freefall on Ross Sterling's investments.

A year later, Sterling sold his namesake Sterling Building, his newspaper the *Houston Post-Dispatch*, and every other business he owned. In all, Ross signed over 40 collateral trust notes aggregating $800,000 to West Production Company. His real estate holdings in seven Texas counties, stocks, bonds, mineral interests and leases were put on the auction block, and they went to sole bidder West Securities for pennies on the dollar – $18,750.[158] One of the land parcels Jim West Jr. came to own was the 1,087-acre Watkins and Parker-Poole piece of the John Crier League, where the current Spread Oaks Ranch lodge is situated. It is doubtful he ever set foot on the property.

The captain of finance would rise again. Ross Sterling built a second fortune as president of the Sterling Oil and Refining Company. His diversified business interests included president of the American Maid Flour Mills and the R. S. Sterling Investment Company, and he was chairman of the Houston National Bank and the Houston-Harris County Channel Navigation Board. Ross Sterling died on March 25, 1949.[159]

Buried deep in the folders and correspondence that make up the historical archives of Ross Sterling, perhaps, is his version of the tumultuous years he spent as a Matagorda County irrigator. Although volumes of material are dedicated to the life and businesses of Ross Sterling, there is not a single mention of V.L. LeTulle and Markham Irrigation – even in Sterling's own autobiography.

The Southern Survey at the Bend in the River

Cattle were first, but it is doubtful that Andrew Olcese Sr. benefitted financially much from the industry. His was a narrow strip of land bounded on two sides by William C. Braman's large pasture holdings that were grazed by A.H. Pierce's herds – either with or without Olcese's consent. By the early 1900s, however, A.H. Pierce's nephew A.P. Borden formalized a grazing agreement with Olcese heir Margaret Olcese.

Rice cultivation was next. Rice had come to Matagorda in 1899, and in 1909, Margaret Olcese's agent and attorney appeared in Matagorda County to execute a lease with J.H. Green, a principal of Green & Sawyer of Bay City, who planned to add the prairie south of Jennings Lake to his rice holdings. In the agreement, "feme sole" Margaret Olcese signed a three-year lease for a yearly payment of $1,200 between 1909 and 1912, giving Green the right to construct "ditches, or canals, fluses [sic], laterals, reservoirs, dams and leveis [sic]." One of its more interesting provisions was "for protection against the introduction of Johnson grass, red rice, or other injurious plants or obnoxious vegetation."[160]

A.P. Borden still had a lease agreement for cattle, and as the first man to cultivate rice in the region, was not optimistic about farmer Green's prospects on the Olcese tract (Fig. 4). In a letter to Green & Sawyer attorney C.R. Johns & Co., he advised: "I do not think there is any rice land in the whole tract, and if you rent it for rice, I would advise you to get well secured paper or money in advance for the rent." But he was willing to surrender part of the lease with the caveat to "give me the balance of the tract, rent free for next year, I will let them take possession of their so-called rice land at once and prepare for a crop next year (Fig. 5)."[161] Then came the drought of 1910, and Green & Sawyer were out of business as soon as the ink was dry.[162]

It took another five years to settle the estate after Margaret died in Alameda County in 1912, the heirs forming the Olcese Estate Company in 1918. In one of its first transactions, the company sold an 11-acre easement to the Markham Irrigation Company (MIC). The right of way was a strip of land 100-foot wide with its center at "an intake cut through a large lake" – Jennings Creek – and the agreement stipulated that the Grantee would reserve "sufficient water in said lake and canal for all stock and domestic purposes at all times and season."[163]

A year later, the Olcese Estate sold the entirety of its 1,476-acre holdings to A.J. Harty for $22,140, the 1919 instrument separating the surface rights from the subsurface mineral rights.[164] The Olcese Estate wisely kept the latter, although the experts of the day thought there wasn't much hydrocarbon potential below the land along the river. Twenty years later, the North Bay City Field was discovered by the Ohio Oil Company McDonald-1

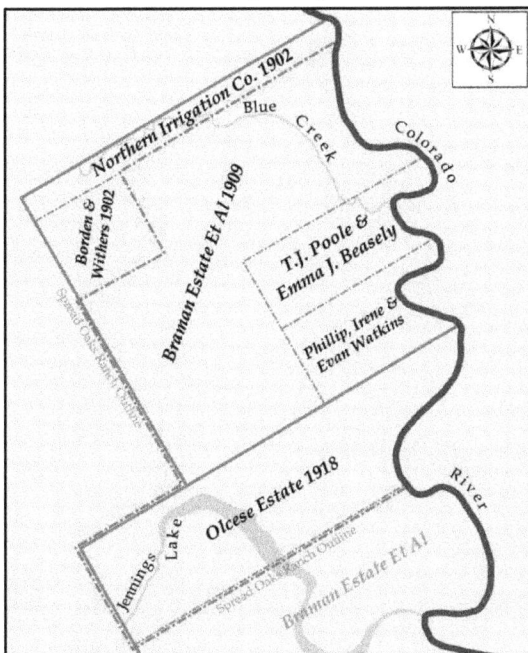

wildcat well.[165] It almost made the descendants of Italian immigrant Andrew Olcese Sr. oil and gas royalty owners. The North Bay City Field accumulation, however, was confined to the center of the original League Survey, and never crossed the Olcese boundary.

The Olcese property, with its Jennings Lake improvements, was at the heart of MIC's 3,500-acre rice reservoir complex. But, apart from the irrigation easement, title to the property was never transferred to the company. It was first in MIC general manager A.J. Harty's name, in 1919. His $22,140 purchase obligated him to four mortgage payments on a $5,000 cash purchase, and in 1921 MIC president Victor L. LeTulle assumed the note.[166]

The Crier tract came into the 20th century with most of its late 1800s owners. Much of the western side remained with the Braman and Pierce heirs. The southern quarter, however, was coveted by the rice irrigators. They had already laid claim to the Olcese parcel to the south, and by 1919 held deeds covering both the Watkins and the Parker-Poole holdings.

Watkins Family. After the Pierce brothers sold the 555-acre Julia C. and J.R. Fretwell tract to Samuel Ward and Irene Clementine in 1882, the Watkins family remained on the land for nearly half a century. Of the seven children born on Samuel and Irene's "Old Hog Ranch," three died between the ages of six and 13. Son Evan, born in 1870, and Samuel Jr., who was born three years later, married sisters – Evan wed Frances Isabel Harris, and Samuel married Jessie Harris, rearing some 19 children between them. As the family grew, they built a second home on the banks of Watkins Lake next to the original family cabin, raising cattle, horses, and hogs, and growing rice. They also made money by selling summer vegetables, the catfish they netted on the river, and the ducks they shot during winter in Bay City after it was founded in the mid-1890s.

Evan and Sam Jr. were in their 30s when they joined the frenzy of early 1900s rice farming. After early profitable years, they expanded their agricultural interests in 1909 through an agreement with the Northern Irrigation Company (NIC). In return for labor and a percentage of the proceeds, NIC would lease them 500 acres, provide seed rice, and furnish irrigation water from its Colorado River pumping plant and canal network.[167]

Then came the unprecedented drought of 1910 (see Section 2, titled *Matagorda Rice*). With the Colorado River at historic lows, NIC was unable to pump irrigation water, and the Watkins' could only watch as their crop withered in the summer sun. Although they sued for $9,000 in damages, the court allowed them just $1,636. That year Evan and Sam Jr. were only two of the many failed area farmers, along with seven irrigation companies that went broke, including the Northern Irrigation Company.[168]

The Watkins brothers tried rice farming again, with funding this time provided from Bay City banker and investor Victor L. LeTulle. The brothers, who could not afford tractors, still broke sod with mules. During a dry spring, their pack animals were unable to turn the packed, hard soil. According to area rancher Tommy LeTulle:

> "One day Sam [Jr.] and all of his boys were looking at a long line of wagons coming down the road toward their house…and drove in Sam's yard and started unloading a lot of equipment, large timbers, binders, twine, harness, etc. Sam walked up to the man who had gotten off the tractor and…he told Sam that V. L. LeTulle had sent them out there to help put in his rice crop. He also told Sam that V. L. had sent orders for him to take care of them."

In Tommy LeTulle's version, the apparent act of good will did not end well. "Well," he wrote, "Sam Watkins [Jr.] made a good crop, but there was not much left when V. L. LeTulle got his cut."[169]

Most of the extended Watkins family continued to live, work, and play at Old Hog Ranch until they sold the property in 1918. By the 1910s, Samuel Sr. and Irene divided their time between land they bought near Matagorda Bay and a home in Bay City purchased so that the grandchildren could attend high school. "Uncle Samuel" Ward Watkins died in 1916, leaving "a large family and connection," and Irene Clementine died in 1920.[170]

Son Evan lived at least part of each year at the family ranch and opened a market with a butcher shop and bakery in El Campo around 1900. After the 1920s he bought and sold cattle. The family says he was a cowboy all his life, competing in local rodeos as a tie-down roper up until his death at age 73. Samuel Jr. also remained in the Bay Prairie area, where he farmed and worked cattle. He was 83 when he died in Markham in 1956.[171]

History is fortunate that some of the Watkins's stories have been recorded, both in print and handed down, by the third generation of Watkins who spent their childhood at Old Hog Ranch. Writer Monty Brast interviewed Ruby Watkins before she died in 1991. Born on the ranch in 1909, Ruby was the youngest of Evan and Frances's 10 children. In her recollections, Ruby told of learning to swim in the Colorado River, red wolves they called "lobo wolves," and travelling on foot or horseback to accompany the older children who attended Blue Creek School. The teacher, Laura Roades, lived with Watkins, her salary paid by Evan and Sam Jr. The site of the Blue Creek school is unknown, only that it was "located near the river."[172]

Ruby was three years old when her parents moved to Bay City, but the family returned to Old Hog Ranch during summer. It was here that Ruby mastered the skill of breaking roughstock, calves, and roping Brahman bulls, often entering rodeos in Bay City. Her hobby, tolerated but not necessarily encouraged by her parents, led to some broken ribs and a broken arm but also some notable rodeo prize earnings. Ruby married V.R. Baty in 1929 and died in 1991.

Neal and Lynn Watkins are the keepers of the family lore handed down from their father, Victor, who was Ruby's older brother and was born in 1903. Neal recalls his father's strong work ethic, instilled at an early age from his ranch work. Vic preferred working in the outdoors to anything related to schoolwork – other than football. He dutifully packed off to Bay City schools each fall but left at the end of football season and quit school for good in the 11th grade.

Rice farming made an indelible impression on Vic's memory. As a youngster, he helped his father and uncle prepare the land with a mule team attached to just a Fresno or plow. At "hog killing time" he recalled the family butchering and smoking pigs then, with no refrigeration, packing the hams in barrels of lard to preserve them. According to his sons, growing up on the farm probably influenced Vic's diet for the rest of his life – he had cornbread, potatoes, tomatoes and vegetables with almost every meal.

During winters, the boys and their father travelled by horse and wagon to hunt ducks along the oak and hackberry-lined banks of Blue Creek. Its dense canopy of trees not only made it easier to sneak up on roosting mallards undetected, but the cover also made it more difficult for the birds to take flight. Game laws outlawing the sale of waterfowl had only been recently passed, but it wasn't until many years later that most rural people took any heed of them. The Watkins' were not the exception when they filled their wagon with ducks and geese to sell in Bay City. Ducks were sold by going door to door. Geese fetched the best prices and were used locally to make goose down pillows. Vic also shot ducks by moonlight, preferring a smaller gauge .410 Lefever to his usual Winchester Model 12 16-gauge – the .410 was quieter, which not only scared fewer ducks, but was less likely to attract the attention of any game wardens (Fig. 6).

When Old Hog Ranch was sold in 1918, 15-year-old Vic went to work for the Pierce Ranch as a cowboy. He told his sons Neal and Lynn how they drove herds from summer pastures to their wintering grounds that ended with a drive down the beach from Matagorda and across Brown Cedar Cut. They often slept on the beach while waiting for an incoming tide – otherwise the herd might be swept into the Gulf – and Vic remembers waking up in the morning to rattlesnakes sharing his bedroll.

During the 1920's Vic went to work for Texas Gulf Sulphur Company, and in 1946 became foreman of the Lobit Ranch near Dickinson before settling in Webster. He continued to hunt and fish for the rest of his life. When Vic married Olive Anne Krause in the winter of 1938, he went goose hunting the next day. Friends and family were curious why he went hunting right after his wedding, to which he replied, "I've been goose hunting a lot longer than I've been married – I'm not going to stop hunting now!"

Evan's brother Samuel Jr. also raised his family on the ranch and had at least seven children that survived to adulthood. Vic's cousin Manley Sexton "Bute" Watkins was the oldest, born in 1901. Bute by the late 1920s lived in Markham, leasing pasture land along the Colorado River and moving his herd that to winter grazing grounds in Collegeport each winter. He was the last of the Watkins to work Bend in the River land, returning in 1949 to work cattle for Tommy LeTulle. Bute was agile in the saddle, a good roper, and an accomplished rodeo cowboy. Although he remained with Tommy for 16 years, LeTulle remarked that he never seemed to adjust his methods of working cattle over dogs.[173] As a Watkins, he was simply more comfortable with a horse, saddle, and a rope.[174]

The irrigators purchased the Watkins' Old Hog Ranch land for a portion of their ambitious infrastructure development on the west side of the Colorado River. Phillip Watkins was the first to sell, his one eighth interest transferred to Markham Irrigation Company's A.J. Harty in 1918. In the deed, the attorney scribed that although Phillip was "now with the American Army in France," he was still a resident of Matagorda County. Irene C. Watkins and Evan Watkins sold the remaining 7/8 interest to A.J. Harty in 1919. Harty turned his interest over to the Markham Irrigation Company (MIC) for an assumption of his note in 1921.[175]

Before the deeds were even finalized, MIC began dredging a series of canals across the Watkins homestead. A waterway was dug from Blue Creek Lake to the south and parallel to the river, cutting through and incorporating what was Watkins Lake. From there the channel was connected to the original Jennings Creek, which was dammed across its middle to form Jennings Lake to the northwest and North Cortes Lake to the southeast. The remainder of Jennings Creek was diverted from its earlier river outflow and dammed to shape Harty Lake, named for A. J. Harty (Section 2, *Matagorda Rice*, Fig. 15).

The Harriet Parker-T.J. Poole Tract. Harriet Parker shared ownership of the north half of the original Alley-Denison piece of the Crier Survey, and her heirs, now the estate of

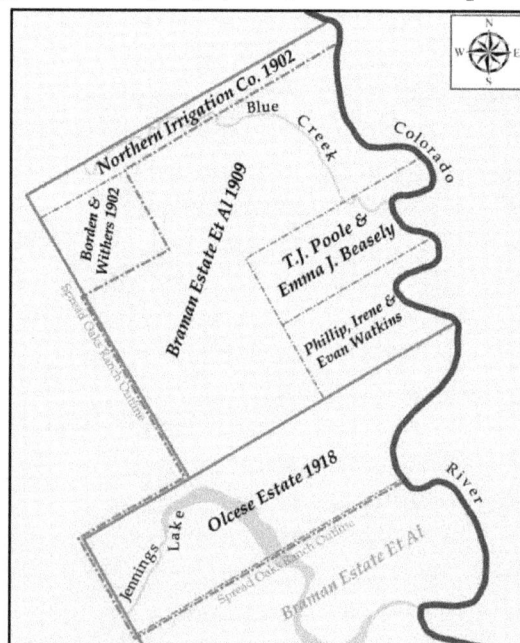

Emma J. Beasely, sold the remaining one-third interest in 1919 to A.J. Harty via intermediary C.L. De St. Aubin. Harty transferred the deed to Markham Irrigation (MIC) two years later.[176] Thomas J. Poole Sr. and his son, of the Poole Cattle Company, were paying taxes on the remaining two-third interest of the 555 acres in 1911, and in 1918 they also sold their remaining interest to Harty, who included this acquisition in his 1921 sale to MIC (Fig. 8).[177]

Thomas Jefferson Poole Jr. There were three Thomas Jefferson Poole's integral to Matagorda County history. The first T.J. Poole worked for the Charles Morgan Steamship Line in New Orleans, relocating to Indianola before the Civil War. For the next 15 years, he led several successful shipping ventures in Galveston, Indianola, and on Palacios Bay and formed business partnerships with cattlemen Sam Allen, A.H. Pierce, and another with W.B. Grimes.[178]

Poole's son, Thomas J. Poole II, was born while his mother, Irene, was living in Mexico during the Civil War. At birth he was named William Lawrence Poole, but his mother changed it to Thomas Jefferson Poole following his father's death in 1875.[179] The widow Irene, daughters Mary and Frances, and son William, lived in Indianola until their house was swept away during the hurricane of 1875. Homeless, they were welcomed at the Tres Palacios WBG Ranch by William Bradford Grimes.[180]

What began as a misfortune evolved into two marriages between the Grimes and Poole families. W.B. Grimes' wife died during childbirth in 1876, and the 51-year-old widower with seven children later married T.J. Poole Sr.'s widow, Irene. The younger T.J. Poole married W. B. Grimes' daughter Fannie Louise in 1881. For their wedding gift, W.B. presented them with the WBG Ranch.[181]

T.J. Poole III was born in 1883 in Corsicana while his mother was travelling from the Grimes Ranch to Kansas City.[182] It was the custom of the day to use suffixes such as Senior and Junior only while the males were living, so T.J. Poole III would always be known as T. J. Poole Jr. His 29-year-old mother died five years later during labor, and young Tom Jr. was relocated to the W.B. Grimes cattle operation near Kansas City. Here he learned the beef business, then returned to the WBG Ranch in Bay Prairie that he inherited after his mother's early demise. Tom Jr. married in 1904, and husband and wife moved to Bay City. When he sold the venerable WBG Ranch, he used some of the proceeds to form the Poole Cattle Company with Tom Sr. Over the years, father and son leased or owned some 40,000 acres of farm and pastureland, and Tom Jr. invested in the Markham rice mill in 1904.[183]

Tom Poole Jr. had a gold-plated resume as a businessman and civic leader. Among his many professional titles was director of the Bay City National Bank and later the Bay City Bank & Trust Co., president of the El Campo Rice Milling Company, a principal in the Coast Telephone Co. of El Campo, a partner in the Brahma Drilling Company and American Water Company, and later purchased the holdings of Northern Irrigation Company. Called the Northern Ranch, he managed its cattle, rice, and oil.[184]

Poole's civic participation was also lengthy. He was a director of the Southwestern Cattle Raisers Association, a founder of the Matagorda County Fair and Livestock Show, and an elder of the First Presbyterian Church of Bay City. He was also president of the White Man's Union Association in the early 1930s. Despite its ominous name, the association during his tenure only functioned to scrutinize city and county budgets.[185] Thomas J. Poole III died on September 2, 1969, and was buried in the Grimes Cemetery.

The A.J. Harty Tract. When Harty purchased the Watkins and the Parker-Poole parcels in 1918 and 1919, it was the first time the southeast quarter of the Crier Survey was held by a single landowner since James Denison answered the sheriff's cry for bids in 1841. The land would change hands again. Harty sold the combined tract to Markham Irrigation in 1921, then V.L. LeTulle purchased it from MIC in 1927.[186] The same day, V.L. turned the deed over to Ross Sterling.[187] MIC principals passed the land between themselves as individuals, as well their company, a total of four times in just nine years, and the benefit of that curious strategy is likely known only to them.

Ross Sterling did not keep the land long, either. In the fall of 1932, Sterling walked into the Houston National Bank of Commerce to deliver a mortgage and collateral trust agreement conveying $17,300 of holdings to brothers Jim 'Silver Dollar' and Wesley West for $10. Part of his Matagorda County forfeiture included the 1,087-acre Parker-Pool tract.[188]

Braman and Pierce Tracts. During the early 1900s, ownership of the west side of the original Crier Survey was as constant as the east side was frenetic. The original W.C. Braman Estate remained in the family for a hundred years. By the 1920s, it passed from Daniel Hawes Braman, his sister Julia Hawes Burkhart, and her husband Harry G. Jr. to a lengthening list of heirs.[189]

A.P. Borden and Mamie P. Withers remained as trustees to the A.H. and Hattie Pierce 139 acres on the northwest part of the Crier Survey (Fig. 8). In 1929, the executors were Lacy W. Armour and her husband H. Laurence, Clive and Mary W. Runnels, Abel Pierce Withers and H.P. Withers, and incorporated as Pierce Estates.

Northern Irrigation Company. Covering a mile of Blue Creek, the value of the northernmost 221-acre tract of the Crier Survey before 1900 was mainly limited to watering cattle. That changed with the advent of rice cultivation and the ensuing contest to control irrigation water. The tract that sold for $475 to Augustus Kountze and transferred to the Texas Land & Cattle Company (TL&CC) in 1893 was bought in 1902 by the Northern Irrigation Company (NIC) as part of a $30,000 transaction that included adjacent properties on the Kountze K and KO Ranches.[190]

NIC's tenure was short, the company filing for reorganization after losses resulting from the drought of 1910. In 1914, the deed to the 221-acre parcel was transferred from NIC to its trustees Albert Anderson, J.C. Carlson, and G.L. Elken. That year, the Markham Irrigation Company (MIC) took control of NIC's assets.[191] MIC manager A.J. Harty operated much of the 18-mile Blue Creek canal network until at least 1927.[192] The reach of the irrigators from the 1910s to the Depression, it seemed, was never far from the Bend in the River.

Epilogue. The dawn of the 20th century brought abrupt changes in technology, transportation, and agriculture to Matagorda County. Between 1900 and 1904, the county

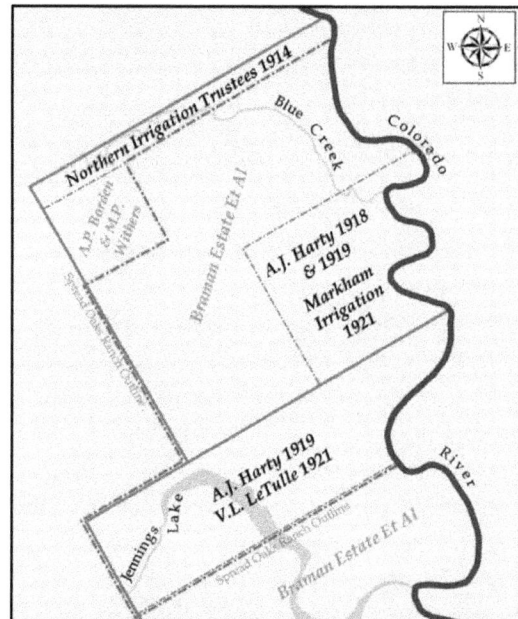

saw the birth of the rice industry, discovered its first oil fields, and laid railroad tracks that linked Bay City to the rest of Texas. By 1905 some parts of the county were connected by telephone, electricity, and residents even witnessed the spectacle of the first automobile. The town of Markham was platted, connected to Bay City by an iron bridge built over the Colorado River in 1902 near the site of Elliott's Ferry. Between 1900 and 1910, the county population doubled from 6,097 to 13,597 residents.

Iron and Steam. Parts of Texas were connected by rail as early as the 1850s, but it was another half century before Matagorda saw its first railroads. When they came, they came fast, crisscrossing the entire county in under two years. Hundreds of convicts from the state prison farm descended on Matagorda in 1901, laying the tracks of the Cane Belt Railroad that reached Bay City from Eagle Lake and Sealy. As the first passenger cars pulled into town, Bay City hosted a great celebration, replete with barbeques, dances, and a rodeo. A year later the rails were extended south from Bay City to the town of Matagorda. The New York, Texas & Mexican Railway, later the Southern Pacific Railroad, completed a second rail line between Van Vleck and Hawkinsville in 1902. In 1903 the line was extended to Bay City and Palacios.

Markham. Rice and railroad led to Markham's founding in 1903. The 355-acre townsite was purchased from the W.C. Moore-Cortes Canal Company, which bought 15,000 acres of A.H. Pierce's holdings west of present day Spread Oaks in 1900.[193] Named for Charles Henry Markham, general manager of the Southern Pacific Lines, the Markham townsite was platted by a hog-proof fence with four entry gates, and a sign with the town name was hung on the side of a boxcar. When the first lots were sold, residents lived in tents until their houses could be constructed.[194]

The first shipment to the new depot town was whiskey, and with it, Markham opened its first saloon. The Moore-Cortes Canal Company moved its headquarters from Cortes to Markham and built the two-story Markham Hotel in 1903. Mrs. Steve Perry was manager of the Markham Hotel. Her husband, Steve Perry Sr., farmed rice on the southern part of Spread Oaks Ranch between Jennings and Cortes lakes.

The town grew to encompass two boarding houses, a bank, five general stores, two drug stores, lumber yards, Northern Irrigation Company's big rice warehouses, a cotton gin, mule barns, feed lots, cattle shipping pens, and blacksmith shops. There was no jail, only a boxcar that was used for temporary confinement until the sheriff could transport its charges to Bay City.[195] The town celebrated when investors, that included T.J. Poole Jr., started construction of the Markham Rice Mill in 1904. It burned to the ground a year later.[196]

Oil. Texas oil was first produced in Corsicana in 1895, but it was the 1901 Spindletop discovery that put Texas on driller's maps. That single find increased the state's production from less than a million barrels a year to nearly five million.[197] As oil men cast their eye across the Lone Star State in quest of the next Spindletop, it caught Matagorda County's Big Hill. Rising perceptibly above the prairie with some sixty feet of elevation, the topography of Big Hill, to the untrained eye, looked like it might be another Spindletop.

Bay City's William Cash and Houston investors spud one of the first wells at Big Hill in 1901. After teamsters negotiated the muddy terrain to construct a derrick and install a cable-tool rig, the rope cable was rhythmically hoisted and dropped until the heavy iron fishtail bit stalled at 840 feet, then blew back uphole. The well discharged millions of cubic feet of hydrogen sulfide into the air, flowing for several months. Cash did not find oil, but he did discover nearly a hundred feet of sulfur. At the time, it had no commercial value.[198]

Dr. P.S. Griffith drilled "on the top of the hill" in 1904, the well blowing out at 1,850 feet. It was a gusher, flowing crude and water above the derrick for so long that Houston sightseers boarded trains to witness the spectacle. Two offset wells brought field production to 40,000 barrels a day, but within two years the rate declined to 300 barrels a day. Big Hill's boom had ended, the workers deserting the field for Ross Sterling's Humble Field, while others headed to the new Clemville Field.[199]

In contrast to Big Hill, Clemville's topographic expression was subtler, and it took a keen eye to notice its five-foot elevation difference over the prairie. Teams of horses and wagons with as many as ten mules moved the machinery to spud the first well, the Hardy-1, in 1908. At 1,365-feet the ground began to shake, then exploded with a gusher that flowed uncontrolled at some 3,500 barrels a day.

Oilmen drilling to the south found what they thought was another accumulation. Called Markham Field, they later learned both Clemville and Markham were part of a single, giant salt dome. Wells couldn't be drilled fast enough. Blowouts were common –investor George R. Burke described seeing five wells blow out at the same time. Streams at the headwaters of Tres Palacios Creek filled with oil, their banks lined with discarded wood and metal. The new fields brought a wave of workers, so many that the town of Hardy, soon renamed Clemville, sprang up with boarding houses, stores, saloons, teamster businesses, and tents before the first shotgun houses were built. Located five miles east of Spread Oaks Ranch, there is no trace of the town today.

A Rise and Fall. About 20 Matagorda County mothers lost sons in World War I, but others benefited from the boost in cattle and agricultural prices. Power lines continued to extend across the prairie, buzzing with current that brought electricity to even more homes. Matagordians saw their first airplane around the time of the first World War, recognizing the new form of transportation might revolutionize travel, much as rail had in 1901 and the automobile in 1908.

In the late 1920s the nation's wealth exploded under President Warren Harding, then imploded as the stock crash of 1929 that marked the beginning of the Great Depression. Franklin Delano Roosevelt became president in 1933, occupying the Oval Office for part of the ten-year period remembered for its poignant images of Americans in shanty towns or soup lines, the haunting look of impoverished children at their sides. These images were only bested by families in the Midwest grappling with dozens of dust storms – the Dust Bowl – that consumed former prairies turned farmland, the great particulate cloud eventually reaching as far as the East Coast.

Matagorda County residents endured the Depression with less turbulence than in other parts of the country. Some industries suffered, such as seafood, farming, and ranching, but those same industries fed the county. They may not have had jobs or money, but they had food. Less fortunate were northern financiers who had invested in the county's oil industry, rice production, and infrastructure, and many left the region.

Like the Texas War for Independence and the Civil War, the Great Depression was a watershed event in Texas and Matagorda County. And like their response to the earlier challenges, they would rise again.

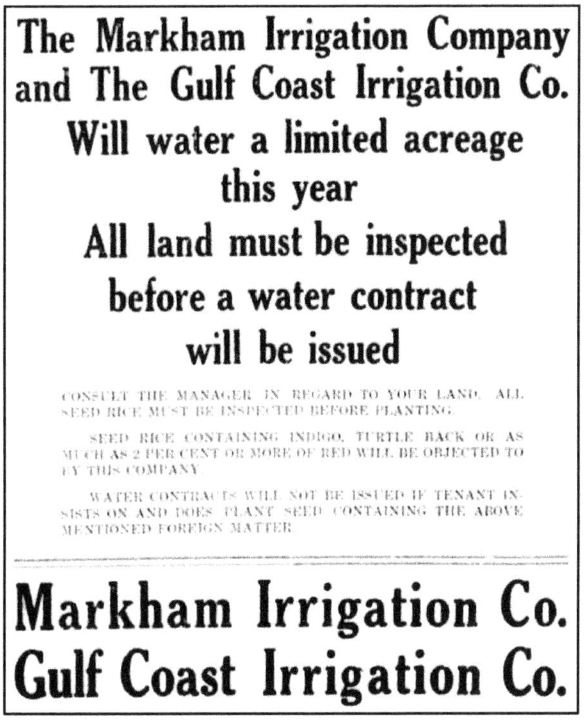

Fig. 1. As the only two irrigation companies remaining in the Bay Prairie area after 1923, Markham Irrigation and Gulf Coast Irrigation Company controlled both rice irrigators and rice growers. *Daily Tribune*, Jan. 28, 1924, https://texashistory.unt.edu/ark:/67531/metapth1365879 /m1/4/, Portal to Texas History.

Fig. 2. A.J. Harty went from genius irrigator, owner of irrigating companies, and a bank to a barbeque restaurant before he vanished from the public eye. *Daily Tribune*, April 9, 1932, *Portal to Texas History*, https://texas hist-ory.unt.edu/ark:/67531/metapth1554632/m1/2/.

LETULLE MERCHANTILE CO.

WHOLESALE AND RETAIL DEALERS IN

Groceries, - Hardware, - Flour

FEED STUFFS

SULKY PLOWS   DISC HARROW

FARM WAGONS

RICE SEEDERS   RICE DRILLS

EVERYTHING IN

CAR LOAD LOTS

BAY CITY.   -   -   TEXAS

Fig. 3. V.L. LeTulle moved from the family farm to Bay City in 1900, a year later opening LeTulle Mercantile Company of Bay City. Catering to the needs of the new, booming rice business, he sold so many plows, harnesses, saddles, rice binders, and threshers that the railroad built a spur to the side door of his store. *Advertiser Weekly*, March 1, 1901.

"Exhibit B"

OFFICE OF THE EXECUTORS OF THE ESTATE OF A.H. PIERCE.

A.P. Borden, Executor
Mrs. Maria P. Withers, Executrix.
Pierce Tex., Dec. 5th 1908

Messrs. C. R. Johns & Co.,
Austin, Texas

Dear Sirs:-

In reply to yours of the 1st inst., beg to say, we have a lane leading from our pasture up the river onto this lease. If your party will run a fence from the east side of our lane across Jennings Creek, and fence in the land they cultivate, as indicated by the dotted line on the enclosed sketch, and give me the balance of the tract, rent free for next year, I will let them take possession of their so-called rice land at once and prepare for a crop next year. I desire this for a watering place and the low overflowed and rough land will do me as well as any. I do not think there is any rice land in the whole tract, and if you rent it for rice, I would advise you to get well secured paper or money in advance for the rent. As I have other lands leased and am depending on this for water, I don't feel disposed to give up the lease at present time, except on the condition as stated above.

If this agreeable, fix up the papers making me the lease rent free for next year of the land indicated and the release to the part wanted for rice and forward to me, and I will execute same.

Yours truly,

A.P. Borden.

Filed for record at 4 O'Clk. P.M. January 6th A.D. 1909
Recorded at 9 O'Clk. A. M. January 14th A. D. 1909

Fig. 4. A.P. Borden's 1909 letter to Margaret Olcese's agent on the prospects of rice production on the Olcese tract. Modified from Matagorda County Deed no. 23484, Exhibit B.

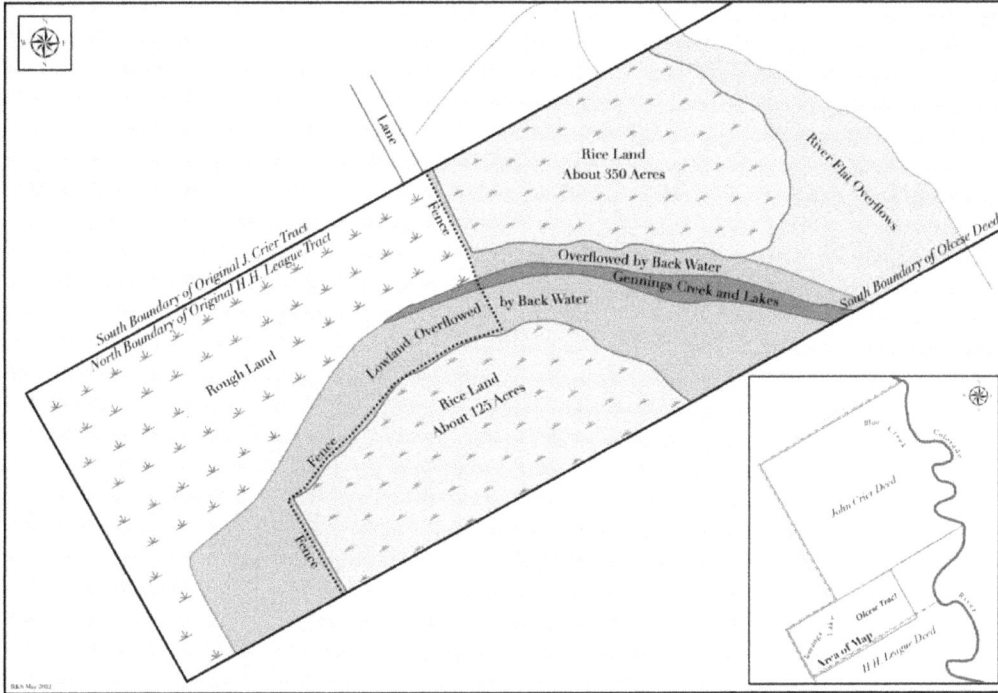

Fig. 5. A.P. Borden's hand drawn map of Jennings Creek – spelled "Gennings Creek and Lakes" – on the Olcese tract. Borden grazed cattle on the "Rough Land," and sketched in the area he thought most prospective for rice cultivation. The cedar fences referred to in his letter (Fig. 4) are still visible today. Braham pastureland is to the north and south. Within a decade, the geomorphology of the creek and floodplain would be reshaped by A.J. Harty and Markham Irrigation. Modified from Matagorda County Deed no. 23484, Exhibit C.

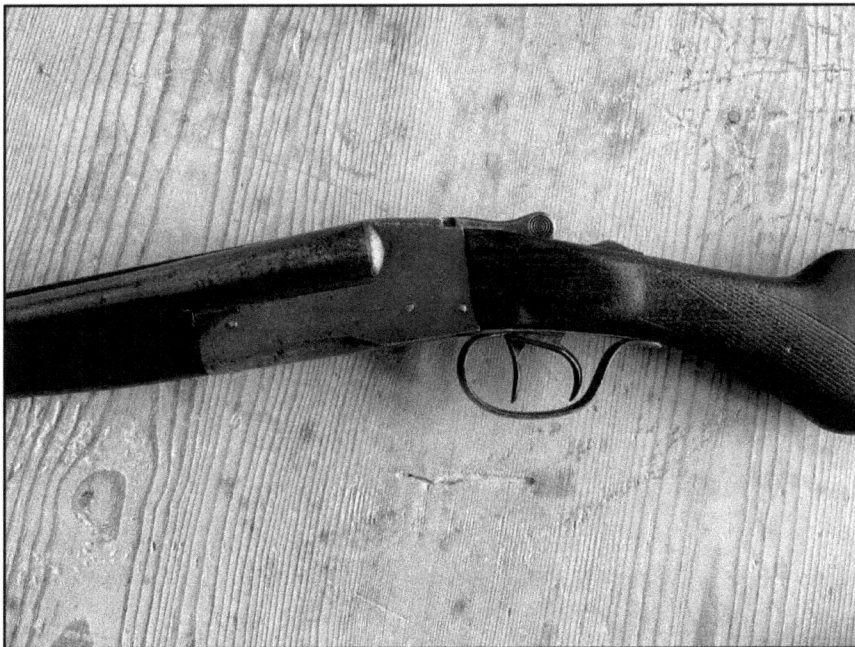

Fig. 6. Victor Neil (also spelled Neal) Watkins' .410 – his dove and "nighttime" duck gun. Vic's sons, grandsons, and great grandsons all learned to shoot with this gun. Courtesy Watkins family.

99

CHAPTER 4

Landowners of the Bend in the River

1930s to 2000

Land purchases at the Bend in the River between 1870 and the 1930s reflected the economies of the time. First were cattle, then rice irrigation and cultivation. By the 1930s, it was oil and gas. When the Olcese Estate sold its League Survey holdings to A.J. Harty in 1919, the instrument was the first at the Bend in the River to separate the surface from the subsurface mineral rights.[1] All future transactions did the same.

An uncountable number of Bend in the River deed and interest changes were filed after the 1930s, the contracts not on the land itself, but what lay beneath it. Or didn't lie beneath it. When the North Bay City Field was discovered by the Ohio Oil Company on the southern part of the original League Survey, it prompted a flurry of leasing activity throughout Bay Prairie. But, as wells were drilled and seismic data acquired, there was little evidence of commercial hydrocarbons below the surface at the Bend in the River.

Perhaps the biggest contribution of oil and gas exploration to the Bend in the River was its improvement to infrastructure. Historically, the west side of the Colorado River was, at times, impossible to traverse. Just upriver of Cayce's then Elliott's Ferry, some eight miles of river's edge terrain was dissected by Jennings, Silver, Blue, Dry, and Jones creeks. Their banks in places were steep, and for a long time covered in dense canebrakes. With too much rainfall the creeks and tributaries carried raging torrents of water. With too little rain, their parched banks opened gaping cracks large enough to lame a horse.

An east to west road was completed between Tres Palacios and the Colorado River to Elliot's Ferry, on the edge of the Braman Pasture, in 1898.[2] But the only north-south road on the west side of the river was a wagon trail located "on the edge of the tree line." For the first 30 years that the Watkins family lived at the Bend in the River, they didn't even bother with the vagaries of the road, instead traveling the last mile or so to their cabin by boat.

Postmaster William Douglas was so thoroughly disgusted with the route that, in 1899, he sent a letter to the *Matagorda County Tribune* resigning his mail delivery position (Fig.1). "I wish to dispose of my mail contract," he wrote, and "will give a good man a bargain." Descriptions of his travails on the river's west side included near drownings and teams that bogged down "in which the mud is saddle skirt deep."[3] When oil and gas companies made their initial drilling forays into the area in the 1930s, they began shaping a network of interior roads connected by iron pipe bridges.[4]

Three Bend in the River ownership changes occurred in the midst of the great Depression, but in two of them, no money was exchanged. The first contract was between V.L. LeTulle and his brother James, who acted as an intermediary in a narrowly avoided violent clash between V.L. and his nephew Tommy LeTulle. The other deed change was less boisterous, but certainly more recognized – the West brother's seizure of former Governor Ross Sterling's acreage. Both transfers occurred in 1932. For the next seventy years, none of the new landowners lived on the ranch. But their ranch foremen and their families did, the names including Lenon Hemphill, Danny Savage, and Manuel Briones. The exception was Tommy LeTulle, a fixture for some 50 years.

After the Depression, Bend in the River deed holders were no longer "just" a cattleman, or rice farmer, or oilman. They were all three. The exception – again – was Tommy LeTulle. In contrast to the other owners, he didn't grow rice or have oil and gas holdings. He steadfastly remained "just" a cattleman, and what he lacked in business diversity he more than made up in color.

The Southern Survey at the Bend in the River

One of the things that set Tommy LeTulle apart from other ranchers was that he wrote his life down on paper. Called the *Memoirs of Tommy LeTulle*, his words left a vibrant record of his half century of life on the southern part of Spread Oaks Ranch. In Tommy's telling, the 1,476 acres of the northern League Survey that became the Tommy LeTulle Ranch, in 1932, was acquired through a deal with his uncle, V.L. LeTulle. Tommy would swap a decade of his farming and ranching labor to his uncle for the promise of his own land. At the end of ten years, however, V.L. changed his mind.

The result of V.L. LeTulle's change of heart was a legendary Bay Prairie feud between uncle and nephew. Tommy wrote that V.L. pulled a knife on him in the middle of Bay City, then threatened to shoot him. Tommy taunted his uncle to come do it, staking himself out and waiting at V.L.'s LeTulle River Farm near Bay City, armed with a shotgun and .44 pistol. V.L. didn't show, but the deed to the 1,476 acres did. Not from his uncle, though, but through his father John James, who hurriedly received the deed from V.L. for "the love and affection I bear to my brother."[5]

That's Tommy's version. There is another account, a bit sneakier and certainly less bold. With Tommy LeTulle's story telling, there was always another version, but his were always more entertaining.

Tommy was born in 1910, the second son of 13 children. When his mother separated from John James in the late 1910s, the future cattleman delivered newspapers and worked in an Austin clothing store, earning $2 a week. He quit school in the 8th grade. For a couple of years he painted movie theater posters before drifting back to Bay Prairie, where he worked as a farm and ranch hand.

Like his father, Tommy had three wives. About all we know of his first wife, Margaret, is that she shot him. "I deserved it" was all he would say of the matter. He thought his second wife would be a better catch "because she was going to church," but instead, he complained that she "liked to doll up and be pretty" and spent money frivolously. After five years of marriage, she ran off with their son Thomas B. LeTulle Jr.

Tommy's third wife, Alta Ree Smith, was one of nine children (Fig. 2). A Markham preacher at first refused to marry them because Tommy already had five children, so the

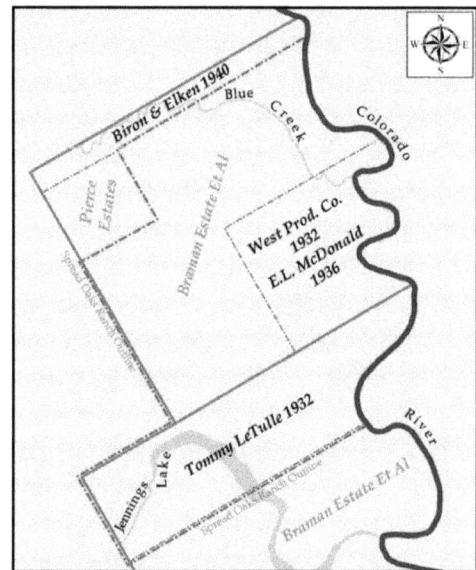

couple hauled the wedding party around the county, knocking on doors, until they found a willing Justice of the Peace in El Campo. Their honeymoon at the Bay City Como Hotel lasted only one night because Tommy had a rice crop to harvest.[6] The newlyweds loaded up Alta's two mules and childhood pony, Sparky, and moved into a wooden shack near Jennings Lake, its location today unknown. The LeTulle shack was replaced in the late 1950s by a modern home – made from concrete. Tommy got the idea from old shellcrete masonry homes built from crushed and heated oyster shells by area settlers.

Much of what Tommy LeTulle did intrigued the Bay Prairie community, and he rarely disappointed. No one was surprised, then, when a continuous line of cement trucks rambled down the road to his ranch. Some stopped their worked and followed the trail. At its end was Tommy's new house, entirely formed up and completed in one continuous concrete pour. With air ducts in its 10- to 12-inch-thick walls and insulated roof, the house didn't have air conditioning but remained tolerable in summer. He proudly said that there was "only a half a pickup [truck] load of lumber in the LeTulle house." Complete with an interior swimming pool, former movie poster artist Tommy covered the couple's concrete walls with painted murals of western themes.[7]

Tommy and Alta shared their homestead with some interesting people. One was his aunt, who in the late 1800s contracted a fever that left her "a slow thinking person, but very kind." Another was Milton Allen, an "old negro" who grew corn in the late 1800s, and later mentored Tommy on dog training and cattle raising. Then there was a ten-year old "little black boy" who appeared at their doorstep in a blinding rain storm. They named him George Washington – never knowing his given name – and he remained with the couple for ten years.[8]

Rancher Tommy. Tommy gave up rice farming in the early 1930s to concentrate on raising cattle with Alta. Alta, Tommy wrote, had grown up on a truck farm on the San Bernard River in Wharton County, and was no stranger to hard work. She became an equal in Tommy's ranching operation, at least in his version. The pair started out with mostly borrowed money to expand their herds, leasing some of the toughest thickets in five counties and, because no one else wanted to work them, he leased at a low price.

His secret to the bottom land country was using mules instead of horses, and cow dogs instead of cowboys (Fig. 3). Horses were too tall to get through the thickets, he found, and counseled that "you can work a horse to death, but not a mule."[9] Two of his mules were named Kate, and many of his dogs. Tommy's mother was also named Kate, and only Tommy knows if his naming convention was a sign of esteem or loathing.

In a country recognized for talented ranchers, Tommy LeTulle was one of the best known – in part because he was very good at it, and in part because, with his mules and cow dogs, he did it differently than everyone else. Tommy raised and trained a slew of cow dogs – half bloodhounds with East Texas cur dogs, collies, red bones, sheepdogs crossed with hounds, and others. "I train all my dogs on a command-reward basis," he once said. "I don't pet 'em, and I don't play with 'em."[10] If one of his dogs was slow to respond, he shot them. He was proud of the ones he didn't have to kill, and they willingly dove into thickets to drive out his cows for branding, castrating, penning, and shipping. He said he trained his dogs as "cow holding dogs rather than cow catching dogs,"[11] but coached a couple as "biting dogs" to latch on to the snout or testicles of any particularly uncooperative beeve.

Danny and Jimmie Stephens remember just how good a cattleman he was. "There was a time when Tommy wanted to cross 200 pairs of cows across the [Colorado] river," they say. "The cheapest way to do it was to bring up the barge, but no one thought Tommy could load those cattle, particularly the calves. He took a mare and fed it on the barge for three days. On the fourth day, he put the calves near the front and when the mare walked on to eat, they followed her." He got the herd across the river, and he did it his way. As for his renowned mule Kate, "Tommy was such a good trainer that he could load that mule in the back of a flatbed truck."[12]

Most of Tommy and Alta's herd were Brahmans, Herefords, and various crosses. Like everything about the cowman's life, he had his own ideas about keeping his animals healthy. He never vaccinated with "store bought" medicine but used a blue Mexican garlic as a vaccine instead. He even used garlic to cure anthrax and swamp fever, known as the "blind staggers." Tommy was adamant about the benefits of winter pasturing his animals on salt grass as opposed to feeding them hay. Salt water that inundated his coastal winter grazing grounds, he believed, provided all the nutrients they needed, and he never used mineral supplements. During their years of cattle raising, he and Alta made dozens of drives to and from Bay Prairie to the salt flats at the mouth of the San Bernard River and Sartwelle marsh near Palacios.[13]

Tommy avoided veterinarians and doctored his own animals, although he conceded that "vets have some good cures, too." He used their "store-bought" medications for stomach worms, and he came to trust veterinary medicine enough to try what he termed "scientific mating," purchasing a field horse that was "shipped down to Bay City from Missouri in a test tube." He only reluctantly took his dogs to a vet, and only when they were so badly cut up by hogs that he couldn't sew them up himself.

Tommy had one foot in old Matagorda and the other in the new. People still describe seeing him on the bench of his chuckwagon, driving a herd to winter pasture down one of the county's asphalt highways. Or his own description of running a herd through an old trail that had become the parking lot of the South Texas Nuclear Plant, the herd getting caught up in the middle of a crew shift, stopping traffic and tangling up dozens of cars.

Citizen Tommy. Writers who interviewed Tommy in his later years used descriptions such as colorful cowboy, unorthodox rancher, rascal cowman, and one-of-a kind-cowboy. It's exactly how Tommy would portrayed himself. By his own admission, he was quick to anger and never resolved a conflict without carrying a pistol or two. "I will tell you one thing," citizen Tommy wrote, "I liked everybody but took orders from nobody, not even my wife." Of his former neighbor, Danny Savage, perhaps says it best – "I was friends with Tommy, but only on his terms," and adds "there could be two books just on him."[14] There's already one, and Tommy wrote it.

At local parades and rodeos, Tommy was often the center of attention, roping calves and directing dancing dogs or his trick horse. Tommy trained the horse himself, and at one time considered going on the road with his act. He didn't want anything to distract from his ranching, however, so "I took the horse home," he wrote, "and never went to another show." Tommy awed the audience one year at the Matagorda County Fair with a penning demonstration performed by his cow dogs. Someone reminded the fair committee that Tommy might just grab one of his underperforming hounds and kill it. The image of Tommy "holding up an empty leather dog collar after he sliced the dog's throat" was too vivid for the family event organizers, and it was the last time Tommy LeTulle was invited to perform.[15]

Men who worked with Tommy remember that he talked to his dogs and sang to his cattle. Tommy was not exaggerating when he said he explained to his dogs what work they planned to do that day – if they knew whether they were working cattle or hogs, they would ignore the trail of one and go for the other. Tommy loved chasing wild hogs on horseback and for that adventure he trained some of his baying hounds as "front end" dogs and others as "rear end" dogs.[16]

Neighbor and retired ranch foreman Danny Savage says Tommy was best the dog trainer he'd ever seen. "But," he recalls, "he had some tricks. Everybody was amazed how the dogs ran under the mule's legs, staying close to Tommy. Well, he had these little scraps of food, and he would toss 'em down to the dogs." Once Danny drove by Tommy and Alta's house "and the back of the place was covered in white. Looked like snow." Tommy's dogs had raided his chicken house. When Tommy returned home, "well, he was pretty hard on those dogs."[17]

Tommy was a man who pondered. He figured things out on his own, usually, and when he did there was no changing his mind. But he was perplexed, he admitted, by "the old wisdom" that a grey mule never dies. He had a grey mule he swore was a remarkable 55 years old. So, here was a mule that seemed to lend credibility to the tale, but he was still torn. Finally he concluded that they did probably die, but then vacillated, because "you never see a dead one."

Tommy also had his own way of looking at people, of judging their worth, and he pronounced his opinion of them in his *Memoirs of Tommy LeTulle*. Not everyone was pleased with his versions of Bay Prairie's social history. But some of those anecdotes included individuals who lived on the Bend in the River, and many do not exist anywhere else. He knew some of the Watkins family history, for example, and Sam Watkins' grandson Bute later worked for Tommy. He also wrote of the "Old Indian" who had a squatter's camp at the mouth of Blue Creek, surviving on what he hunted, trapped, or caught on his trotlines. Tommy remembers anytime he visited him, the Old Indian was always ready with a plate of "roast coon" and sweet potatoes. No one knew his name, or what became of him (Fig. 4).

Tommy told the tale of the McMann family, who lived between Blue and Dry Creeks in a log cabin they built around the time of the Civil War. They were also evidently squatters, and in Tommy's account, during the late 1800s A.H. "Shanghai" Pierce instructed the sheriff to evict them. The sheriff and his men followed the wagon road up the Colorado, served the papers, and moved all their furniture into the yard. When they left, the McMann's simply moved back in.

After the McMann parents died, the remaining three boys were forced to fend for themselves. According to Tommy, they had little contact with the outside world and grew "wild," losing their ability to speak and uttering only guttural sounds. If they saw outsiders, they scampered into the dilapidated house to peep through the windows or "ran like deer through the woods."

When the Kenyon Dredging Company moved onto the banks of the Colorado River in the late 1920s, dredging foreman Tony George observed the boys. Their clothes were worn out. They didn't have food. He brought them groceries, and alerted Sheriff Joe Mangum. The sheriff thought it wiser to resettle them than leave them in the wild, although the best he could do was haul them off to county jail. No one today seems to know what became of the "wild boys of Blue Creek."

Tommy in Perpetuity. A.H. "Shanghai Pierce had one. Why not Tommy LeTulle? Tommy was silent on his motivation to commission a statue of himself, but certainly the towering edifice of the Cattle King down the road had entered his mind. Tommy laid out his "LeTulle Ranch Cemetery" in 1982, complete with "walkways, drives, lots, and grave spaces" and in 1986 gifted three acres to Matagorda County for use as a public cemetery.[18] In 1985, he contacted local Markham sculptor Danny Stephens. He wanted a life-size statue of himself on his mule Kate, with a handful of cur dogs trailing obediently behind him, as the centerpiece for his Bend in the River mausoleum and cemetery.

Danny Stephens and his wife Jimmie remember that the only way they could reach Tommy was by leaving a message at the Bay City Feed Store. Jimmie says they would leave the first message. Then Tommy would respond, and the Stephens had to go back to retrieve his instructions.[19] Tommy had a telephone, Jimmie says, but it was in the barn. It wouldn't have mattered – the odds were that Tommy wasn't going to answer it wherever it was.

Danny Stephens got his sculpting start when he was showing quarter horses in Oklahoma. He met an artist there, and jokingly told Jimmie that his work did not compare to Frederic Remington. Jimmie not only challenged her husband to show what he could do, she brought home some clay. His first piece was a horse and a boy, and it showed promise. Then he encountered renowned western theme sculptor Jim Reno, who was willing to help the young artist. When Danny brought him pieces, "Jim would take a toothpick and he scratched every place that needed to be fixed in the clay," Danny says. "I knew I'd arrived when one day Reno was looking at a piece and didn't scratch it at all."[20]

It was a long process to capture Tommy LeTulle in bronze, and the Stephens' recall they enjoyed their time with Tommy. Danny measured every inch of Tommy and his mule Kate, "but nobody could measure the dogs, they were too wild" (Fig. 5). The measurements were used to create a maquette, a miniature of the piece that was "pointed up," as it is called, to cast the full-size version. The process, Danny explains, is to form the sculpture in clay, then cover it in liquid rubber and plaster of Paris to make a mold, after which it's cast with wax. The final step is to fill it in with bronze at the proper scale. The piece was cast at a Santa Fe foundry, and because of the size and weight, each piece was molded separately then welded back together again. One of the artist's tricks was to sculpt Tommy's head larger than it was because of the focal point down below.[21]

The foundry had intended to deliver the finished piece to the cemetery, but the mausoleum wasn't done. Instead, they delivered it to the Stephen's home, where it sat under a tree for a month. Cranes were needed to unload onto a flatbed trailer – the horse alone weighed half a ton. The project garnered a lot of interest, particularly in Texas newspapers, and Tommy loved the attention (Fig. 6). The project "cost me $105,000," he announced. Of the cur dogs, he confessed that he wanted more, "but they cost me $8,000 apiece." Sculptor Danny didn't correct Tommy at the time, but 40 years later he said, "they were actually $3,500."[22]

Tommy LeTulle died in 1988 at the age of 79. At his funeral, mourners saw him return from the dead, briefly, on videotape. He had filmed his own eulogy. Alta Ree joined him beneath his statue a few years later, under the inscription that reads "Dedicated to my wife Alta Ree Smith Le Tulle."

Matagorda County and Spread Oaks Ranch owner Forrest Wylie maintain the cemetery today. And every so often, Danny Stephens (Fig. 7) comes out and cleans off the bee nests, the spider webs, and mud daubers from his bronze work of art. Sometimes Tommy's acquaintances come by to pay their respects. Every one of them has a Tommy story they want to share, and each is colorful. The statue is a favorite destination of visitors to Spread Oaks Ranch, as well. Tommy has not been forgotten, and it's just what he wanted.

The Northern Survey at the Bend in the River

The SE Crier Tract. After former Governor Ross Sterling was forced to forfeit his 1,087-acre Bend in the River land in 1932, its next owners were brothers Jim 'Silver Dollar' and Wesley West.[23] Four years later, the West brothers sold the surface rights to Esker L. McDonald. George Townsend was the next landowner, followed by Joel E. Morrow.

Wesley and Jim 'Silver Dollar' West. The West brothers were the sons of one of the wealthiest men in Texas as the owner and president of the West Lumber Company and South Texas Lumber Company with investments in cattle and oil.[24] Sons James Marion Jr. and Westley Wendall West were born in 1903 and 1906, respectively, and grew up in Houston.

James Marion Jr. was the antithesis of the man he bankrupted. Ross Sterling was an outwardly modest, self-made businessman who built then lost his fortune, and then remade it. West came into money, and although his resume was as replete with accomplishments as impressive as Sterling's, he was attention-seeking and eccentric. Although he was a skillful attorney, oilman, and cattle rancher, he preferred to display his meticulously cultivated 'Silver Dollar Jim' image. He tipped only with silver dollars. He was known to fling a handful of the coins on the floor of a bar or restaurant, then watch the wait staff scramble for them. Wherever there was a swimming pool, patrons could be assured that West would toss a few coins into the water to see who would dive for them.[25]

West was obsessed with law enforcement, accompanying the Houston Police Department on patrols in one of his 40 Cadillacs – all painted blue and stuffed with pistols, shotguns, and rifles – and he monitored law enforcement calls on his state-of-the-art radio equipment. He even held a Texas Ranger's Commission, wearing his Ranger badge as part of a wardrobe that sported monogrammed cowboy boots, gold belt buckles, and assorted diamond accessories.[26]

Jim West Jr.'s lifestyle – and the public's infatuation with it – was a distraction to his gifted resume. He was president of West Production Company and vice president of West Securities, president of two cattle companies, chairman of South Texas Lumber Co., a trustee in the charitable West Foundation, director of the Texas National Bank, and a chairman of the Texas Law Enforcement Foundation. As a lawyer, he was licensed to practice before the US Supreme Court.

West suffered from severe diabetes and spent so much time with Hermann Hospital doctors that he moved into his own hospital suite. The sign on the door of room number 574 read "Do not open this door without knocking – and be sure you do not ever knock on it." Inside, West installed a rose-colored carpet, damask curtains, and his own furniture that included an electric stove and refrigerator.[27] Diabetes contributed to Silver Dollar Jim's death at 54 years in 1957. As estate executors were surveying his Houston home, they found a quarter million dollars' worth of silver coins in the basement.[28]

Brother Wesley was as successful in business as Jim Jr., but a much less flamboyant figure. He was a rancher and oilman, founder of Wesley West Minerals that bought and sold mineral rights and interests, and a principal in other family-owned oil and gas entities that included West Securities and West Production Company. West, who was a co-owner of KBTC radio in Austin, sold his interests in the station, renamed KLBJ, to future president Lyndon B. Johnson. He and his wife Neva Yvonne were generous donors to the arts, medical research centers, and several Texas universities.[29]

E.L. McDonald. When the West brothers' West Production Company sold the Sterling tract in 1936 to E.L. McDonald, it included the former Markham Irrigation Company easements and right-of-ways. The time had passed for those strips of land that, just a decade earlier, were so critical to the irrigators.[30] The new shining financial star was petroleum, and McDonald negotiated a 50% interest in the oil, gas, and other minerals rights. West Production kept the remainder. Sun Oil Company signed a 7-year oil and gas exploratory lease the same year.[31] Every well that Sun and succeeding operators drilled were either dry holes or non-commercial discoveries.

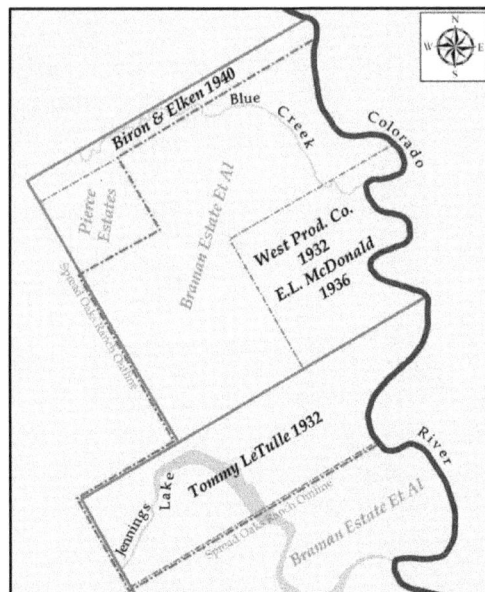

Esker Louis McDonald was born in 1896 to Elizabeth and the Reverend Eli McDonald, who preached throughout the Bay Prairie area while E.L. was a youth. E.L. graduated from college with a law degree and played semi-professional baseball. After E.L. married Elmore Rugely Hawkins in 1927, he hung his shingle as lawyer and worked for the First National Bank in Bay City.[32]

For the next 40 years, he invested in land, farming, and mineral royalty interests, most with banking partner and brother-in-law James C. Lewis.[33] His business holdings included Lewis & McDonald Rice Co., Buckeye Ranch Co., Smith & McDonald Cattle, and Matagorda County Land and Cattle Company.[34] By the time he died in 1973, E.L. owned 121 tracts of land and mineral royalty interests in over a hundred producing and non-producing properties.[35]

McDonald purchased the Bend in the River tract along with land to the east, across the Colorado River. He built a substantial cattle operation, raising a herd that at one point reached 800 cows, calves, bulls, and heifers. His ranch foreman, Roy Williams, worked for him for several decades. When the Matagorda County Fair and Livestock Exposition Association held their first show in 1943, E.L. was one of its first directors.

Esker L. McDonald sold his west side of the Colorado River holdings to Bay City's George W. Townsend in 1950. His estate, however, retained, his portion of the mineral rights.

George Townsend. George William Townsend was born 1911 in the East Texas town of Groveton. His father, Warren C. Townsend, relocated to Bexar County by the 1920s and worked as a farmer and oilfield pumper. Son George initially followed in his father's footsteps, starting as an oilfield roustabout in the 1930s. By 1940 he had married and moved to Matagorda County, working as a roughneck for Skelly Oil and as a ranch foreman.

Like many men in the years during and following the Great Depression, Townsend developed a diverse resume to survive and later thrive. In the 1940s it was farming, ranching, and the oilfields. By the 1950s, he was a construction foreman and founded George Townsend Lease Service, an oilfield service company, in Bay City. His former ranch foreman Danny Savage recalls that Townsend got his break when "Skelly Oil passed him over for job he should have had. So he quit. He went right to Rugely Chevrolet and bought a truck and went to work for himself. He's the one who brought oil field boards to this country, and he built a lot of 'em."[36] In 1975, Townsend added banker to his resume as a director of the Bay City Bank and Trust Company.[37]

Bay City knew George Townsend well. He served as a Bay City Chamber of Commerce director in the 1950s and was its vice president in 1957.[38] He held numerous positions with the Matagorda County Fair and Livestock Exposition Association, acting as its director, executive committee member, and its president from 1954 until his death in 1982. His 28-year tenure overlapped with other Fair and Livestock volunteers and Bend in the River landowners, T. J. Poole Jr., and E.L. McDonald.

Farmer, rancher, oilfield pumper, and bank director Townsend's passion was quarter horses. In the early 1960s, he was a co-founder of the four-county Texas Mid-Coastal Horse Breeders Association. Located at the Wharton County Fairgrounds, Townsend planned its stock horse exhibition facilities with a track and stalls and promoted a futurity program for quarter horses and other registered breeds. Categories included racing, cutting, roping, reining and barrel racing, as well as halter futurities for weaning quarter horse colts and fillies.[39] As a sponsor of competitive youth horse shows, Townsend donated use of both his Bend in the River land and another ranch he owned in Wharton County for FFA and 4-H events.[40]

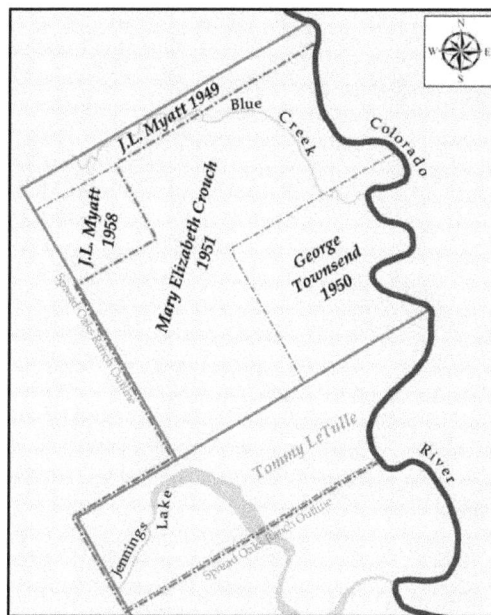

In addition to the SE quarter of the John Crier Survey, Townsend purchased another ranch near Wharton, and in 1957 leased a large ranch west of San Antonio near Rocksprings called the V.A. Brown Estate Ranch. When his Bay Prairie ranch foreman Crawford Mitchell moved there to operate its cattle and stock horse operation,[41] Danny Lee Savage took his position on the Bend in the River property.

At some 80-plus years old, Danny Savage knows Bay Prairie and cattle. He didn't start out that way. Born in 1936, the future ranch foreman never had the opportunity run cattle as a boy. He did own a horse, but since he had no access to pastures, "I just set him by the side of the road."

Area newspapers first carried his name not as a cowboy but as a running back who scored two touchdowns for the Tidehaven Tigers High School team in the mid 1950s. It was the first time Tidehaven ever beat rival Palacios. Asked about his winning touchdowns

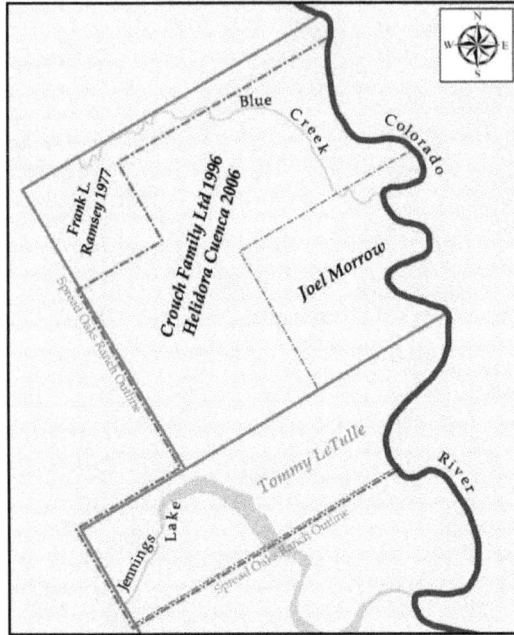

in the locally famous game 70 years later, Danny says "They weren't pretty. Really just three-yard plunges!" After High School, he volunteered to work for anyone in the area who was penning or vaccinating cattle. He got practice, he says, at Bay City's amateur roping events. "Every Friday night, you could pay $2, and Bay City gave you three calves you could rope. But you had to bring your own horse." One of his first paying jobs in the saddle was with preacher Melvin Harper at Buckeye Ranch, and that was where he learned how to rope.[42]

In the early 1960s, Danny heard George Townsend was looking for a foreman, and he says he was surprised when he got the job. "I drove to the ranch my wife and baby, and I ended up staying there a long time." Danny recalls that Townsend, who lived and worked in Bay City rather than moving to his Bend in the River land, came out every Sunday to inspect the calving operation.[43] Townsend built several houses on the property and painted them green. Three are still in use today but are pastel yellow.

When Townsend died in 1982, his son William Allen moved from Rock Springs and remained at the ranch for about a year before moving to Bay City. Danny Savage continued to handle the Townsend cattle until the ranch was sold to Joel Morrow in 1993.

Joel Morrow. Joel Eugene Morrow was born in 1941 in Bay City and died in 2019. His father, Joel Wayne Morrow, owned several small businesses in Bay City, and was active in the community as a Boy Scout district director, volunteer on annual Rice Festival committees, and the Chamber of Commerce-sponsored annual fishing tournament.

Joel Jr. left Bay City for college and later relocated in Richmond, west of Houston, and founded several Houston area businesses. He returned to Bay City in 1990 and bought the Townsend tract in 1993. He was taken by the number of live oaks on his new property, and gave it the name Spread Oaks Ranch. Nearly everyone who visited the family remembers that the walls of the main house were covered in big game mounts and skins, many from his trips to Africa. Joel Morrow hired Manuel Briones as ranch foreman, and Manuel still holds that title today.

Manuel has been in the saddle most of his life, beginning as a young boy on his grandfather's farm in Mexico. When the lure of opportunity on the other side of the Rio Grande beckoned him, he crossed the river to begin a new life. The journey nearly killed him. "My mother told me not to go," he remembers. "I crossed the river and walked for seven days. I had no drinking water or food for three days. I almost died. And all I could think about when I was so sick was my Momma's words, telling me not to go." Life north of border began to look more promising when he got his first ranching job in Brazoria County, then in Matagorda County. Now, as he phrases it, "I've spent the last 35 years at the end of Tommy LeTulle Road."

Manuel's storytelling includes the time a big canebrake rattler rose next to his horse, its head surgically removed at the tip of a bullwhip. And when his first blue heeler Abbie

110

splashed into Silver Lake in pursuit of a raccoon but was killed by an alligator. He'll tell you about his mentor, Chico. He and Manuel worked a lot of cattle together, and in all their years of roping, Manuel says he only saw him fall off a horse three times. Chico didn't retire from the saddle until he was 87 years old. Then there is Manuel's horse, Billy. He says only that the horse is a little frisky, but the truth is that no one on the ranch could ride him. They couldn't even saddle him.

In October 2012, the Morrow Holding Company sold its 1,168 acres to the Wiley family.

Braman Tract. Mary Elizabeth Braman Crouch would figure prominently in the next chapter of the Bend in the River. She was the daughter of Victoria doctor Daniel Hawes Braman and his wife Myrtle Barnes. Born in 1910, she was named after the Mary Elizabeth Braman who navigated the Braman holdings after William Cheever Braman's passing in 1899.[44] Mary E. married oil man Crockett Louis Crouch in 1929, and by the 1940s lived in Lockhart, south of Austin. She took title to the family's portion of the Crier Survey in 1951.[45]

Lenon Hemphill was Crouch Ranch foreman from 1952 to 1988. Born William Lenon Hemphill in 1918 in Red Rock, between Lockhart and Bastrop, Lenon in the 1940s was a prize-winning rodeo cowboy. He was 34 years old when he moved to the ranch with his wife Bernice, in 1952, and raised three children there. Son Danny was born on the property in 1952 and followed in his father's footsteps. He was seven years old when he first competed in the 1959 Calhoun County Youth Rodeo, entering the tie down, breakaway, bull riding, barrel races, team ribbon roping, and bareback riding events.[46] Danny continued to compete for years, placing and winning top honors in most events. By the time he was 13, he was so proficient at breaking horses that people came from across Bay Prairie to hire him.

The Crouch Ranch headquarters, Danny says, consisted of four houses and a cutting horse arena located near where the entrance gate to Spread Oaks Ranch is today. The Crouch home was adjacent to theirs, and they visited regularly from Lockhart. Mrs. Crouch loved roses, and Danny got his first job caring for her dozens of rose bushes when he was eight years old when. Mrs. Crouch always drove a purple Cadillac, he says, and fondly recalls her as a "fantastic lady."[47] Husband and wife spent winter weekends at the property, inviting guests to hunt deer and hogs.[48]

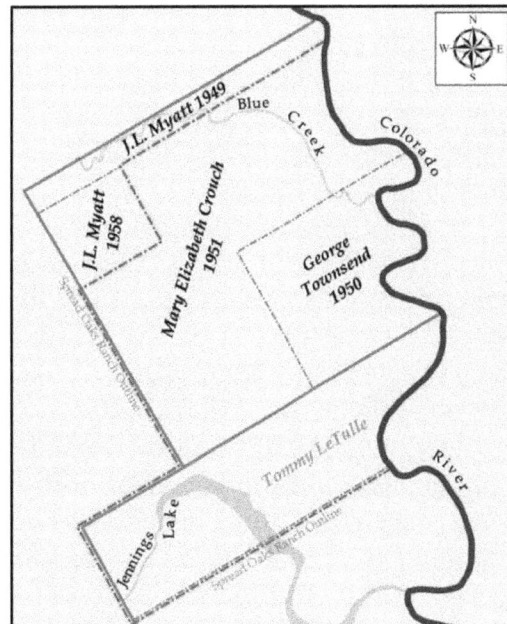

The Crouch piece was mostly grazing pasture, but when cattle prices dropped in the late 1960s to early 70s, his foreman father leased 600 acres for rice. Danny worked cattle with this father, and he says, "if Dad couldn't do it from a horse, it didn't get done." Seventy years later Danny still remembers the number of windmill wells on the property – eleven – and he pulled pipe on each one to make repairs at least once. He recalls the original Blue Creek bridge made from oil field pipe that was decked with heavy boards spaced with a large gap between each. The gap was so large that, when he moved cattle across it, some refused to go. "I hated that," he says, "because then I'd have to rope 'em and drag 'em.

Of the Hemphill's neighbor, Tommy LeTulle, Danny says that when Tommy and his father got into an argument, the young boy worried they might kill each other. Danny often fished on Jennings Creek, and a favorite memory of Tommy is the day that he rode up on a mule and paid him a visit. Danny offered him a sandwich, and the man and boy sat for a long eating and fishing, not saying much, but enjoying the moment.[49]

Mary E. Crouch transferred the property to the Crouch Family Limited Partnership in 1996 and died the next year.[50] Lenon died in 1995 at 77, and his wife Bernice lived to be a hundred. Heliodoro Cuenca owned the 2,807-acre tract for a few years after 2006,[51] then sold it to the Wylie family in 2013.

The Northern Tracts. Throughout most of their history, the northern tracts of the Crier Survey were mostly an extension of the Pierce and Braman holdings, regardless of the name on the deed. That changed in the 1940s as more of the Bend in the River land was fenced in by individual ranchers. J.C. Carlson was the sole survivor of the Northern Irrigation Company (NIC) trustees in 1940.[52] That year, he sold the surface rights of the original Crier 221-acre tract to NIC trustee heirs, who transferred ownership to J.L. Myatt in 1949.[53] The adjacent 139-acre Pierce Estates tract was also sold to J.L. Myatt, in 1958.[54] After he died in 1970, his wife deeded the tracts to family members, including daughter Leola Mae and husband Frank L. Ramsey. In 1977, the land title for both tracts were transferred to Ramsey.[55]

J.L. Myatt. Jesse Lee Myatt was born in Tennessee 1888 and moved to El Campo in 1914, marrying Jackson County native Minnie Atkinson in 1918. Myatt was a rice farmer, rancher, and invested in oil leases. As a rice man, he was elected to the American Rice Growers Association board of directors in 1922. He raised Herefords and quarter horses on the Jesse Myatt Ranch near Columbus and, in 1959, his Myatt Ranch *Macamdo Man* entry was named champion gelding at the first annual Victoria Quarter horse show.[56] Myatt was 70 years old when he entered and competed in senior division quarter horse reining and roping contests.

Jesse and Minnie Mae Myatt kept the Northern Irrigation and Pierce tracts for 29 years, until 1977, when the surface deed was transferred to son-in-law Frank L. Ramsey.[57] Jesse Myatt lived a long life, dying of heart failure at age 82 in 1970. Minnie Mae lived until 1993.

Frank L. Ramsey. Frank Lovic Ramsey was born in Mississippi in 1916, moving to El Campo in the 1930s. By 1940 he married Jesse L. Myatt's daughter, Leola. For a long time, spouse Leola had no idea if her 2nd lieutenant husband was dead or alive. During World War II he was a US Army Air Corps navigator, his B-17 shot down over Germany. All Leola knew from a single military issued telegram was that he was missing in action. Later, she was told he was a German PWO, and he returned home at the War's end.[58]

During the 1950s Ramsey worked the oilfield and grew rice and cotton. He held posts with the Rice Marketing Association and South Texas Cotton & Grain Association, and in 1957 signed on with the Eisenhower-era Farmer's Home Administration and Agricultural Stabilization Conservation Service (ASC), first with the Wharton County ASC, and then as Director of Texas State USDA ASC. With responsibility for government cotton subsidy allocations, Ramsey expected his job would be pretty much routine. He was wrong.[59]

In June 1961 his boss, ASC Chief of Production Adjustment Henry H. Marshall, was found shot to death at his farm in Franklin, his death ruled a suicide by Justice of the Peace Lee Farmer. Farmer's conclusion was curious given that Marshall had five rifle bullets lodged in his stomach, all fired by a bolt-action .22.[60] Later, when a grand jury had his remains exhumed, a Houston pathologist added a severe blow to his head and carbon monoxide in his blood stream to the list of injuries. If Marshall's wounds were self-inflicted, he had worked very hard at it.[61]

Agricultural chief Henry Marshall had uncovered accounting improprieties, the finger pointing to Pecos County wheeler and dealer Billie Sol Estes. Two Oklahoma agricultural department agents, Marshall learned, received bribes as part of an Estes subterfuge to transfer cotton allotments from farmers whose land was condemned for public projects.[62] It was the just the tip of the iceberg. Within months of the Marshall killing, the full extent of Estes' nefarious financial empire, built largely through manipulation of federal subsidies, was subject to investigations by the FBI, four grand juries, the IRS, The Department of Agriculture, two Senate and House investigating committees, and the Texas Rangers.[63]

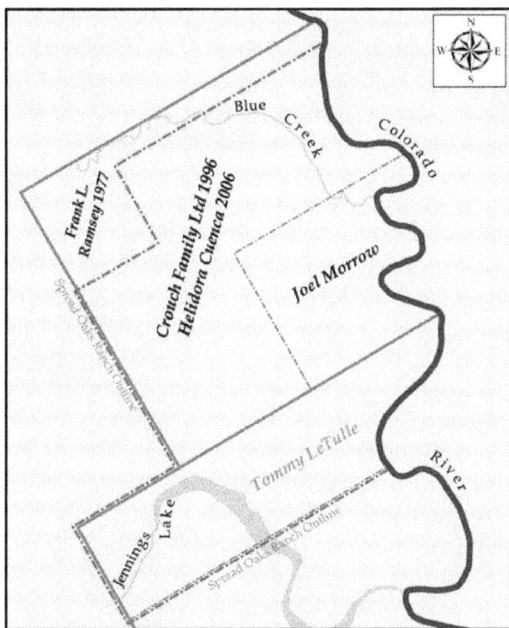

The grand jury hearing for the Henry H. Marshall killing was held that June in Robertson County.[64] Frank Ramsey was called to testify for the government, but star witness Estes pleaded the Fifth Amendment for protection against self-incrimination. After five weeks, the jury concluded there was insufficient evidence to link Estes or anyone else to Marshall's demise, and confirmed his death was a suicide.[65] In one of the oddest twists and turns of the saga, Estes – the man linked to the death of Henry Marshall and under siege by the FBI, IRS, assorted grand juries, and Senate and House investigating committees – was named by the Kennedy administration to the Federal Cotton Advisory Committee.[66] Frank L. Ramsey was one of many who resigned from the Department of Agriculture during 1961 and 1962.[67]

The El Campo farmer who put his government bureaucrat position behind him was elected by his peers the next year as president of the Wharton County Cotton Association. Ramsey continued farming and ranching, raising a sizable herd of registered Herefords. The family had a passion for rodeos, with Frank competing in quarter horse barrel racing and daughters who held various rodeo queen titles. His horses won titles on the Texas and national circuit, such as the Texas Bred Futurity, La Bahia Downs, Kansas Derby, and All-American Derby held in New Mexico. Frank Ramsey died in 2003, and the property today is still owned by the family.[68]

Epilogue. During the last 70 years of the 20th century, the "Golden Age of Radio" and the coming of television brought the outside world into the living rooms of Matagorda residents. World War II was to touch every American community, and in Matagorda County it produced the heartbreak of 120 Gold Star mothers. Post-war technology supplanted horses and mules with gasoline powered tractors, and automobiles came to replace the trains that were so eagerly anticipated just decades earlier. County residents suffered severe hurricanes in 1942 and 1961. A hundred years earlier, the measure of a hurricane's wrath was in the number of ships lost at sea and a human toll, but by the mid-20th century that measure was the damage done in dollars, and it was tens of millions.

WW II. Life during the war for Matagorda County residents who remained at home was in some ways like the rest of the US. There was a ration on gasoline, sugar, rubber, and other commodities. No new cars were sold between 1942 and 1947. On the streets, all the young men were gone. There were practice blackouts, and a 24-hour air raid alert system. Boys collected scrap iron, wives and mothers sponsored fund raisers for the USO and rolled bandages.[69] They rushed to read the morning newspapers to get the latest information on the war and stood by the railroad tracks to watch troops trains passing through Markham to and from Palacios' aerial artillery instructional center at Camp Hulen.

Many days it sounded as if the war was at Matagorda's doorstep. In 1941 the US Army took over Matagorda Peninsula as a bombing and machine gun range, with planes taking off from Camp Hulen and strafing targets placed in the dunes or offshore. Well Point, to the southwest of Camp Hulen, was an anti-aircraft firing range. Both aerial gunning sites made it challenging for local fishermen, who had to remember to get clearance to use the waterways before they set sail.

There was a German POW camp in Bay City, with tents and oyster-shell lined roads, that at its peak numbered 400 residents. The first soldiers who arrived there were still wearing their uniforms after capture in North Africa. The Army contracted the POW's out as a labor force, some 20 to 25 at a time under an armed guard. With most of the farm labor off at war, many of the POW crews worked Bay Prairie's rice fields.

A Pair of Hurricanes. Matagordians took their eye off the war only when the hurricane of 1942 stormed ashore. Inland towns such as Bay City and Markham were largely spared but in Palacios, nearer the coast, 100-mph winds splintered houses and blew off sections of roofs and walls. Shrimp boats were piled up on the bayfront along with mounds of debris. Camp Hulen was badly damaged, and two soldiers drowned when their truck was overtaken by high water along Tres Palacios Bay. In the surrounding countryside, cotton bolls were blown from their stalks, and half the rice crop was destroyed. Rural residents went days without electricity or water.

There was damage to every structure in the town of Matagorda, and nearly all the houses on the east side were wiped out. The Red Cross and other relief organizations remained in Matagorda for weeks after the storm. A protection levee was approved around the town after the storm with elevation improvements that, 20 years later, were completed the day before Hurricane Carla bullied its way into town.[70]

In September 1961, coastal Texans held their breath as Carla, a Category 5 hurricane with winds of 175 mph, set its sights on Corpus Christi. Then it changed course, weakening some, and made landfall at Matagorda Island on September 11 with 145 mph winds. The towns of Matagorda and Palacios suffered sustained winds of 115 mph and a storm surge of 16 feet. Bay City was inundated with over 17 inches of rain.

Buildings in Matagorda were badly damaged, but the new levee shielded the town from the worst of the punishing surge. Palacios was not as fortunate. Houses across the town were demolished, the tidal waters picking some up, floating them over fences, and depositing them in fields. All the port buildings were wiped out, and shrimp boats that were ripped free of their moorings washed over the highway. Damage in Palacios was estimated at over $12 million.

Half the cattle in Matagorda County drowned, the work crews assigned to remove their carcasses sorting through rubble and rattlesnakes. A tangled mass of wire, cable, and broken poles was all that remained of the telephone and electrical infrastructure. Fifteen highway bridges were damaged. Hurricane Carla did almost half a billion dollars in damage across the state.[71]

The End of the Century. The 1960s brought a nuclear standoff with Russia, the shooting of President John F. Kennedy, racial integration, and the assassinations of Robert Kennedy and Martin Luther King. The country followed its first astronauts into space and witnessed a man land on the moon. Much of the nation supported the Vietnam War, although it later divided many families as a conflict the US couldn't seem to win. Color TV brought nightly images of the war's carnage into American homes, as well as anti-war protests and riots that rocked the country. President Richard M. Nixon was toppled by Watergate, and his successor Jimmy Carter wrestled with US hostages in Iran, gasoline shortages, and rampant inflation.

The late 1970s and 80s saw a return to political conservatism and capitalism, the "supply side economics" of one president termed "voodoo" economics by another. The nation's school children tuned in to watch the first teacher in space disintegrate over the Atlantic Ocean. During the last decade of the 20th century, Bill Clinton became the second US president to be impeached while in office and Monica Lewinski was a household name. IBM and Apple's personal computers quickly transformed the world, and cell phones replaced the once-revolutionary technology of push button landlines. The Dow Jones doubled between 1966 and the "New Millennium," as it was called. The world got faster. And the Colorado River still flowed through Bay Prairie.

A CARD TO THE PUBLIC.

The road in the bottom west of the ferry is impassable. There are places in which the mud is saddle skirt deep. There is no use to abuse the mail-carrier or his team. If the people want the the mail, the roads must be fixed at once. I can get through in the mornings by going around through the lakes, sometimes so deep it runs into the bed of the hack; but at night I can't see to pick my way through lakes and timber, and I have no right to risk losing the mail, which I have had to do many times, and risked my life as well; as in some places those lakes are swimming. A little money spent on the road would make a safe passage for the mail. Or, a new road could be cut out. It is not a "heavy dew" that stops me. But I can't do impossible things. There are places that the best of teams bog down in.

Respectfully,

WM. DOUGLAS.

Fig. 1. Postman William Douglas lamented the difficulty of delivering the mail on the west side of the Colorado River in 1899. His "bottom west of the ferry" refers to Elliott's Ferry, near the present site of the Highway 35 bridge. His reference to "the lakes" is to Jennings Creek and Blue Creek, which in times of heavy rainfall were certainly large water bodies. *Matagorda County Tribune*, Dec. 23, 1899.

Fig. 2. Newlyweds Tommy Beach and Alta Ree LeTulle, circa 1950. LeTulle, Tommy, *The Memoirs of Tommy Beach LeTulle* (Houston: Kemp & Co., 2019).

Fig. 3. Tommy LeTulle's stationary, with reference to "South Texas Best Bottom Rancher." LeTulle, Tommy, *The Memoirs of Tommy Beach LeTulle* (Houston: Kemp & Co., 2019).

Thomas B. LeTulle

South Texas Best Bottom Rancher
P. O. BOX 123 . . . . . . MARKHAM, TEXAS

Fig. 4. The "Old Indian" of Blue Creek. LeTulle, Tommy, *The Memoirs of Tommy Beach LeTulle* (Houston: Kemp & Co., 2019).

Fig. 5. Sculptor Danny Stephens, with the clay model at the New Mexico foundry in 1985. Courtesy Danny and Jimmie Stephens.

Fig. 6. Tommy LeTulle by his bronze likeness. Photo was taken by Danny Stephens on the day the monument was erected. Courtesy Danny and Jimmie Stephens.

Fig. 7. Forty years later, Danny Stephens with his bronze Tommy tribute at Spread Oaks Ranch.

CHAPTER 5

The Coming of Spread Oaks Ranch

Forrest Wylie pointed his pick-up truck down the dirt road, mud splashing on the running boards, the truck rattling through every pothole. It was 2011 and, in a way, he was making the journey to the edge of the Colorado River that day as a sort of tribute to his childhood. Those black land river bottoms were important to him growing up. He camped, fished, learned about nature and, he confesses, snuck back in the wintertime to shoot a few ducks. Some 40 years later, when he learned that the 1,100-acre Morrow tract – the Morrow's Spread Oaks Ranch – was on the market, he was drawn from Houston to look.

At the end of the dirt road he parked by a couple of barns and was greeted by a bronzed Mexican man with an infectious grin beneath a distinctive handlebar mustache. Ramrod straight in blue jeans and cowboy boots, Forrest says "that was when I met Manuel Briones for the first time. He had been working cattle for the Morrow family. We rode horses to the river and were picking some pecans from a tree along the way, and I noticed two bald eagles feasting on a raccoon. And as we looked over the river, I saw Manuel was grinning. 'I cannot believe people pay me to be on this land,' he said. I pretty much knew right then and there I wanted to buy the land, and I wanted Manuel to ranch it for me."

Audrey Wylie remembers that what caught her eye were the oak trees. "We had looked at a number of properties," she says, "but we knew right away this was the right one." Their initial purchase in 2011 was part of the Morrow Estate that encompassed the bottom third of the original John Crier headright. Other acreage was added over the next few years, including most more of the Crier tract and the top third of the League headright that Tommy LeTulle had ranched. Today Spread Oaks Ranch, the name given by the Morrow family to the Wylie's core acquisition for its mottes of live oak trees, covers approximately 5,500 acres with over five miles of riverfront. Forrest Wylie no longer trespasses to shoot a few ducks.

The Wylie's didn't yet know about the deep connection between their land and Texas history, but it was a journey they wanted to take. Along that path they would learn of the litany of the colorful, earlier landowners, the role of Jennings Lake in Austin settlement history and the Texas War of Independence, of the river steamer *Kate Ward* that passed by their land to clear the river banks, the longhorn herds that once driven through their pastures, and the significance of the Colorado River log jam on 1800s river commerce and to the early days of rice irrigation.

The trees along the Colorado River have grown back a century and a half after the *Kate Ward* cleared its banks. Remnants of the rice irrigator's canals cross the landscape, the sharpness of their levees dulled with time, appearing more like a natural drainage system than one wrested from the prairie by man and machine (Fig. 1). And still the river, winding through the heart of the property, depositing new land as point bars from erosion of the high ground by cut-back bank processes, and a navigation beacon to countless flocks of birds migrate down the riverine artery each winter (Fig. 2).

Creating a Legacy. The Wylie's vision of the land was, and is, to integrate ranching, farming, and wildlife. "That's the way I remember the land when I was growing up,"

Forrest explains. They also wanted to share it with others, and a hospitality piece was developed alongside the ranching, agriculture, and wildlife cornerstones.

Ranching. Forrest and Manuel went to work on the ranching piece first. With a cattle trailer in tow, they traveled to auctions in Dallas, Fort Worth, and other towns to build a herd of Brangus cattle. Forrest saw how expert Manuel's eye was for selecting the best beeves from any herd on the market. "Too much French," he'd grumble if a cow had more Angus qualities than Brahman. Sellers soon learned that if Manuel was doing the cutting, they were going to have a bad day.

From an initial herd of 120 head, Spread Oaks today has over 500 "mama cows," as Forrest calls them, and around 30 bulls (Figs. 3 & 4). The selection of Brangus on the ranch, Forrest continues, is because "the Brahman part of the cows allows them to take the heat, but the Angus part gives the best meat. Manuel runs registered Angus bulls on everything, so we're certified Angus beef. And out here we're all grass-fed. We sell 'em at around 800 pounds and keep a few to slaughter. That's what we eat at the ranch."

Cowboying is a big part of the ranch culture – Manuel and his hands still drive the herd between pastures from the backs of quarter horses, the way it's been done on the property since the early longhorn drovers (Fig. 5). It's a step back in time as the sound of a bullwhip cracks, dust rises, cattle bay, and one of Manuel's cow dog's darts between the legs of the moving mass to keep the breakers in check.

In 2019 Forrest and Manuel added a herd of Katahdin sheep, a mix of St. Croix and Dorper lines from the Caribbean that are well suited to Texas heat (Fig. 6). The herd grew from the first 30 head to 50 within six months. All the range animals are rotated in ranch pastures to meet their specific feed requirements. Sheep, for example, will eat weeds but cattle won't, so both can feed on the same pasture. The quarter horses, however, have different needs than cattle, and this gives rise to what they call "cow hay" and "horse hay."

Farming. When the Wylie's bought their first tract of land, only about 200 acres were in cultivation. Today the ranch has 2,000 acres in agriculture. The ranch currently grows and cuts nearly 2,000 round hay bales that are used to feed livestock through the winter. Each fall a fleet of tractors crisscross the fields to cut and bale, then move the bales for storage into mammoth-sized barns (Fig. 7).

Spread Oaks manages the hay, while the rest of the crops are grown by area farmers who produce wheat, cotton, soybeans, and corn (Fig. 8). Several fields on the property have been planted with another kind of crop – native Texas prairie grasses. Its success results from leadership provided by the Wildlife & Habitat Federation, with part of its funding and technical expertise offered by the US Fish & Wildlife Service, Quail Forever, and Natural Resource Conservation Service. One of the benefits of this restorative project is to optimize cattle grazing and rotation, and it also provides a sanctuary for the plants and animals of a vanishing rangeland ecosystem.

Wildlife. Spread Oaks Ranch's forests, fields, and river bottoms have always been ideal habitat for wildlife, both native and migratory. The buffalo, bear, red wolf, and ocelot are gone, but not the wild deer, coyotes, bobcats, and wild hogs. The wild turkey and prairie chicken are also gone, along with most of the bobwhite quail, but the land supports two pairs of nesting bald eagles, large flocks of songbirds, a variety of colonial and wading birds, shorebirds, mourning doves, and migratory raptors and waterfowl (Figs. 9 & 10).

Construction and improvement of waterfowl habitat has been a major ranch focus (Figs. 11 & 12). Moving and retaining water efficiently is remarkably specialized, and each spring, large machines of all shapes and sizes grumble to life, their mission to create new waterfowl impoundments, repair old ones, improve the network of canals that move water, install pumps, and repair wells and water control structures. As of 2023, the ranch managed 174 acres of year-round water and 460 acres of ephemeral wetlands in about 30 units. Only Jennings Creek (Figs. 13 & 14) and part of the original Watkins Lake are natural water bodies, the others man-made.

Annual wetlands are disked before the pumps are turned on. Filling the units requires a balance of timing, rate, and volume to reduce noxious vegetation and encourage growth of native aquatic and emergent seed grass – duck food. In the natural wetlands, the biggest challenge is managing non-native invasives, such as Chinese tallow and alligator weed, and noxious vegetation like sesbania, senna beans, and water primrose. Spread Oaks Ranch duck habitat was developed with partners Ducks Unlimited, Wildlife Habitat Federation, US Fish & Wildlife Service, C-GRIP, the Texas A&M Aquatic Wetlands Professional Development Program, and many other contributors.

Ranch whitetail deer benefit from native grass plantings and careful management through enrollment in the Texas Parks & Wildlife Managed Lands Deer Program (Figs. 15 & 16). It's not unusual to see a hundred healthy deer in a single morning on Spread Oaks Ranch. Ranch habitat managers are optimistic that the native rangeland grass program will improve the declining quail population. As for the numbers of wild hogs, everything the ranch is doing seems to be right – and they wish it wasn't! Introduced species such as feral hogs and nutria have been costly to control, and the battle is nowhere near won.

Keeping it Whole. One of the reasons the Wylie's are committed to improving the natural environment is because the ranch will remain in its ranching, agricultural, and wild state in perpetuity, through a conservation easement with Texas Parks & Wildlife's Texas Farm and Ranch Lands Conservation Program. With baseline studies and administrative assistance by the Coastal (Katy) Prairie Conservancy, the Wylie's land will be protected from housing developments, solar farms, and wind turbines, and it can remain a working farm and ranch while providing critical habitat for birds and other wildlife, and native plant communities in perpetuity. They know what they do today will impact tomorrow (Fig. 17).

The Lodge. Its limestone façade rises above the landscape, imposing, yet integral. Audrey Wylie is only partly joking when she says that Forrest "had the vision of going back to his roots with ranching, farming, and hunting, while I had the job of bringing culture and class to our project!" The Wylie's chose the site for the lodge to capture the sunrise behind it – over the ranching piece of Spread Oaks – and the sunset in front, over the farming operation. It took a little under two years to build the lodge, which was completed in October 2017 (Figs. 18 & 19).

Audrey hired residential designer Brandon Breaux for the building plans and Ginger Barber Interior Design to turn the structure into a home. Brandon calls the lodge architectural style "Texas Ranch" with its mix of detached buildings constructed of Lueders limestone, its "courtyard feel," and Spanish Mexican influence. According to Forrest, the interior theme is based on "the strength of rock and stone," but tempered by wood and light. The rock portion of the theme is the fireplace facades, cut from a "large boulder that Forrest and I picked out," Audrey relates, and hoisted into a place using an A-frame pulley system with block and tackle. Rather than sharp edges and clean cuts, a crew of masons chiseled each block to give it a "rough cut" form, as it is called. It took them eight months.

As for the interior wood, it has a history. The beams are all Louisiana cypress and cedar, some hand-hewn that retains its original tongue and groove construction, and other pieces that originated from some of the first sawmills in the state. It's probably between 150 and 200 years old. The wood floors are all restored French oak.

The idea of providing a comfortable and memorable lodge experience was born from the Wylie's interest in sharing the outdoors with others, whether for entertainment or learning, or both. They added an eight-room guest house to the grounds in 2020, its exterior and interior designed to work seamlessly with the lodge (Figs. 20 & 21). In a nod to the ranch's history as an original Stephen F. Austin headright, the guest house was dubbed the "Old 300."

The ranch kitchen is not contained within the lodge walls but oozes out across the fields, trees, and lakes. Daily menu offerings embody the meaning of field to table. Walk-in refrigerators and freezers are stocked with certified Angus beef, cured hams and bacon, ranch lambs, sausages, and wild deer and hogs. Many of the meats are prepared in the ranch's charcuterie room and cured in its smokehouse. A hoop house shade garden bursts at the seams with ranch-grown greens such as kale, spinach, mustard greens, and cabbages, and its greenhouse is replete with seasonal herbs, peppers, tomatoes, and hydroponic cucumbers, okra, parsley, and thyme. There's even a century-old chuck wagon to use for a unique outdoor dining experience (Fig. 22).

Epilogue. If the Wylie family believed in ghosts, they wouldn't have to look far (Fig. 23). They'd almost certainly find them at Jennings Creek, where the first of the Austin Old 300 colonists built a log cabin in 1821. Called Jennings Camp, the structure provided respite for the earliest of the Austin settlers travelling upriver to San Felipe. The camp and adjacent creek was named for Jacob Jennings, who died in 1822 and was buried nearby, the location of his grave as unknown as the site of the cabin.

The unsettled soul of Hosea League would be among the apparitions. He failed as an empresario, was vilified when he was a Mexican Texas *regidor*, and spent months in chains as an accessory to a murder he did not commit, guilty of no more than being the wrong person at the wrong place at the wrong time. It cost him everything.

The spirits might include the Texian volunteers who made-up Stephen F. Austin's ragtag volunteers that camped beside Jennings Creek before marching to Gonzales and the first battle of the Texian Revolution. Brimming with optimism, the same campsite was occupied just 15 months later by Mexican General José de Urrea's force of about 1,100 cavalrymen and infantry. Had Santa Anna given the order, theirs was part of an army that Sam Houston would have faced at San Jacinto, and it would have changed history.

Then there was the ferry, first called League's and then Cayce's. The Texian volunteers crossed it, the Mexican Army burned it, and somewhere in between it was crossed by the shuffling retreat of the refugee Texians during the Runaway Scrape. Like the bones of Jennings and the relics of his cabin, the remnants of the ferry are lost to history.

Landowner apparitions might include those who died early from the quiet killers of the day, like James Worland, who departed life at age 26 in 1840 from a fever. Maybe Jacob Briggs, who drowned when the steamship *Varuna* broke up in a storm off the Florida coast. Perhaps, too, the ones who died violently, like George Cayce, who was killed at the Council House Fight in a melee between Comanche and Texas Regulars, or his brother who died after he was kicked by a horse.

There could be benevolent ghosts. Three generation of Watkins with more children than their grandparents could count. A.J. Harty, whose first ethereal activity would probably be to inspect the remnants of his irrigation handiwork at Jennings Lake. Mary E. Crouch and her roses. McDonald, Townsend, and Morrow with their cutting horses and cattle. Somewhere between the good ghosts and the unsettled ones would be Tommy LeTulle, and he would have a lot to say.

Maybe the nighttime messengers wouldn't be ghosts at all. Maybe just sounds. Perhaps the whistle of the steamer *Kate Ward*. Or, in the distance, the thunder of hooves. First bison, then longhorns and mustangs. Maybe also the piercing night-time sound of the apex predators who once secreted its canebrakes –cougars, red wolves, and bears.

The sun is setting orange on a horizon broken only by oak mottes in front of the lodge. Spring is coming, but there's still a chill in the air. Two swallow-tailed kites hover over the lake edge, and a flock of teal jet past the bass pond behind the lodge. The Wylie's find comfort in the new but have an appreciation of the ghosts of the past. Spread Oaks is just that kind of place.

Fig. 1. The Colorado River at Spread Oaks Ranch, looking north. Photo by R.K. Sawyer.

Fig. 2. A.J. Harty and the rice irrigators dug miles of canals across Spread Oaks Ranch. A hundred years later, their levees and waterways today look more like part of the natural environment than an industrial-scale irrigation network. Photo by Les Tompkins.

Figs. 3 & 4. Brangus hooves on the ranch follow in the footprints of bison and longhorns.
Photos by Karen Sachar.

Fig. 5. Cowboys and cutting horses are still a big part of the Spread Oaks Ranch culture. Photo by Karen Sachar.

Fig. 6. Katahdin sheep, a mix of St. Croix and Dorper lines that are well suited to Texas heat. Photo by Karen Sachar.

Fig. 8. Each year, about 2,000 acres wheat, cotton, soybeans, and corn are grown and harvested by area farmers. Photo by Karen Sachar.

Fig. 9. American bald eagle. Photo by Jerzy Trybek.

Fig. 10. Blue-winged teal over a ranch wetland unit. Photo by Nate Skinner.

Figs. 11 & 12. Over a mile of underground pipes deliver water to duck ponds (left) in addition to miles of surface canals and ditches. Electric wells and diesel pumps move water from reservoirs (right). Photos by R.K. Sawyer.

Figs. 13 & 14. Jennings Lake, looking north (top). Remnants of the original cypress trees were visible during the 2022 summer drought (bottom). Photos by R.K. Sawyer.

Figs. 15 & 16. Spring fawn (top) and a late summer buck (bottom). Photos by Les Tompkins.

Fig. 17. Aerial overview of the main lodge and surrounds. Upper left, following the road and telephone poles, is the division between the original League Survey and Crier Survey. Jennings Lake is just visible in the far upper left. Tommy LeTulle was the previous owner of this land. In the distance, center, is the Pierce/Braman Pasture with the addition of a modern cutting horse arena. The lodge is situated near the site of the circa 1880s Watkins Cabin. To its right is the "Old 300" guide quarters, and in front is the clay target field that overlooks one of the ranch's two stocked bass ponds. Photo by R.K. Sawyer.

Figs. 18 & 19. View of the main lodge exterior from the bass pond (top) and interior of main room (bottom). Photo by Nate Skinner.

Figs. 20 & 21. View of the "Old 300" guest house looking towards the river (top) and interior (bottom). Top photo by R.K. Sawyer; Bottom photo by Nate Skinner.

135

Fig. 22. A century old chuck wagon is the centerpiece for fine dining in a rustic setting. Photo by R.K. Sawyer.

Fig. 23 (next page). The location and artefacts from Jennings's cabin, League and Cayce's ferry, and many other early historical structures have been erased with time. Some of the features discussed in the text that can be observed today are:

BCC: Bass Club Chimney. Intact chimney from a 1950s era bass fishing club.

BF: Borden's Fence. Posts from A.P. Borden's 1909 fence remain after a hundred years.

CRH: Crouch Ranch Headquarters. Only some of the foundations are visible today.

EBCB: East Blue Creek Bridge. Built by Joel Morrow in 2010.

LOF: Location of Old Pump. Site of a relift pump dating from at least the 1920s.

MCC: McMann Cabin. Home of the wild boys of Blue Creek. Location only approximate.

OBCB: Old Blue Creek Bridge. Only parts of its foundation have survived.

OI: Old Indian Cabin. Location is approximate but close.

OP: Old Pump. Remnants of an irrigation relift pump.

OWBC: Old West Blue Creek Bridge.

TLH: Tommy LeTulle Home. Tommy and Alta's concrete house. Not much is left today.

TLM: Tommy LeTulle Monument.

TRH: Townsend Ranch Headquarters.

WBCB: West Blue Creek Bridge. Built by the present ranch owners.

WC: Watkins Cabin. Location is approximate but close.

WL: Watkins Lake. Location before it was drained and channeled in 1918.

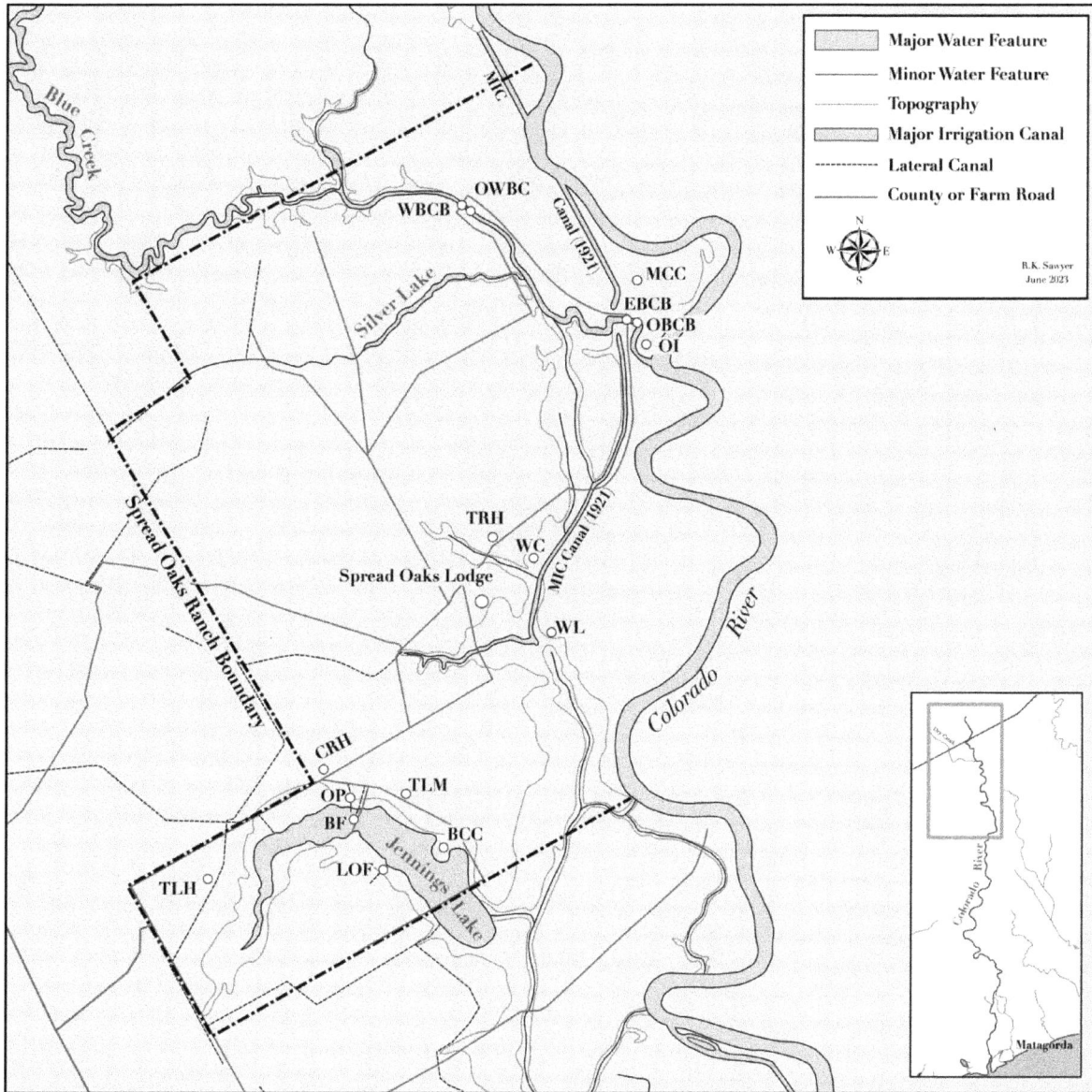

Fig. 23. Location of some of the man-made features on Spread Oaks Ranch discussed in the text. See caption on preceding page.

SECTION 2

Historical Narratives

Preface. The previous section is a compilation of the people that owned Bend in the River land. Section 2 is an account of historical topics, chosen either because Bend in the River landowners played an important role in them, or because the topic was important to the history of the land. Usually it was both. Section 2 includes overviews of early Texas settlement, the Texas War for Independence, the Colorado River log raft, Matagorda's cattlemen and cowboys, and the early rice and irrigation industry.

Early Texas Settlement. The land that would be Spread Oaks Ranch was granted to the first wave of Texas emigrants – Stephen F. Austin's "Old 300" – and the deeds were signed by Stephen F. Austin and Mexico. It didn't take long for the cultural gap between the Mexican government and those who accepted their invitation to settle Texas to come to an impasse, and the result – war – was probably inevitable. The chapter is called *From Spain to Texas*, and it is a story about the founding of the Texas Republic. What's remarkable is how many times the Lone Star protagonists came dangerously close to failing.

Texas Revolution. Texians were by no means in concert before or during the Texas War for Independence. Disparate factions not only fought Mexico, but within themselves. The chapter is called *The Battle for a New Republic*, and it documents the surprising amount of friction between the period players, and the internal strife and questionable decision-making that nearly cost them the war. Spread Oaks Ranch landowners who fought in the Texas Revolution include Thomas Alley, Elijah Flack, and the Cayce family. Every Cayce male of age volunteered for the War's duration, and their ferry and guest house were integral to the Texian and Mexican armies, and by Texian families uprooted by, and retreating from, the Mexican army.

The Colorado River Raft. The Colorado River should have been a prosperous route for commerce between the coast and inland towns. Instead, it was a major barrier. The chapter *Water and Wood* explores the reason – a logjam that closed the artery to maritime travel. For nearly a hundred years, men and machines grabbled with its removal.

Matagorda's Cattlemen and Cowboys. The theme of the chapter titled *Matagorda's Cattle and Cowboys* is Bay Prairie's long-horned cattle – the first important post-Civil War industry to a part of the country whose plantation and slave-based economy was ravaged after the Northern victory in 1865. Bay Prairie cattle filled northern cattle trails after the Civil War until about 1900, and Matagorda County and the Bend in the River were at the heart of it.

Early Rice and Irrigation. Rice irrigation was another of Bay Prairie's financial windfalls. *The Early Years of Matagorda Rice* tells the story of rice farmers and irrigators who transformed the area's native grasslands into miles of canals and reservoirs, creating an irrigation network connecting the Colorado River water source to rice fields that stretched along the western side of the river. The future Spread Oaks Ranch was at the center of it, and nearly all deeds that changed hands between 1901 and 1920 were in some way related to rice and its infrastructure. Thousands of acres of waving green crops belied the challenge, and the fight, to access the limited resource of Colorado River waters.

CHAPTER 6

From Spain to Texas

1820 to 1835

For many Americans, western expansion of the United States was not only justifiable – it was ordained by God. One day it would have a name – Manifest Destiny. Even before the phrase was coined, it was the principle that guided 19th century America in land consolidations such as the 1803 Louisiana Purchase and the annexation of Spanish Florida in 1819. There was nothing unique about it. Man, since the beginning of civilization, had demonstrated that land and riches were the rewards for flexing the muscle of a superior fighting force over a lessor one. The New World, although a relative newcomer to the global stage, was following historical precedent.

Craving Texas. Possession of Spanish Texas was a logical step in western expansion. Originally extending north to what would become the Utah Territory and west to the Tamaulipas Territory at the Nueces River, Spanish Texas formed an arcuate belt approximately 200 miles inland from the coast. On maps of the day, it was bordered by lands to the southwest known for their "droves of wild horses." To the northwest lay the "range of the Comanche Indians" with its "herds of buffalo," and south of the Red River was the land of the "Choctaw Indian."[1]

Thomas Jefferson and others held the popular belief that the United States already acquired Spanish Texas under the terms of the Louisiana Purchase, their dreams dashed when President John Adams, instead, drew the boundary only as far as the edge of western Florida. From then on, there were Americans determined to conquer Texas. They would have to wait in line. A Mexican insurgency, with far more at stake than America's expansionist dream, was actively waging war on Spain's remaining New World possession.

Intent on independence, Mexican nationalists harassed the Spanish Royalist regime from 1810 until their victory in 1821. Easiest for Spain to put down were the internal, mostly peasant rebellions. More troubling were military incursions, both by land and sea, often financed by American expansionists. Called filibustering campaigns, their ranks were filled by former US soldiers lured by the promise of bonus money and land. The first campaign was the 1812 to 1813 Gutiérrez-Magee expedition, followed in quick succession by the those of Juan Pablo Anaya and Francisco Xavier Mina with Henry Perry, another by Frenchman and privateer Louis Michel Aury, and two expeditions commanded by James Long between 1819 and 1820.

Moses Austin and Spanish Texas. Moses Austin had owned mining operations in the Missouri Territory but was now bankrupt. Arriving in San Antonio de Béxar during the fall of 1820, the former miner sought a consultation with New Spain Governor Antonio María Martínez. His goal was to enlist the governor's support to convince Spain to appoint him as an immigration agent, or *empresario*, and permit colonization of 300 American families between the "Brassos" and Colorado rivers.

Austin's idea was not new. Spain, nearly as weary of indigenous Indian depravations as it was rebel's intent on an independent Mexican state, was bleeding money as it tried to maintain control over its northern frontier. In 1820, it finally permitted foreigners to settle parts of Texas under terms in which, in return for generous land grants, they would become Spanish citizens, practice Catholicism, and develop the land.[2] As importantly, they would assist in defending the territory.

Anglo settlement was not without controversy, and Austin's petition would go unanswered by Governor Martínez. The history of Texas Anglo-American colonization would be markedly different had not Philip Hendrik Nering Bögel – the self-described Dutch nobleman using the title Baron de Bastrop – intervened on Austin's behalf.[3] The Dutchman oversaw his own successful empresario ventures in Spanish Texas, and with Bastrop's endorsement Governor Martínez ultimately agreed to Austin's proposal.

Moses Austin's return to trip to Missouri would kill him. After his mules, stores, and powder were stolen, he subsisted on mostly berries and roots, his journey troubled by rains and swollen rivers, and he was even attacked by a panther.[4] Austin arrived home a sick man. When he died of pneumonia a few months later, the duties of the Texas enterprise were inherited by his son, Stephen F. Austin. The young empresario left New Orleans for Texas in the spring of 1821 to tour the country and finalize his father's settlement terms with Martínez.

Stephen F. Austin's expedition, like his father before him, was replete with the hardships of missing mules and horses, unfordable rivers and inlets, fevers and sickness, scarce potable water, lost guides, and native Indian scares. Yet he marveled at the splendor of the land and its copious resources. Choosing the boundaries for the new settlement between the San Jacinto and Lavaca rivers,[5] it would be called Austin's Colony. It was the first of several settlement contracts that would spread across Texas during the next 15 years, and was later named renamed First Colony.

Stephen F. Austin and Mexican Texas. During his first tour of Texas, Austin learned that the rebellion against Spanish rule, begun 11 years earlier by priest Miguel Hidalgo y Costilla, had been decided by former royalist army officer Agustín de Iturbide. The Treaty of Córdoba, signed in August 1821, proclaimed the new Empire of Mexico to the world. Austin wasn't concerned that Mexico's independence might be a threat to his father's Spanish land grant.[6] But as arrangements stalled in the fall, he was informed that Mexico would have to refer the matter to the nascent national government for approval.[7] When Stephen F. Austin settled his first colonists anyway, he was taking a terrible gamble.

One of the first of Austin's settlers was Jacob Jennings, who arrived on the schooner Lively and settled at the Bend in the River on the Jennings Tract, later the Hosea League Survey.

The earliest of Austin's settlers journeyed to Texas overland from Natchitoches and via the Gulf of Mexico from New Orleans in December 1821. Austin remained in the colony until March, then traveled to Mexico City to appeal to Agustín de Iturbide and the provisional government. He was not alone. A cast of characters were in the city that also aspired to settle Mexican Texas, the list including representatives from Tennessee, an entourage from Ireland and Germany, and even the duplicitous James Wilkinson. A former American war hero, Wilkinson had been a Louisiana Territory governor and Spanish double agent known for his role in the capture of former vice president Aaron Burr on treason charges. Wilkinson was to die in Mexico City in 1825, still waiting for approval.[8]

The Mexico City that greeted Austin during the spring of 1822 was in a celebratory mood. She was free of Spain, and the rebel factions that fought for independence had, at least for the time being, bowed to Iturbide's rule as head of a constitutional monarchy. The rattle of muskets and the ringing of church steeple bells greeting Iturbide's designation as Mexico's first emperor.[9] Austin shared the city's optimism, writing to Joseph H. Hawkins in New Orleans that Congress, "though rather slow," would "sanction all that has been done." He was confident he would return to his First Colony soon.[10]

That fall, however, Austin was still in Mexico City and had lost much of his enthusiasm. In November, he wrote that the National Constituent Congress seemed to be headed towards anarchy and was already split into three factions: "one for the Bourbon King, one for an emperor from this country, and the other for a Republic." Congress refused to relinquish any powers to Iturbide, he continued, and the ruler "could do nothing so long as Congress existed without its sanction." Then a plot to dethrone the monarch was uncovered, and it involved members of Congress. Iturbide dissolved the body, imprisoning some who were "dragged from their beds at midnight" at the "pointed end of a bayonet." Then he formed his own assembly, the Junta Instituyente.[11]

Austin concentrated his lobbying effort on the Junta Instituyente, and the body approved his colonization plan. All that he needed next was Iturbide's approval, but Iturbide took his time. It was time, it turned out, he didn't have. Former supporter General Antonio López de Santa Anna was scheming with the army and Iturbide's enemies, and it culminated with a revolt against the emperor. Approval of Austin's Texas colonization venture occurred during the narrow window between Santa Anna's coup and the king's abdication.[12] Iturbide was executed in 1824.

As Mexico charted its new course as a republic between 1823 and most of 1824, the country was ruled by a provisional triumvirate government.[13] Having disposed of the European model for a king and monarchy, the future of the retitled Republic Mexico would be guided by two competing ideological factions, the federalists and centralists. The federalists drew their government blueprint from the United States, advocating a liberal platform with the dispersal of power to largely self-governed, autonomous states. Much of their support was from the people who had few rights under Spanish rule – Mexican-born Spaniards, or *criollos*, and mixed-blood Indians and Mexicans, the *mestizos*.

In contrast, the conservative centralists, composed mostly of a ruling class of clergy and landowners, favored a strong central government supported by the military. The philosophical differences between the parties, combined with a minority number of former royalist soldiers ready to rise if Spain acted on its repeated threats to reclaim the republic, would lead to political cross currents, intrigue, and divisions that would threaten Mexico's stability for the foreseeable future.

Texas in the Republic of Mexico. In just two years, Stephen F. Austin had negotiated his colonization plan with three governments – New Spain, the Empire of Mexico, and now the Republic of Mexico. A weary Austin again postponed plans to return to his new colony.[14]

Trusting that a stable Mexico was in the best interests of his settlement ambitions, Austin directed his immense intellectual energy – and growing influence – to Mexico's governing structure. The result was *A Project of a Constitution for the Republic of Mexico formed by Stephen F. Austin of Texas – City of Mexico March 19, 1823*, a remarkable essay with some 225 articles covering government organization by a legislature, senate, and congress, as well as elections, laws, executive powers, the army and navy, judicial system, and religion.[15] He started for home in late April after a prolonged, tumultuous year.

Austin's draft became the basis for the 1824 *Federal Constitution of the United Mexican States*, authored by Ramos Arispe[16] and approved by the constitutional congress in October that year. The document, following the Spanish model before it, organized Mexico into states divided into departments that were headed by a provisional chief who oversaw municipalities (Fig. 1) governed by an *ayuntamiento*, a council consisting of an *alcalde* (chairman), *regidores* (councilmen), and *síndico procuradors* (jurisprudence).

Bend in the River landowners Hosea H. League and Thomas Cayce served as regidores to the San Felipe Ayuntamiento.

Texas and its neighboring interior province, Coahuila, were combined into a single state with its capital in Saltillo. Although the number of departments within Coahuila y Texas grew over time, there were initially three: Monclova, Saltillo, and the Department of Béxar (Fig. 2). The latter encompassed the boundaries of Spanish Texas and was usually referred to as the Department of Texas and was locally administered from San Antonio de Béxar.[17]

In October 1824, the Mexican Republic elected its first president, Guadalupe Victoria. Victoria was a federalist whose liberal party ruled a nation mired in debt, its treasury kept afloat by British loans. Like Iturbide before him, his administration soon came under siege, this time a revolt led by centralist vice-president Nicolás Bravo. Swift military intervention by generals Antonio López de Santa Anna and Vicente Guerrero restored stability long enough to hold elections. When the contest winner was disputed, centralist Manuel Gómez Pedraza ended the stalemate by inserting himself in the presidential palace. Santa Anna and other liberal supporters marched on the capital, forcing Pedraza to flee the country. The federalist candidate, Vicente Guerrero, filled the void.[18]

A Brief Battle With Spain. Guerrero's first presidential term, already on shaky ground, was put to the test when Spain determined to take back its former possession. On July 5th, 1829, Spanish General Isidro Barradas, with a fighting force of some 3,500 men, sailed from Cuba for the Mexican port of Tampico.[19] With its limestone bluffs and surrounding lagoons bordered by mangrove and salt grass flats, Tampico was a position easier to defend than to assault. But that was exactly what General Santa Anna, the self-appointed defender of the Mexican Republic, intended to do.

At the behest of President Guerrero – but before congress sanctioned the action – Santa Anna marched for Tampico. With no time to raise funds or troops from the government, his campaign was one of forced conscription and confiscation. Santa Anna's outnumbered cavalry and navy struck the Spanish stronghold, but his bloody offensive failed. He next adopted a siege strategy. The Spanish troops were slowly ravaged by malaria and yellow fever, their supplies and ammunition destroyed by a hurricane. When Santa Anna demanded and received Commander Barradas's unconditional surrender, the architect of the Spanish defeat was hailed a national hero.

Santa Anna's military triumph had little impact on the longevity of Guerrero's government. Guerrero had been granted dictatorial powers by congress during the Spanish invasion, but he had no proclivity to relinquish them. His detractors charged that he was more of a tyrant than a republican. Guerrero's centralist vice president Anastasio Bustamante, backed by the military, resolved to remove the leader. After congress voted Bustamante as Mexico's third president, he summarily executed his former rival.

Mexico in just nine years had been a Spanish possession ruled by a European king, a Mexican monarchy with a reigning emperor, a republic governed by a provisional government, then three presidents as well as two interim presidents. The latter, together, ruled less than 13 days.[20] Transfer of power in Mexico had been turbulent, the product of a revolution, three coups, and at least one dubious election. But there was one constant – Antonio López de Santa Anna.

Santa Anna. Born a Criolla in 1794 in Vera Cruz, Santa Anna began his military career as an infantry cadet in the Spanish Royalist Army. He rose to the rank of general in the new republic, showing a genius for military maneuvers and political mastery, able to exploit their effect because he lacked both compassion and enduring loyalty. He was the royalist soldier who turned against Spain just as the Mexican rebels seemed likely to be victorious. He was the Mexican warrior who masterminded the overthrow of his mentor Agustín de Iturbide, then conspired with President Guadalupe Victoria to crush Nicolás Bravo's coup. He won the support of the Mexican people when he defeated the Spaniard invasion at Tampico. Up to this point, Santa Anna had avowed liberal, federalist principles, but this was to change. When it did, it would alter the course of history.

It was against this backdrop of government mutations that Stephen F. Austin – as persistent as Santa Anna was cunning – attempted to build and perpetuate his colony. Despite the challenges, Austin was largely successful. That success would be tested, though, as a result of anti-colonial decrees passed after the conservatives gained control of Mexico in 1830, and again in 1834 that would put him, and Texas, on a collision course with Santa Anna.

Reconsidering Texas Colonization. Many in Mexico were ill at ease with Anglo-Americans, whether outside its boundaries or within. Outside of its borders, there was persistent tension with its northern neighbor, the United States, which made its expansionist intentions known covertly and sometimes overtly, such as President Andrew Jackson's overtures to purchase Mexican Texas, but a willingness, if necessary, "to seize it."[21] Within its borders, Mexico's worst colonization fears were realized when empresario Haden Edwards' East Texas colony rose in defiance, claiming the eastern portion of the state and drafting their own Declaration of Independence. Called the Fredonian Rebellion, it was put down in 1827. But not without consequences.

The Fredonian Rebellion helped validate the conservative's growing anti-colonial view, motivating Mexico to reevaluate its immigration policy. Integral to the effort were General Manual Mier y Terán and the Comisión de Límites, or Boundary Commission. Initially assigned to survey the state's flora and fauna, mineral resources, and to refine its boundary maps, the commission's duties were quietly expanded to include a commentary on the status and intentions of its Anglo colonists.

Terán's 1829 report concluded that hundreds of illegal Anglo immigrants – "shrewd and unruly" squatters who violated Mexican laws with impunity – were settling Texas. Playing to one of the conservative's greatest suspicions, he expressed concern that large numbers of Anglos were advocating for a separation of Texas from the state of Coahuila.[22] Another on the boundary commission accused the liberal government of doing nothing to prevent Texas from "being stolen by foreign hands," and of ignoring the "imminent danger of the ambitious North Americans," who are a "lazy people of vicious character."[23]

Terán and foreign minister Lucas Alamán proposed reforms that were incorporated into President Anastasio Bustamante's Law of April 6, 1830, a remarkable turn in policy that shook the foundation of the more than 20 colonization enterprises either planned or already in effect. The edict suspended all future settlement contracts, prohibited further immigration from the United States, and encouraged settlement by Europeans, Mexican "convict-soldiers," and "Mexican families" who would be "assigned the best of agricultural lands." It also authorized government commissioners to oversee existing empresario contracts for conformity to the colonization law, refined existing language forbidding the importation of slaves, and authorized a military occupation of Texas.[24]

Anglo response to the Law of 1830 nearly precipitated the Texas Revolution. Although some of the rulings would later be repealed, Mexico had shown her hand. The touchstone for the first bloodshed between the colonists and Mexico was Bustamante's policy for the collection of trade tariffs "with foreign countries," meaning mostly the United States. Although intended to help fill the country's depleted treasury, colonial taxation was a deeply unpopular measure. Worse, it would be enforced by hundreds of troops sent to construct new forts, reinforce existing garrisons in Nacogdoches, San Antonio de Béxar, and La Bahía Goliad, and to provision custom houses along the coast at Copano, Matagorda, Velasco, and Anahuac.[25]

First Skirmishes. The first conflict would occur at Anahuac, where General Manual Mier y Terán – principal author of the Law of 1830 and now commandant of the eastern interior provinces – had posted Col. Juan Davis Bradburn with orders to establish a town, custom house, and garrison.[26] Summer had turned to fall as Bradburn sailed north through Galveston Bay and into Trinity Bay, lightering his troops to shore at the channel leading to Lake Anahuac.

Bradburn, a former Virginian and American filibusterer rewarded by Mexico with a military appointment for his role in the Spanish revolt, would be a central character in the back and forth of the political tide between Terán's conservative reforms and the liberal policymakers that had shaped Texas since Mexican Independence. In one incendiary move, Terán installed George Fisher, a controversial figure of constantly shifting allegiances, as Anahuac's port administrator. Fisher, who took a rigid view of Mexico's new tariff policy, ordered captains of merchant ships who resisted to be detained. Bradburn dealt with their protests by declaring martial law and closing all Texas ports of entry except at Anahuac.[27]

Bradburn also clashed with federalist land commissioner José Francisco Madero over legacy land titles, pronouncing that any signed by Commissioner Madero's hand were invalid. He then threatened military force against Madero's *ayuntamiento* office headquartered at Liberty, on the Trinity River.[28] Terán supported Bradburn in the Madero issue by relocating the land office to Anahuac, then ordered Madero's arrest. Next, Bradburn nullified the licenses of several Anglos who were practicing law, he said, without a sanctioned government certificate. The rumblings of discontent grew louder.

South Carolinian William Barret Travis was one of the many Anglo transplants who flourished in Mexican Texas. In the short time after his arrival, he purchased land and was practicing law at Anahuac with Patrick C. Jack. Now, because of shifting centralist sentiment, his immigration status was illegal, the validity of his law practice was endangered, and his land title was voided. Travis didn't have a lot more to lose.

145

William Travis and Patrick Jack organized the first resistance to Bradburn and the centralist decrees. Forming a volunteer militia at Anahuac, they orchestrated a plot to return escaped slaves that were under Bradburn's protection. When Bradburn had the pair arrested, they joined other colonists who were incarcerated in a brick kiln "for slight and trivial offenses, [their] trial by the civil authorities refused."[29] One of those rebuffed civil authorities was San Felipe Judge William H. Jack, brother of Patrick Jack, who traveled to Anahuac in the late spring of 1832 to negotiate prompt trials for the accused.

Turtle Bayou. Judge Jack's diplomacy failed, the angry judge responding by calling for organized resistance to the "arbitrary and unprincipled conduct" of the "odious" Bradburn.[30] A small army of volunteers answered his call. Marching towards Anahuac, the rebel Texians made camp at Turtle Bayou on Lake Anahuac, fortuitously capturing a unit of cavalry they intended to exchange for Bradburn's prisoners. Bradburn initially agreed to terms, then changed his mind. As the stalemate extended into summer, the Turtle Bayou camp swarmed with horseflies and mosquitoes, the cover of oak mottes and stands of cypress along the shoreline the only escape from the summer sun. There was little food or supplies, and even fewer arms. They would have been justified if they chose to scatter to their homes. Instead, they remained.

A committee was formed in camp to outline their grievances, their resolutions recorded in a document known as the Turtle Bayou Resolutions. The first article charged the current Mexican administration with repeated violations of its country's constitution, using terms such as "total disregard of the law" and "military despotism." In another, they validated their actions as patriots who pledged their lives and fortunes in support of Mexico and its laws.

Then they rolled the dice. For nearly half a year, Santa Anna had been waging a war against the conservative Bustamante regime under a call to arms proclaimed by his Plan of Vera Cruz. The rebels declared for the general in another resolution that praised the "manly resistance" of the "highly talented and distinguished chieftain" in his defense of their "adopted and beloved country."[31] Staking their fortunes – and lives – on the success of the author of the Plan of Vera Cruz was a bold move. Now, it was not only up to Santa Anna to triumph, but the warrior politician would also have to believe their hyperbole.

Brazoria alcalde John Austin was dispatched from the Turtle Bayou camp to Brazoria to procure artillery and ammunition for the anticipated conflict with Bradburn at Anahuac. But a formidable obstacle stood between them and their goal – Fort Velasco. Under the command of Domingo de Ugartechea, only months earlier the Brazos River custom house and adjacent fort were fortified with about 100 troops supplied with muskets, a smooth-bore swivel gun, and an eight-pound cannon.[32]

Fort Velasco. During his march from Turtle Bayou, Austin raised a legion of some 150 volunteers with plans to reduce the fort. The plan called for a river assault on the fort's west side, with land forces attacking from driftwood breastworks stacked along the Gulf shoreline and trenches dug between the fort and East Union Bayou to the north.[33] Securing the American schooner *Brazoria* upriver from the fort, a pair of cannons and a battery of six-pound cannons were mounted, the ship's decks then fortified with a breastwork of cotton bales. Munitions were hastily forged – slugs formed from chains and square bar iron, and jars filled with buckshot.

During the night, the *Brazoria* lowered the stars and stripes from her masthead, hoisting in its place a Mexican flag with the word 'Constitution' sewn across it in large letters.[34] As the vessel tacked downstream, the darkness was pierced by the discharge of the fort's big cannon, the first shot passing through *Brazoria's* spars. Henry Smith, one of the land division commanders, wrote that after the initial salvo "the fort seemed to be one continued blaze of fire," with "their bullets cutting in every direction."[35] A white flag fluttered over the fort in the morning – Ugartechea and his force had run low on ammunition. The Texians allowed the garrison to march out peacefully, Commander Ugartechea and others signing an agreement that they would not take up arms against Texas again.

Velasco was the first engagement between Texian Anglos and soldiers of the Republic of Mexico. Between 7 to 10 Texans were killed with 27 wounded with, in Ugartechea's command, 35 killed and 15 wounded. It was a decisive victory for the Texian volunteers, although Henry Smith later wrote the fighters were "totally undisciplined, badly armed, and under a heavy fire" as they struck a larger, more disciplined army, their actions "more of a reckless hardihood than of true courage."[36]

John Austin was free to sail for Anahuac, but he didn't go. The Mexican government had prudently removed Bradburn from his Anahuac command and released the prisoners. It is doubtful that Austin could have delivered those cannons anyway. The *Brazoria* was so badly damaged it couldn't sail, the underwriters billing the Mexican government for the loss.[37]

Averting a War. The rebels of Anahuac and Fort Velasco expected their day of reckoning, and it came with Santa Anna's orders for Brigadier General José Antonio Mexía and 400 troops to sail from Matamoros and quash the Texian uprising. Dropping anchor at the mouth of the river, Mexía surveyed the damage at Fort Velasco, then continued upstream to Brazoria for a parley with Stephen F. Austin and the rebel principals. They insurgents pled their case. Their actions and the wording of the Turtle Bayou Resolutions, they argued, were consistent with Santa Anna's Plan of Vera Cruz. Mexía and his army stood down.

Mexía had intended on an invasion, but it became, instead, a celebration. Cannons and muskets fired salutes, the Texians at Brazoria organizing a public gala replete with a dinner and ball dedicated to Santa Anna. Glasses were raised to the general, the leader who "started as the Washington of his country, and [should] continue to do so to the end." Mexía, in his toast, pledged to promote the future prosperity of the colonies and "to prevent the exercise of caprice by the government towards emigrants." Although lost amidst the revelry, among Stephen F. Austin's salutes was an ominous "the connection between [Coahuila y Texas] is unnatural and ought to be dissolved."[38] It was a bold proclamation from the usually statesman-like empresario, and it foretold the future.

The approximately 150 men who answered Judge Jack's call to arms during the spring of 1832 could very well have been initiated the Texas Revolution, and it might have ended that day with Mexía's army at Brazoria. Probably the only reason it didn't was its timing. Had the Anahuac uprising occurred earlier, Bustamante may have succeeded in uniting his countrymen to a common cause, putting an end to both the rebellion and Anglo colonization. But Santa Anna had already eroded much of the president's popular support, and the success of his Plan of Vera Cruz gained momentum at the critical moment when the rebels – maintaining that the revolt was a show of allegiance to Mexico, the constitution, and Santa Anna – could be believed.

The Players. Of the men who played critical roles in the events of 1832, some would reappear in history while others would not. The originator of the Law of 1830, General

Manual Mier y Terán, remained loyal to Bustamante, taking up arms in his defense against a later Santa Anna coup. When Bustamante was defeated, Terán on July 3, 1832, made a dramatic exit by falling on his sword. The place he chose was the courtyard where former emperor Agustín de Iturbide, the rebel leader he supported during the fight for Mexican Independence, had been executed.[39]

Anahuac commander Col. Juan Davis Bradburn was relieved of duty on July 2. He fled Anahuac for New Orleans with a Texian posse at his heels, losing his horse and swimming the Sabine River as he made a narrow escape. He would return to Texas and retire in Mexico. As for his nemesis William Travis, Travis would reappear at Anahuac in 1835 and would, again, be instrumental in the closing of its tariff house. Eight months later he would die defending the Alamo.

Connecticut native John Austin was a distant cousin to Stephen F. Austin and a rising star who first came to Texas as part of the failed Long filibustering expedition. Captured, he spent time in a Spanish prison. He received a land grant in Harrisburg. Active in civil affairs, Austin was a port officer, alcalde of the Brazoria Municipality, an elected militia general, and a delegate to the Convention of 1832. Austin died during the 1833 cholera epidemic along with his two children. His Buffalo Bayou land grant became the city of Houston.

Velasco commander Lt. Col. Domingo de Ugartechea, despite agreeing not to take up arms after his Velasco defeat, returned to Texas as commander at San Antonio de Béxar in 1835. Here he would be linked to another cannon episode, giving the order to dispatch cavalry to reclaim a six-pounder in the possession of DeWitt colonists at Gonzales. His action resulted in the first battle of the Texas Revolution and the famous flag of the rebellion with its inscription 'Come and Take It.'[40]

José Antonio Mexía, remaining a steadfast federalist to the end, sided with the Texians during the onset of the Revolution. Captured during a failed attempt to overthrow Santa Anna and the national government in 1839, he was executed. Henry Smith would become Texas' first but troubled governor, and later served under Sam Houston as the Secretary of the Treasury. He followed the lure of California gold, dying in 1851 in a mining camp.[41]

A cautious Stephen F. Austin returned to San Felipe and penned a statement to the colonists. There was discontent in the settlement, he wrote, fomenting because of the Law of 1830 and because many colonists were concerned that the Anahuac and Velasco agitators could have jeopardized all they had worked for in Texas. Yet he addressed the returning rebels not as traitors but as "Fellow Citizens and Soldiers of the Santa Anna Volunteer Company," rationalizing that the uprising embodied their duty as Mexican citizens. Now, he counseled, was a time to rejoice with the return to the "free democracy of the nation under the banner of the distinguished patriot and leader, General Antonio Lopez de Santa Anna."[42]

1832 had been an unsettled year for Mexico and its centralist president, Bustamante. In addition to the implications of his call for military actions in the colonies, his treasury was empty, and he made powerful enemies by abolishing freedom of the press and marching several popular republicans before firing squads. Santa Anna was systematically whittling away at his support, and in Zacatecas, lawyer Valentin Gómez Farias had led the state in revolt.[43] A month after the battle of Velasco, Bustamante vacated the presidency. He was replaced by interim president Melchor Muzquìz who, in turn, was quickly traded for Manuel Gómez Pedraza in what was his second unremarkable term as president.

Legislating for an Independent Texas. 1832 was as eventful for Austin as it was turbulent for Mexico. Austin expended enormous energy in defusing the potential consequences of Anahuac and Velasco. Next, he turned his attention to organizing the Convention of 1832. Fifty-five delegates assembled that fall in San Felipe, their objective to craft a petition calling for the authority to organize militias and establish safety committees, to repeal of the Law of 1830, and most importantly, to demand a separation of Texas from the State of Coahuila y Texas. The Constitution of 1824 included language allowing Texas, at a future date, to become a state within the Republic of Mexico. Austin was not alone when he resolved that the time was now.

In Austin's version of the Convention of 1832, the Anglo Texians and Mexican Tejanos "all united as one man."[44] That was not true. There weren't any representatives from the Tejano districts, and their omission was not lost on the Mexican government. Ramon Muzquiz, political chief of Texas, was so incensed that didn't present the petition to congress, rebuking its authors by charging that the convention was an illegal gathering and "derogatory to the supreme government."[45]

The failing was a strong reproach for Austin, and for a short time, he despaired. In his response to Muzquiz, he wrote that "I have but little hope of obtaining anything from the government of Mexico," and although the condition of Texas "is bad, we may fear to see it still worse." A pessimistic Austin then added, "I am settling up all my business and in April I will go to the north for six months or one year. There is little to be hoped for in Texas." He didn't go.[46]

By December, Austin had regained his vigor, and this time wisely included Tejano leaders in plans for a second convention. He again advised them of his goal to separate Texas from Coahuila and asked for support on reparation for "all the insults offered to Texas, and all her grievances, and to demand full satisfaction." Then he presented an ultimatum: "If our grievances [are] not fully redressed by the first day of March next, Texas would then proceed immediately to organize a local government."[47]

The Tejanos pledged their support for a Texas separate from Coahuila but would have no part of his threat to form an independent government. Neither would some of the Anglo colonists, notably Anahuac alcalde John A. Williams, who disparaged Austin for his inflammatory rhetoric.[48] A year later, those same sentiments would have Austin arrested.

Richard Royall, father of Bend in the River landowner James Royall, represented Matagorda in the 1833 Convention and was chairman of the Matagorda Committee of Public Safety and Correspondence.

Austin's address to the second convention, held in April 1833, was unflinching. The nation, he said, was "torn and broken asunder by political parties" coveting "the supreme executive power of the nation by the force of arms," but in the end creating only "confusion and bloody discord."[49] He criticized the "evils" of ignorant and corrupt alcaldes who occupied the highest official office in Texas, although one "seldom sought by those who are most qualified to fill it." He railed against civil jurisprudence, in which matters had to be appealed 700 miles distant in Saltillo, the process so burdensome as to "amount to a total denial of justice" by a tribunal that "knows not nor cares not" about the "lives, liberty, and honor of the accused."[50] Importantly, his earlier threat to form a sovereign government did not surface.

Another New President. During the spring of 1833, Mexico was again preoccupied with presidential politics and in no mood to entertain Anglo demands. It was an election that would change history. Antonio López de Santa Anna became Mexico's new president and avowed federalist Valentin Gómez Farias its new vice-president. For his part, Santa Anna preferred the battlefield to the presidential palace, but there was never any uncertainty about who was running the country.[51]

Undaunted, Austin took the convention proposals in Mexico City. Traveling from the coast in July by stagecoach, the Mexico he saw was in chaos. He was detained because his passport, signed by one Mexican general, was rejected by authorities loyal to another. A military siege by centralist general Gabriel Durán caused another delay. President-elect Santa Anna and General Mariano Arista had moved to suppress it, but then Arista traded sides for Durán. For his part, Santa Anna was at one point taken hostage, then somehow later emerged as a hero. The insurrection was quelled by General Guadalupe Victoria, who relied on his support from the local militia because the regular Mexican Army joined the revolt.[52] Had it not been so deadly, the affair might have been comical.

Austin's Troubles. Austin would spend months in Mexico awaiting action on the second convention. During that time, he nearly died from cholera then recovered long enough to lobby for the convention reform articles and watched as former president Bustamante and the hapless General Arista, with about 300 others of "the banished," sailed into exile. He met several times with President Santa Anna who, he said, "speaks very friendly about Texas."[53]

While Austin waited, he penned a letter repeating that, if the convention's application was refused, Texas should organize an autonomous government, but wisely added: "on the basis that it is part of the Mexican Confederation."[54] To this point his correspondence was personal, but by October the impatient empresario formally directed his opinions to an official office, the Béxar Ayuntamiento. Surprised by his words, the Ayuntamiento upbraided Austin for opinions "exceedingly rash," "injurious to the colonists," and potentially treasonous.[55] Then they forwarded his communication to acting president Farias.

Farias had heard these words in conversations with Austin before, but now they were part of the official record. In January of 1834, Farias had empresario Stephen F. Austin arrested for treason. Of the 18 months Austin would spend in prison, five were in the "dungeons of the Inquisition" – Mexico City's infamous Palace of the Inquisition – with part of that time in solitary confinement.[56] Later, Austin would write that Farias became "the most violent and bitter enemy I had."[57]

Appeasing Texas. Although vice president Farias and his congress did not formally recognize the Convention of 1833, they certainly understood the consequences if they continued to ignore it. Conceding to convention calls for increased government representation within Coahuila y Texas, a Brazos Department was established with administrative headquarters in San Felipe de Austin, and a Nacogdoches Department added. The government seat of the original Béxar Department was unchanged. Revisions to the judicial system included an appeals court and trial by jury. English was permitted in schools and public matters, and religious freedoms were granted. Perhaps most importantly, the Law of 1830 article restricting immigration was repealed.[58] These were big steps, enacted in a remarkably short time. But there was a crucial omission – Mexico would not recognize separation of Texas from Coahuila.

Although they weren't yet apparent, there would be repercussions to other legislation passed during late 1833 and 1834. One was relocating the Coahuila y Texas capital from the conservative stronghold of Saltillo to federalist dominated Monclova. The other was the deferral of import tariffs for a year that, while initially considered constructive, only served to postpone the inevitable dissent to 1835.[59]

Waiting for Austin. Austin languished. It wasn't until June – six months after his arrest – that he finally appeared for a hearing before a military tribunal. That body, however, determined the matter was a civil offense. Another three months passed before a civil court concluded that the charges were not in their jurisdiction. Next, the case was reviewed by a federal district judge who decided that, since Austin did not reside in his district, he, too, had no authority to render judgment. Finally, the charges were presented to the Supreme Court of the United Mexican States – not to hear the case, though, but to resolve which court had the authority to handle the indictment.[60]

Leaders in Texas were unsure of what to think. Austin's legal challenges were taken up in Monclova, where the Coahuila y Texas congress penned a "spirited and highly honorable" appeal to the general government on the empresario's behalf.[61] The Matagorda Ayuntamiento petitioned Mexico City to communicate the specific nature of the charges against Austin, as up to this time they had only heard the "popular rumor" that Colonel Austin had been "rendered obnoxious to the general government in consequence of statements" made "against his fidelity to the union."[62]

Then Austin confused them. In an unexpected admission published by the *Texas Republican* in November 1834, Austin wrote that he had never advocated for a Texas independent of Coahuila. It was not him, he said, but others who sought "to excite public opinion in favor of that measure." The man who had clamored for a resolution to injustices with such vigor that he strained the support of Tejanos and Anglos alike was suddenly advising his countrymen to take no part in any inflammatory plans or pronouncements, and to "preserve a dead silence." At face value, his was a remarkable change of heart. More likely, he was trying to appease his captors. Austin wanted to go home.[63]

Austin was released on Christmas Day 1834 after congress extended a general amnesty for prisoners charged with political crimes.[64] Although Austin was free from prison, he was not allowed to return to Texas until late summer, 1835. During his time away from the colonies, confusion – the hallmark of Texian and Mexican politics since its birth as a nation – had spread closer to home, to the state of Coahuila y Texas. The principal architect of the disorder was President Santa Anna.

Santa Anna's Change of Heart. Santa Anna kept his eye on the pulse of the nation as Farias's liberal reforms took flight. They were popular in the northern frontier, but the military, Catholic church, and moneyed landowners writhed in discontent. Outlining their demands in a document titled the Plan of Cuernavaca, the conservatives broke with the government in the spring of 1834, pledging Santa Anna singular authority over the military and the government if he embraced their cause.[65] It was a prize too great to squander. The former champion of the republican federalist party seized the opportunity and switched political loyalties.

Now, as quickly as the Farias-championed reforms were affected, Santa Anna had them repealed. Then he ordered all the citizen's militias to disarm. Protesting the president's not so veiled threat of force against them, the Mexican congress and most of the state's legislatures were impelled to adjourn.[66] Now, running as head of the centralist party, Santa

Anna secured the popular vote during the fall 1834 presidential election. He returned to Vera Cruz in the winter of 1835, installing Vice President Miguel Barragán in Mexico City as acting president[67] while he prepared, again, for the battlefield. During the election, the warrior-politician had carried most of the Mexican states. Only Zacatecas and Coahuila y Texas were steadfast in their opposition. He had a plan for them.

Moving Towards War. The Texas Revolution was probably inevitable. From the Anglo point of view, it was – after all – Manifest Destiny. From the Mexican side, the recently avowed centralist Santa Anna was prepared to dispose of the democratic model and its liberal reform supporters. The only unknown was *when* the confrontation would occur. That uncertainty was reduced by parallel events that combined to propel the conflict towards sooner rather than later.

Central to the Revolution's timing was the decision to move the capital of Coahuila y Texas from conservative Saltillo to republican Monclova in 1833. Aligned with Farias just as the centralists regained power, Monclova's administrators quickly antagonized the national government. Most offensive were their strategies to raise money through speculation in land they did not own, and their persistence in forming militias that were contrary to law. Both themes played out in a theatre of high stakes political intrigue that resulted in the final splintering between conservatives and liberals in Mexico's northern frontier. Then there was the Anglo response to the reimposition of tariffs, as divisive in 1835 as it was in 1830. Any one of these affronts was enough to provide Santa Anna with the justification, if he needed any at all, on a course of subjugation. Combined, they were incendiary.

Monclova's Land Speculation. One of acting president Farias's decrees tendered vacant public lands to the highest bidder, the proceeds intended to supply Mexico's treasury. On paper, it made sense. But the edict allowed the governor and legislature to engage in the real estate business, the potential for political and financial reward so great that it brought out the worst in both elected officials and Anglos near to the administration.

Monclova's first land decree, penned in 1834, offered vacant land incentives only to Mexican companies.[68] Some of the nominated parcels, however, were hardly vacant. Many included settlers still awaiting clear land titles in Milam's and Wavell's colonies. They didn't get them. That year the Monclova administration rendered their claims invalid, then sold the land with the edict that "its occupants must yield to the eleven league claimants."[69]

Controversy continued to build with two more public land acts. The first, passed in April 1834, involved the sale of 400 leagues. A year later a second allowed for the governor, at his sole discretion, to peddle another 400 leagues. Charges of political bribes, graft, and corruption were leveled by both Texians and Tejanos alike. The good fortune of Monclova insiders who amassed large land holdings, such as Stephen F. Austin's business partner Samuel M. Williams, John Durst, Robert Peebles, and Francis W. Johnson, would be short-lived.[70] Soon, they would become enemies of the state.

Mexico City's response to Monclova's scheming was strong. The national congress, reaffirming that only the general government had the authority to approve land dispositions, immediately annulled Coahuila y Texas's second land act. Newly seated Monclova governor Agustín Viesca continued selling land certificates anyway.[71] Viesca's disregard for the federal colonization law was illegal and even treasonous, but he still hadn't played all the cards in his hand.

Monclova's Militias. Monclova's government speculators took payment for land not just in cash, but in exchange for establishing, or serving in, the Coahuila y Texas militia. The action was justified as vital for public defense, a necessity to "restrain the arrogance of wild Indians," and "repress the ferocity of the savages." Santa Anna, however, correctly viewed militias as a potential threat to his government, banning them in May 1834 and again by official decree the following year. Monclova's refusal to dissolve their militias put the Coahuila y Texas capital yet again on the wrong side of president. If it had allowed it to continue, Monclova would have grown a sizable army. As part of their land contract, for instance, Williams, Peebles, and Johnson promised Viesca they would raise a force of 1,000 volunteers.[72]

> ***Early Bend in the River landowner Thomas Alley was elected a lieutenant in the First Company of the Austin Battalion civic militia under Colonel Stephen F. Austin.***

A Struggle of State. In June 1834, the Coahuila y Texas executive counsel at Monclova boldly denounced Santa Anna and the Plan of Cuernavaca. The next month, principals from the former capital, Saltillo, declared against Monclova and its constitutional congress, establishing their own opposition government that voided all laws passed in Monclova after 1833.[73] The two rival capitals replaced their elected governors with military officers and prepared for civil war.[74] Before much blood was shed, both factions turned to Santa Anna for arbitration. His decision in December 1834, ratifying Monclova as the seat of government, was calculated. Although he could argue his position on constitutional grounds Monclova, he knew, would give him pretext to resolve the Texas problem. It did.

The sparring between Monclova and Saltillo spread to Texas, and it forced the leadership to take sides. In September, Superior Judge of Texas Thomas J. Chambers, José Antonio Vásquez, and Oliver Jones – the Texas delegates to Monclova – prepared an address describing the Coahuila y Texas situation as one of "universal and frightful disorder and confusion." Seeking to "save the country from anarchy," they called for a provisional congress. The usually restrained Tejanos in San Antonio de Béxar, led by alcalde and political chief Juan Nepomuceno Seguín, endorsed the plan.[75]

The task of soliciting delegates to attend the convention and form a provisional government, scheduled for November 15, 1834, went to political chief of the Brazos Department Henry Smith. Few were willing to follow his lead. The Nacogdoches Department termed the assembly unconstitutional, and both the Brazoria and Columbia municipalities voted overwhelmingly against Texas adopting any form of its own government.[76]

The central committee of the Brazos Department prepared a formal response to Seguín and Smith's proposal in an October meeting at San Felipe. In a document titled *Address to the People of Texas by the Central Committee*, they called the separatists position "violent, reckless and ambitious," their views "weak counsel" and warned that the "wanton, ungrateful violation of Constitution and Laws which we have sworn to support" would lead to "consequent ruin."[77] The composition of the central committee was intriguing. Some were undoubtedly sincere, trusting their actions were consistent with the still absent Austin. But among the members were William H. Jack and William B. Travis, who only four years earlier had hazarded the future of Texas at Anahuac. The roster also included Francis W.

Johnson and Robert Peebles, who stood to lose fortunes in lands amassed from their Monclova dealings.[78]

Samuel M. Williams wrote that "the demagogue" Henry Smith suffered "a mortifying defeat" in his attempt to rally support for the separatist cause.[79] As Austin's business partner, Williams's apparent loyalty to Texas and the Mexican federation was understandable. But he went further in correspondence directed to Colonel Juan Almonte, exposing names of those whose actions were contrary to Mexico's central government. Williams's patriotic fervor was not altruistic. Like Johnson and Peebles, he had a lot to lose – notably his hundreds of leagues of land granted by Monclova – if Texas claimed independence.[80]

No Turning Back. Events in April and May of 1835 accelerated rapidly. That spring, Santa Anna was busy brutalizing both rebels and townspeople alike in the rebellious state of Zacatecas, a move that shouldn't have been lost on Coahuila y Texas. William B. Travis forced the surrender of the tax collector and garrison at the port of Anahuac. Saltillo again broke from Monclova and its governor, Agustín Viesca, who continued to push Mexico City to its breaking point.

In response to the uncertain political landscape, the colonists organized the first Committee of Safety and Correspondence at Mina that May. By August, over a dozen more were formed across Texas. That month General Martín Perfecto de Cos, Commandant General of the Eastern Interior States, was readying his army at Matamoros for Coahuila y Texas. The last remaining federalist state in the Republic of Mexico knew he was coming, but they weren't prepared.

Reducing Zacatecas. Like Coahuila y Texas, Zacatecas remained steadfast to republican principles and the Constitution of 1824. More importantly, it also refused to disarm its militia. Santa Anna set his sights on the insubordinate federalist state in April 1835. Zacatecas, a rich silver-mining region situated southwest of Coahuila, was bordered to the west by the rugged topography of the Sierra Madre Occidental and the east by the high plains of Guadalupe. It was here that Zacatecas Governor Francisco García, with 4,000 militia and a line of artillery, prepared to take a stand against Santa Anna's 3,400 regular troops.[81]

García's refusal to accept Santa Anna's surrender offer was met by a thrust that struck the defenders simultaneously on five fronts. In Santa Anna's account, just two hours of "continued exertion" were enough to "secure the victory," the field afterwards presenting "a most horrid picture." His triumphant army next moved on the capital, its troops pillaging the city as their reward. In just three days, the army took 2,700 prisoners, amassing a body count of over 2,000 militia and townspeople, the latter including women and children. Relishing his success, the general wrote of the rebel's "misfortune" but how, ultimately, they would "be accountable to God and to the nation, and on them will fall the consequences in due time."[82]

As Zacatecas smoldered, the jubilant Supreme Commander paraded his army through the countryside, celebrating in cities along the route to Mexico City. Had Santa Anna abandoned the bravado and chosen, instead, to march to Matamoras and reinforce General Cos as he readied for the Texas campaign, the outcome of the Texas Revolution might have been very different.

Anahuac and Travis, Again. Mexico's northern frontier suffered from too few ships, no cavalry, and few arms. Texian and American shipping merchants seized the opportunity.

Smuggling ran rampant until, in January 1835, Captain Antonio Tenorio was ordered to reestablish the Anahuac custom house (Fig. 3). Provided with a detachment of just 34 troops, Tenorio recognized the folly of his "deplorably isolated" posting. His soldiers deserted, and many who remained were paid more as Anglo spies than they received in military wages. Relations with the colonists were at best indifferent – nearly all refused to provide Tenorio with any supplies – but, at worst, he feared that they might attack the garrison at any time.[83]

Tenorio was reinforced in May, finally flexing his military muscle with the confiscation of two ships by the Mexican schooner *Moctezuma* for a minor bureaucratic offense, a lack of clearance papers. The action was not well received. Twenty colonists framed a petition resolving to prevent collection of any future tariffs, complaining of the "poverty of the citizens" and the inequity of duties not collected in other ports. Tensions rose a month later when Tenorio arrested Andrew Briscoe and DeWitt Clinton Harris on an alleged smuggling charge.[84]

That spring, General Cos was in Matamoros preparing his army to reinforce the Anahuac custom port. His May 26 missive detailing his plans was intercepted at San Felipe, however, the communication serving to eliminate any doubts the colonists might have had whether troops were about to move on Texas. Then a second letter, couriered from Texas military commander Ugartechea, was seized. It not only confirmed the plan but carried his threat that "these revolutionists will be ground down."[85]

In response, James B. Miller, the new political chief of the Department of Brazos, called a consultation of the central committee at San Felipe on June 22. Miller, one of the hawks in the Texas "war party," considered the seized dispatches sufficient evidence to raise a militia and advance on Anahuac before Cos could arrive with reinforcements. The committee voted him down. Miller and the war party then went around the committee, and in a secret meeting authorized William Travis to assemble a company for the Anahuac undertaking. Travis set sail from Harrisburg in less than a week.[86]

A fresh breeze carried the sloop *Ohio* from her moorings in Buffalo Bayou, past Morgan's Point and into Trinity Bay. Dropping anchor outside Anahuac, Captain Travis brashly rowed ashore to offer surrender terms. Tenorio asked for time. Instead, Travis and his company advanced. Rather than defend their position, Tenorio and his troops scattered for the trees, bayous, and prairie. Without firing a shot, Travis's 30-man volunteer company succeeded in subduing a garrison of 44 regular soldiers in less than an hour.

After the rebels freed Briscoe and Harris from the unoccupied fort, Tenorio reappeared from hiding and agreed to surrender. The Anahuac custom house grew smaller on the horizon as the *Ohio* returned to Harrisburg with its prisoners. It was the Fourth of July, and the rebels invited Tenorio and his men to a barbeque and a ball, where Tenorio "waltzed and talked French all evening" with one of the ladies in attendance.[87]

Travis did not receive a hero's welcome. Instead, his actions were condemned by an Anglo population mostly still loyal to the "peace party" and still optimistic in negotiating with Mexico.[88] Travis had put those goals at risk, just as he had in 1830. A livid General Cos ordered James Miller "to proceed immediately and without excuse to the apprehension of the ungrateful and bad citizen W.B. Travis." He railed that Travis's "scandalous attack upon Anahuac criminal [was] in every point of view," and would not "pass with impunity." He ended the communication with a warning to the colony – "that by chastisement of the delinquent, no doubt may be entertained of the good faith of those necessary to their prosperity, and to the increase of their well acquired property."[89]

Monclova on the Run. William B. Travis was just one name recorded on General Cos's arrest warrant. Others added to the lengthening list eventually included the influential separatists Robert M. Williamson and Moseley Baker, Coahuila y Texas legislator José M.J. Carbajal, Santa Anna's fallen ally Lorenzo de Zavala, and land speculators Samuel M. Williams, Francis Johnson, and John Durst.[90] At the top of the list was Monclova governor Agustín Viesca.

Viesca had only just taken the oath of the governor's office when he assembled his growing militia to march on rival Saltillo. General Cos threatened bloodshed if they didn't immediately disband. A week later the governor and his legislature abandoned Monclova, relocating the seat of government to the perceived safety of San Antonio de Béxar. Here they should have been repelled, but San Antonio de Béxar military commandant declared his small force no match for the rebellious Tejanos. General Cos dispatched two detachments from Nuevo León to provide support, certain that the "conceited foreigners will realize that the Supreme Government has sufficient power to suppress them."[91] Viesca and several in his legislature were intercepted and arrested by one of Cos's detachments.

The Mexican army, albeit only a small part of it, was at last on Texas soil. Most Texians were indifferent. Many did not believe the news – it was only a rumor, they thought, spread by land speculators who hoped to profit "by an agitation of the people."[92] As for Viesca's capture, no Tejano or Texian army was raised to secure his release. Loyalists mostly perceived him with disgust, a result of his "shameful bartering" and "highly obnoxious" sacrifice of valuable public lands.[93] It was spring of 1835, and Texas had not yet found an excuse to go to war.

Summer. Advocates of the war and peace parties debated the future of Texas during the summer of 1835 at public meetings and through the local Committees of Safety and Correspondence. The war party argued that the colonists were blind to the obvious.

Only months earlier, Santa Anna had crushed Zacatecas for offenses of arguably less magnitude than Coahuila y Texas. They contended that the two war department dispatches seized in May demonstrated that a Texas invasion was imminent. Then there was Cos's July circular to the Texas military departments warning that those subscribing to the "excitement of some bad citizens" and who forgot their duties to the nation that "adopted them as her children" would be repressed "with [a] strong arm." Cos added the chilling phrase that "the inevitable consequences of the war will bear upon them and their property."[94]

The peace party remained on the side of caution. Stephen F. Austin was still detained in Mexico, and many worried for his safety. They dismissed war party cries that the Mexican army was intent on "the purpose of compelling you either to leave the country or submit to an imperial government" and to "keep you in subjugation."[95] Most peace party advocates had no reason to doubt the explanation proffered by both Cos and Ugartechea at various times– that troops were only settling the Saltillo-Monclova quarrel and ending the "squandering of public lands."[96]

As the Texians debated, General Cos was implementing his war strategy. In July, he ordered the sloop of war *Correo Mexicano* to Anahuac in response to Travis's treasonous venture. In preparation for the arrival of his army, he installed Colonel Nicholas Candelle as the new commander at La Bahía. Candelle, described as "a man of barbarous antecedents," immediately jailed La Bahía's alcalde, extorted thousands of dollars from the treasury, stripped the townspeople of their arms, and pressed its citizens into manual labor for his detachment.[97]

Fall. Texians seemed to view their future in terms of black or white – they were either in the war camp or the peace camp. Stephen F. Austin, at last setting sail for Texas after more than a year and a half, was more visionary. Although not ready to share his beliefs in political circles, he did voice them in a letter to his cousin, Mary Austin Holley. Texas, he wrote, "ought to become part of the United States," an opinion he kept to himself because he did not want "anything [to] transpire in the public prints to alarm the Mexican government." Austin's Texas must be a slave state – not for economic reasons, but to provide stability to neighboring Louisiana as it grappled with "the overgrown slave population of that state." Of Santa Anna, he wrote that the general "told me he should visit Texas next month – as a friend." But he was at last suspicious of Santa Anna's intentions, opining that "his visit is uncertain – his friendship more so. We must rely on ourselves, and prepare for the worst."[98]

Austin landed at Quintana in the first week of September aboard Thomas McKinney's merchant schooner *San Felipe*. Ironically, he arrived just as the sloop of war *Correo Mexicano*, ordered to Anahuac by Cos the previous July, was boarding the captured American brig *Tremont*. The *San Felipe* squared off, cannons roared, and the damaged *Correo* disengaged. Overtaken, it surrendered to the Texas ship. Cos's captain and crew were charged with piracy and locked in chains.[99]

Over a thousand colonists swarmed Brazoria to pay their respect to Austin. The peace party quickly offered their leader the chair of the Brazos Department central committee. War and peace parties alike pressed Austin for his sentiments on the upcoming consultation at Washington-on-the-Brazos. Austin was asked if he supported its tenet "to secure peace if it is to be obtained on constitutional terms, and to prepare for war if war is inevitable."[100] He did. Austin had written those same words to Mary Austin Holley a week earlier, but now he expanded on them in his speech at a banquet given in his honor.

In his Brazoria address, Austin voiced his support for letting the people of Texas decide, through elected representatives, if they were prepared to "relinquish all or a part of their constitutional and vested rights under the Constitution of 1824." It was a constitution, he orated, that was "about to be destroyed," potentially subjecting the country to "unlimited dictation." His next words horrified the peace party. Should Mexico send an armed force to Texas, he said, war would be not only an "inevitable consequence" but a "solemn duty" and a "sound and correct moral principle".[101]

Only days later General Cos's armed warship, the *Veracruzana*, passed through Aransas Bay and lowered her sails on the north shoreline of Copano Bay. Two other ships followed, that together, brought his army to between 400 and 500 troops. Mexico had sent an armed force to Texas.

As Long as it's a Row. As Cos and his army organized, Stephen F. Austin authored a circular on behalf of the San Felipe central committee calling for "every man in Texas" to take up arms and "take to the field at once." They were to rendezvous on the 28th of September "in the low country" at "League's old place on the Colorado" and at a second location at "James Kerr's on La Baca" (Fig. 3). For those unable to join the advance, he wrote, they "are required to unite with the reserve and report themselves to the committee of safety in this place and be ready for marching orders."[102]

The two places Austin selected as muster points that late September effectively marked the beginning of the Texas Revolution. "Leagues old place on the Colorado" referred to the Bend in the River land originally granted to Captain Jacob Jennings, and by 1835, to the former Revolutionary War hero Thomas Cayce. Austin's choice of the location was a practical one – Cayce operated a ferry that crossed the Colorado River on the main road connecting Brazoria and Columbia to La Bahía (Goliad). A mix of prairie and oak mottes provided suitable troop encampments between the ferry and, just downriver, the original Hosea H. League plantation house.

> ***"Leagues old place on the Colorado" referred to the Bend in the River, the land originally granted to Captain Jacob Jennings, then Hosea League, and by 1835 to former Revolutionary War hero Thomas Cayce.***

The second site, "James Kerr's on La Baca," was the league of land granted to James Kerr that was situated between the Lavaca River and Navidad River above the Atascocita-La Bahía Road near Guadalupe Victoria. Both Kerr and his cabin were well-known to Texians. Kerr had been a delegate to the 1832 and 1833 Conventions, his homestead a landmark to settlers in DeWitt's and DeLeon's colonies. Importantly, Kerr's place was near the action. Just as crucial was that the area's colonists had, at a meeting they called the previous July at William Millican's gin house, already made it known they were organized and prepared to fight.

Located on the Navidad River north of the town of Santa Anna – soon to be renamed Texana – Millican's gin house was crowded on that steamy July day. The Texians who arrived by boat, horse, or carriage all came for the same reason – the Committees of Safety and Correspondence had alerted them that General Martín Perfecto de Cos was preparing to crush Texas's insurrections. Alarmed, emotions were high as the men gathered to plan a course of action.[103]

Their discussion was spirited, but the assembly quickly and unanimously declared Texas an independent sovereignty. They penned their tenants in a document known as the Navidad Resolutions – considered the precursor to the Texas Declaration of Independence – and it was couriered to most of the other Texas municipalities. Its supporters knew their words were treasonous, punishable by death. Before they disbanded, the men agreed to form a militia and prepare for hostilities. It was these men that Austin believed he could rely on now.

> ***Bend in the River landowner Thomas Alley was at the Millican Gin House in July, and with brothers John and William, were members of the assembly that declared Texas an independent sovereignty and volunteered to form a militia.***

The volunteers who answered Austin's call were ordered to prevent General Cos and his army from reaching Béxar. They didn't know whether they were about to face 50 troops or 500. They also didn't know what, exactly, they were fighting for. In the words of historian Noah Smithwick, the volunteers had no "distinct understanding as to the position we were to assume toward Mexico. Some were for independence; some for the Constitution of 1824; and some for anything, just so it was a row."[104]

Gonzales – the Lexington of Texas. Express messages fanned out across Texas from the coast with the news of General Cos's arrival at Copano Bay. Matagorda and Bay Prairie settlers first received word from James W. Fannin Jr., who appealed for volunteers to return with him to Copano and engage Cos's army before it reached Béxar. Then he changed his plans. The Texian militia, he learned, was facing off against Mexican cavalry at Gonzales (Fig. 3). Fannin turned north.[105]

Located in DeWitt's Colony in the rolling plains below the Balcones Escarpment where the San Marcos joined the Guadalupe River, Gonzales had little military value to either side. It did, however, possess a small six-pound brass cannon issued by the Mexican army for defense against Indian depravations. San Antonio de Béxar military commandant Ugartechea wanted it returned. It was late September when an ox cart convoyed by five riders stopped at the edge of the Guadalupe River. There its leader, Corporal Casimira de León, sent a dispatch to Gonzales alcalde Andrew Ponton requesting surrender of the ordnance.

Gonzales's 18-man militia decided to make a stand. Resisting de León's directive and stalling for time, riders were sent throughout the countryside to seek reinforcements. In response, Ugartechea ordered Lieutenant Francisco de Castañeda from Béxar with a hundred horsemen. During his advance, the lieutenant learned that the town's militia snuck across the river, taking de León and the cart drivers' prisoner.[106]

Castañeda, on one side of the river, scribbled messages while the Texian militia guarded the opposite bank. Their hedging continued – "the alcalde was away", came a reply, or "the department political chief would have to be consulted." Finally, the message came that the Texians would only yield the cannon through force.[107] During the delay, volunteers had rallied to Gonzales, their numbers growing from 18 to approximately 140. Among them were Col. John H. Moore with a company from LaGrange, the Minute Men of Lavaca under Thomas Alley, Capt. George M. Collinsworth with the Matagorda Volunteers, James Fannin's Brazos Guards, and Robert M. Coleman with the Bastrop Company.[108]

Captain Thomas Alley owned the southeast corner of the Crier Survey where Spread Oaks Lodge is located. He raised a militia called the Minute Men of Lavaca and was one of the first to reach the action at Gonzales.

With his army now approaching nearly 200 men, Castañeda moved west along the river, seizing cattle, crops, and gorging on ripe watermelons before reaching the homestead of Ezekiel Williams. While the Mexicans slept, the Texians at Gonzales took a vote, overwhelmingly favoring an assault on the Mexican position. Command Colonel Moore organized an effort to unearth the divisive cannon buried in a nearby peach orchard, hoisting it into a two-wheeled cotton cart (Fig. 4). Blacksmiths readied the weapon, forging iron balls into shot and hammering "ugly-looking missiles" from pieces of chain. Armed with artillery, Bowie knives, and long, single-barreled, muzzle-loading flintlocks, the volunteers marched along the river under the cover of darkness on October 2.[109]

It was a humid night with a fog that settled over the river and prairie. A brief skirmish between the Texians and Castañeda's pickets alerted the Mexican camp, and they took their positions. Through the morning's dim light, they at last got a look at their opponents. The Texians couldn't have made much of an impression. Standing before them was little more than a rag-tag collection of rebels garbed in mostly ill-fitting buckskin breeches, their headwear a menagerie of military hats, sombreros, and coonskin caps with tails, their backs burdened by a bedroll of either quilts, blankets, buffalo robes, or "gaudy counterpane woven by tender hands." Their mounts were equally haphazard, an assortment of mules, skittish mustangs, small Spanish ponies, and large American quarter horses.[110]

The Texians undisciplined appearance in the field did not carry to their countenance. The infantry formed into battle lines with the cavalry to the right, the disputed cannon front and center. Colonel James C. Neill fired the initial cannonade, and as rifles mostly missed their mark, the Texian infantry charged. At the end of the action, one Mexican lay dead in the field among crippled and dying animals.[111]

The Battle of Gonzales was of more political significance than military importance. Castañeda withdrew to Béxar, unwilling to press the engagement without orders from Ugartechea. For their part, the Gonzales volunteers failed to attack the army during its retreat. There was hope among the nascent Texas leadership that Gonzales would be a touchstone proclaiming an independent Texas to the world, and that the United States, if not Great Britain, would rally to their cause. The conflict, however, mostly succeeded in announcing their intentions to Mexico. Santa Anna, for one, heard it.

Of War and Peace. Austin wrote to the Committees of Safety and Correspondence at Gonzales's conclusion. "Public opinion has proclaimed against military despotism," he pronounced, and "war is declared." He called for the people of Texas "to be of one spirit and one purpose" and "to take Béxar, and drive the military out of Texas." He then very wrongly added his opinion that Texas would quickly "have peace, for the present government of Mexico have too much to do at home…to send another army to Texas."[112] This passage suggests that Austin was either keenly naive – unlikely – or that he was being deliberately untruthful, perhaps to rally support for the war cause. The latter seems probable given his words to David G. Burnet the same day. Advocating "war in full," he wrote that he "hoped to see Texas forever free from Mexican domination," but "it is yet too soon to say this publicly."[113]

While Austin spoke of war, Colonel Ugartechea talked of peace. Writing to Austin after the Gonzales skirmish, he advised that the supreme government wished "to adopt measures fit to procure a permanent and firm peace," but only if the "enemies of order" were surrendered for their "crimes and abominations" and the Gonzales cannon returned. Without these measures, he would use a force "of every description of arms, sufficient to prove that the Mexicans can never suffer themselves to be insulted." The consequence, he wrote, would be military action in "a war declared by the colonists."[114] That, it seemed, is exactly what Austin was now hoping for.

General Cos marched through Refugio on October 1, arriving in La Bahía Goliad the next day (Fig. 3). On the 5th, he hastened to San Antonio de Béxar to reinforce Ugartechea, the 400-strong infantry battalion of Morelos arriving four days later.[115] Eighty miles away, volunteers were still arriving at Gonzales, their numbers growing to 300 men. On October 11th, they were joined by Stephen F. Austin as the newly elected commander-in-chief of the Volunteer Army. His tenure would last just three weeks.

Some of the men at Gonzales wanted to head off General Cos on his push to San Antonio de Béxar. Others took a more cautionary tactic. Cos had posted only small detachments at Goliad and at Fort Lipantitlán, and the more prudent Texians thought these better targets. They were right.

First Goliad. Goliad was a larger town than Gonzales. Founded on the edge of the San Antonio River, it was comprised of dozens of small *jacales*, which were stone houses with flat roofs, shuttered glassless windows, and floors of hardened mortar, and a *presidio*, or fort, adjacent to the Catholic Church. Constructed of limestone blocks, the flowing arches of the church's belfry and doorways were at odds with the hard lines of the fort's defensive parapet. Those walls would provide an unwarranted sense of security to Mexican Colonel Juan López Sandoval and his 30 men.

There was no carefully prepared military plan for the events after Gonzales. Instead, independent actions on the part of both Texians and Tejanos seemed to converge into a collaborative campaign along the 30-mile corridor between Guadalupe Victoria and Goliad. John J. Linn and Victoria alcalde Plácido Benavides, both part of the Victoria Committee of Safety and Correspondence, originally intended to move on Béxar. Instead, they chose Guadalupe Victoria when they learned Capt. Manuel Sabriego was intent on apprehending Coahuila y Texas legislator José M. J. Carbajal, and mark off a name on Cos's arrest warrants.

Several Texians volunteer companies, on their way to Goliad, joined the brief action at Guadalupe Victoria. Among them was Captain George M. Collinsworth. In a dispatch to Austin on October 8, Collinsworth advised that the Matagorda Volunteers were marching towards Goliad with 47 "good and effective men" that, he thought, were "sufficient to take that place."[116] But he was joined by many more, including prominent De Leon Colony merchant Phillip Dimmitt, and Brazoria's Ben F. Smith and William H. Jack. Austin, writing from Gonzales on the 11th – his first day as commander-in-chief of the Volunteer Army – also advised Captain John Alley, with another 40 men, to march with the Lavaca volunteers (Fig. 5).[117]

In 1821, Phillip Dimmitt built the cabin on Jennings Creek with Jacob Jennings that was used by early Austin colonists as they travelled inland from the Gulf of Mexico.

It took less than an hour for Collinsworth's advance to drive Colonel Juan López Sandoval and the Mexican garrison from the *presidio* at Goliad. The Texians did not lose a man. Sandoval lost three, and 21 were taken prisoner.[118] The Victoria and Goliad campaigns proved an undisputed victory for the militias and volunteer army. Only a week had now passed since the events at Gonzales.

After Guadalupe Victoria and Goliad, the Texians concentrated on Fort Lipantitlán (Fig. 3). Located at the Laredo Road crossing on the Nueces River, it was the only remaining post along the interior route linking the supply base on the Rio Grande at Matamoros to the army at Béxar. Captain Dimmit was the plan architect, but he remained in charge of the occupation of Goliad while his second in command, Captain Ira Westover, took to the field with a Texian force of about 60 men. The strength of the Mexicans under Capt. Nicolás Rodríguez was about 80. In the November 4th skirmish, Rodríguez's detachment abandoned the field with five killed and about a dozen wounded, retreating to Matamoros. Only one Texian was wounded.[119]

Far from the Front. Mexican federalist general José Antonio Mexía and Hungarian-born George Fisher were men without a nation in 1835. Only three years earlier, Mexía was sent by Santa Anna to settle matters with the Texians after the battle at Velasco. Now, he was another fallen ally of the general, forced into exile after a futile two-month offensive against him in the state of Jalisco.[120]

George Fisher had failed at most everything he tried to do to this point in his life. He was a member of James Long's unsuccessful filibustering expedition. He had empresario ambitions, but his colonization application was snubbed. The San Felipe department provided him with a minor government role, a job he lost when he was suspected as a spy. His next posting was as customhouse administrator in 1830 during the first troubles at Anahuac, after which he was forced to flee to Mexico. He did not remain long there either, expulsed over liberal views he circulated in publications.[121]

Mexía and Fisher took sanctuary in New Orleans and continued their scheming against Santa Anna. Sympathetic southern rallied to their call to support "the Texians, and the defense of their rights," raising $7,000 in military aid. Some of the monies were used to promote Mexía's plan to overtake Tampico and divert Santa Anna's attention from Texas. Both Stephen F. Austin and the war-time government were in support of the expedition, with Austin advising that "even a rumor of such a thing would keep troops from being sent to Texas."[122]

In November, Mexía and 130 men left the Mississippi River docks for Tampico aboard the schooner *Mary Ann*. Although optimistic that the "public sentiment is generally in our favor," there were a host of logistical pieces that could have gone wrong. Most of them did. The expected republican support in Tampico never materialized. The schooner beached outside the harbor, and during the portage from the vessel to town, powder and ammunition were ruined. Worse, Mexican commandant Gregorio Gomez's company of 250 knew they were coming. As Mexía's command marched to the city, they were forced to scatter for shelter in the sharp skirmish that followed. Mexía did not remain with his troops, retreating instead to the harbor and sailing away, justifying his actions as "most prudent" to "abandon his position and go to Texas."[123]

The 28 remaining men of Mexía's command, left to their fate, were taken prisoner. Some were soldiers and mercenaries, a blend of Creoles, Americans, French, and Germans who answered the "invitation to join in a reaction against tyranny." Others claimed ignorance of the campaign. They weren't soldiers at all, they extolled, simply emigrants who thought they were headed to Texas but, instead, were pirated by a "shameful abduction or deception practiced on us." These men, who trusted "the clemency and mercy of authorities," would be disappointed. On December 14, a priest dutifully recorded their "dying statement" before they were paraded out and shot. On that day, 600 miles away, a defeated General Cos was preparing to abandon San Antonio de Béxar and march his troops back to Mexico.[124]

Siege of Béxar. When Captain George Collinsworth moved on Goliad during the first week of October, he had a force of some 160 men.[125] Austin next hastily ordered them on toward the real prize – General Cos's army and its occupation of San Antonio de Béxar. John Alley, Ben F. Smith, and Plácido Benavides turned their companies from Victoria and Goliad towards Béxar on October 14, while Captain Collinsworth headed to Matagorda to enlist more recruits.

The road to San Antonio was jammed with volunteers eager to advance the Texian cause. Bivouacked on the outskirts of town, the army that General Austin commanded had grown into an amalgamation of fighters from different points of origin and with diverse cultures. There were Mexican nationalists and Coahuila y Texas Tejanos who, in addition to Benavides, included Juan Seguín, José Carbajal, and Salvador Flores. Both factions were fighting not for an independent Texas, but for the Constitution of 1824.[126] There were the volunteer auxiliary corps, organized from nearly every state of the Deep South, as well as Tennessee, Kentucky, and Ohio. Each division, despite where it originated, was composed of an assortment of men from different states and even from overseas.[127] Lastly were the Texian volunteers. Austin had a deep respect for them but found they were impossible to lead. They were, he said, made up of "discordant materials" in a fluid "volunteer system" with desertions and the arrival of newcomers daily.[128]

Mexican deserters along with reconnoiters by James Bowie and James Fannin provided Austin with intelligence on General Cos's army. He learned the position of redoubts that blocked that he town's *calles*, or streets, that radiated out in a grid pattern from two central plazas. Building rooftops were fortified "with unburnt brick" and portholes for riflemen. At least nine cannons bristled from buildings on both sides of the San Antonio River where it made a wide meander separating the town from the Alamo courtyard *presidio* and chapel. General Cos, he was informed, now had a force of at least 300 infantry and 400 cavalrymen, and at night he kept a strong patrol of 60 sentinels and 80 mounted scouts.[129]

For nearly two months Austin was intent on storming the town. Each time he gave the order, however, either the men or their commanders declined to muster. At least part of his challenge was because the influential Sam Houston vocally opposed his plans, expressing his doubts that the assault could be won.[130] With the offensive at an impasse, Bowie and Fannin suggested a siege aimed to "shut in the enemy" and "starve them out." They knew provisions were in short supply because the "bean crop was destroyed, the peas were not yet ripe, the corn unharvested, and the town had few stores of beef."[131] Also, with Austin's forces spread out around the outskirts of town, foraging forays were risky. For the next almost two months, as the army continued to debate the best course of action, a siege became the de facto strategy.

The impetuous Bowie and Fannin, the West Pointer, were at times no more inclined to follow Austin's orders than the Volunteer army. Instructed to rejoin Austin's command after they separated on one reconnaissance mission, they instead elected to make camp. The site they chose was south of the city at the juncture of the San Antonio River and San Pecario Creek, near the Concepción mission. When's spies informed General Cos that the rebel army was divided, he dispatched Col. Ugartechea with 275 men and two cannons to engage. The Texians, with only 90 men, should have been overwhelmed on that October day. But the Mexican's notoriously inaccurate flintlock muskets were no match for the Texians and their Kentucky rifles. Ugartechea lost 14 killed and 39 wounded. Texian losses in the Concepción battle amounted to only one killed and another wounded. Austin wanted to press the fight, counselling for an immediate assault on the town. Once again, he was overruled.

On December 3, the Texian army on the outskirts of Béxar finally agreed on something – to disband and return to their homes. As they packed, Ben Milam entered camp after a scouting trip and achieved what Austin, and his replacement Edward Burleson, could not. Fuming at the turn of events, he uttered his famous impassioned call to arms – Old Ben was willing to fight alone, but would others follow him? His appeal was answered by 300 men. Two commanders were chosen, Ben Milam and Francis W. Johnson.[132] Johnson, a peace party member only weeks earlier, had changed his stripes after he learned that Cos determined to hunt him down along with other Monclova land speculators.

The army organized at the Old Mill, northeast of the town, after dark. Milam and Johnson's divisions headed south along Calle de la Acequia (Main Street) and Calle de la Soledad (Soledad Street), while Neill's Battalion was to advance on the Alamo. Under heavy fire, the two divisions succeeded in occupying the town center. Here they dug trenches and battered holes in house walls to open shooting windows. The fighting was hot as grape shot and bullets tore away fencing, doorways and windows, and the walls of buildings. For several days, much of the battle was house to house, the flash of silver as knives and bayonets found their mark.

Over the course of five days there were three arenas of battle – the town, the Alamo, and the army reserve camp outside of town. Cos lost each of them. His troops first abandoned the town for the safety of the Alamo walls, but here they were surrounded. Four companies of cavalry rode off against orders rather than continue the struggle. Then Edward Burleson, who had replaced Austin Commander-in-chief of the Volunteer Army, successfully defended the reserve camp.[133] A flag of truce fluttered over the Alamo on December 11.

Bend in the River landowner Thomas Alley, with brothers William and John, led companies at Béxar during the two-month siege and were with Ben Milam when he fell.

The Siege of Béxar was a major Texian victory. Five or six Texians were killed, including Ben Milam, with less than 35 wounded. Cos lost a total of 150 killed or wounded.[134] It was the largest bloodletting between the Mexicans and Texians since the Battle of Velasco in 1832. General Cos and roughly 1,100 soldiers were allowed an honorary surrender with quarter. As they marched from the Alamo towards Mexico, they were considerably more fortunate than those who would lose another battle there just three months later.

At the close of 1835, the Texians had driven the Mexican army entirely from the countryside. Many thought the war was over and most of the volunteers went home. Few had any idea that, some 400 miles away, Santa Anna was gathering an army of roughly 4,000 soldiers. He intended to finish what he started at Zacatecas the previous April.

A Wartime Government. The Gonzales skirmish was less than two weeks distant when, on October 11, the Texians met to form their first government. It was a challenging time to try and build a nation. The first government was called the Permanent Council, its nucleus the San Felipe Committee of Public Safety and Correspondence with delegates elected from each of the Texas municipalities.

Permanent Council. The Permanent Council never reached a quorum because most of the elected delegates were in the army. But according to historian Rupert Richardson, the body served well. Matagorda delegate and chairman Richard R. Royall was elected its chairman. Royall and the council were largely successful in supplying the army, commissioning privateers to the fledgling Texas Navy, closing the insidious land offices, and establishing a postal system. Additionally, they authorized an agent to travel to the United States to solicit men, money, and supplies. The Permanent Council governed Texas for only three weeks.[135]

Bend in the River landowner John Royall was only two-years-old when he travelled by wagon to Texas with his father, Richard Royall, in 1830.

Consultation. The second government during the Revolution, the Consultation, went into session on November 3 with a quorum of 55 delegates out of 98. Only 12 municipalities from the departments of the Brazos and Nacogdoches were represented. Notably absent were the districts of Béxar, Goliad, Refugio, Victoria, and San Patricio. As a result, the Tejanos were not represented, the exception the single voice of Harrisburg delegate Lorenzo de Zavala. Conspicuous as well was the absence of Stephen F. Austin.[136]

The most heated debate of the Consultation was what the Texians were fighting for. The war party declared for independence, the peace party as a separate state within a federalist Mexico. There was logic to both sides. The war party argued there was no Republic of Mexico to return to – Santa Anna had nullified the Constitution of 1824. The peace party, including a pragmatic Sam Houston representing the Nacogdoches district, reasoned if they pressed for separation, they would lose the support of the Tejanos and liberal Mexicans. The delegation voted 33 to 15 against independence, but compromised, adding an article that Texas retained the right to withdraw from Mexico if it was no longer governed by a "constitution and laws." Notable in opposition to any compromise was Henry Smith – who would become the first governor of Texas.[137]

Provisional Government. The Provisional Government, the third administration in as many months, was formed by a subcommittee of the Consultation. Brazos political chief Henry Smith was named chairman,[138] and no one thought it a conflict of interest when chairman Smith was nominated as Texas's first governor – and won it handily – in a contest against the absent Stephen F. Austin. Next, the delegates of the 13-member council were chosen. None were Tejanos. A new major general was named for the regular Texas army – Sam Houston.[139]

On November 14, as the Consultation handed the reins of government to the new governor and council, a rider was dispatched to Béxar to deliver a message to General Stephen F. Austin. It carried the news that, although his request to resign as the leader of the Texas army was granted, he would not be governor. Instead, Texas's senior statesman was ordered to report to the Provisional Government as a commissioner to the United States to lobby for Texas funding, support, and troops.

The Consultation sanctioned General Sam Houston to raise a force of 1,200 men for a duration of two years, the soldiers receiving a cash bounty and land grants for their service. All able-bodied men between the ages of 16 and 50 were required to assemble in their respective municipalities that December. The Consultation also agreed to maintain a volunteer army, over which Houston had no control. The oversight would have serious implications when Santa Anna and his 4,000-strong army thundered into Texas.[140]

The First Declaration of Independence. At the close of December 1835, Matagorda alcalde Ira Ingram and a committee that included Goliad commander Phillip Dimmitt took it upon themselves to write a Declaration of Independence. The text was unsolicited, poorly timed, not representative of the views of most Texians or the presiding government – and would be replaced by a second Declaration of Independence penned two months later. But on that cool December day, their document, promulgating a "free, sovereign, and independent State" was celebrated with cheers, rifle shots, and the hoisting of the famous "bloody arm" flag that Dimmitt made for the occasion (Fig. 6).

As quickly as the Goliad declaration was dispatched, its proclamations were retracted. One reason was that Stephen F. Austin, only days earlier, had written the Provisional Government warning against independence. The skirmishes of 1835 convinced Austin that

165

Texas, alone, could not win the war. To that end, he was negotiating for the support of Tejanos and liberal Mexican nationalists, whose loyalty was not to a sovereign Texas, but to federalist Mexico.[141] Two weeks later, in a letter to Richard Royall, he added another concern – that an independent Texas was unlikely to secure support from the United States. Austin was proven right on both points.[142]

There may have been other reasons. First, the document was Anglo-centric. The framers opined that the Mexicans, which they termed the "Creole population," were "strangers to the blessings of regulated liberty" and lacked the vision for any institution other than that "of their ancient tyrants." Enlightened government, they wrote, only "belongs to the North-Americans of Texas," and although they could set an example for Mexico's people, "we need not expect or even hope for their cooperation." None of this was language that would motivate any person of Mexican blood to the Texian cause.

Second, its passages were filled with political bombast. The writers chafed at decisions made during the 1835 campaign and used their Goliad document to air their discontent. The volunteer army, they wrote, was led by "men more desirous of being honored with command than capable of commanding" and who were "busy aspirants for office running from the field to the Council House, and from this back to the camp, seeking emolument and not service, and swarming like hungry flies around the body politic." Their warning of the "danger from this…insinuating, secret, silent, and unseen influence in our councils, both in the field and in the cabinet" gives the impression that the Texas leadership was as much the enemy as those bearing bloodied bayonets. It was language that had no place in an essay pronouncing the emergence of a progressive and democratic Texas to the world.

When the declaration stayed on topic, there were some convincing discourses. One paragraph argued that "the laws and guarantees under which we entered the country as colonists, tempted the unbroken silence, sought the dangers of the wilderness, braved the prowling Indian, erected our numerous improvements, and opened and subdued the earth to cultivation, are either abrogated or repealed, and now trampled under the hoofs of the usurper's cavalry." In the end, the Goliad Declaration of Independence was ferreted away "to remain in the files of the secretary without further action."[143]

Governing Themselves. The Provisional Government of Texas had the opportunity to show themselves, and the world, their resolve in administering Texas in a way that Mexico never could. It didn't happen. The blame for the failing was a rivalry between Governor Henry Smith and the presiding council. It was a short feud. The first Provisional Government of Texas reigned for less than three months.

Calling himself not governor, but the "Supreme Executive of the free and sovereign state of Texas," Henry Smith proved to be a legislative barrier at a time when Texas, foremost, needed action. His preferred stalling tactic was the veto, and he used it with abandon. He rejected most of the council's appointments. He vetoed relocation of the capital to Washington-on-the-Brazos. Although approved by the Consultation articles, the governor refused a war-time loan from Texas patriot and peace party advocate Thomas F. McKinney. In another attempt to secure war funding, the council created the offices of auditor and comptroller. The governor vetoed them. Smith, it was noted, even vetoed his own authority to veto.[144] Ultimately, the council resorted to secretly drawing from the treasury without the governor's knowledge.[145]

Smith's extreme intolerance of Mexicans was as detrimental to the fledgling nation as his inaction. He declined offers from prominent Tejanos or Mexican federalists who

166

aspired to join the war against Santa Anna. When the council agreed to include more Tejano representation in its body through a vote by "all free white males and Mexicans opposed to the central government," Smith objected. He considered it "bad policy to trust Mexicans in any matter connected with our government." Smith had a particular problem with "the inhabitants of Béxar." They had "every opportunity to evince their friendship by joining our standard," he advised, and because they didn't, it was evidence "that they are really our enemies."[146]

In early January 1836, after just six weeks, the nascent Texian government was in anarchy. Governor Smith fired the first salvo, accusing the council of being "Mexican-like," and "ready to sacrifice [their] country at the shrine of plunder." There were Judases among the council, he wrote, "vile scoundrels" with a "sneaking sycophantic look", a "meanness of countenance" and a "sympathetic tickling and contraction of the muscles in the neck" as if they were anticipating "the rope." Then he made his move. At noon the next day, Smith advised, he would cease communication with the council. Their services would no longer be needed.[147]

The council responded by deposing the governor. Their charges against him included malfeasance and misconduct, violation of the principles of the Federal Constitution of 1824, "official perjury," assuming dictatorial powers, a "general disorganization" and, chafing from his insults the day before, "slanders and libels upon the general council." In their view, Smith was officially unseated, and named lieutenant governor James W. Robinson acting governor.[148] When the council demanded the ousted governor surrender the records of office, Smith ignored their order, demanding the same of the council and threatening arrest of those who refused.[149]

The government impasse wasn't resolved until March, when both Smith and the council presented their versions of the bitter affair to a war-time convention. Rather than take sides, a resolution was adopted to replace them all. The governor, lieutenant governor, and the council of the first Provisional Government of Texas were terminated.[150]

History begs the question that, had Stephen F. Austin retained a leading role in its first government, whether he might have stewarded a better outcome. He was never given the opportunity. Austin had made enemies, particularly his use of his influence to secure the outcome of various land dealings, and they would collapse his political future. Most damning was his role, with partner Samuel Williams, in acquiring the former Leftwich grant of the Texas Association.

Located north of the El Camino Real and between the Colorado and Brazos rivers, the Leftwich Colony had seen three failed empresarios in just over two years. In 1830 the role passed to a fourth, Sterling C. Robertson. Robertson met with Austin, requesting him to intercede with the Saltillo legislature on his behalf and, with its six-year term lapsing, extend the contract. Robertson would be disappointed. The Law of April 6, 1830, had nullified the venture and then, a year later, political chief of Texas Ramon Muzquiz ordered the eviction of all families that Robertson introduced.[151]

The southern survey of the Bend in the River was owned by Hosea H. League, who was one of the failed Leftwich Colony empresarios.

Austin, relying on his ability to court favor in Mexico when others failed, had his own designs on the territory.[152] He and Samuel Williams successfully petitioned Saltillo for the award, renaming it their Upper Colony. Robertson in June 1831 wrote a brief letter to Austin asking for confirmation that "our colony is given to Mr. Williams."[153] It was.

consignment. He found influential allies, such as Superior Judge of Texas Thomas J. Chambers, who represented Robertson as attorney and agent.[154] Robertson and Chambers vilified Austin in a public campaign, slandering him as "corrupt and tyrannical" and a man who operated with "treachery and malice."[155] Keenly aware that powerful political enemies were using his land ventures against him, Austin wrote Williams that "I am of the opinion that the upper colony will totally ruin me," adding "cursed be the hour I ever thought of applying for that Upper Colony."[156]

While Austin was imprisoned in Mexico during 1834, Robertson and his supporters found favor in Monclova and reclaimed the Leftwich contract, in part with "a bribe of about thirteen hundred dollars."[157] Settlement efforts were initiated immediately. In their first promotional circular, Robertson and partners debased Austin with phrases such as "justice has at last gained a triumph over perfidy" in a land long "kept a wilderness by fraud and chicanery."[158]

The next move was Austin's and Williams's, who petitioned Agustín Viesca – Monclova's third governor in less than a year – for Robertson's removal. Their success would cost them deeply. Austin made lasting adversaries during the Leftwich Colony ordeal, and they surfaced first in 1835 when the Provisional Government backed Henry Smith over him as governor, and again in 1836 as the Republic of Texas leadership was selecting its political roster, passing over Austin as its president. Ironically, the president-elect, Sam Houston, was a stockholder in Robertson's Texas Association and Nashville Company of the former Leftwich grant.

As towns fell like dominoes before Santa Anna during the winter of 1836, Texas barely had a functioning government. Decisions made or deferred during this period would be costly to Texas and her defenders of independence. Historian Roy Smith, in fact, presented arguments that the ineptness of the Provisional Government was the cause of what could have been avoidable tragedies at places that live long in Texas lore – the Alamo and second Goliad.

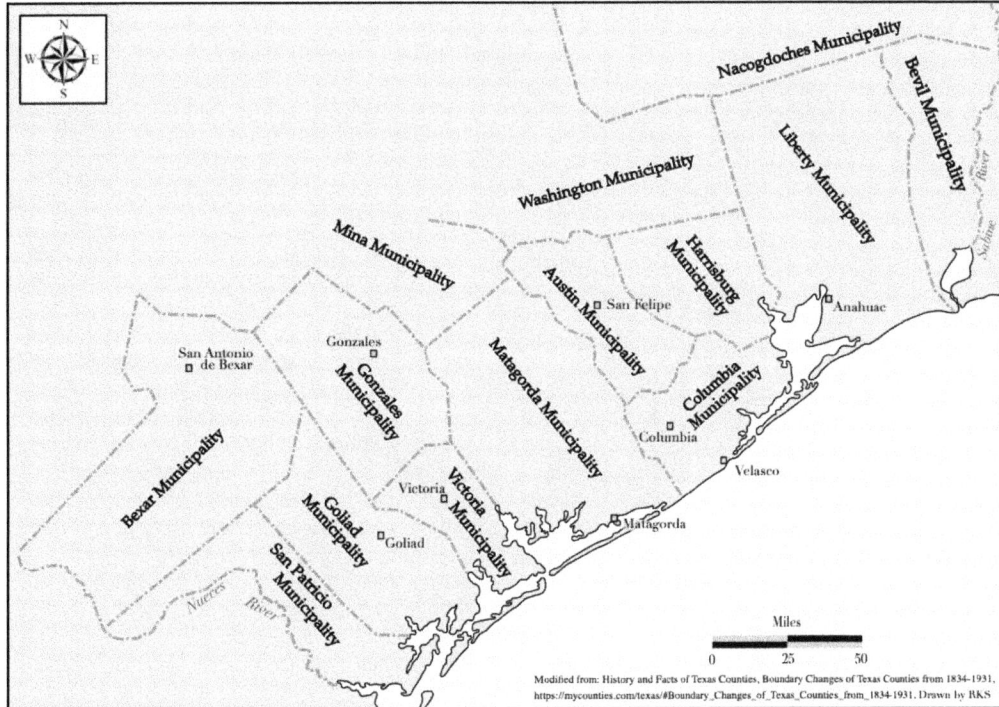

Fig. 1. Municipalities as they existed in Mexican Texas 1834. Parts of Wharton and Jackson counties were later derived from the Matagorda Municipality.

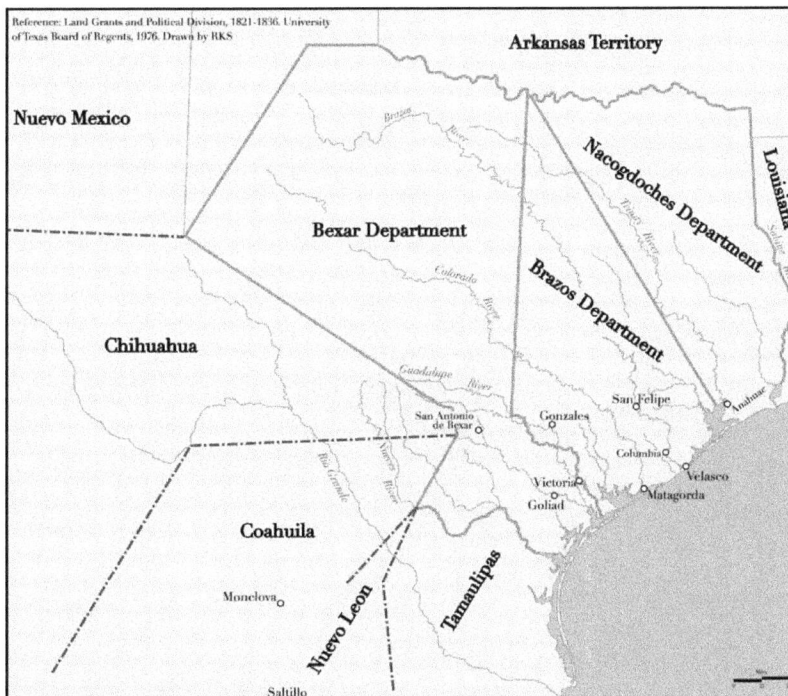

Fig. 2. The military organization of Mexican Texas was administered as departments. The Department of Texas was created in 1827 with its headquarters in San Antonio de Béxar. By 1834 Texas was divided into three departments within the State of Coahuila and Texas, called Coahuila y Texas. Its capital was Saltillo from 1824 until 1833, when it was relocated to Monclova.

169

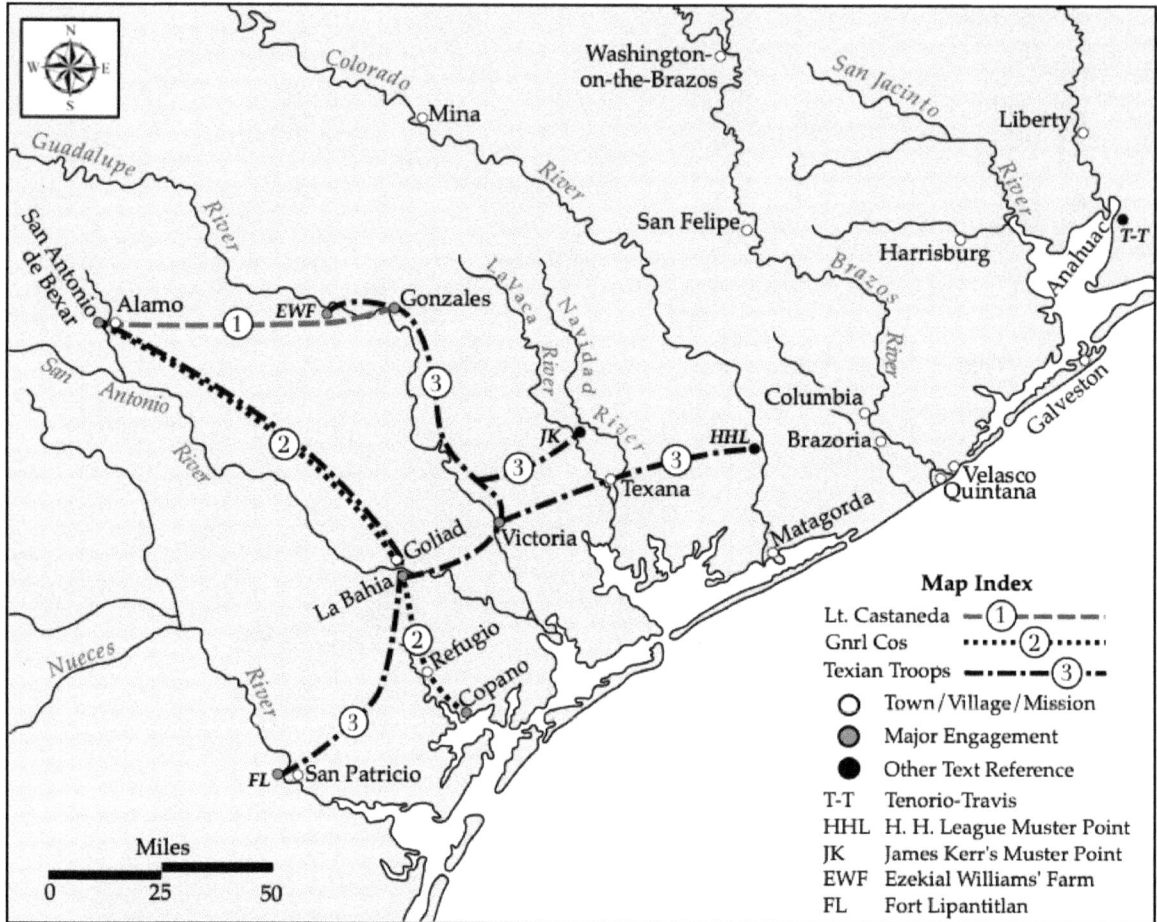

Fig. 3. Map showing the places, routes, and major engagements during the Texas War for Independence in 1835. The two places Austin selected as muster points effectively marked the beginning of the Texas Revolution. One was "Leagues old place on the Colorado," which was at or near present day Spread Oaks Ranch. The land was originally granted to Captain Jacob Jennings, then Hosea League, and by 1835 the former Revolutionary War hero Thomas Cayce. Austin's choice of the location was a practical one – Cayce operated a ferry that crossed the Colorado River on the main road connecting Brazoria and Columbia to La Bahía (Goliad). A mix of prairie and oak mottes provided suitable troop encampments between the ferry and, just downriver, the original League house.

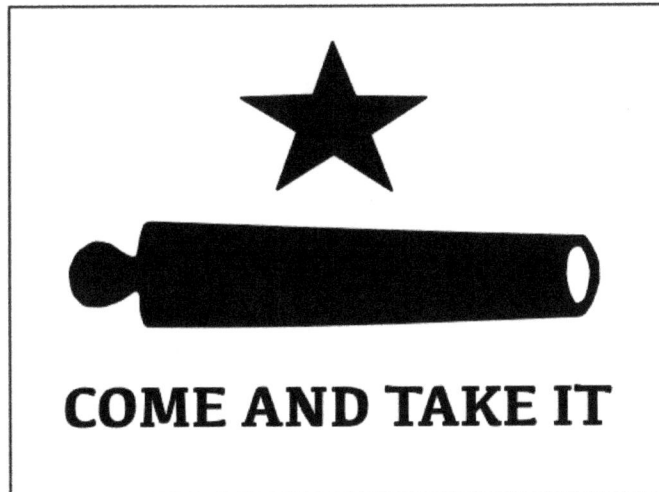

COME AND TAKE IT

Fig. 4. Popular legend has it that the Texians flew the 'Come and Take It' flag over the cannon cart on the Gonzales field of battle. Equally likely is the version narrated by DeWitt Creed Taylor, in which a committee of officers hoisted it for the first time as they prepared to advance on **San Antonio de Béxar**. There may be truth that the patriotic ladies of Gonzales offered to sacrifice their silk dresses and even curtains to fabricate the celebrated flag, and that it was sewn by Sarah Seely DeWitt, wife of late Empresario Green DeWitt, her daughter Evaline, and Caroline Zumwalt, from fabric cut from Naomi DeWitt's wedding dress. Ricks, Thomas L., *Gonzales Come and Take It Cannon*, TSHA Handbook of Texas, https://www.tshaonline.org/handbook/entries/gonzales-come-and-take-itcannon; *Houston Chronicle*, Oct. 2, 2018; DeWitt Colony Flags, 1700-1846, Sons of DeWitt Colony Texas, http://www.sonsofdewittcolony .org/dewittflgs2.htm.

Excerpt from a letter from Stephen F Austin to James Kerr and John Alley, October 3, 1835.

I regret that there are no Guns to be had in this quarter for the supply of Capt. Alley's Company. There is public powder at Matagorda which you can get by applying for in my name to the committee of that place, as they informed me they would hold it subject to my order.

Fig. 5. Bend in the River landowner Captain Thomas Alley and his brothers participated in most of the 1835 campaigns. The brothers were at La Bahía – the first battle of Goliad – where recently promoted Captain John Alley commanded 111 men from Victoria. During the skirmish they had enough volunteers but were plagued by a lack of supplies. Stephen F Austin to James Kerr and John Alley, Oct. 3, 1835. Eugene Barker, ed., *The Austin Papers*, (Austin: University of Texas Press, 1927), v. 3, p. 152-153, http://digitalAustinpapers.org/document?id=APB4906.

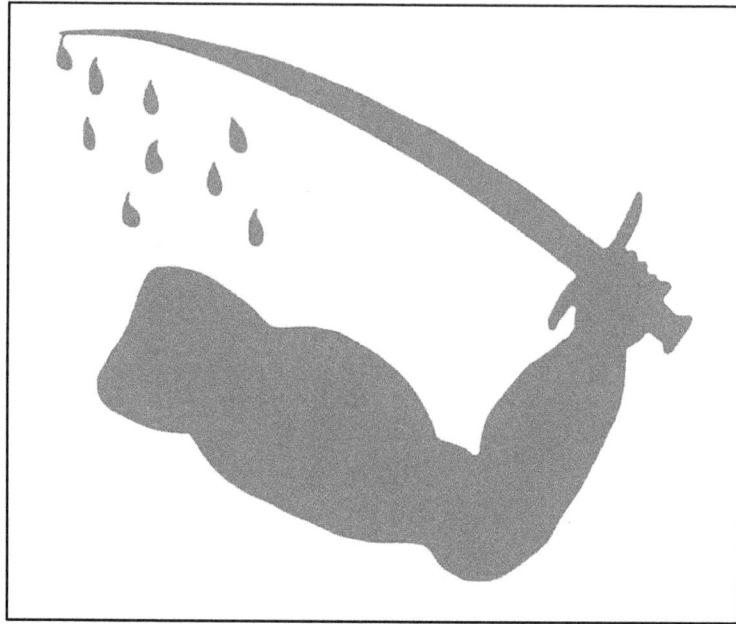

Fig. 6. At the close of December 1835, Matagorda alcalde Ira Ingram and a committee that included Goliad commander Phillip Dimmitt took it upon themselves to write a Declaration of Independence. The text was unsolicited and would be replaced by a second Declaration of Independence penned two months later. But on that cool December day, their document, promulgating a "free, sovereign, and independent State" was celebrated with cheers, rifle shots, and the hoisting of the famous "bloody arm" flag above the La Bahía Goliad presidio that Dimmitt made for the occasion. As it unfurled for the first time it was immediately pierced with a gunshot from the streets outside the wall. Stephen F. Austin to the Provisional Government, Dec. 14, 1835, The Digital Austin Papers, http://digitalaustinpapers.org/document?Id=APB5075; Goliad Flag Severed Arm, Bloody Sword 1836, http://texasflagpark.com/texas-flags/goliad-flag-severed-arm-bloody-sword-1836/.

CHAPTER 7

The Battle for a New Republic

1835 to 1836

When the supreme commander of the Mexican Army, General Antonio López de Santa Anna, stormed into Texas in February 1836, its leader was confident of victory. He would have been more certain had he fully appreciated the state of his opponent. The Texas Provisional Government was not only challenged by a lack of finances, supplies, and soldiers, it was crippled by a crisis of leadership.

During the winter of 1836, Santa Anna's adversary had a barely functioning government, its governor and council hopelessly divided. One of its most effective statesmen, Stephen F. Austin, was out of the country, assigned to diplomatic duty in the United States. The regular army's new commander-in-chief, Sam Houston, had left the field for East Texas. It seemed as if everyone in the new government was jockeying for status, a title, or leadership. That was especially true in its three separate armies – one regular, another volunteer, and a third auxiliary. With too many chiefs but not much insight, they were spread across the countryside. Santa Anna, it seemed, was poised for an easy triumph.

The generalissimo devised a two-prong strategy for the Texas invasion. General José de Urrea would lead a division along the coastal, or southern route. Under him was Colonel Domingo de Ugartechea, intent on honor after his litany of failures – defeat at Velasco in 1832, the standoff at Gonzales, the humiliating rout at the battle of Concepción, and his retreat from Béxar barely two months earlier. General Santa Anna and his northern division would penetrate Texas north of Laredo (Fig. 1). His second in command was Italian-born Texas empresario Vicente Filisola, and another of his divisions was led by General Martín Perfecto de Cos, the disgraced architect of the failed 1835 Texas campaign.

Rather than risk delivering men and supplies to the Texas coast through the Copano port, the Mexican Army crossed the scrub and prickly pear desert during the winter of 1835 and 1836 with a supply train comprised of 1,800 pack mules, 33 wagons, and 200 carts.[1] Unaware that Santa Anna's massive war party was moving north, the Texas Provisional Government thought it had time to spare. Time enough to quarrel among themselves. Enough time to send its commander-in-chief to East Texas to negotiate with the Cherokee and other Indian tribes instead of leading its regular army. Time enough to send an expedition to Matamoros instead of strengthening and defending its own forts and settlements. It was time, it turned out, they didn't have.

Matamoros. Most of Texas' political and military leaders were obsessed with invading the Mexican river port town of Matamoros. Everyone, it seemed, except Sam Houston. The strategy to bring the battle to Mexico was theoretically sound, but it was a terrific gamble – the expedition would consume limited resources desperately needed for the defense of Texas if the Mexican army moved north. It had.

José Antonio Mexía, encamped at Quintana after his earlier failed assault on Tampico, volunteered to command the Matamoros expedition that December. The provisional government enthusiastically backed the proposal, but Governor Henry Smith objected to the choice of leadership. Mexía was no patriot, he said, and his only motivations were to rob the "seaports west of us" in a struggle "to recuperate his own desperate fortunes."[2] Smith instead instructed General Houston and Colonel James Bowie to proceed to Matamoros by way of Copano.

Houston chafed, writing Smith of the folly to attempt another foreign maritime invasion. Mexía's "disaster of Tampico," he counselled, should "teach us a lesson."[3] Instead, he convinced the governor to concentrate on a defense closer to the Texian front. But the presiding council circumvented Smith, sending Houston their own orders to renew the Matamoros venture. Already encumbered with too many military chiefs, Houston ignored them.[4] The council next conspired to undertake the mission with commander-in-chief of the Volunteer Army Francis W. Johnson, Coahuila empresario Dr. James Grant, and Colonel James W. Fannin Jr. When the governor learned of the proposal, he vetoed it. The council went around him, again.

Smith and Houston were committed to strengthening Texas fortifications, but the Matamoros expedition leaders were just as intent on undoing them. Grant, as he was preparing to march south from San Antonio de Béxar and its mission-fort, the Alamo, absconded with over half of the garrison's troops, munitions, horses, and winter provisions on December 30.[5] Given the fate of the Alamo defenders two months later, Johnson's admission that he left only a force "barely sufficient to hold the post" was chilling. Stripped of his resources, Béxar commander Lt. Col. J.C. Neill wrote of the deplorable condition of the town and fort in a dispatch on January 14, imploring Houston to send aid.[6] It was the first largely unfulfilled request of many by the beleaguered commander over the next seven weeks.

Alarmed at Johnson and Grant's ravage of Béxar, Houston rode quickly from Goliad to Refugio to prevent them from pillaging his southern defenses. He was too late. They had already moved from Refugio, and with a company of 100 men, were headed for the Nueces River and San Patricio. Nearly a month had passed since the Matamoros expedition was organized, yet its leaders had covered no more than 100 miles. Another 175 miles lay ahead.

Mexican General José de Urrea was less measured. He had not only already reached Matamoros, but in just nine days moved to the Nueces River. That an army of nearly 700 men could intercept them without a trace of their coming was entirely lost on the Johnson and Grant. With their units divided, they hardly knew what hit them. Johnson's annihilation at San Patricio was first, on February 27, followed by Grant's on March 2 at Agua Dulce Creek (Fig. 1). Out of 90 men, 83 were "cut to pieces."[7]

Delayed in joining Johnson and Grant, Fannin arrived at Refugio on February 7 with 400 men. Fannin needed to make a decision. He was committed to supporting the Matamoros venture but had knowledge, now, of Santa Anna's imminent Texas invasion. The news prompted him to write the general council and Governor Smith's recent replacement, Lt. Governor J.W. Robinson, recommending his troops defend the Texian front instead of joining Johnson and Grant.[8] It would be the first of many vacillations in the coming weeks.

The Alamo. On January 17, General Houston ordered Col. James C. Neill, the man who fired the first cannon of the conflict at Gonzales, to destroy the Alamo mission and remove its artillery. It was an order that Neill, even if he was so inclined, could not obey –

Grant, on his way to Matamoros, had appropriated too many teams and wagons.[9] James Bowie, who left Texana for the Alamo with about 30 volunteers, carried the same instructions. But Bowie was a volunteer, and Houston was regular army. When he reached Béxar on January 19, Bowie had little hesitation in choosing his own course of action. He would defend the town.

Writing to Governor Smith on February 2, Bowie explained that "the citizens of Bejar [sic] have behaved well. [Lt.] Col. Neill and myself have come to the solemn resolution that we would rather die in these ditches than give it up to the enemy." He added that "the salvation of Texas depends in great measure in keeping Bejar out of the hands of the enemy," but "a large reinforcement with provisions is what we need. It would be a waste of men to put our brave little band against thousands."[10] Governor Smith concurred but, far from providing large numbers of reinforcements, ordered just 26 men under Lt. Col. Travis to Béxar. Travis was followed by famed frontiersman David Crockett with 12 Tennessee volunteers.

The issue of 'who was in charge' had always plagued the Texian's quest for independence, and it arose at Béxar immediately. Texian volunteer Jim Bowie was the soldier's commander of choice over regular army Travis, with Bowie celebrating his election by getting drunk and parading through town. Travis, who nearly resigned his commission over the Béxar posting in the first place, was appalled at the new commander's actions. The two settled the leadership issue when a freshly sober Bowie agreed to command the volunteers, and Travis the regulars and cavalry.[11]

Santa Anna, with some 1,500 cavalrymen, reached San Antonio de Béxar on February 23 (Fig. 1). A messenger was sent to the mission requesting a parley and Bowie carried their terms – surrender – back to Travis.[12] Travis replied with a cannon. The 12-day siege began almost immediately, the smoke from the first artillery rounds at times obscuring Santa Anna's red banner signifying no quarter, surrender, or mercy. Somewhat less than 150 Texas soldiers now peered over the parapets at a Mexican force numbering some 2,000 troops.

For days, the sound of cannon blasts resonated across the usually silent countryside. Thirty-two volunteers from Gonzales followed it, slipping through the siege to reinforce the beleaguered Alamo defenders. They were the last. At dawn on March 6th, a cavalry unit was posted outside the Alamo and prepared to cut anyone down who might escape.[13] Then General Cos – the commander who the Texians allowed to march to freedom from the same fortress just months before – ordered his infantry column to scale the Alamo walls. The battle lasted just over an hour, its finale when the survivors were either cut down after their surrender or huddled against the Alamo barrack wall and hoisted over the soldier's heads on the end of bayonets. The final curls of smoke from the funeral pyre of stacked Texian and Tejano bodies marked the culmination of a brutal victory for the general who showed no quarter.

Second Goliad. Between February and early March, Sam Houston, the commander-in-chief of the regular Texas army, was far from the front. The previous November, Houston and the Consultation prepared a treaty ceding lands to the Cherokees of East Texas in exchange for their neutrality in the conflict. That December, the provisional government sent Houston to convince the Cherokees to support it.[14] While the Alamo at Béxar was under siege, the army's leader was in route from Nacogdoches to Washington-on-the-Brazos.

With Houston preoccupied, Colonel Fannin was the highest ranked military officer in the Texas army. After abandoning the Matamoros undertaking, he chose the La Bahía mission across the river from Goliad to make a stand. Here Fannin received desperate messages from the Alamo, soliciting him to bring his army to their relief. On February 28 he set off towards San Antonio de Béxar, infamously retiring his march just a short distance from where he started. Citing insufficient oxen, carts, provisions, and certain of the need to man La Bahía before an attack, Fannin returned to the fort.

In Fannin's communications, the highest-ranking officer in the patriot army wasn't giving orders, he was begging for them.[15] When he did receive them, they were either delayed or contradictory. Acting governor Robinson advised him on March 6 to "use your own discretion to remain where you are or to retreet [sic] as you may think best for the safety of the brave Volunteers Under your command." Two days later Fannin was ordered by Houston, who finally reached Washington-on-the-Brazos, to reinforce Travis at the Alamo. Houston had no idea it was too late. When he did, he instructed Fannin to destroy the La Bahía stronghold and fall back to Guadalupe Victoria.[16]

Fannin's decision-making left him in no position to withdraw. Although aware that General Urrea held Refugio, on March 12 he sent a party of 30 men under Captain Amon B. King to the Refugio mission. No match for Urrea's troops, and rather than retreat, King fortified himself in the town's stone church and requested reinforcements. Fannin dispatched Lt. Col. William Ward's Georgia battalion, with 120 troops, to his relief. As a result, two of Fannin's units, many of his carts and teams, and several express riders were strung out between Goliad and Refugio (Fig. 1). After a delay of several days, Fannin reluctantly headed to Victoria and left them to their fate.[17]

Fate would be unkind to Ward and King. Ward did arrive at Refugio to support King, but they disputed command of the combined units, settling the matter by dividing their forces. King's small detachment was massacred by Urrea's troops after they surrendered. Ward was able to slip away to Guadalupe Victoria, but Urrea held that village, as well. After a short but vigorous contest, Ward's ammunition ran low. A white flag of surrender preceded the prisoners march to the La Bahía mission.

Fannin fared no better. On his painfully delayed withdrawal from the La Bahía mission on March 19, his 300 men bivouacked on the open prairie near Coleta Creek (Fig. 1). It was a poorly chosen position, the force quickly swarmed by more than 1,000 infantrymen and cavalry. The Texians repelled charge after charge by Urrea's troops, their lancers, muskets, and bayonets taking a heavy toll. In the morning, the survivors delivered a white flag of surrender, believing they signed terms capitulating with quarter. History shows it was at discretion.[18] Lt. Col. Ward did at last rejoin Fannin – as prisoners at the La Bahía presidio.

It was Palm Sunday, March 27 when the prisoners were ordered to form a line and marched from the mission's stone walls in three directions. Gunfire echoed across the prairie as the men were summarily executed, their rifled and bayonetted bodies piled in wagons and burned. The wounded who remained at the presidio were dragged out and killed. From a total of about 344 who died that Palm Sunday, Colonel Fannin was the last.

Victors and Vanquished. In just 30 days, Santa Anna's southern and northern divisions won six encounters and killed about 650 of their enemy. Most of the dead were not killed on the field of battle, but after their surrender. The list of those who perished in the winter of 1836 were not only Texians and Tejanos, but fighters from Louisiana,

Mississippi, Alabama, Georgia, South Carolina, Missouri, Tennessee, Kentucky, and the northern cities of Philadelphia, Boston, and New York. They toll included several from overseas – Scotland, Denmark, Holland, Ireland, England, and Wales.[19] There were professional soldiers, but most were volunteers who, in civilian life, were shoemakers, plasterers, blacksmiths, store clerks, lawyers, or doctors.

Nearly 40 years later, Santa Anna blamed the annihilation of the Alamo's defenders on "the obstinacy of Travis," because he would not enter "into any capitulation, and his responses were insulting." He added that their fate might have been different if they had surrendered, but because they chose to fight, it caused "the death of the whole of them."[20] In his statement, he conveniently forgot the extermination of those who *did* surrender – Lt. Col. William Ward's Georgia battalion at Refugio, those at the Alamo, and Colonel Fannin on the prairie east of Goliad.

A New Government. One hundred and seventy miles away, as cannons roared and the Alamo walls crumbled, 59 delegates gathered in a small cabin at Washington-on-the-Brazos. It was the first week in March, and with temperatures that dropped to near freezing, the only protection from the brisk north wind was a covering of cotton cloth tacked to the frames of open doorways and windows.[21]

Bankrupted Bend in the River landowner Hosea H. League, now a judge in Harrisburg, was on the committee that selected delegates to the 1836 Washington-on-the-Brazos Convention.

The first order of business at the Convention of 1836 fell to George Campbell Childress, a Tennessee lawyer and nephew of Leftwich Colony empresario Sterling C. Robertson. Childress chaired and authored the Texas Declaration of Independence, starting his draft while in route to Washington-on-the-Brazos and completing it on March 2, only a day after the convention was called to order. The document was read and unanimously adopted without amendment in less than an hour (Fig. 2).[22]

Sterling Robertson visited Bend in the River landowner Hosea League in 1830 when he was in prison for murder. It was here he signed the Leftwich Colony over to its new empresario, Robertson.

Dispatches poured into Washington-on-the-Brazos from the field, the most disturbing from Travis at the Alamo. The delegation was torn. They were anxious to build a wartime government, but the war continually distracted them. They worked anyway. New Jersey born David G. Burnet was named as interim president, and Santa Anna's fallen ally, Lorenzo de Zavala, vice president. George Childress and Robert Hamilton were commissioned as "Special Agents to the US" to gain recognition of "the Sovereignty and Independence of Texas."[23] In one of their last pieces of business, Thomas J. Rusk was nominated as Secretary of War before the convention was abandoned on March 17. The Mexican army was coming, and most sought the perceived safety of Harrisburg.[24]

Bend in the River landowner Hosea League was interim Republic President David Burnet's law partner before the Revolution.

Sam Houston left the proceedings at Washington-on-the-Brazos, finally arriving on March 11 at Gonzales to join his army. He had just 350 men.[25] Houston had received Travis's missives and, unaware of the Alamo's fate, was anxious to reinforce him at Béxar. He was too late. Just four days later, with General Antonio Gaona's troops to his north and Santa Anna close on his heels, Houston began backtracking his steps. The panicked citizens of Gonzales followed him. Not willing to leave anything that could be used by the Mexican army, the town and its stores were burned.

Houston recrossed the Colorado River, his strategy to put that obstacle, raging from recent rains, between the Mexican army and his own army Although he was now burdened with the fleeing citizens in his charge, the tactic bought him time. Within a week after arriving at Ross's Prairie on March 17, his force swelled to as many as a thousand men.[26] He initially determined to meet the Mexican forces on the Colorado River,[27] then changed his mind, retreating during the night of March 26 for San Felipe.

On March 17, General Houston camped at John Crier's homestead on Ross Prairie before moving south to Beason's Ferry. In addition to these holdings, Crier also owned the north part of present day Spread Oaks Ranch.

The Runaway Scrape. After their Alamo victory, the Mexican army divided into three forces – General Gaona headed north to Bastrop, Santa Anna to San Felipe de Austin, and General Urrea continued his march on the coastal prairie route. The Texian citizens in line with Urrea's southern advance were the first to take to the mud-filled roads. Next, fearing Santa Anna's retribution and with no protection from Houston's army, were residents of the upper prairie. All would go east, some to Louisiana, others to Galveston Island. If they made it, they had no idea what was next. But it would certainly be no worse than what lay behind them.

Accounts of the exodus, known as the Runaway Scrape, paint a pitiable picture. Texian and Tejano women, children, the infirmed, and the aged slogging in small groups along muddied roads or riding in ox-drawn carts, hauling no more provisions and personal belongings than they could carry. They travelled mostly without speaking, the unnerving quiet interrupted only by shouts for news from those they passed, or the crying children, and the occasional wails of surviving family members at the death of a loved one. Those who died during the passage were hastily buried among broken or bogged down wagons, stranded mules, oxen, and horses, and effects cast along the route.

Cayce's Ferry was an important crossing during the Runaway Scrape. With the Cayce men in the field, wife Hannah, daughter Mary Ann, and the Cayce slaves and servants joined the flood of Texian families as they slogged east.

The Trail to San Jacinto. Behind the exodus of travelers, General Urrea was making rapid progress. After Fannin's failed resistance on the prairie outside of Goliad, he had few obstacles. Urrea took possession of Guadalupe Victoria on March 21.[28] Next on his march was the mid-coast – Texana, then a Colorado River crossing at Cayce's ferry, then the towns of Matagorda, Columbia, and Brazoria. It was here that Urrea's army, consisting of about 1,165 infantry and cavalry, would prepare to march on Velasco and Galveston and complete their conquest (Fig. 1). Assembling his forces on April 22, a rider delivered a message. The architect of the successful coastal campaign was, instead, ordered north.[29]

The Mexican cavalry and infantry stretched across the Bay Prairie horizon at the Cayce Ferry crossing, located either on or immediately south of the present-day Spread Oaks Ranch boundary.

Santa Anna's progress, in contrast, was slow. During Houston's retreat, he ordered towns and stores burned, the prairie grasses necessary for the army's horses torched, livestock destroyed, and all means for river crossings – bridges, ferries, and boats – scuttled. It wasn't until April 5 that Santa Anna's advance force crossed the Colorado River – nearly two weeks behind the rebel army.[30] General Houston was one river ahead of him.

Houston reached the Brazos River plantation of pioneer settler Jared E. Groce between San Felipe and Washington-on-the-Brazos on April 4 (Fig. 1).[31] Groce's Bernardo Plantation was a godsend to the general grasping for any small advantage, availing him not only a place to camp and drill his units, but a hospital for the sick and abundant stores of grain and beeves. The army remained in the vicinity of Groce's until Houston, now with 700 troops, crossed the river on the steamboat *Yellow Stone* along with 200 horses, ox-teams, wagons, and two six-pound cannons.[32]

Since the first day at Gonzales when Houston began marching east and away from the Mexican army, his actions were dogged by dissention. Uncertain if he intended to fight or continue his retreat until he reached Louisiana, his detractors dubbed Houston the leader of a coward's army. Camped at Groce's, the general received a letter from Texian president Burnet. "Sir," he scribed, "the Enemy are laughing you to scorn. You must fight them. You must retreat no further."[33] Burnet even ordered Thomas Rusk to the field to prevent further retreat, giving him the authority to take control of the army, if necessary, to follow the mandate.[34] The rank and file were equally critical, and increasingly vocal. In the days before San Jacinto, Houston dealt with their threat of desertion by digging two graves. Notice was given that the next soldier to disobey orders would be shot.[35]

Passing through the burned remains of San Felipe on April 7, Santa Anna was unaware that the rebel army was camped only a short distance, about 20 miles, to the north. The crossing, made impassable by Houston's snipers of Captain Moseley's detachment, slowed his passage. The generalissimo was forced to head south and parallel to the Brazos River, towards Old Fort, arriving at the west bank on April 11. When a lone ferryman poled Santa Anna across the Brazos with some 700 infantry, 50 cavalry, and a single cannon on April 12,[36] the general violated a basic military tenet. He had divided his army, leaving wagons, stores, artillery, and most of his troops behind him.

Perhaps he was impatient. More likely, Santa Anna was certain of victory over an adversary that had not yet shown a willingness to fight, and he wanted to horde its glory. The general, however, always said that his bold move was a strategy to quickly end the conflict. In his preferred version, word had reached him that some of the rebel government conspirators, still fleeing east from Washington-on-the-Brazos, were in Harrisburg. Rather than continue a game of cat and mouse with the retreating Houston, he said, his small force would instead capture its leaders.[37]

April 15 dawned cool and wet as Santa Anna approached Harrisburg, its streets empty and buildings largely abandoned. His quarry, the Texian government, had just hours earlier boarded the steamer *Cayuga* and sailed for New Washington, Colonel James Morgan's fledgling town between Houston and Galveston. Apprehending the Texian government was justification enough for the move, but Santa Anna had another purpose. American land speculators were as prominent on the general's list of enemies as treasonous rebels, and foes of both camps were allegedly collected in New Washington. It was a target too rich to ignore.

David G. Burnet and Lorenzo de Zavala, now the leaders of the upstart Texian administration, had been on the wrong side of Santa Anna before. In the late 1820s, the Saltillo legislature gave the pair part of the failed Edwards' Grant.[38] Both empresarios, however, struggled for funds and had little hope for success after the 1830 anti-colonization law, and they sold their holdings to the New York-based Galveston Bay and Texas Land Company. It was an act viewed by the centrists in Mexico as illegal as it was offensive. When the authorities declined to recognize the Galveston Bay and Texas Land Company's legal land titles, their representatives bitterly complained in a letter to Mexico City land administrators. The rebuttal was written by none other than Santa Anna himself, and he was not sympathetic to their position.[39]

Many of the same players in the Galveston Bay and Texas Land Company were behind Colonel James Morgan's development of New Washington – including Lorenzo de Zavala.[40] New Washington, with its pastoral setting overlooking the San Jacinto River and Trinity Bay, would not go unscathed.

Santa Anna remained in Harrisburg long enough to see it burn, ordering Colonel Don Juan Nepomuceno Almonte and his dragoons ahead to New Washington.[41] Almonte reined in his mount at the sandy bay shore. The Texian government, including Zavala, had again eluded their pursuers. Except for one. David Burnet was rowing a small skiff furiously towards the channel and the safety of the schooner *Flash*.[42] It was an easy shot. But Almonte, a soldier who followed a strict code in affairs of war, ordered his soldiers not to fire. Burnet was with his daughters and wife, and Almonte would not endanger noncombatants.[43]

Santa Anna arrived at New Washington on April 18, personally inspecting Colonel Morgan's warehouses and stores. Then he took as prisoner a free woman of color, Emily West. In Texas lore, West would later be immortalized as the Yellow Rose of Texas. Santa Anna again set his sights on Houston's retreating army and prepared to move north to the San Jacinto River east of Harrisburg. Before his march, he set fire to every structure in New Washington.[44]

On April 19, Houston abruptly headed south towards Buffalo Bayou on the west side of the San Jacinto River. The reticent warrior was now in possession of captured army orders that detailed the enemy's position and, more importantly, its strength. He was prepared to make a stand before Santa Anna received reinforcements from Old Fort. In a dispatch that day from Harrisburg, he wrote: "We go to conquer. It is wisdom growing out of necessity to meet and fight the enemy now. Every consideration enforces it. No previous occasion would justify it."[45]

Both generals were now aware of the position of the other. The only unknowns were when and where, and both uncertainties were narrowing quickly. Santa Anna even delivered a message to Houston, written in English by his field translator Almonte: "Mr. Houston, I know you're hiding in the bushes. As soon as I catch the other land thieves" – a not too subtle reference to Burnet and Zavala – "I'm coming up to smoke you out."[46]

The two armies recognized the strategic importance of the nearest passage over the San Jacinto River, Lynch's ferry. It was along this route that they first collided on April 20. After a brief skirmish, the Mexican army withdrew to fortify their position by the San Jacinto River. The Texians moved to their lines with their backs to Buffalo Bayou – an unwise tactic for a defensive position, but an indifferent location for an offensive one. Houston knew the passion of his soldiers was such that the stream would remain far behind them.[47]

The Texian and Mexican forces spent the night camped just a mile apart. Early the next morning General Cos arrived from Old Fort with another 500 reinforcements, nearly doubling the size of Santa Anna's army. Throughout the day, Houston calmly consulted with Rusk, then the officers in his ranks, and finally the rank and file. That afternoon, he prepared his attack plans. The infantry would be led by colonels Burleson and Sherman, and Lt. Col. Henry Millard. The artillery would be commanded by Colonel George Hockley, and the cavalry by newly promoted Col. Mirabeau Lamar.[48]

Late in the afternoon, the Texians made their move, attacking with cries of "Remember the Alamo!" and "Remember Goliad!" The Mexican army didn't see them coming. The infantry quickly overwhelmed the enemy's right, and the cavalry broke the army's left. Cannons in the center of line ceased firing after the Mexican artillerists were reduced by accurate rifle fire and overrun by the infantry. The fleeing Mexican fighters, dogged by a savage Texian offense, made for the river, swamps, or hid in oak mottes flanking Peggy's Lake. Not taking the time to reload their rifles, the Texians killed with gun stocks and pistol butts that doubled as war clubs, stabbed madly with Bowie knives, or slashed with swords until their steel blades were broken.[49] It was said that Houston, while observing the savagery of soldiers, quipped that he praised "his soldier's valor [while] damning their manners."[50]

Sixteen-year-old Shadrack Cayce left the Bend in the River to fight for Texas independence. General Sam Houston sent him back from the front lines during the Battle of San Jacinto because of his young age.

Santa Anna made only a brief attempt to rally his panicked soldiers then, accompanied by General Cos, aide Ramon Martínez Caro, and a portion of his personal guard, he mounted his horse and sprinted west, towards Vince's Bayou, intent on crossing its bridge and rejoining General Filisola at Old Fort.[51] The bridge, however, had been strategically demolished that morning. The victors pursued their quarry, killing some along the bayou banks. Although General Houston did not know it yet, Santa Anna was taken prisoner just before dark.

The battle of San Jacinto was a rout, and it lasted just 18 minutes. In his official dispatch on April 25 to "his Excellency David G. Burnet, president of the Republic of Texas," General Houston reported eight killed and 14 wounded to Santa Anna's 630 killed, 208 wounded, and 730 prisoners.[52]

A Fragile Victory. General Houston slowly descended from his saddle. During the fight he had two mounts shot from under him, and his ankle was shattered by a musket ball. His recent injury was yet another to add to previous wounds he received in battle, the injuries including a bullet in one shoulder and an arrow in his thigh. With the chaos of the closing hours of battle and nightfall approaching, he had boundless battlefield decisions to make. They were important, yet distractions. To the victorious general, only one question really mattered: Where was Santa Anna?

Houston was keenly aware that his victory was a fragile one. To the west, some 4,000 Mexican troops could strike his small forces at any moment. If Santa Anna had escaped and got word to them, the moment would be sooner rather than later.[53]

After a slow march, Gaona's forces arrived at Filisola's Old Fort position on April 21, the day of the battle of San Jacinto. Couriers dispatched the news that Santa Anna had suffered a major defeat. If reports were also true that the generalissimo had been taken captive, then Vincente Filisola was now the de facto commander-in-chief of the Mexican army. His first piece of business was to order General Urrea, at Brazoria, to abandon his eastern march and reconnoiter with the main army on the road west of Old Fort and await news.[54]

General Antonio López de Santa Anna was captured and brought before Houston on April 22. As he faced his adversary, his demeanor was dignified but feigning. He was no enemy of Texas, he offered. He wanted to prevent more bloodshed. The man who had put so many to their deaths seemed willing to say anything to avoid their fate.

Barely a month earlier, Captain Thomas J. Rusk was elected Secretary of War at the Washington-on-the-Brazos convention. Now, at San Jacinto, he returned to the military with a promotion to Brigadier General. It was Rusk who joined Sam Houston to decide the fate of their famous prisoner. Both men believed the general was more useful to the infant Republic alive than dead, and Santa Anna ultimately agreed to an armistice that preserved his life. The agreement carried the conditions that he order General Filisola's withdraw from the Brazos River to Victoria at the Guadalupe River, protect Texian property during the countermarch, and to release prisoners under their guard.[55]

Fight or Flight. Three days after the events at San Jacinto, General Filisola addressed his troops at Old Fort. He spoke boldly. Although Santa Anna was defeated, he orated, it was just a "small, but notable event" at the hands of "a cowardly and disloyal enemy," their success only "quite by chance." He spoke of continuing the war, declaring that "our nation's honor compels us to avenge it's illustrious son, General Santa Anna."[56] His words were inconsistent with history.

The Mexican army regrouped at the widow Powell's homestead on the edge of the San Bernard River, holding a consultation the next day. Its leaders tacitly agreed to honor Santa Anna's directive and withdraw to the Colorado River and solicit instruction from Mexico City. The widow Powell's dogtrot dwelling and outbuildings were put to the torch as they moved west.[57] Heavy rains slowed their movements.

Tres Villas Battalion of 200 infantrymen – the last of the Mexican army retreating after San Jacinto – crossed Cayce's Ferry at the Bend in the River in late April. They torched it and the Cayce's home on the Colorado River.

On the afternoon of April 27, the Mexican commanders received another dispatch from the Santa Anna. "I find myself a prisoner of war among the insurrectionists," he wrote, the result of "having had a disastrous encounter." Then he directed generals Gaona and Filisola to San Antonio de Béxar, and General Urrea to withdrawal to Guadalupe Victoria. More importantly, he advised that an armistice was agreed upon "while negotiations are underway to bring the war to an end forever."[58]

After San Jacinto. In the days following the conflict, Houston and his adversary camped in adjacent tents on the San Jacinto battlefield. By day, the two generals conversed, their words translated by Colonel Juan Almonte and scribed by clerk Ramon Martínez Caro. The backdrop to their conversations were post battle sounds familiar to both warriors – groans of the wounded, hushed chatter of prisoners with their guards, the sound of shovels burying the dead, and the baying of pack animals groaning under the weight of wagons bearing supplies and medicine or ferrying the wounded across Buffalo Bayou to Lorenzo de Zavala's estate and makeshift hospital. At night, odd shadows were cast from bonfires lit so guards could watch their charges. The illumination of the flames caught, as well, fleeting images of red wolves emboldened by the abundance of carrion.[59]

Bend in the River landowner Andrew Crier was with army surgeon general Dr. William P. Smith during the Battle of San Jacinto and was a camp guard.

The San Jacinto camp was abandoned on April 30 and moved three miles up upriver to George M. Patrick's dwelling, the relocation necessitated to "escape the offensive odors"[60] of decomposing men and animal carcasses. At Patrick's, the 122-foot-long steamboat *Yellow Stone* arrived on the first of May, bearing interim Republic President David Burnet, Vice President Lorenzo de Zavala, and other Texian leaders who had, a week earlier, fled New Washington for Galveston.[61] Sam Houston recognized the riverboat immediately – it was the same vessel that ferried his troops and supplies across the Brazos River from Groce's Bernardo Plantation just two weeks earlier.

There was much news to share. General Houston informed Burnet of the treaty terms that he and Rusk drafted between Santa Anna and the Provisional Government. Burnet at first reeled from the information but was shortly convinced of its wisdom. Houston learned that General Cos had been captured and was held in Galveston at makeshift Fort Travis. Then, citing Houston's incapacitation from his battlefield injury, Burnet told the victor of San Jacinto that Thomas J. Rusk would replace him as commander in chief of the Texas army. On May 5, Houston wrote his troops, confiding that his leaving inflicted "many painful sensations," but asked their support of Rusk, a soldier worthy of the position due to "his valor, his patriotism, and his wisdom."[62]

An Uncertain Captivity. On May 6, Burnet and most of his ad interim cabinet boarded the *Yellow Stone* to move Santa Anna and his entourage – Almonte, Ramon Caro, and Colonel Gabriel de Ortega Núñez – to Galveston. Their personal disdain never far from erupting, Burnet denied the wounded Houston passage but demurred at the instance of Houston's doctor. Houston would leave from Galveston to receive care in New Orleans. Vice president Zavala, visiting his family across Buffalo Bayou, would join Burnet later at Velasco. Rusk was also not among them now, moving towards Victoria with the remnants of the army to monitor Filisola's withdrawal.[63]

To the prisoners on the *Yellow Stone*, the barren sand dunes and covering of scrubby spartina grasses as they approached the eastern edge of Galveston Island were not a cheering sight. There were no structures, only makeshift lean-tos and rows of tents crowded with a disparate collection of troops, Mexican prisoners, and refugees of the Runaway Scrape. Fort Travis was only partly completed, its construction under the direction of Colonel Morgan, still chafing from the burning of his New Washington plantation.

Anchored in the deepwater harbor, the detainees were transferred to the schooner *Independence* while the less celebrated prisoners were rowed ashore and slept in the sand.[64]

Santa Anna's time in the staterooms of the *Independence* was short, sailing May 10 on the steamboat *Laura* for the provisional capital of Texas, Velasco, at the mouth of the Brazos River. Because the agreements outlined by Houston and Rusk at San Jacinto were made with the military, not by the government, they were not legally binding. That authority was Burnet's, and he was still willing to maintain that Santa Anna was the only person with the influence to end the war and secure Mexican recognition of Texas independence. Residing in a small building in Velasco, the unlikely collection of men formalized the drafts that became known as the Treaty of Velasco.

Burnett and Santa Anna signed two agreements on May 14, one titled simply 'Public Treaty,' the other the 'Secret Treaty.' In the ten articles of agreement of public version, Santa Anna agreed not to take up arms against the people of Texas, to cease hostilities "both on land and water," evacuate its invading army, protect Texian property during the retreat, return private property taken during the hostilities, and agreed that prisoners on both sides would be released.[65]

In the secret treaty, the fallen generalissimo promised he would never again take up arms against Texas, that the entirety of the Mexican army would vacate Texas, that he would use his influence in the Mexican government to acknowledge the war for independence settled all matters between the belligerents, and that the border between Mexico and Texas was established at the Rio Grande. For his concurrence, Texas would promptly and safely land Santa Anna at Vera Cruz.[66]

Had the contents of the secret agreement been shared with the people of Texas – particularly its army, still incensed by the injustices at the Alamo and Goliad and still clamoring to hang their perpetrator – the next chapter in Texas history might have been very different. Instead, after the surrender of the supreme commander of the Mexican army, the conduct of Republic of Texas patriots contributed to a peculiar chapter in the Lone Star State's formative years.

President Burnet initially honored the Velasco agreements, permitting Santa Anna and his entourage to board the Texian schooner of war *Invincible* on June 1, their destination Vera Cruz. Lorenzo de Zavala and Treasury Secretary Bailey Hardeman, as commissioners for the Republic of Texas, would accompany the group to Vera Cruz and then Mexico City. Liberated and jubilant, Santa Anna penned a letter titled "Farewell of General Santa Anna to the Texian Army." Addressed to "My Friends!" he wrote: "I have been a witness of your courage in the field of battle, and know you to be generous." They would, he scribed, have no reason to regret any kindness shown to him and signed it with "your grateful friend."[67] Santa Anna's enthusiasm would be short lived.

The *Invincible* was at anchor in the Gulf when, on June 2, Brigadier General Thomas J. Green and 130 volunteer troops from the United States made port. Green's soldiers found the streets of Velasco thronging with people and in a state of "great confusion" over Santa Anna's imminent freedom. At one public meeting that day, the crowd listened to a speech by Mirabeau Lamar, Rusk's replacement as Secretary of War, who presented his support of the amnesty. Lamar was heard courteously but his position disregarded. Most in the audience had made up their minds, their positions buoyed by General Benjamin W. Henderson, future Attorney General of the Texas Republic, and interim Secretary of State James Collinsworth, the pair whipping up popular frenzy in opposition to the release of the celebrated prisoner. It was something of a paradox that Collinsworth, just two weeks earlier, had represented his government during the signing of the Treaty of Velasco.[68]

Other than the date, June 3, there is no general agreement to the events that happened next. In some accounts, a captain named Hiram A. Hubbell, under General Thomas J. Green's command, organized the rabble at Velasco, seizing the prisoners and forcing them ashore. In Hubbell's words, "there was at first some objection, but [the prisoners] at last complied." When Burnet heard the news, he directed General Green to accept Captain Hubbell's "speedy resignation," one that "would be very cheerfully accepted."[69]

In a second version, Burnet countermanded his own order and directed the captain of the *Invincible* to bring the entourage ashore. Generals Green and Henderson, Treasury Secretary Hardeman, and a Colonel B.F. Smith Foote boarded the ship to bring the charges off "dead or alive."[70] Regardless of which account is closest to truth, they both ended that day with the resignation of the first vice president of the Republic of Texas, Lorenzo de Zavala, citing that the government had lost the "moral confidence of the people.[71]

By mid-June, Burnet admitted he bowed to public sentiment. The embattled Republic president explained that the government lapsed its agreement because of the "highly excited popular indignation" at the many atrocities at the hands of Santa Anna and his Army, notably "the barbarous massacre of the brave Colonel Fannin and his gallant companions."[72] In another proclamation, he conceded that the treaty terms "received an almost universal condemnation by the citizens of Texas." But, he explained, holding Santa Anna prisoner "gave to us advantageous which years of active warfare might fail to confer." Burnet ended the missive by blaming the affair on Sam Houston. He was livid, he wrote, when he learned Santa Anna had escaped immediate execution, a fate that that "the world would have sanctioned." But after General Houston invited his prisoner "to the hospitality of his camp," it was a decision that he begrudgingly supported.[73]

As the prisoners were ferried ashore once more, Burnet rightfully worried for their safety. His solution was to deliver them back to sea – ironically to the *Ocean*, one of the two army transport ships that brought Thomas J. Green and company to the Brazos River in the first place. They were quickly removed to more secure quarters at Quintana by Galveston merchants Thomas F. McKinney and Samuel May Williams. The latter, only recently, was one of the names on Santa Anna's arrest warrants as a result of his land speculation offenses.

Mexico's Dilemma. Between late April and the middle of May, General-in-Chief Vincente Filisola was abiding by Santa Anna's wishes and, by most accounts, the evacuation terms of the armistice. Despite negotiating waist deep mud and unfordable rivers and streams, his soldiers and stores reached the west bank of the Colorado River by May 9. On the 23rd, the army was between Victoria and Goliad, and as May turned to June, he reached the Nueces River.[74]

Throughout the army's withdrawal, Mexico's Secretary of War José María Tornel's communication with Filisola vacillated from supportive to threatening. In his first correspondence after San Jacinto, penned May 15, Tornel expressed the importance of the safety and liberation of Santa Anna and other prisoners. He made a short reference to the necessity of "preserving" San Antonio de Béxar, then added a warning not to agree to an independent Texas, "as the nation would not allow it." Tornel, however, made no mention of restoring the battle in Texas.[75]

Tornel soon changed his tone, writing that he viewed Filisola's retreat "with the greatest indignation." Filisola may have been following Santa Anna's orders, but as a prisoner of war who did not consult his government, Santa Anna represented neither Mexico, its commander-in-chief, nor acting president José Justo Corro who, Tornel asserted, disapproved the Velasco Treaty. He charged the general with abandoning a position he was ordered to "preserve at every cost" and for this, he continued, "you will have to answer before a Council of War." In closing, Filisola was ordered to surrender the command of the army to General Urrea and return to the capital "to be tried for your conduct."[76]

Tornel changed his strategy and his tenor in another vaguely worded dispatch. Appealing this time to military honor, the war chief encouraged Filisola to press the battle rather than return to Mexico. But, he counseled, he would not have the support of his government – its war chest was empty, and its administration was split on continuing the conflict. His reward, however, would be the personal glory of restoring Texas to the Mexican Republic. Filisola kept marching.[77]

A Change of Heart. Commander-in-Chief Rusk was charged with monitoring Filisola's retreat, but also to avoid colliding with his army. Throughout May, he traversed the same road to Victoria and Goliad that the Mexican army had so recently travelled. He viewed the devastated countryside with dismay. Towns and bridges were burned. He found few supplies for his army, and little forage for his horses. At Goliad, Rusk paused long enough to bury the scattered bones of the dead.[78]

On June 3, the same day that Velasco was in the throes of civil disorder, Rusk held an honors of war ceremony in front of the Goliad La Bahía mission. He spoke of the martyred men who had relinquished "the ease, peace, and comfort of their homes, leaving behind them all they held dear, their mothers, sisters, daughters and wives," and subjected themselves to "deprivation in the name of liberty." Their only reward was death after capitulation. Then, he told of consolations. One was that most of their murderers were killed at San Jacinto. Another was that their chivalrous deeds would be remembered by history. A third was more chilling. "We can still offer another consolation," he said. "Santa Anna, the mock hero, the black hearted murderer is within our grasp."[79]

Rusk's return to the scene of the Coleta Creek slaughter outside of Goliad was a watershed for the soldier who, with Sam Houston at San Jacinto, had authored the armistice granting Santa Anna his freedom. Now, he had a change of heart. Commander-in-chief Rusk seethed when he learned of Burnet's immediate plans to release the illustrious prisoner, ordering Captain William H. Patton to prevent their departure. On June 15, Patton relieved Burnet of the charges and transferred them from Velasco to William H. Jack's two-room house upriver at Bell's Landing.[80]

Divided Amongst Themselves. The military, government, and the public debated Santa Anna's fate throughout June and July. Popular sentiment was for a military tribunal at Goliad, where Santa Anna would be symbolically executed at the place Fannin fell.[81] Others argued for due process – to them, violation of an agreement that existed between representatives of the government of the new Republic of Texas and any other country was unfathomable.

Commander-in-chief Rusk was the highest-ranking officer in the military, and his opinion helped stoke the embers of dissent. One who felt its heat was Captain Mosely Baker, who was with Rusk when he buried his comrades at Goliad. Baker, writing that "the disposition to be made of General Santa Anna is the all absorbing question at this moment," railed that Texas had no need for Santa Anna to secure peace in Texas. Instead, the "haughty despot when in power, and the cowardly sycophant when in adversity" deserved "the ignominious death of the vile felon." Like Rusk, Baker sought vengeance for the spirits of "Travis and Fannin and their murdered compatriots," and justice could only be served when the perpetrator was "hung by the neck" above the Goliad graves.[82]

The Texas civilian government remained divided on the issue. President Burnet's view and that of the recently resigned vice president, Zavala, in support of the armistice, was widely known. Secretary of War Lamar vacillated between immediate execution, at first, to due process. In contrast, Secretary of State James Collinsworth and his successor William H. Jack, and Treasury Secretary Hardeman, were ardently opposed to amnesty. The cabinet's divisiveness inspired Lydia Ann McHenry, later known for her role in establishing the Methodist Church in Texas, to utter the words: "our Cabinet is perhaps the most imbecile body that ever sat in judgement on the fate of a nation. Weak, corrupt, and orderlous [sic].[83]

On May 31, Stephen F. Austin boarded a train from Washington D.C. to Louisville, Kentucky, then embarked on a river steamer bound for Texas. His tenure representing Texas as an emissary to the United States was over, and he had been gone for nearly six months. One of his first orders of business was to visit Santa Anna at Patton's place. The Texas statesman became entirely convinced of his former adversary's "fairness, sincerity, and magnanimity" in fulfilling the Velasco Treaty obligations. Keenly aware that the Texas government and military were hopelessly at odds, he suggested Santa Anna correspond with Andrew Jackson, and request the president to mediate between the new Texas Republic and Mexico.[84]

Santa Anna's letter to US President Andrew Jackson was symbolically dated July 4, 1836. In it, Santa Anna offered that "Mexico cannot retain Texas" and pledged to "avert further evils from his country, by terminating an expensive and useless war." But, he wrote, he was entirely unable to influence his countrymen while in captivity.[85]

City of Houston founder Augustus Chapman Allen was one who saw the wisdom in Austin's arbitration strategy. He voiced his opinion in a decree "to my fellow Citizens in arms and the Volunteers from the United States," writing that "I have learned that this army have resolved to bring Santa Anna [to Victoria], and try him by Courts Martial for his life, for the savage and murderous deeds he has committed." Wouldn't it be wiser, he implored, to wait until President Jackson had weighed in on the subject? On July 27, he couriered a copy of his suggestions to commander-in-chief Rusk.

Almost Treason. The fate of Santa Anna was not the only issue dividing the new Republic that summer. On July 16 a plot was initiated, orchestrated by unnamed army officers in Victoria, to arrest David G. Burnet and deliver him for a military trial. Execution of the order was given to one of the schemers, Lieutenant Colonel Henry Millard, of the First Regiment of Infantry.[86]

Captain Amasa Turner was assigned to Millard's company, and who, in May, had charge of the guard command assigned to the prisoners aboard the *Yellow Stone* on their journey from Buffalo Bayou to Galveston. Now it was August, and Millard handed Turner a new order: "You are hereby commanded to proceed forthwith to the house or office of David G. Burnet, President of this Republic," it read, "and arrest the person of said David G. Burnet and him safely keep. You are also commanded to take into your possession all the books and papers of the Secretary of State, Secretary of War, Secretary of the Navy and Secretary of the Treasury, and them safely keep and deposit."[87]

Captain Turner defied his orders, and in a carefully crafted deception, turned the tide against the conspirators. As the plot evolved, a company of Rangers and a volunteer militia assembled at Velasco to resist any forces Millard might muster. The scheme quietly dissolved. Fortunately for most of the Texans, overthrow of the civil government by the military was not an acceptable resolution to the Santa Anna problem. Texans might not agree with their president, but they were decidedly against "the danger of anarchy."[88]

Many historians who handled this chapter in Texas history downplayed it. Names and actions were omitted. The role of commander-in-chief Rusk in the affair, it seems, was never debated. Euphemisms were used such as a "tug of war between the civilian government and the military" for an event that was, bluntly, an act of treason. Millard was suspended from the army but quickly resurfaced as a chief justice in Jefferson County and as a colonel in the Texas militia.[89]

Plotting and Poison. Santa Anna and the Mexican detainees were in unceasing danger, their antagonists not just in the government and military, but within its citizenry. They lived in an atmosphere of constant intrigue, one not just defined by physical threats, but also from well-meaning schemers who organized several escape attempts on their behalf.

Still under the charge of Captain William H. Patton at Bell's Landing, a drunk loyalist attempted to shoot Santa Anna, his volume of whiskey ensuring that the bullet widely missed the mark, passing between Colonel Juan Almonte and Colonel Núñez. A few days later, a Spanish woman visited the general with an elaborate escape plan hidden in her linen glove. It outlined how she had delivered a bottle of wine spiked with an elixir to drug the guards so the prisoners could make their escape to waiting horses kept nearby for the occasion. If the plot failed, a second wine bottle contained poison for the general to consume at his discretion.[90]

Patton responded by moving his charges further upriver to the perceived safety of Orozimba Plantation on July 30, but it did little to stem the tide of conspiracy. Two weeks later, Spanish native Bartolomé Pagés arrived at Columbia on the schooner *Passaic* from New Orleans. As the perpetrator of yet another escape plot, Pagés delivered a bottle of bitters which contained opium, the "deleterious liquor" to be administered to Santa Anna's guards. When the plot was uncovered, Pagés confessed, further detailing an earlier failed liberation scheme financed by Santa Anna supporters in New Orleans. Pagés escaped confinement in September, was retaken, and appeared in Velasco court to a judge who, curiously, absolved him of all charges.[91]

Santa Anna's Freedom. In late July, interim Republic President Burnet issued a proclamation for the election of a new president and cabinet. Burnet was tired, and his son was ill. At the First Session of The First Congress, Sam Houston defeated Stephen F. Austin and former governor Henry Smith in the September election, and the new president was inaugurated on October 22. In November 1836, President Houston signed an order allowing Santa Anna to travel to Washington D.C. and meet with outgoing president Andrew Jackson. Of the original captors, only Santa Anna and Almonte remained. Ramon Martínez Caro was released in September and Colonel Gabriel de Ortega Núñez was moved to New Orleans.

The two men and their Texas entourage began their journey along the coastal route on horseback, passing north of Galveston Bay. Here they traversed the San Jacinto battlefield to Lynch's ferry, where few words were spoken on either side. Reaching Baton Rouge, they boarded steamboats up the Mississippi and Ohio rivers to Kentucky, reaching the nation's capital on January 18, 1837.

Santa Anna and the Texas emissaries met with Jackson and newly elected Martin Van Buren. Neither side of the travelling party got what they hoped for. Jackson remained firm that the United States would not intercede between Texas and Mexico, a position that he had already communicated in a belated response to Santa Anna's July 4th appeal. In it, he explained that the US "never interferes with the policy other powers." Further, the Mexican government had warned the president that, so long as Santa Anna was a prisoner, "no act of ours will be regarded as binding."[92]

As for the Texans, US annexation would take another eight years. Although the populace voted overwhelmingly for annexation in 1836, the United States was not prepared to admit another slave state, nor was it prepared to take an antagonistic stand against Mexico.

After eight days in Washington, Santa Anna and Almonte boarded a US frigate *Pioneer* at Norfolk, bound for Veracruz.

Epilogue. After the drama of Santa Anna's surrender and incarceration, some of its main characters rose while others fell, but none remained the same. David G. Burnet's infant son, Jacob George Burnet, died at Velasco "of the whooping cough"[93] shortly after the first Republic president left office. Over the next 34 years, Burnet held minor government roles and raised crops but died broke in 1870.

Stephen F. Austin, passed over in 1836 as president of the Republic of Texas, succumbed to pneumonia in December 1836. Interim Republic vice president Lorenzo de Zavala died the previous November. Republic Treasury Secretary Bailey Hardeman died from a fever in 1836. In 1838, former Secretary of State James Collinsworth drank himself into Galveston Bay and was buried in the new city of Houston.[94]

Sam Houston held numerous roles in Texas government. He was a two-term Republic president and served in the House of Representatives, then after annexation was a Texas senator from 1846 until 1859. A controversial figure with a long list of enemies, his anti-slavery sentiments created many more, and he was defeated in his run for governor and the senate in the late 1850s. He won the governor's chair again in 1859 but was forced from office when Texas voted to join the Confederate States of America in 1861. Houston retired in Huntsville and died three years later.

Rusk's replacement as Secretary of War, Mirabeau Lamar, would be elected Sam Houston's vice president in 1836 and succeeded him as president. He was defeated after one term. Interim Secretary of War and army commander-in-chief Thomas J. Rusk held a variety of military leadership positions, practiced law, was chief justice of the Texas Supreme Court, elected to the US Senate, and had other roles in education, railroads, and the postal system. After his wife died in 1856, he committed suicide.[95]

The two antagonists in the plot to arrest David G. Burnet, Lieutenant Colonel Henry Millard and Captain Amasa Turner, had distinguished careers after the events at Velasco. Millard was suspended from the army for his potentially treasonous actions but quickly resurfaced as a chief justice in Jefferson County and as a colonel in the Texas militia.[96] Captain Turner lived in Galveston, where he was custom's officer, then moved to Lavaca County where he served as a representative to the legislature and senate, then finally settling in Gonzales after the Civil War.[97]

Santa Anna received a warm welcome when he landed at Vera Cruz. Four years later he again became president of Mexico and renewed hostilities with Texas. General Antonio López de Santa Anna, the man who agreed to everything and anything to avoid execution – and convinced many notable Texians of his sincerity – had meant none of it.

President Santa Anna and the Mexican government were still intent on recapturing Texas. Theirs would require a delicate strategy, one strong enough to test the Texas response, but not so strong to incite United States intervention. Santa Anna's first move was to authorize a raiding party under the command of Ráfael Vásquez. Vásquez marched through Goliad, Refugio, and captured San Antonio in March 1842 before quickly crossing back into Mexico.

During the 1842 raids by Mexican generals Ráfael Vásquez and Adrián Woll, Bend in the River landowner James Denison served as a private in Colonel Clark L. Owen's Regiment of Albert C. Horton's Volunteer Company.

The Vásquez expedition was followed by a second, commanded by French-born Adrián Woll who, with some 1,400 infantry, cavalry, and artillery took San Antonio in September. In a sharp engagement, 41 Texas volunteers were killed, and several prisoners taken, before Woll retreated during the night.[98]

Henry Petty Cayce, who lived at the Bend in the River on the League and Cayce tracts, fought in both 1842 Mexican invasions of Texas, and at Matamoros under General Zachary Taylor during the Mexican American War.

Texas was admitted into the United States in 1845. Mexico, however, still refused to recognize Texas or its boundary claim to the Rio Grande (Fig. 3). US President Polk turned to the fallen Santa Anna, now exiled to Cuba by his countrymen for the crime of "excesses," and who promised to negotiate Mexico's sale of the disputed territory with his government. Once again, powerful period players were duped by his words. Sailing as a free man through the American blockade, Santa Anna instead led the resistance. It was called the Mexican American War, and the general and his army were resoundingly defeated. The result was the Treaty of Hidalgo that added 525,000 square miles of western lands to the American nation. It was Manifest Destiny.

Bend in the River landowner Andrew Crier volunteered for wartime service during the Mexican American War, enlisting in Capt. Caleb C. Herbert's Colorado County Mounted Rifle Company and Captain Price's Texas Mounted Volunteers.

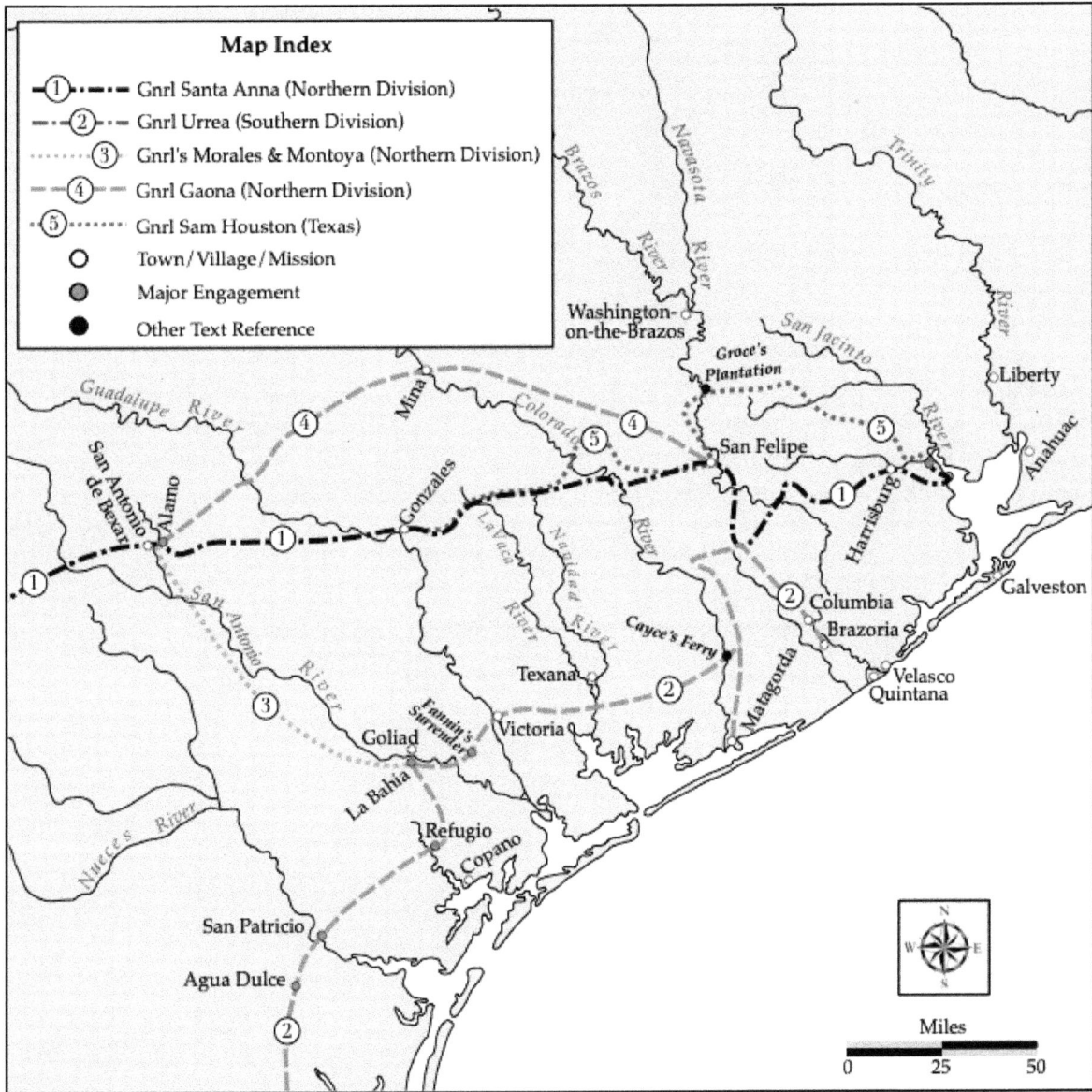

Fig. 1. Generalized routes taken by the Texian and Mexican armies, 1836. Multiple references, including Kendall, W.T., *Texas and Mexican Army Troop Movements*, March 28 – April 20, 1835, San Jacinto Museum of History; Dimmick, Gregg J., *Sea of Mud* (Austin: TSAHA, 2004), 362 pp.

Fig. 2. The first official flag of the Republic of Texas, accepted by the March 1836 convention at Washington-on-the-Brazos. Interim Republic vice president Lorenzo de Zavala is credited as its designer and was adopted in a motion by George Campbell Childress, author of the Texas Declaration of Independence. Greer, J.K., *The Committee on the Texas Declaration of Independence*, Southwest Quarterly, v. 30, no. 4, April 1927, p. 251, https://texashistory.unt.edu/ark:/67531/metapth117142/, The Portal to Texas History; First Flag of the Republic De Zavala Flag 1836.

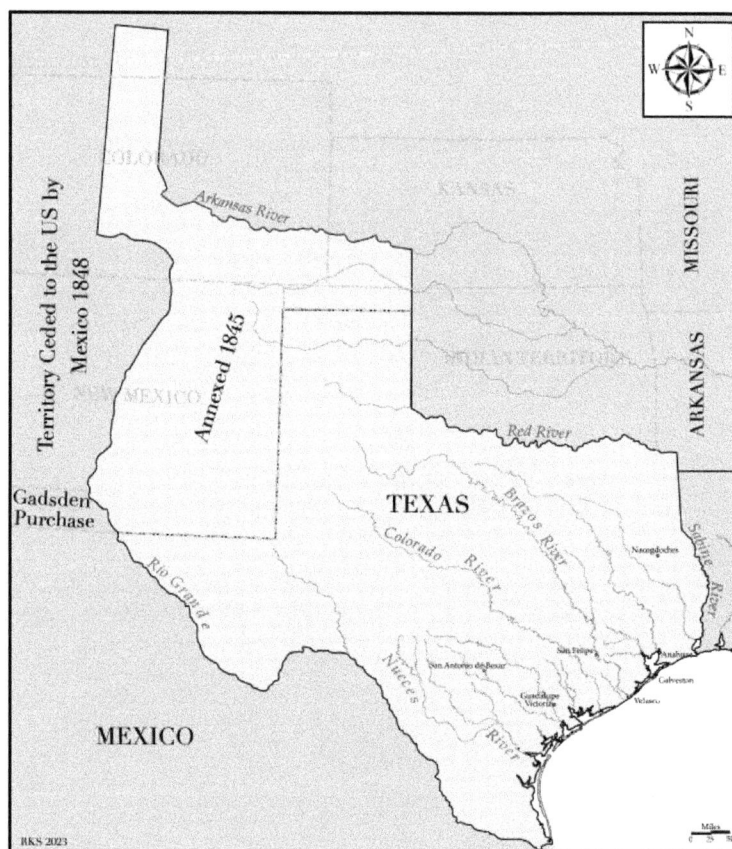

Fig. 3. Texas boundaries after admission to the United States in 1845. Mexico refused to recognize Texas sovereignty or its claim to lands between the Nueces River and Rio Grande. After the Mexican American War, the United States added the territory from Texas to the Pacific Ocean. Map from various sources.

CHAPTER 8

Water and Wood – The Colorado River Log Raft

Other than the sound of cross-cut saws as slaves cleared timber, the banks of the lower Colorado River in the early summer of 1845 were devoid of man-made noises. But not at the old Jennings and League Survey on the Bend in the River at Cayce's Ferry crossing, which nearly always bustled with activity. Here, the silence was broken by the shouts of flatboat men poling upriver, or the rumbling of stagecoaches and ox-drawn carts horses moving to and from the landing, now operated by blacksmith George Elliott and his son.

The smattering of people along the river weren't concerned by the gray smoke billowing over the riverbank. They had seen it before, as slaves burned the canebrakes to plant sugar cane or corn. But the shriek of the whistle was alien, and the men abandoned their work, and the women and children deserted their chores, scrambling to the edge of the river where they stood, transfixed, as the first steamboat to traverse the Colorado River – the *Kate Ward* – chugged past. As a result of the Colorado River log jam, or raft, riverboat navigation was a long time in coming, and most cheered or waved. Then, as the smoke from her boiler stacks settled on the horizon and her transom faded around the next riverbend, they went back to work or play.

During the formative years of the Texas Republic, the great Colorado River log jam was the barrier to the dream of turning the town of Matagorda into a center of commerce between Gulf shipping and inland markets upriver. In fact, one of the reasons that Republic of Texas President Mirabeau B. Lamar selected Austin as its capital was his certainty that riverboats would connect the seat of government to the Gulf of Mexico at Matagorda. It never really came to pass. Matagordians may have tamed a harsh land, but for over a hundred years, it seemed they were unable to conquer logs.

Log rafts on the Colorado River were first recorded in 1690 in an expedition by Alonso de Leon and were mapped by his cartographer, Manuel Joseph de Cardenas. The raft they encountered was not large, blocking only a single branch of the Colorado River delta. When Stephen F. Austin's colonists arrived 130 years later, a raft had again collected near the mouth of the river. By 1837, the head of the raft extended upstream about 10 more miles. For Matagorda town it was beginning to be a barrier to river commerce.[1]

1838 marked the first recorded traverse of the Colorado River when a Captain Wren piloted the keelboat *David Crockett* downriver from Bastrop. Keelboat trade, however, was far from ideal. The small flat boats had to be poled downstream, guided by rudder and poles. Then, if they weren't dismantled and sold for lumber, they were sailed and poled back upriver. It was a laborious, time-consuming journey, and the amount of cargo they were able to haul, compared to steamboats, was insignificant. Although the enterprising Captain Wren managed to cover a remarkable 300 miles in five days, he only reached as a far as the head of the log raft above Matagorda town.[2]

Matagorda planters and merchants, as early as the 1830s, lobbied vigorously for the removal of the raft, proposing that the value of the timber it contained offered considerable inducement to contractors. The Texas senate and house agreed, approving incorporation of the Colorado Navigation Company (CNC) to improve river navigation in 1837. Signed by

Sam Houston and Mirabeau B. Lamar, the act provided for raising an ambitious $125,000 in capital stock (Figs. 1 & 2). A year later, they hadn't raised the money.[3]

Matagorda's river port plans were dashed again when, in 1842, high water delivered another round of driftwood that clogged the section of river at two broad meanders above Cazneau's Island. Called the "Raft of '42,"[4] it was the catalyst for renewed interest in river navigation. In January 1844, the Texas senate and house rechartered CNC, authorizing the sale of $100,000 in common stock.[5] Engineers inspecting the raft thought it was impractical to remove the floating masses, proposing instead to dam tributaries and creeks flowing into the river. (Fig. 3) This, they thought, would increase flow in the main river channel, scour out the debris, and float it to the Gulf. Now, they needed to find a vessel suited for the job.

Matagorda businessman Trowbridge Ward and Austin entrepreneur Joseph W. Robertson, both commissioners in CNC, founded Ward & Co. in 1844, intent on designing a shallow draft steamer capable of navigating the Colorado.[6] Co-owners in the syndicate included Samuel Ward, a principal in the Matagorda dry goods firm Ward & Ingram, and his brother George W., a Matagorda commission merchant and delegate of the 1842 CNC Committee.[7] The venture, they thought, might capitalize on CNC contract work, but more importantly, if successful they would monopolize maritime trade between the coast and towns upriver.

Construction of the Ward & Co. steamboat began in the spring of 1844 at the head of the raft above Cazncau's Island. The site had evolved into a bustling – but entirely unplanned – river port. Because of the persistent log jam, coastal freight destined for inland towns was offloaded and lightered from Matagorda Bay by teamsters with horse, mule, and ox-drawn carts, then shuttled across the prairie to the head of the raft. It was the same for goods moving from the other direction, downriver, via keelboats and later river steamers bound for the coast. The lightering practice was both time consuming and costly. There were delays due to labor or weather, particularly during rains. A newspaper editorial expressed the common sentiment that "our friends in the interior are tired of sticking in the mud with their ox teams on a road running parallel to with one of most beautiful streams in the union, and of paying out one-fourth of the avails of their crops for transportation."[8]

For Matagorda, a port town with ambitions to advance its Gulf and inland trade, the raft was maddening. Matagorda was a prosperous antebellum town, its alabaster oyster shell streets lined with the summer homes of plantation owners, restaurants, theatres, and hotels, the latter including the 20-room Colorado House with its Chippendale chairs, ornate fittings, and polished wood furnishings (Fig. 4). But its civic leaders could only watch as the logs continued to gather, powerless as, increasingly, shipping traffic headed for the head of the raft by-passed the town. Worse, a railroad was chartered from Tres Palacios Bay to head of the raft and it, too, would entirely pass Matagorda.[9] Meanwhile, the coastal ports of Galveston and Indianola expanded their hold on shipping markets at Matagorda's expense. A lot was at stake as the Ward & Co. riverboat neared completion.

It was "a lively, cheerful, and gay scene" on that June day in 1845 as people from throughout the Colorado River valley collected to witness the Ward & Co.'s inaugural steamer voyage. Dubbed the *Kate Ward* for incorporator Samuel's sister, the christening ceremony was completed by the steamer namesake herself, Kate Ward.[10] The vessel was a side-wheel steamer, between 110 and 115 feet in length, 24 feet at the beam, with two decks, two engines, and iron boilers. Importantly, she drew only 18 inches of water when empty and, fully loaded with 600 bales of cotton, would not draw more than 3-feet water.[11]

Piloted by Captain William J. Ward, the riverboat began her career carrying freight from the head of the raft as far as La Grange. Its crew included her pilot, Captain Ward, ship agent Trowbridge Ward, ship mates, three engineers, several "wood choppers," a butcher, and a wagoner to handle short-distance drayage. Manifests from landings at river towns and plantations listed her main cargo as cotton bales, bags of wildfowl feathers used for pillows and mattresses, lumber, shingles, plows, weighty limestone millstones for grinding grain, animal hides and deer skins, sacks of salt, oyster shells, pecans, and barrels of molasses and currant. Captain Ward's scribed bills of ladings provide a glimpse of life aboard the river steamer. In addition to staples such as clothing, boots, and shoes, he purchased tobacco sold by the plug, tin cups, gunny bags, whiskey by the gallon, whetstones for sharpening knives and tools, gunpowder, and mosquito bars.[12]

Confined by obstacles between LaGrange and Cazneau's Island, Captain Ward's real prize lay many more miles upstream – Austin – and another that was further downstream – Matagorda. With his eye always on the river level, Ward made his move towards Austin in the early spring of 1846. When the *Kate Ward* ascended the river north of Bastrop, the Austin prize seemed within his grasp. The capital city knew Captain Ward was coming, and a throng of townspeople lined the riverbank in anticipation of his maritime miracle. On March 8, as the steamer appeared on the horizon, the vessel was met with cheers, huzzas, "and every demonstration of rejoicing." US Army Major Beall and his detachment of dragoons fired an honorary salute.[13]

Newspapers throughout the south promulgated news that the *Kate Ward* – the first to steamer to run "the difficulties" of "an untried stream" – had reached Austin.[14] The feat, pundits implored, "formed an era in the history of Western Texas.[15] The capital of Texas was at last "connected with the rest of the world by a new link" that would unlock the "treasures of the mountain frontier."[16] The Texas legislature even gifted Captain Ward a league of land.[17] Then, planning for the future, towns along the river route announced that "arrangements have been made to keep on hand a constant supply of good wood at convenient points" so that "inferior wood," which had to be hauled from the river banks by the ship's crew, would not slow the steamer's next journey.[18]

Firewood cut and stacked along the river for the *Kate Ward's* two boilers would go unused. Just a month after its Austin return, the steamer ran aground near Columbus and remained there until the river rose. Low water persisted through much of the summer, restricting the *Kate* to only a few trips between the head of the raft and La Grange. The low river level continued into fall, terminating trips above Columbus. Planters expecting to ship their cotton by river were, instead, obliged to use teams. Meanwhile, the Ward & Co. financiers were falling deeply into debt.[19]

Higher river levels during winter and early spring in 1847 permitted the *Kate Ward* to make several successful forays to La Grange.[20] Captain Ward, however, was still eager to round the raft and prove he could reach Matagorda and the Gulf. An attempt after a summer "freshet" failed,[21] however, and the vessel spent several weeks lodged in the raft above Matagorda.[22] A low river stage persisted into fall, and its owners were again forced to dry dock the steamer. Observers opined that the "steamer will rot to pieces before her enterprising proprietors will obtain an income sufficient to the interest on the capital they have invested."[23]

Inactivity again plagued the riverboat venture through much of 1848. That spring, the *Kate Ward* grounded on a shoal. Freed, she spent much of summer wedged between two sections of the raft.[24] Ward & Co. principals, now convinced of the folly of Colorado River navigation, accepted a $1,000 offer from a Victoria syndicate headed by riverboat captain and entrepreneur Jesse O. Wheeler to move their operation to the Guadalupe River.[25] All that stood between the *Kate Ward* and her new career was the log jam, but it remained a formidable obstacle.

Then it happened. In the fall of 1848 torrential flood waters roared down the river, inundating the prairie at the head of the raft. With its flow blocked by the log jam, the current was diverted east of the barrier, where it scoured a new channel. Captain Ward eyed the landscape, then made his move. Steam and smoke billowed skyward as the crew stoked her boilers and held her steady against the current. Gripping the helm, Capt. Ward pointed *Kate's* bow downriver into the temporary channel. The hull cleared the first shoal, but in other places creaked and groaned as it grounded hard on the bottom. In less than 15 minutes he achieved what was previously not possible, traversing some two and a half miles around the raft and landing in the main channel. Negotiating the eddies where the original channel joined the Kate Ward Chute, as it came to be called, Captain Ward headed to sea and up the Guadalupe (Fig. 5).[26]

Between her inaugural sail and 1848, the *Kate Ward* had achieved some important maritime milestones, but had not contributed to any meaningful navigation improvements. She was primarily a river trader, and not a particularly profitable one. Her role would change, and the *Kate Ward* would again return to the Colorado River, but in 1849 her future seemed limited to removing obstructions in the Guadalupe River and trading between Port Lavaca, Indianola, and Victoria (Fig. 6 & 7).[27]

The Colorado Navigation Company, still intent on opening the river, held conventions in LaGrange and Columbus during early 1849. Nothing had come of earlier plans to dam river tributaries and creeks and committee members debated their next move. Although the *Kate Ward* was now plying the Guadalupe River, her surprising success in by-passing the Colorado River raft was the foremost topic. Many committeemen backed a proposal to deepen the Kate Ward Chute and extend it upriver. The canal idea, however, was tabled because it would have to cut "through a heavy tenacious soil."[28] Their plan, instead, was to remove the raft.[29]

Company delegates solicited sealed bids to clear the entirety of the river from the foot of the raft at Matagorda Bay to Austin (Fig. 8). That July, southern newspapers advertised the proposal under the heading "Notice to Capitalists!"[30] Editorials endorsing the endeavor espoused its benefits to residents "in the valley of the Colorado" who "are alive to the importance of being connected with the Gulf of Mexico." Reaching Austin, the "highest navigable point in the whole west" was a worthy goal, but "every blow struck to clear out the river is that much in favor of a route from some point upon its waters to California."[31] Despite the hyperbole, the proposal did not receive any bids.

The CNC was undaunted. They would do the job themselves, with funding provided by the sale of $25 certificates. Now, just as in 1844, they needed to find a vessel suited for the job. And again, like 1844, they would turn to the *Kate Ward* for the job.

Although the *Kate Ward* was doing brisk business as a steam freighter between Indianola and Victoria, the steamboat venture was still unprofitable. Creditors dogged the operation. Former Victoria patron Jesse O. Wheeler filed a lawsuit – it eventually reached the Texas Supreme Court – charging the Ward & Co. partners of accounting improprieties.

The *Kate Ward* owners were ready to sell, and in the winter of 1850/51, she became the property of CNC for the sum of $6,000.[32]

The Ward & Co. principals never returned to river navigation. Owner and ship agent Trowbridge Ward moved to Bexar County. Merchant Joseph W. Robertson remained in Austin. Samuel Ward left Texas in 1847 and by 1854 was "a citizen of the state of New York." George W. Ward, who earlier followed the lure of California gold, died there in 1851.[33]

Captain William J. Ward remained at the *Kate Ward*'s helm, his freighter now converted to a snag boat fitted with an engine able to hoist 20 tons "for the purpose of removing the logs and trees in the raft."[34] When the *Kate Ward* returned to Colorado River in the spring of 1851 the raft, described as "snags and rafts, floating in some places and in others a solid bed of timber" had, in just three years, stretched upriver another six and a half miles to the "Bluff Landing on the Reese tract of land."[35]

The CNC assembled its work force, posting advertisements in area newspapers soliciting "negroes to work on the raft, for whom high wages are offered"[36] and "parties of smart axemen [*sic*]."[37] Work started at the foot of the raft and a channel was quickly cleared through 20 miles of river, including the worst section of timber and floating logs along a continuous seven-mile section at the head of the raft.[38] Just as the *Kate Ward* seemed destined for Austin, the project was halted. The CNC was out of funds. That year, and into early 1853, the *Kate Ward* remained in drydock at Matagorda harbor.

The Colorado Navigation Company's coffers got a boost with a $20,000 appropriation under the Rivers and Harbors Act in 1852. The US Corps of Engineers and Topographical Engineers had made their first survey of the Colorado River in 1850, concluding that improvement of the Colorado River was necessary more for military reasons than for commerce.[39] Two years later, project supervisor Lt. William H.C. Whiting travelled to Matagorda. One of his first orders of business was purchase of the *Kate Ward* and to offer Captain Ward – a man he commended as "an excellent practical engineer of great energy and sound judgement" – the helm. Repairs to the steamer started immediately (Fig. 9) but were delayed by "a pestilence at New Orleans and in Texas."[40]

Kate, now the property of the US government and newly fitted with snag boat "tackle and machinery," returned to the river in the summer of 1853.[41] The government plan was to dredge a channel around the worst section of the log jam, assigning US Corps of Engineers Lt. W.H.C. Stevens to the venture. Stevens announced the work would entail connecting "certain lakes together, on the route in which the steamer *Kate Ward* got out of the river several years ago. There are three large lakes, which when so united, will not only form a good channel but make a considerable cut off."[42]

While confident of his technical recommendations, Lt. Stevens had doubts about the available work force. Cynically – even for the times – he warned that labor was a critical weakness "in the execution of any project in this country. Planters are unwilling [to permit] their slaves to leave their cotton and sugar. White labor," he added, "is objectionable here. It can neither be controlled nor supported as well as slave labor. The executive officer depending on white hands is constantly liable to be left at any critical period of his operations."[43]

Prejudices aside, what the lieutenant failed to consider was how formidable a task the *Kate Ward*'s crew faced in their daily work. The raft could be treacherous – although thick and stable in some places, it was more often a floating, fluid mass that, as the morning sun heated its surface, could be alive with cotton mouths, water snakes, and the occasional rattlesnake. Operation of the primitive snagging rig could remove an arm or leg in an instant, and a man caught in the mud mill – a rotating chain with dredging boards powered by the ship's steam boilers – might quickly drown.

The terrain was demanding as well. Paths along the riverbank used by mule and horse carts to deliver supplies were cleared by hand through dense stands of *Arundinaria gigantea* – canebrakes – that towered to heights of 25 feet. Wagons overturned in steep ravines, and nearly always bogged down in mud. Throughout most of the year laborers suffered cold, heat, or rain, their work plagued by gnats, mosquitoes, and horseflies.

Stevens's disdain for the Southern work ethic proved to be unfounded. The *Kate Ward* commenced its efforts in November 1853 and finished clearing the river in just five months. She dredged a new canal above the raft, later part of the Thorpe Canal, and completed a second section extending downriver to the foot of the Kate Ward Chute. Covering over four and half miles, the two canals by-passed the western meanders of the original channel, redirecting the river through a new channel to the east.[44] When a flood in June 1854 further deepened the channel and "washed it out much wider," it allowed passage for "the largest class boats without the slightest difficulty."[45]

Two hundred and eighty-one miles separated Austin and Matagorda Bay. Although keelboats and river steamers were able to navigate about 260, the dream of sailing the last 20 or so to Matagorda had always remained elusive. But in March 1854, the *Kate Ward* made the vision a reality. Steamers could at last traverse the Colorado River, connecting the port towns of Galveston, Matagorda, and Indianola to inland towns upriver.

Boats that made the journey included the *Betty Powell, Lareno, Moccasin Bell, Colorado Ranger*, and likely several others,[46] but the *Kate Ward* was not one of them. Lt. Stevens proposed to dispense of surplus government property, and with her work complete, he offered the *Kate* back to the Colorado River Navigation Company for $4,000. The old steamer, he thought, might continue to be useful for removing snags, clearing overhanging timber, and dredging shoals.[47] Instead, a syndicate of Lavaca merchants purchased the *Kate Ward* in August.

Kate steamed down the river to the Gulf during early September.[48] Captain Ward likely had a hint of remorse as he by-passed the raft through the channel that bore his vessel's name, then headed to Matagorda Bay through the river's west channel. Here he met the hurricane of September 18, 1854, and broke apart in the breakers off Dog Island, adjacent to the west branch of the Colorado River.[49] Three survivors were found four days later clinging to one of her paddle wheels. Eleven other seamen on board drowned, including Captain Ward and an unnamed brother.[50] The "mangled bodies" of Ward and his brother were found on a "desolate beach" – probably Matagorda Peninsula – several days after the wreck. Captain Ward's widow "suffered on" until she died in the late 1850s.[51]

That fall, cotton boats and steamers passed through the Colorado River channel cut by the *Kate Ward*, their routes connecting inland towns as far as Austin with the port towns of both Matagorda and Indianola. Then, between 1860 and 1863, driftwood began rafting opposite the Williams League above the Kate Ward channel.[52] This time, however, Texas could not turn to the federal government. The Lone Star State had cast its lot with the Confederacy after the first cannonades of the Civil War.

In 1870, a "Colonel Thorpe" – probably J. L. Thorpe, Matagorda representative to the State Democratic Convention in the 1850s – was enlisted to remove the most recent raft, putting "a force of negroes to work with axes and poles," cutting loose "the tangled mass of driftwood and pushing it off downstream." With progress slow he determined, instead, to "put them to ploughing and scraping" a canal around the raft. Called Thorpe's Canal, the new waterway was short-lived, cut-off by floating logs and again shutting down river commerce. It would be another 50 years before removal the log jam was again given serious consideration (Fig. 10).[53]

Notice to Boat Builders.

PROPOSALS for Building TWO FLAT BOATS will be received at the Office of the Colorado Navigation Company, for ten days. Plan and dimensions to be seen at the Office.

By order of the Board of Directors,

C. A. BULLARD, Secretary.

Matagorda, April 18th, 1838.

Fig. 1. Colorado Navigation Company advertisement for flatboats. *Matagorda Bulletin*, April 25, 1838, Univ. of North Texas Libraries, The Portal to Texas History, https://texashistory.unt.edu/ark:/67531/metapth80348/.

NOTICE

OF THE

Colorado Navigation Company.

SEALED Proposals, for removing the Raft and other obstructions in the Colorado River, and rendering it navigable according to the provisions of the Charter for this Company, will be received at their office for ninety days.

By order of the Board of Directors,

C. A. BULLARD, Secretary.

Matagorda, April, 18th, 1838.

Fig. 2. Colorado Navigation Company's initial call for bids to clear the river raft Colorado Navigation Company. *Matagorda Bulletin*, April 25, 1838, Univ. of North Texas Libraries, The Portal to Texas History, https://texashistory.unt.edu/ark:/67531/metapth80348/.

MR. EDITOR—Sir, in giving you a discription of the "Colorado" river, I would say that in my opinion, it is the best in the country for navigation, for the reason that it furnishes more water at a low stage, than any other—and with the improvements which are required on all streams of this kind, will become a good one for navigation as high as this place. The improvements required, are the cutting away the hanging timber on the banks, and blocking up the small passages which take the water from the main channel of the river. There is no place where the water is confined to one channel, which will not admit of Steam-boats running at low water successfully.

WM. J. WARD.

Austin, March 10th, 1846.

Fig. 3. The state of the river in 1846 according to *Kate Ward* Captain William Ward. *Texas Democrat*, March 11, 1846, Univ. of North Texas Libraries, The Portal to Texas History, https://texashistory.unt.edu/ark:/67531/metapth48311/.

Fig. 4. Lithographic letter sheet of Matagorda Texas, circa 1860. The drawings were done by Helmut Holtz and sent to Hamburg, Germany lithographer Eduard Lang. The Colorado House is in the center. Matagorda was a quintessential antebellum town, with several summer homes built by plantation owners, as well as restaurants, theatres, and hotels, the latter including the 20-room hotel, the Colorado House. Built from cypress, the hotel featured Chippendale chairs, ornate silver, copper and brass fittings, and mahogany, cherry, and walnut furnishings. Matagorda town visitors could travel by a weekly stagecoach line to and from inland Texas cities, or travel by sea via the steamship *The Yacht*, the first commercial steamer between Galveston and Matagorda. *The Yacht* was quickly followed by large steamships of the Harris and Morgan Line, and stately sailing brigs began to arrive from the East Coast as early as 1848. The Colorado River raft prevented Matagorda from realizing its full economic potential. Collection of Jim Moloney.

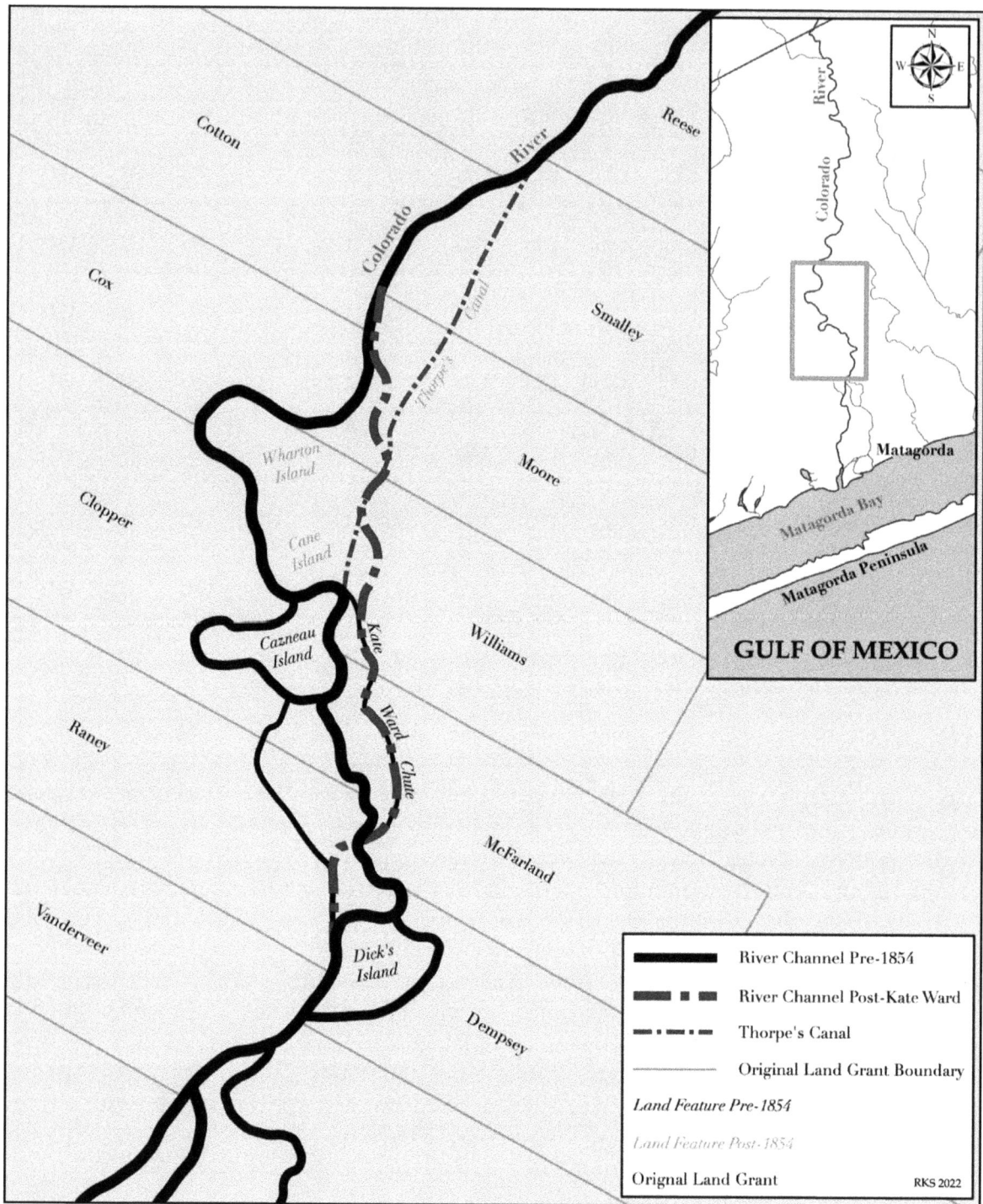

Fig. 5. The original Colorado River course and the "Kate Ward Chute," with the later Thorpe's Canal. Center of map is about 11 miles south of present day Spread Oaks Ranch. Base map modified from The Texas General Land Office, Matagorda County Rolled Sketch 11, ca. 1908 to 1912, doc. no. 8348.

YANKEE BEANS & PICKLED PORK—
will arrive by the "Kate Ward."
JOHNSON & CO.

Fig. 6. By 1850, the *Kate Ward* was trading on the Guadalupe River between Port Lavaca, Indianola, and Victoria. *Texian Advocate*, Aug. 30, 1850, Univ. of North of North Texas Libraries, The Portal to Texas History, https://texashistory.unt.edu/ark:/67531/metapth 180349/.

JUST received por "Kate Ward"
    New Cranberries
    Dried fruit, Currants,
    Peaches,
    Apples,
    Raisins,
    New Codfish,
    Mackerel No. 1,
For sale cheap for cash, wholesale and retail.
May 3, 1850—1   JOHNSON & CO.

Fig. 7. Inventory of goods shipped by the river freighter *Kate Ward* in 1850. *Texian Advocate*, Dec. 5, 1850, Univ. of North Texas Libraries, The Portal to Texas History, https://texashistory. unt.edu/ark:/67531/metapth180357/.

Notice
TO CAPITALISTS.
PROPOSALS
WANTED FOR CLEARING OUT THE
RAFT
AND OTHER OBSTRUCTIONS
ON THE COLORADO RIVER,
IN THE STATE OF TEXAS.

PERSONS wishing to contract for the same will give in their bids, under seal, to Thos. Wm. Ward, at Austin, and to John Rugeley, at Matagorda, in said State, previous to the 15th of October next, naming such securities as he or they may be able to give, upon entering into a contract with the Directors for the completion of a part or whole of the work.

It is desired that the estimate for removing the Raft should be made separate from the other obstructions reaching from the head of the Raft to the city of Austin.

Notice is hereby given that the sum or sums contracted to be paid, will be turned over by reasonable and regular instalments as the work progresses.

The Raft, from the report of the Delegates appointed by the Convention to survey the same, and under whose authority and that of subscribers we now act, was found to consist in lineal measure, of about 3250 varas, being about 3000 English yards. The most of it is supposed to be loose and floating, is in small detached parcels and lies only fifteen miles above the mouth of the River.

Those wishing to contract however, will satisfy themselves by examination or otherwise, of the extent of the Raft and the difficulties to be surmounted.

(Signed)   THOS. J. HARDEMAN,
Chairman of Convention

Fig. 8. Colorado River Navigation Company was still seeking bids to clear the river from the foot of the raft at Matagorda Bay to Austin in 1849. *Colorado Times*, Oct. 15, 1849, Univ. of North Texas Libraries, The Portal to Texas History, https://texashistory.unt. edu/ark:/67531/metapth80434/.

MATAGORDA:

SATURDAY, MAY 10, 1851.

☞ The steamer *Kate Ward* started up the river on Monday last, in order to commence operations on the Raft, but during the heavy gale on Monday night sustained some injury to her chimnies, and was compelled to return here on the following morning for repairs.

Fig. 9. The *Kate Ward* was converted to a snag boat and returned to Colorado River in the spring of 1851. *Colorado Tribune*, May 10, 1851, Univ. of North of North Texas Libraries, The Portal to Texas History, https://texashistory.unt.edu/ark:/67531/metapth80435/.

Fig. 10. Colorado River log jam looking north from the old wagon bridge on the original Cayce headright towards Spread Oaks Ranch, 1910s to early 1920s. Courtesy Matagorda Museum, File No. 1994.56.225G.29.

CHAPTER 9

Matagorda's Cattle and Cowboys

1860s to 1900s

Long-horned Iberian cattle were initially brought to the New World by the Spanish, who maintained large herds on the open range of the southwest plains of North America. The men who worked those herds were vaqueros, and they laid the foundation for the American cowboy. During Texas colonization, longhorns roamed freely throughout the lower prairie and coastal marshes, and those early wild herds quickly carried the brand of Matagorda cattlemen. By 1850, the fledgling cattle industry counted 35,000 head in Matagorda County.

With a mostly undeveloped transportation infrastructure between the 1840s and mid 1860s, coastal Texas beef had limited value. Cull cows and heifers were unceremoniously rounded up and killed locally for their hides and tallow, while healthy steers were turned back on the range. The relatively few trail drives during those years headed to the Midwest, sometimes California, but mostly to New Orleans. The alternative to the overland drive to Louisiana was by steamship from Indianola. Here, herds were grazed along the saltgrass flats of Powderhorn Bay before they were moved down the town's oyster-shell road to its long wooden loading dock and into specially fitted cargo holds of the Morgan Steamship Line. A remarkable 21,685 beeves and 42,599 hides, together valued at $600,000, were shipped from Indianola in 1860.[1]

No one was minding cattle in the years between Fort Sumter and Appomattox, and longhorns proliferated in Texas. It was said that the bulls on the northern Great Plains "put their backs to the northern wind and sleet and walked south."[2] By 1865, as many six million head roamed the Lone Star State. The greatest number of wild and claimed cattle were in the coastal grasslands and blackland prairie between the Sabine and Guadalupe rivers. Meat prices fell from the abundance, but it hardly mattered. No one in Texas had any hard currency.

Low beef prices were one of the reasons cattle were still mostly sold for hides and tallow after the Civil War. Walruses or swamp angels – old cows and beeves not worthy to pasture – were driven into chutes, killed, then hoisted by their hind legs and skinned. Hides were salted and the deboned meat discarded, hauled away to points where hundreds of vultures circled like black clouds. Residue called hash was thrown to the pigs. Steam vats rendered the valuable tallow to the surface and were packed in wooden kegs. There were at least three tallow operations in Matagorda County. The largest was W.B. Grimes's "W.B. Grimes Tres Palacios Rendering and Packing House," which processed between 25 to 100 cows a day. It was a "sad" and deplorable" business, according to Grimes's daughter Fannie, but it sustained him and others in the business through the late 1860s.[3]

Beef prices headed higher by about 1868, but only the North had hard cash. A beeve in Texas was then worth about $4, but that same steer could fetch $40 in meat packing plants up north. Southerner cattlemen eager to sell their commodity had to find a profitable way to access Northern markets. Railroads in Kansas or other points could move their product swiftly to cities throughout the North, but the challenge was getting them there. The legend and lore of the great trail drives, and the cowboys who got them there, was born.

Initially called beef drives to differentiate steers destined for markets from cattle raised for their hides and tallow, the first route north used by cattlemen from Matagorda and other Texas coastal prairie pastures was the Shawnee Trail. The route ended at Missouri and Kansas rail depots, where cattle were loaded and shipped to eastern slaughterhouses and meat packing operations. Quarantine laws aimed at curtailing the spread of "Texas fever" caused the closing of the Shawnee Trail to Texas longhorns. The trail then moved further west, first to the Chisolm, and later to the Western Trail.

The trail boss and his drovers faced a myriad of obstacles between Texas and Kansas. Nature dogged the trailers with droughts, floods, snowstorms, lightning storms, and raging rivers. Then there were the challenges of human nature – rogue Indians, rustlers, fence-building settlers and farmers, resentful northern cattlemen, and government inspectors that could quarantine an entire drive. For most cowboys, the herds were less trouble than the trail itself.

Cattle were to provide Texas with its first large scale money-making opportunity after the Civil War, whether for hides, tallow, or beef. Word spread of the seemingly limitless unbranded "slicks" available for the taking. Called mavericking, it was the catalyst for what became Matagorda's "Wild West," when the county attracted a cast of characters with nothing more in common than an eagerness to stake their fortune. Many of the newcomers were War veterans, both Yankee and Confederate, some were Anglos wet behind the ears with more boldness than sense, and others were freed blacks and men of Mexican descent from both sides of the Rio Grande. Their resumes were equally colorful, the less reputable among them portrayed as horse thieves, renegades, desperados, and men with "a range of temperaments." It could be a rough livelihood, one in which a man guilty of no crimes might be murdered because of the company he kept, or the gold in his pockets.

In addition to the large numbers of unbranded longhorns, many that did carry a brand were miles from their origin. But not all of them. The first brand was supposed to settle its ownership, but it was a wild, unfenced land, and a newcomer could make money a lot faster from the "running iron" – counter branding. To some extent, just about everyone did. Brands were changed, cattle were rustled, and many were skinned before anyone looked to see who they belonged to. The contest between established cattle operations and rustlers would be a violent one, the credit for the bloodshed on the hands of both (Fig. 1).

Vigilante Justice. Rustlers rarely had their day in court, their due process of law decided, instead, by the ruling justice system of the prairie – vigilante committees. A trial rarely lasted longer than it took to wrap a rope around the limb of a tree. Vigilante justice was so prevalent that, when the Lone Star State established the Frontier Battalion of the Texas Rangers in 1870s, one of its initial responsibilities was to see that cattle rustlers made it to the nearest judge alive.

Some Matagorda vigilantes had associations to cattle outfits, while others were outlaws with affiliations only to themselves or their gangs. The killing of suspected rustlers rarely ended with their hanging or shooting – it spawned a trail of revenge that stopped only after more killings.

When A.H. Pierce and other Matagorda cattlemen hired some 200 "regulators" to enforce their kind of order to the cattle business, it was the start of a conflict with battlegrounds that covered the West. Jack Helms, a former state police captain, headed the regulators. Helms was a man so violent that, in 1870, he shot a free black man between the eyes for whistling Yankee Doodle, the wrong tune to a former Confederate. One of Helms's regulators was Jim Sutton, who was killed in front of his wife at Indianola by Jim Taylor. Taylor's brother, Billy, shot down another Sutton associate, Gabe Slaughter. Helms set out on a trail of reprisal but was gunned down by Jim Taylor ally John Wesley Hardin. Gunslinger Hardin was later killed by a John Selman who was killed by George Scarborough.[4]

During the summer of 1870, John M. Smith, a sometimes-law-abiding cow hand and sometimes rustler who rode with the Taylor-Harding clan, sent word he was going to shoot A.H. Pierce, at least in part because of his connection with Jack Helms. Smith didn't get the chance. When Pierce's cow hands caught him with Ed and Wilbur W. Lunn skinning a calf with the wrong brand and rustled cows filling a broken-down cart, A.H. was at the head of the men who meted out their punishment. Ropes were tossed over an oak limb and around the offender's necks, their horses nudged out from under them. Wilburn Lunn was fortunate to have escaped the hanging, but his freedom was short-lived. He was jailed for an unrelated murder in 1872.[5]

Charles Siringo was another part-time rustler early in his career (Fig. 2). A contract killer named Sam Grant shot him in 1875, but the 20-year-old survived. No prosecutions were made, but Siringo suspected Grant was hired by one of Matagorda's "wealthy cattlemen on account of my boldness in branding mavericks and killing stray bulls for their hides."[6]

Pointed North. Outlaws and violence were only a small part of the cattle business. For most Matagorda cowboys, it was a life in which months were spent pasturing herds, an easy rhythm to their days that was only interrupted by storms, predators, wandering stock, and occasional confrontations with rustlers. Their time was often spent alone, their possessions what they could pack on a horse or mule. They cooked for themselves, their fare meager, mainly biscuits or cornbread, salted or dried meat, occasional wild game or a calf, and coffee.

The logistics of going "up the trail" was a different matter. Weeks of planning and stocking went into preparation for the journey. Pack animals and a supply of ponies were secured. Wagons were readied. One or more supply wagons were loaded with items such as oak and hickory wood to repair wheels, spokes, and axles; strips of iron that could be hammered into felly rims, wheel hubs, and various wagon fittings; and raw leather for reins, bridles, and saddle repair. Last came the crew's personal supplies, such as bedrolls, extra saddles, firearms, and ammunition.

The chuck wagon was the beating heart of trail drives and took the longest to ready. The canvas bonnet and bow hoop supports were tuned, the brake lever and brake block checked along with the double and single trees, and yoke, affixed to the tongue that connected to the teams. A toolbox, jockey box, water barrels, ropes, coffee grinder, and lanterns found their place along the exterior sideboards. Lastly, the wagon was loaded with dried and salted meat, and staples such as flour, beans, molasses, coffee, and lard.

West Texas rancher Charles Goodnight is credited with conceiving the chuck wagon and its hinged wooden cupboard in 1866. Located at the rear of the wagon, the cover of the chuck box unfolded to form a working surface for food preparation and provided access to shelves and drawers filled with utensils and medicine. Cast iron skillets, pots, and Dutch ovens were stored in a compartment below the chuck box called the boot (Fig. 3).

Cowboys before the drive busied themselves inspecting such things as metal spurs and rowels, and tack for signs of wear. Saddles were tweaked, particularly its flocking and accessories like stirrup width, that had to match the size of the rider's boot. Much attention was given to their lassoes, made from twisted grass, rawhide, or hair from a horse's mane and kept limber by alternately drying and greasing. Personal items like clothing were nothing more extravagant than denim, canvas, and wool beneath leather chaps and leather boots. About the only thing they changed when they moved from the Texas heat to Midwest cold was their hat. Straw was the preferred material in summer and in winter, if they could afford it, it was made from animal fur, particularly silverbelly beaver felt.[7]

For Texas coastal prairie cowboys there was only one breed of horse – the mustang. Derived from colonial Spanish stock, they were still caught wild south of the Rio Grande. Each year, the cattlemen's pony herd was replenished from wild stock, and they had to be broken before trailing. It took an experienced wrangler. According to Charles Siringo, the horse had to be roped and thrown before it was fitted with a hackamore, or rope halter, and a leather blind. When the horse stood, it was saddled for the first time and the blind removed. The horse would then "wear himself out bucking around the corral." Next, it was ridden, and "the bucking and running began again." It "often required two hours to get him docile and back into the corral." After being ridden for several days and a bridle put in his mouth, "he was broke."[8]

Cattle were rounded up on horseback. The heifers were sorted and held back as breed stock, and steers and "slicks" – the name used for any cow without a brand – were penned. Bulls were the most challenging, with many taking to canebrakes and deep timber that had to be extricated, roped, and tied. Some of the wildest timber cattle, called mossy horns, could be 20 years old. The roughest ones were pinned, their eyelids sewn shut so they wouldn't break for cover again. It took about two weeks for the thread to rot.[9] Sometimes, a sharp axe was used to cut half of each horn to reduce goring when steers were packed into steamship holds and overloaded rail cars, or when an angry bull repeatedly spiked a rider's pony. Bulls, once branded and castrated, were left to pasture.

Trailing herds nearly always carried a mix of brands, and to prove ownership across state lines, every steer had to be roped and thrown for "road branding." It could be done by one cowboy, but safer with two. To throw a steer, a 30-foot rope was securely fastened to the saddle horn. The first rope went over the bull's head, and a second cinched up his hind legs.[10]

After roundup and penning, the herd was trail ready. Matagorda and Wharton County drover Willie LaBauve remembered that the big herds would go up in late April or "as soon as the grass sprouted," and arrive in Kansas June or July. The larger cattle operations typically moved 4,000 to 5,000 head at a time, and traditionally employed a dozen men or more. An overland journey from Gulf Coast pastures to Kansas or Missouri covered nearly 700 miles and, at rate of 10 to 12 miles a day, spanned three to four months.[11]

The uncertain business of driving a herd to market was mostly worth the risks. Although cattle prices fluctuated widely, based not only on the quality of the animal but market conditions, the price per head that the cowman received doubled between 1872 and 1882. During the same time, the extension of the railroad system cut transportation costs by half. According to the *Fort Worth Daily Democrat*, over 500,000 southern Texas cattle were shipped from northern railheads in 1883. By the time drives dwindled in the early 1890s, somewhere between six and ten million cattle had gone "up the trail."[12]

Cattle Trailing. The first organized cattle trail was the Shawnee Trail that reached northeast Kansas and central Missouri. Established in 1840s, it started near Austin and ended at railheads of the Missouri Pacific Railroad in Kansas City, Sedalia, and St. Louis. (Fig. 4) Its tenure was short. Kansas and Missouri legislatures passed quarantine laws that effectively closed the Shawnee in the 1850s after northern cows began succumbing to Texas fever. Texas longhorns were resistant to the tick-borne disease, but it was deadly to cows without immunity.[13]

Cattlemen who had spent months on the trail stood to lose a substantial investment not just in time, but in money, to quarantine regulations. Some herds were confiscated by officials and others saw them stampeded by angry locals. Historian Chris Emmett wrote that northern stockmen were incensed as their grazing land and markets crowded with Texas longhorns – fever or no fever – and they resented the invasion. Some made real on their warning that "we will be justified," by "forcible means, if necessary, to prevent any further admission of such cattle into our country." One newspaper reported that "the citizens are fully aroused, and I don't think it would be safe for a Texas steer to be seen in these parts."[14]

Matagorda cattleman A.H. Pierce knew the risks when he chose the Shawnee route long after it was closed to Texas cattle, but he had always found a way around it. On one drive, when his customary payoff didn't work, he changed his strategy. Pierce recounted how he held up his drive at the edge of a Missouri town, then:

> "with us in back of them old longhorns," we "charged 'em waving our slickers and chaps, yelling and shooting off our guns." But "them old critters had an idea'r of their own. They went down into the village rather sudden, and they waked them people from their tranquility. The rumble was like thunder. A dense cloud of dust and all hell broke loose on 'em at once. Citizens took shelter where they could get the quickest. Some climbed gate posts, some went up trees. Others looked at my passing herd from rooftops. Fences went down. Clotheslines disappeared. Flying destruction went through there on the horns of my cattle, and you know, Sirs, all of us were out of Missouri and into Kansas before them Longhorns quit runnin'."[15]

Quarantine laws were the main reason that, by the late 1860s, most herds headed north to central Kansas railyards by way of the Chisholm Trail (Fig. 4). The Chisolm started near Austin, then ran west of the Shawnee route through Waco and Fort Worth before crossing the Red River at Spanish Fort, or Red River Station. According to Charles Siringo, the route was laid out by "half-breed squaw-man" Jesse Chisolm, who was awarded a government contract to establish supply routes from the Red River north through Indian Territory.[16]

Millions of hooves would follow Chisolm's route after Illinois cattle buyer Joseph McCoy built stockyards at the Abilene railhead on the Kansas Pacific Railroad, choosing the site in a sparsely populated region without – yet – the imposition of enforced quarantine laws. So many Texas cattle were trailed up the Chisolm that it was known to most drovers as the Texas Road.[17] The Atchison, Topeka & Sante Fe Railroad (AT&SF) soon built a parallel track to the Kansas Pacific that intersected the Chisolm Trail some 80 miles south of Abilene. Rail depots and stockyards were established at Wichita and Newton that shaved a week off the cattlemen's drive.

Pioneers continued to push west into central Kansas and quarantine regulations followed. For a brief time, herds driven up the Chisolm only had to pass inspection. Charles Siringo related the tale of a state cattle inspector from the Red River Station who presented himself at several camps. The trail-hardened cowboys had little time for the bureaucrat, especially after he announced a fee for his service of ten cents a head, and his obligation to cut all the strays from the herd. He was invited for a cup of coffee. Then he was thrown to the ground, hog tied, and deposited downriver in a plum thicket. The herds were crossed without further delay. As for the inspector, he was retrieved two days later and was last heard from in Kentucky.[18]

Like the Shawnee before it, the Chisolm Trail was a short-lived route, its demise after Kansas closed its borders to Texas cattle in 1873. By then, more than one and a half million Texas cattle and "a half million Spanish mares" had passed over it. Parts of the Chisolm route through Texas and what would become Oklahoma were still in use until the 1880s, but its days were numbered as well, a result of increasing settlement, farming, barbed wire, more railroads, and the US government's changing policies in Indian Territory.[19]

Life on the Trail. Cowboys spent days and nights in the saddle to keep the herd moving, grazed, and watered, and there was the constant wrangling of strays (Figs. 5 & 6). Although exposed to heat, rain, mud, cold, and snow, their main complaint was the swarms of flies and mosquitoes that clouded the herd. In the early years, trail riding was a primitive affair. At the day's end, dinner was usually calf ribs from the fire, a Dutch oven filled with loin, sweet breads, and heart, and a side of corn bread with molasses followed by coffee. Meals were eaten from the blade of Bowie knife. Some carried a bedroll, and others slept on the ground under a canvas or wagon sheet.[20]

The trail boss often rode a day or so in front of the herd scouting for water, pastures, or trouble. Behind the trail boss were the supply and chuck wagons, then the spare saddle horses, called *remuda*. The herd was next, and if the beeves were behaving, it was worked in a formation. At the lead were a couple of waddies or trail hands, called point men. Flankers rode on the sides, and swing men moved around as they needed to make the herd turn. A couple of drag men brought up the rear, which was considered the worst job because of the dust.[21]

For experienced cowboys, herds were relatively easy to manage – until they weren't. One of the most vulnerable parts of any drive were river crossings (Fig. 7). A dominant steer on a trail drive was invaluable for swimming rivers, as a hesitant leader could slow the whole herd. One trail hand was even known to "go in among the cattle" and seize a big steer by the horns, then "back it into the river, turn it around, hold on to the horns and swim across the river with him. The other steers of the drove would follow."[22]

When rivers roiled with flood waters, drovers had no choice but to camp and wait. Charles Siringo wrote of a drive halted at the Red River by a raging torrent nearly a mile wide. For days, some 20 different camps lined its banks, waiting to cross, "and at night the air rang with the voices of singing cowboys." Between powerful currents and the risk of being "struck by a swift flowing log or tree," the dangers in crossing flooded streams were very real, and it killed cattle, horses, and drovers.[23]

Another trailing risk was stampedes, and they were regular affairs along the route. Nature was the catalyst for some, particularly storms with thunder and lightning. Man caused others. It might be the crack of a rifle or pistol, but often, it was deliberate. Settlers and farmers stampeded herds as retribution for cut fences and trampled crops, and northern cattlemen as a deterrent to their tick fever fears. Indians, if they were refused a herd toll for crossing their lands, sometimes stampeded herds. Anything could set a herd off, day or night, and experienced cowboys slept with their boots on. At least part of the crew stood guard after dark, their best defense against a stampede their "singing and whistling to the restless cattle."[24]

Public corrals were a necessity near settlements and quarantine areas, and it took cowboys hours to enclose the herd by "yelling and the beating of quirts against leather chaps." Some "fighting mad steers" ran for the timber and had to be tied down using a "hobble rope." Only their back legs were bound, so that the animal would be ready to trail at dawn. Public corrals were round so that, if the herd did stampede, cowboys could push them into a milling circle until they were exhausted.[25]

Plow Men. Settlement, particularly farming, was a bane to cowboys whose livelihood depended on the open range. According to Charles Siringo, the Chisholm Trail was too sacred to be scratched with plow. But, by 1880, the Texas piece of the Chisolm was no longer passable for large herds as "fool hoe-men" had "squatted all over it."[26] Siringo wrote of conflicts with homesteaders who followed the Texas & Pacific Railway after it reached Fort Worth in the mid 1870s, when trail hands increasingly stared down the barrel of a rifle or shotgun wielded by a planter incensed by hundreds of hooves that thundered through new crop land. Loaded guns were soon replaced by the barbed wire, but it only made things worse. Fences were cut, and they were trampled.

Siringo also saw many of the traditional watering places "fenced up" by newcomers. "We paid no attention to the fences," he wrote, and "shoved the herd right through them." He painted a colorful picture of longhorns running through fences in a cloud of dust with barbed wire wrapped around horns and tails.[27]

Charles Siringo observed the transformation of another Texas cattle town, Amarillo. On early drives, he recalled "a million buffalo in one black mass" watering at Wild Horse Lake. He never saw another buffalo after settlement and barbed wire followed tracks of the Fort Worth & Denver City Railway across the Panhandle in 1887.[28]

Between settlement and quarantine restrictions, drovers continued to push west, at first using branches off the Chisolm. Then the new Western Trail was laid out, with railheads at Ellsworth on the Kansas Pacific line and Dodge City on the AT&SF. The problem with the Western Trail, at first, was the Red River War.

Indian Territory. The land between Texas at the Red River and Kansas was Indian Territory (Fig. 4), and each of the three principle trailing routes crossed it to reach Missouri or Kansas railheads. Branches of the Shawnee Trail crossed Choctaw, Creek, and Cherokee Nation lands. The Chisolm traversed the Red River into Chickasaw land, then the Cimmaron River before the southern boundary of the Cherokee Outlet and finally to the quarantine grounds on the Kansas border. The Western Trail crossed Cheyenne and Arapaho lands along the Canadian River before it reached the Cherokee Outlet. In addition to the cattle highways, Indian Territory was spanned by a network of military supply trails, wagon roads, and telegraph right of ways dotted with Indian villages, military and cattle camps, corrals, and branding pens.

Within Indian Territory, large-scale conflicts between Native American tribes and trailers were rare. Renegade bands stole cattle, ponies, and mules, but mostly reservation tribes either exacted tolls to cross their land or collected a pasture fee, paid in cattle or coin. If their demands were refused, many responded by stampeding the herd during the night.[29]

Outside of Indian Territory, on the Southern Plains, it was a different story. The Medicine Lodge Treaty of 1867 designated the Territory as a reservation for the Comanche and Kiowa, and a second for the Southern Cheyenne and Arapaho tribes. For their cooperation, the US government promised housing, food, supplies, rifles, and the right to continue their tradition of buffalo hunting south of the Arkansas River (Fig. 8).[30]

The agreements looked good on paper, at least to Washington officials. The reality, however, was that reservation Indians suffered ration shortages, as well as growing numbers of Anglo settlements and the intrusion of White buffalo hunters into their sanctioned hunting grounds. In response, bands from the Comanche, Apache, Arapaho, Cheyenne, and Kiowa tribes joined to form a loose confederacy but with a common goal. They would abandon Indian Territory and return to the Texas Plains, following the bison and, wherever they encountered settlers, drive them out. Persistent mayhem followed.[31]

Former Civil War army leader William T. Sherman was largely responsible for the strategy to end the defiance. The ebb and flow of the bison herds were the lifeblood of the Southern Plains Indians, and in a move reminiscent of his scorched earth campaign that brought the Confederate cities of Atlanta and Savannah to their knees just seven years prior, Sherman advocated annihilation of the West's great herds. In 1874 buffalo hunters, with deadly efficiency, began their slaughter. They succeeded in exterminating most of the big animals by 1878 (Fig. 9).

Sherman also declared all Indians outside of their designated reservation boundaries as hostiles. The outcome was a string of sharp skirmishes, called the Red River War, that played out between the army and the insurgents in the rolling plains and incised canyons of the Texas Panhandle. It didn't last long. A practiced military would ensure that the nation's westward settlement – its Manifest Destiny – would prevail.[32] Most of the rogue warriors who had abandoned Indian Territory returned by the spring of 1875. Their defeat meant business as usual for cattlemen, who were able to drive up the restored Western Trail and again, for a while, dodge quarantine challenges.

The Red River War may have been Indian Territory's most violent chapter, but the landscape remained troubled throughout the late 1800s, increasingly caught in a struggle between the competing interests of fickle government Indian resettlement policies, expansion of Anglo settlement, competition between northern and southern cattle syndicates, and clashes with Native American tribes. Government efforts to appease the disparate interests in the region was to partition and reassign lands. The result was a profusion of transitory boundaries. Areas designated within Indian Territory consisted of the Cherokee Strip in southern Kansas, the Cherokee Outlet, which was always, mistakenly, called the Cherokee Strip, and the Cherokee Nation. After the Red River War, dozens of smaller parcels were ceded to over 20 different tribes. Other lands carried the names Neutral Lands, "No Man" lands, Unassigned Lands, and later "Land Run" tracts.[33]

Indian Territory seemed to be a land in which dreams were dashed. For Native Americans, it represented the loss of freedom and bison hunting grounds, and in the late 1880s and 90s, the vexing issue of "land runs" that opened treaty areas to White settlement. For cattlemen, the biggest worry was the disposition of the Cherokee Outlet. Located south of the Kansas border, the Cherokee Outlet was hugely important to the cattle industry after Kansas imposed its 1873 quarantine restriction on southern cattle. Because the state waived its quarantine to Texas herds that were pastured during winter for three months or more, the significance of Indian Territory was elevated to a new level. The race to control the Cherokee Outlet was on.[34]

In deals made with the Cherokees, several large southern cattle operators were already leasing pastureland in the Cherokee Outlet, the arrangements bringing in as much as $100,000 a year. But, after the 1873 restrictions were announced, those contracts were voided – not by the Cherokees, but by Kansas cattlemen who formed the Cherokee Strip Association. The association leased six million acres from "the government and the Cherokee Nation" and, although they continued grazing contracts for a few Texas cattle companies, their control succeeded in eliminating southern competition. The Cherokee Strip Association now had a monopoly on US cattle markets.[35]

Armed fence riders hired by the Cherokee Strip Association began turning away Texas herds with impunity. On a drive to Nebraska in 1884, Rockport founder and Coleman-Fulton Pasture Company cattleman Thomas H. Mathis was turned back at rifle point by the association's hired hands. Mathis made an urgent appeal to the US Interior Secretary, and "received assurance that the trail should be kept open." For a short while, it was, although the Cherokee Strip Association responded by demanding pasture tariffs.[36]

Cattlemen weren't the only Whites clamoring for a piece of Indian Territory. Homesteaders put enormous pressure on the federal government to allow access to treaty lands. Popular sentiment seemed always on the side of settlers, and western policymaking increasingly reflected it. Cultivators brought families, one newspaperman wrote, their settlement contributing to the building of towns and communities. In contrast, the stock raiser was a nomad who "lives on the rim of human society, and his profits depend on unlimited free pasturage." Cattlemen were less generous in their praise – settlers were squatters, nesters, and the new name for homesteaders – Boomers.[37]

Initially the Boomer's runs were unsanctioned, their stake-claiming accompanied by the burning of ranches, killing of stock, fence cutting, and the torching of grazing land. Soldiers kept them running out until 1889, when the first great land rush was sanctioned by the US government. The Boomers came in wave after wave between 1889 and 1893. By 1893, 100,000 Whites had settled the Cherokee Outlet.[38]

Anticipating the land rush, Washington officials nullified the Cherokee Strip Association lease, ordering all its holdings returned to the Cherokee Council. The Kansas cattlemen stalled. Their deal was made with the Cherokees, lawyers said, not the government and they could only be ejected by the government through a treaty with Cherokees. They were wrong. Then, in another failed strategy, the Cherokee Strip Association tried to preempt government policy by offering the Cherokee's twenty million dollars for their land.[39]

In 1890, the original "Government Lands" and the western part of "Indian Territory" became the Oklahoma Territory. The proclamation, signed by US President Benjamin Harrison, directed removal of all cattle from "the Cherokee Strip or Outlet." That year the Cherokee Strip Association thought it wiser to shift its allegiances to, and stop antagonizing, Washington. In support of the president's proclamation, they "concluded to take a hand in the enforcement," hiring an overseer to patrol the Strip and help to extricate all cattle – except for those with an association brand.[40]

Lawless. It was rough on the trail, but probably rougher at towns on the end of the trail. The major towns that lasted long in the lore of the Old West were Abilene, Wichita, and Dodge City, and smaller or shorter-lived towns such as Newton, Ellsworth, and Caldwell

(Fig. 4). The towns had much in common – they were initially established as cattle loading depots in response to shifting quarantine laws, they experienced meteoric growth and an equally rapid reputation for lawlessness, and just as quickly faded away. What followed in the wake of the cattlemen was usually settlers.

The economy of each railhead town was driven mainly by the needs and whims of drovers and a sprinkling of cattle buyers and railroad men. Usually, one part of town was the "respectable" section, its dusty streets lines with hotels, hardware stores, merchants, livery stables, hat and boot makers, saddlers, horse peddlers, and the office of the marshal or sheriff. A second district was replete with saloons, gambling halls, brothels, and boarding houses. On the outskirts of town was always a "boot hill" cemetery, so named because its occupants died "with their boots on," a euphemism for an end by a bullet.

Kansas City, Sedalia, and St. Louis were established before the Civil War as railheads on the Missouri Pacific Railroad. After the Civil War, when trailers moved from the Shawnee to the Chisholm, the end of the line was Abilene at the Kansas Pacific Railroad. At first, the town had no lawmen, and the tenure of its earliest marshal, Thomas J. Smith, was short. Hired in 1870, he was shot dead a year later. The next Abilene lawman was Marshal "Wild Bill" Hickok, known as much for his dexterity with a pistol as with a deck of cards.[41]

With a population of 2,000 and about "the same number of transients," Abilene in 1871 had but one first class hotel. W.B. Grimes family friend Booth Jordan provided a description of the entertainment district of the town. It was "deplorable" place, he wrote, where ladies of respectable families "never stir outside of their houses for fear of being insulted." There was "plenty of gambling" and dance houses, but "the supply of women on hand is not equal to the demand." The "fairer sex," he continued, "are all diseased and there are hundreds of Texas boys who are sorry that they ever saw this place for they can never marry if they have any respect for the woman they love."[42]

More than 40,000 head of cattle were shipped from Abilene in 1871 before it lost its freighting dominance to quarantine laws and increased settlement. New cattle towns were established at Newton then Wichita on the Atchison, Topeka & Sante Fe Railroad, and west of Abilene on the Kansas Pacific Railroad at Ellsworth.

Wichita, with a population around 2,500, wore the freight crown between 1873 and 1876. Wichita's lawmen were among the best known in the annals of the Old West – Wild Bill Hickok moved there after his year in Abilene, and Wyatt Earp served on the Wichita police force in 1875 and 1876 before moving to Dodge City. Gunslinger John Wesley Hardin shot one of his own cowboys on the streets of Wichita over his choice of hats. Quarantine laws and the "foolish farming hoe men settling up in the cattle country" contributed to Wichita's decline.[43]

Dodge City was next on the trailer's maps, and for nearly a decade, its freight yards moved as many as 75,000 head a year. Charles Siringo called Dodge City the "toughest cattle town on earth," its streets a mix of "free-and-easy-girls, long-haired buffalo hunters, and wild and wooly cowboys." It was a place where too much whiskey flowed and it "stirred up the devil" in a cowboy.[44]

Dodge City had the most impressive list of gunmen and lawmen of any town in the West. Wyatt Earp, the Masterson brothers, and "Doc" Holliday all resided in Dodge at some time in their careers. The town was equally famous for its Boot Hill Cemetery, with the graves of 81 men who "died with their boots on, except for one."[45]

Caldwell was Dodge City's challenger, and the town rose to prominence in 1880 and persisted until 1885. Its lawmen, Sheriff Henry Newton Brown and Ben Wheeler, were as notorious as the outlaws they were hired to subjugate. Brown, before he pinned his badge, killed a cowhand in a gunfight, rustled cattle and horses, and rode with Billy the Kid. His respectability as Caldwell marshal was in question after he shot an "Indian Chief" named Spotted Horse, and a cowboy named Boyce. Brown left no doubt when he and his deputy, Ben Wheeler, rode to the town of Medicine Lodge and held up its bank, killing the president and cashier. After a shootout, Brown and Wheeler were captured. Marshal Brown was shot by a mob that swarmed the jail, and Wheeler was hung from an elm tree.[46]

Advocates of the Open Range. As Texas's cattle business prospered, so did the cattlemen's political influence. Their tool was stockmen's associations, and while their conventions were bawdy, their message was earnest. Rustlers were among the earliest issues tackled by the Stock Raisers Association of Western Texas, the group in 1875 adopting a resolution that "cattle thieves and hide purloiners should disappear, if to do this, it is necessary to call in the gallows." For the next 25 years, although they softened their rhetoric, the group tackled the many obstacles to their thriving livelihood. They used their influence to encourage passage of legislation on branding issues, penalties for theft and fraud, fencing, quarantine laws, Indian Territory, railroad transportation, and "a system of sanitary laws" to protect cattle from contagious diseases.[47]

The Northwestern Cattle Raiser's Association had 238 members in 1884, its membership counting holdings of 1,400,000 head. Averaging at the time about $22 each, and not including the land they owned, association members controlled over thirty million dollars – worth almost a billion dollars today. It was the kind of money that could buy a lot of votes, but it was no match for progress.[48]

The open range and the great trail drives of the American West were in decline during the late 1880s and 1890s. Crippled by quarantine regulations and barbed wire, they finally succumbed to settlement. The nation's beef market would, of course, prevail, its ally the growing web of railroads linking cattle raisers directly to the nation's markets. Then, with the advent of the refrigerated boxcar, livestock was no longer loaded live for the journey to market but was butchered instead, their chilled carcasses transported across the country at speeds never thought possible.

By the early 1900s, cattle were grazed and worked on pastures surrounded by miles of fencing, complete with corrals and other infrastructure. The longhorns mostly disappeared by 1910, having become the pariah of the plains for their ironclad immune systems that allowed them to fight off the tick fever pathogen but remain a carrier. Too, in the words of cattleman Woodlief Brown, the longhorn carried "too much bone, leg, and horn in proportion to beef."[49] Texas ranchers began to experiment with and embrace breeds such as Herefords, Aberdeen Angus, and Durham shorthorns, often crossed with Brahman purebred stock for hybrid vigor and heat tolerance.

A Few of Matagorda's Cattlemen. Matagorda County was home to many well-known ranchers, their rich history often the subject of entire books and articles. Some of the Bay Prairie cattlemen, like A.H. Pierce with his brother Jonathan, built dynasties, and others, like A.P. Borden, bettered them. The cattle king A.H. Pierce and his brother J.E. were Bend in the River landowners, and their stories appear in that section. Some of A.P. Borden's accomplishments are mentioned in the chapter on rice farming and throughout this chapter.

The names of two other Matagorda cattlemen are known throughout the United States – Charles Siringo and Sam Maverick. Siringo's legacy was his writing, and it brought the trailing cowboy to life for generations. Sam Maverick was an important figure in the development of early Texas and had a propensity for finding adventure or for it to find him. He wasn't a cattleman, yet his name lives on in the lore of cowboy history.

Sam Maverick. Sam Augustus Maverick had a knack for being in the center of momentous events in Texas history, even when he tried not to. At the beginning of the Texas Revolution, in 1835, he lived in San Antonio de Béxar when General Cos occupied the town. He was arrested, suspected as a spy, and in one popular version, was marched to the courtyard to be shot but saved only by a dramatic last-minute reprieve. When Maverick either escaped the city or was granted amnesty, he reconnoitered with the Texian forces, and was the scout who led the ill-fated Ben Milam and his column into town.[50]

Two months later Maverick was at the Alamo, narrowly avoiding the fate of its defenders at the hands of Santa Anna because he was travelling to Washington-on-the-Brazos as a delegate to the Texian convention. Here, lawyer Maverick was one of the signers the Texas Declaration of Independence.[51]

He had only been in Texas a few short years, but already the Maverick name was synonymous as much for his contributions to the Texian cause as for cheating death. He would cheat it again. As a land investor who often joined surveying parties, he had just left camp on one excursion when the company was butchered by Indians. On another occasion, Maverick was in a sailboat that capsized during a storm in Lavaca Bay just before nightfall. He was rescued, lucky that an observant person onshore with a spyglass witnessed the incident.[52]

After the Texas War for Independence, Maverick was San Antonio's mayor. Mayor Maverick lived adjacent to plaza when the courtyard erupted in a hail of arrows and bullets during the Council House Fight. As the Council House repercussions swept south to Linnville on the mounts of Chief Buffalo Hump's Comanche warriors in 1840, it cost Maverick most of the family's possessions – for a second time. The first was during Mexican occupation of his San Antonio home. This time, he had shipped two years of supplies to a Linnville warehouse, and they were among the goods that were ransacked. He later learned that his law books were strung as ornaments from some of the raiding Indian's saddles.[53]

Lawyer Maverick was in a San Antonio courtroom in September when Mexican General Adrián Woll seized the town in 1842. Maverick and others fought from the walls and roof of the Maverick home before surrendering. He was among the over 50 prisoners marched to Mexico, where he remained for seven months.[54] When the family returned to San Antonio, they found their possessions plundered – now for a third time – by occupying troops.

Samuel A. Maverick would have been remembered for his prominent role in Texas history, but his name also endures in the diction of the American cowboy. Ironically, he wasn't a cowboy, never worked a herd, and was a reluctant cattleman, at best.

Always on the move, Maverick resettled his family from San Antonio by way of La Grange to Matagorda Peninsula at Decrow's Point in 1844. Farmer and rancher Charles Tilton paid a debt to Maverick in 400 head of cattle at the price of $3 each. Maverick left their upkeep to a caretaker who had about as much interest in them as Maverick. Unbranded and unpenned, the beeves became wild and unmanageable – many wandered away and just as many succumbed to the running iron. Concerned citizens wrote letters to Maverick about his errant herd, but to no avail.[55]

In 1853 the Maverick longhorns were relocated to the San Antonio River, but the result was the same. Maverick's wandering herd was so well known on the Texas prairie that the joke was that any unbranded beeve probably belonged to Sam Maverick. The name became a staple in cattlemen's vernacular. Although the formal definition of a "maverick" was intended to define a stray or a beeve whose parentage was undetermined, the most accepted designation was "a calf you find and get your brand on before the owner finds it and gets his on."[56]

In the Maverick tradition of narrowly avoiding his demise, he had moved his family and cattle off Matagorda Peninsula just months before Decrow's Point was devastated by the hurricane of September 18, 1854. Bay and Gulf waters converged across the narrow spit during the tempest, leaving only the ribs of the highest sand dunes protruding above the sea. Decrow's resident James Green, a veteran of the Battle of San Jacinto, hauled his eight children by buggy up the beach, burying the youngsters in hastily dug holes to prevent them from blowing away. When the family crawled from the sand and returned to Decrow's, every structure was leveled or washed into the sea.[57] One of the casualties of the storm was the first steamboat to negotiate the Colorado River and pass the Bend in the River in 1848, the *Kate Ward*, that wrecked near the mouth of the Colorado River, killing eleven seamen.

Although not by design, Sam Maverick had a strong connection with the Bend in the River. On the day G.W. Cayce was killed at the Council House Fight in 1840, he was a guest at the Maverick home. Two years later, after Maverick surrendered to Adrián Woll's troops, Henry Petty Cayce was one of the volunteers who drove out the invaders and tried to free their prisoners. The Texas troops were too late. Among Maverick's fellow prisoners was Andrew Neill, who was stationed at Cayce's Ferry in the mid 1830s.[58] During his travels in later years, Maverick was acquainted with and stayed at the homes of the Alley family in Colorado County, and with Thomas Cayce at his Cedar Grove plantation in Brazoria County. His travels also often took him to Port Lavaca, where he lodged at the Stanton House, his host in the 1850s Bend in the River landowner Juliette Fretwell.[59]

Sam Maverick served in the Texas legislature and was a player in another theatre of Texas drama during the prelude to the Civil War. A staunch supporter of the Union, he was one of many conflicted Texans when he grudgingly voted, in 1861, for Texas succession.[60] The old pioneer, lawyer, mayor, senator, and reluctant cattleman died in 1870.

Charles Siringo. Charles Angelo Siringo first "saw the light of day" on February 7, 1855. He was born on Matagorda Peninsula to an Irish mother and Italian father, Antonio Siringo, who died when the boy was a year old. By the time he reached the age of 11-years old, Siringo was working herds near Austin Lake and Bay Prairie for $10 a month. Later he recalled a Matagorda prairie that was teeming with wild mustangs and longhorns.[61]

Lugged north by his widowed mother's new husband, he fled the whiskey-imbued stepfather to roam the heartland of America until he returned to Matagorda County in 1871. The 16-year-old boy started work as one of A.H. Pierce's Rancho Grande cowboys under Tom Nye, the crew branding 25,000 mavericks and calves that year. The next year he worked herds on pastures near Palacios Point before the steers, 500 at a time, were loaded on steamers. At the end of each successful shipment, the Pierce hands celebrated by drinking, then making a mad race to the camp house and leaving a trail of drunken cowboys who had fallen off their horses.[62]

By the summer of 1872, Wiley Kuykendall encouraged Siringo to put his own brand on a few mavericks. "This made me bold," he wrote, and he branded more than he should have. He wasn't the only one who was changing AP and BU brands with a "running iron." Pierce brother-in-law Kuykendall was doing the same thing, and even while he was engaged in the duplicity, Kuykendall was being cheated by other hired hands who employed the same technique. During fall that year Kuykendall quit Pierce. So did Siringo. After he paid what he owed at Pierce's range supply store, Siringo's year and a half tenure netted him 75 cents.[63]

Freelancing Siringo rode the prairie with two branding irons – one with his registered brand and one that was unrecorded, but similar to a brand from a North Texas herd that had wandered south. In the spring of 1874, he hired on with W.B. Grimes to gather and move herds to the Grimes' Tres Palacios tallow factory and had responsibility for the operation's cattle ponies. Siringo was on his own again when, during the winter freeze of 1874-75, thousands of dead cattle littered the sloughs surrounding Tres Palacios Bay and Hamilton Point. Siringo's skinning knife was at work for days in the cold, the hides fetching $5 a piece. That spring, he worked for B.Q. Ward, gathering and "road branding" 1,100 "old mossy horns" that he drove "up the trail" from the Navidad River in Jackson County to Kansas.[64]

Charles Siringo built a substantial resume by the time he was 20 years old. It nearly killed him to get it. He had been dragged behind raging bulls and broncos, negotiated powerful currents during river crossings, was bitten on his foot by a rattlesnake, and in the spring of 1875, was shot by contract killer Sam Grant who tried to put a bullet in his heart. Wounded, he was taken to Yeaman's Ranch and Pierce's Rancho Grande to recover. The two or three people who knew who hired the assassin carried the name to their graves, but Siringo knew it was "on account of my boldness in branding mavericks and killing stray bulls for their hides."[65]

When he healed, Siringo worked for Sam Allen on Sims Bayou – the site is now in the heart of Houston – then returned to Indianola. He didn't remain there long either, his house washing away during the hurricane of 1875. In early spring, 1876, Siringo drove a herd of 2,500 Grimes cattle up the Chisolm Trail to Kansas, making $30 a day. He made another drive in 1877, but remained that year near Wichita, Kansas, to fatten the herd on grass for the fall market before returning to Texas.[66]

Siringo's Matagorda County connection was largely severed by the time he was 22. Still yielding to his wanderlust, he tried his hand as a fur trapper before heading south to work cattle at the LX Ranch in the Texas Panhandle near Amarillo. Siringo spent over two years in Caldwell, Kansas, as a merchant and as town marshal, then moved to Chicago in 1886. While in the Windy City he applied to Pinkerton's National Detective Agency and the company hired him as a "cowboy detective" to work the western cattle ranges from their Denver office. Siringo remained for 22 years. One of his last law enforcement jobs was in 1916, when he worked as a New Mexico Ranger with oversight of seven counties "to run down outlaws and stock thieves."[67]

Charles Siringo returned to Matagorda in the winter of 1913 (Fig. 10). The town of Bay City now stood at the place where, he recalled, he rounded up four old mavericks when he was just 12 years old. He visited Palacios on Hamilton Point, where he had spent a cold winter in 1874-75 skinning dead cattle from sunup to sundown. Jonathan Pierce visited him, and they spent a week reminiscing at Pierce's Blessing Hotel. He paid his respects to A.H. Pierce's gravesite, and visited the grave of his father, Antonio Siringo. In Midfield, he observed Fred Cornelius's longhorn herd, still wearing the T5 brand that Siringo had sold him 40 years earlier.[68]

Then, Charles A. Siringo married Helen Partain of Bay City, who was one of his childhood sweethearts. Siringo was 58 years old, and his wife, it was said, was "pretty for one of 51 years of age."[69]

Siringo lived a life rich in the traditions of the Old West. In addition to exploits in the saddle, he counted among his acquaintances and adversaries Sheriff Pat Garrett, Billy the Kid and his Lincoln County gang, gunfighter Clay Allison, Dodge City Marshall Wyatt Earp, gambler and part-time lawman Bat Masterson, and Butch Cassady and his Wild Bunch – "one of the worst gangs of murderers, train and bank robbers."[70] He also wrote of his experiences. His first book, *A Texas Cowboy*, was published in 1888, and was followed by the *History of Billy the Kid*, *A Cowboy Detective*, *The Song Companion of a Lone Star Cowboy*, and *Riata and Spurs*. Using his expression for the passage from life to death, Charles Siringo went "under the sod" in California in 1928.

A.P. Borden. Abel Pierce Borden, nephew of A.H. Pierce, came to Texas from Rhode Island in 1884 when he was 18 years old. Among his many achievements was establishing the Brahman breed in Texas. The first experimental introduction of the iconic humped-back cows was as early as 1860, when a few Brahman crosses were shipped to Hays County. By the 1870s, a few bulls were pastured in South Texas and around Galveston, and John Keeran and A.H. Pierce later bought five bulls at Indianola. Pierce, in his first dealings with Brahmans, had been convinced of their near invincibility – they handled the Texas heat better than other breeds and were able to travel longer distances from water. Most importantly, they were highly resistant to ticks that carried Texas fever.[71]

In 1904, US Agriculture Secretary James Wilson visited A. P. Borden at Pierce Ranch. Like Borden and the late A.H. Pierce, he was certain that the humped cattle of India – *Bos indicus* – was the future of Texas cattle raising. Wilson issued a permit to Borden for their importation.[72] Borden and South Texas rancher and financier Thomas M. O'Connor organized the logistics, their first order of business to locate a quarantine yard. The site they selected was a salt marsh flat in the bay on Simonson's Island between Staten Island and New Jersey. Quarantine was a necessity because of the potential to import a variety of diseases, with surra of most concern. First reported in India in 1880, surra was usually fatal to livestock.[73]

A stipulation in Borden's permit required that a Department of Agriculture inspector accompany him to India to examine and certify each cow. The men arrived in 1906, touring the countryside by rail to build the herd and diversify the bloodline, which was accomplished by purchase of seven different breeds and three different color variations. Each animal was loaded onto a disinfected rail car and shipped to Bombay, where they were boarded on a steamship destined first to Germany and then Simonson's Island. In total, Borden purchased 51 Brahman cattle – 46 bulls, three heifers, and two calves. After nearly three months at sea, hooves never touched the soil as they were transferred to the Simonson's Island quarantine station by way of cages hoisted from the ship deck to a waiting barge.[74]

Borden didn't lose a single animal in transport, but he nearly lost the entirety of his herd during quarantine. When some of the cattle tested positive for surra, the decision was made to destroy every animal. A barrage of telegrams quickly crisscrossed the county between Borden's Texas and New York lawyers, the Department of Agriculture, and Texas and Washington politicians, but without result. Then the Borden camp went around the bureaucracy and directly to President Theodore Roosevelt. They struck a deal. Borden agreed to have all the infected cattle destroyed – which caused "unforgettable wails" from the Hindu cowmen hired to tend them – and erected a barn for the herd at his expense during extended testing on Simonson's Island. Five months later 33 Brahmans were delivered to Pierce and split about evenly between Pierce Ranch and the O'Connor Ranch.[75]

Borden reported that the first 300 calves carried no ticks to maturity and were 50 percent heavier than ordinary Herefords range calves. He was impressed that the breed had "the courage to look you in the face when you go about them."[76] Free of Texas fever, those Brahmans were to change the Texas cattle industry when they were cross bred with Shorthorn, Herefords, Angus, and other breeds. The Texas longhorn, with its colorful names such as walruses, swamp angels, Pierce sea lions, and Shanghai Pierce coasters, were mostly relegated to back pastures to live out their days (Fig. 11).

After Borden died in 1934, his wife built a memorial chapel in Makunda, India, to honor his Brahman achievement.[77]

$500 REWARD!

The Matagorda and Wharton Counties Cat-tlemen's Protective Association

OFFER the following rewards for information leading to the arrest, conviction and punishment of any person or persons for the following offences, whenever the same are committed in connection with the property of any member of said association:

Theft of cattle by a white man,	$500.00
Theft of cattle by a negro,	250.00
Cutting wire fence (when a felony),	100.00
Burning pasture or grass (when a felony)	100 00
Butchering beef without complying with the law	50.00
Skinning cattle or having possession of hides unlawfully,	20.00
Leaving gates open or tearing down fence,	10.00

Fig. 1. Fines listed by the Matagorda and Wharton County Cattlemen's Protective Association's for rustlers and fence cutters were better than the vigilante alternative. *Matagorda County Tribune*, September 23, 1899, The Portal to Texas History, University of North Texas Libraries, https://texashistory.unt.edu/ark:/67531/metapth1346130/.

Fig. 2. Charles Siringo, circa 1890. He was a 16-year-old boy when he started work as one of A.H. Pierce's cowboys. During his life he was cattleman, detective, and author. Courtesy Matagorda Museum, File No.43.1986.04 10DS -43.

Fig. 3. West Texas rancher Charles Goodnight is credited with conceiving the chuck wagon and its hinged wooden cupboard in 1866. Located at the rear of the wagon, the cover of the chuck box unfolded to form a working surface for food preparation and provided access to shelves and drawers filled with utensils and medicine. The image is of W.B. Grimes' trail hands in Oklahoma Territory, 1890s. Courtesy Matagorda Museum, File No. 2007.11.99.33.

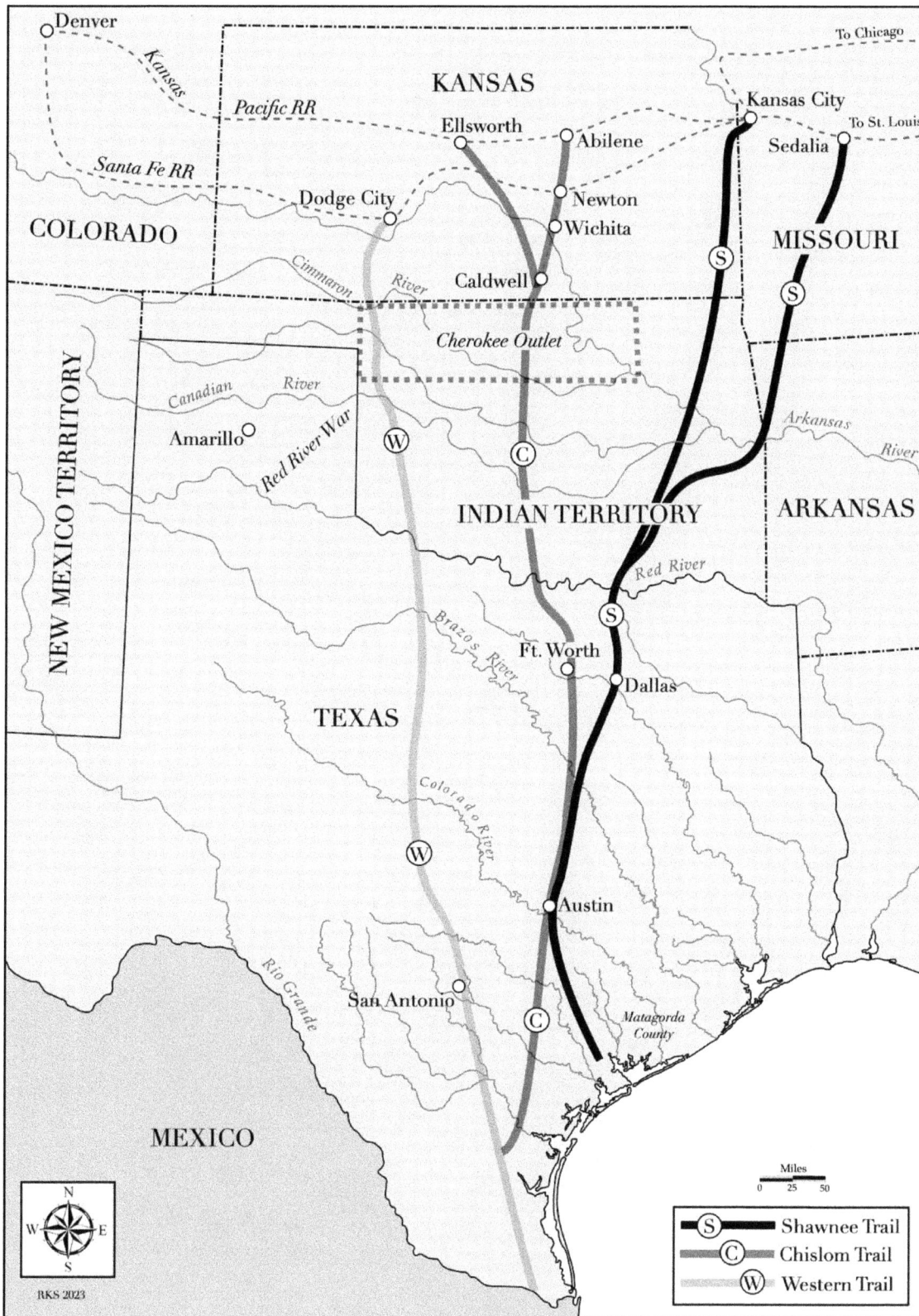

Fig. 4. The Shawnee Trail was established in 1840s and the Chisolm Trail in the late 1860s. After quarantine laws closed them both, the Western Trail was the most travelled.

Fig. 5. W.B. Grimes trail hands, ca. 1880s, after Grimes left Matagorda and moved his operation to the Midwest. Courtesy Matagorda Museum, File No. 2007.11.99.32.

Fig. 6. Part of a W.B. Grimes herd in Oklahoma, late 1800s. Courtesy Matagorda Museum, File No. 2007.11.99.34.

Fig. 7. Swimming the herd, Colorado River, Matagorda County. Courtesy Matagorda Museum, File No. 1994.77.99.35.

Fig. 8. Ponca Indians skinning a buffalo, 101 Ranch, Bliss, Oklahoma. Library of Congress image https://lccn.loc.gov/90710330.

Fig. 9. An image of excess – bison skulls and bones, the result of buffalo hunters, who succeeded in exterminating most of the big animals by 1878. *The Red River War, 1874-1875*, courtesy DailyHistory.org, https://dailyhistory.org/The_Red_River_War,_1874-1875.

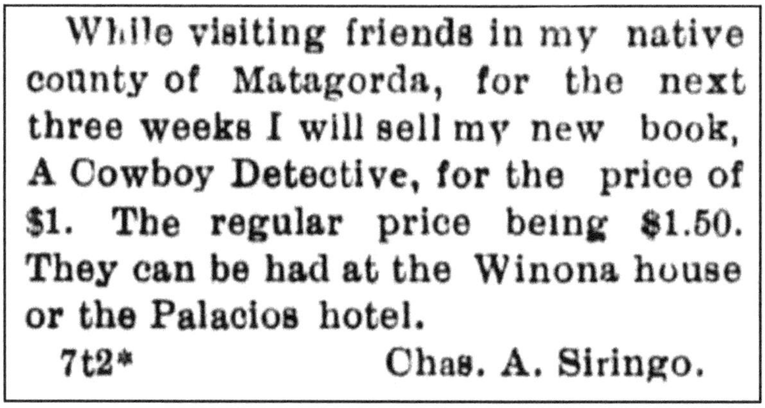

While visiting friends in my native county of Matagorda, for the next three weeks I will sell my new book, A Cowboy Detective, for the price of $1. The regular price being $1.50. They can be had at the Winona house or the Palacios hotel.

7t2*   Chas. A. Siringo.

Fig. 10. During his return to Matagorda County, cowboy and author Charles Siringo offered his most recent book for sale. *Palacios Beacon*, Feb. 21, 1913, The Portal to Texas History, Univ. of North Texas Libraries, https://texashistory.unt.edu/ark:/67531/metapth760452/m1/.

Fig. 11. Brahmans and longhorns, Matagorda County. Courtesy Matagorda Museum, File No. 1989.09.100.3.

CHAPTER 10

The Early Years of Matagorda Rice

In the late 1890s, rice production in Louisiana and Texas was hailed as "the agricultural marvel of the age," yet just a decade earlier, few would have predicted it. Rice had been a labor-intensive crop that relied on unsophisticated farming practices and was expensive to produce. Its rapid rise to economic viability was a combination of improvements in farming technology, a shipping network provided by America's advancing railroads, and a late 1800s cattle price collapse that had many from the Gulf Coast scrambling to find a new source of revenue.

America's industrial age brought new tools and efficiencies to agriculture in the late 1880s. At the forefront of the rice industry were Louisiana growers who began using implements and machinery initially developed for farmers in other parts of the US, but that they adapted to Gulf Coast rice planting and harvesting. Combined with modernized irrigation consisting of mechanized pumps, levees, flumes, and sluice gates, the result was more acres in cultivation and at a lower cost.[1]

Growing shipping infrastructure – railroads – was as important to the economics of Gulf Coast rice as mechanized farming. The first trainloads of grain from the Gulf Coast to eastern markets were shipped from Louisiana in 1884 by the Southern Pacific. Recognizing the potential of the new enterprise, the carrier developed marketing strategies to increase consumer demand. One tactic was a free publication distributed from all its passenger stations that contained hundreds of rice recipes. Another was promotion of a joint Texas and Louisiana "rice kitchen" at the 1901 Pan-America Exposition in New York as a way of "acquainting the masses with rice and its adaptability as a food.[2]

The Gulf Coast rice industry in the late 19th century was also influenced by a decline in cattle prices. In 1897, wholesale prices of cattle raised for meat production dropped over 50% from earlier peaks. In parts of Louisiana and Texas, cattle herds of the lower coastal prairie occupied black gumbo soils– the same earth best suited to rice cultivation – and it facilitated the shift from ranching to farming. According to long-time Colorado River irrigation man Earl Eidebach, Matagorda County's "Bay City boys" turned to rice because "they were unable to sell cattle as meat," and were "vitally interested in getting something going where they could make a profit."[3]

First Sprouts. Early rice crops relied entirely on rainfall before farmers began to divert water by cutting ditches with wooden buck scrapers attached to teams. Neither rainfall nor rudimentary diversion practices produced a predictable yield – there were some good crops, but just as often it either withered in the sun from not enough moisture, or the seed or crop washed away from too much water.

Field preparation was equally primitive. Tilling was done by a horse or mule and eight-inch plow, then seeds were broadcast from the back of a horse or wagon. Workers reaped the mature crop by hand with a sickle or scythe, then bundled the cut crop to dry in the field. Next, seed heads were separated from stalks by manual mechanical agitation, called threshing, before the grain was separated from the chaff by winnowing. It was a time-consuming – and back-breaking – process.

Advances in rice farming progressed quickly, its epicenter the coastal parishes of Louisiana. In just ten years the state evolved from local-scale production to the largest rice growing and shipping region in the world. Its progress caught the attention of writer and agriculturist W.J. Marshall, who toured south Louisiana's rice belt in 1896. Marshall's account, published the next year in *Texas Farm and Ranch*, is credited with introducing modern rice farming practices to states outside of Louisiana – particularly in Texas.[4]

The thousands of Louisiana rice acres in cultivation, Marshall wrote, were the outcome of a revolution in irrigation – the centrifugal pump – comprised of an impeller and diffuser driven by a steam engine. Instead of rainwater, crops were now irrigated by large steam pumping plants capable of filling a network of canals by moving as much as 75,000 gallons per minute. Marshall also wrote of another innovation, the horse-drawn self-binder, that transformed the harvest by cutting and binding the stalks with twine, a process that reduced wastage and eliminated some of the harvesting manpower. There was only a single self-binder in Louisiana in 1884, but over 4,000 by 1893.[5]

The centrifugal pump and self-binder weren't the only technological adaptations made by Louisiana planters. Canal excavation was improved by modifying the design of the Fresno – an iron bucket attached to a team – to create what they called a 'ditcher' – a "monstrous plow" attached to "two yokes of oxen." They adapted machines for planting from the Midwestern grain belt – a disk harrow to prepare the soil, a wagon-mounted broadcast seeder, and finally a "common harrow" to bury the seed. Most implements were drawn by oxen, but in the mid-1890s, steam-driven machinery was making its appearance.[6]

First Texas Rice. The first commercial rice in Texas, planted in Jefferson County before the Civil War, was called "provident rice" because its only irrigation source was rainwater. By the latter part of the 19th century, Jefferson County closely paralleled Louisiana in its rice-growing advancements, notably the adaptation of canal systems for irrigation. Beaumont was also home to Texas' first rice milling enterprise when Joseph Broussard, in 1892, converted his grist mill into the Broussard Rice Mills.[7]

It was probably not a coincidence that, after W. J. Marshall published his glowing *Texas Farm and Ranch* account, Texas rice cultivation spread quickly from its Jefferson County roots to another dozen Lone Star State counties. William Dunovant, who harvested 300 acres of grain at Eagle Lake in 1899, planted the first commercial Colorado River Valley rice crop. As Dunovant's grain headed to mills to the east, another train, the Southern Pacific, was heading west. Lumbering to a stop at the Pierce Station west of the Colorado River, Wharton County rancher Abel Pierce Borden eagerly inspected its cargo – a 162-lb shipment of rice seed from Japan.[8]

Borden located his "experimental rice farm" on the west side of the Colorado River at Long Point, south of the Bend in the River on the Thomas Cayce Survey. In the spring of 1900, Borden contracted county surveyor J.C. Carrington to "run levels" and Wharton farmer T.A. Johnson to "break" the first 300 acres of "black hog wallow prairie" using a half dozen teams and "riding plows." A gasoline engine and centrifugal pump was shipped to Pierce Station and hauled south by teams to construct a pumping plant on the river and fill Long Point Lake. A lateral was dredged to divert water from the Long Point reservoir to irrigate the crop. That September, Borden's harvest of 160 acres yielded 68 bushels per acre, and the $1.25 he was paid per bushel covered costs with a profit.[9]

Borden Rice Company's crop was one of two planted on the Colorado River in 1900. Franz and Louis Huebner, on a cattle drive between Colorado County and Bay Prairie two years earlier, had inspected William Dunovant's first rice crop in Colorado County. Dunovant's irrigation water was sourced from Eagle Lake, and the men correctly figured the Colorado River was an equally viable supply.[10] The Huebner's were principals in the Bay City Bank, and interested their banking partners D.P. Moore, Henry Rugely, and N.M. Vogelsang in the idea. The future rice men did their homework, first meeting with Dunovant in Eagle Lake, touring a Beaumont rice mill, and they ended their fact-finding mission in the rice fields of Louisiana. On their return, they not only brought back a load of Honduran seeds but also a rice farmer to mentor them in their Texas venture.[11]

Within months of forming the Matagorda County Rice & Irrigating Company (MCR&IC), the Bay City Bank partners shipped an "engine, boiler, and pump" and five McCormick self-binders by rail to Wharton, then floated the machinery down the Colorado River by barge.[12] In January, MCR&IC hired E.E. Wells and his brother Walter to break 500 acres of land east of Bay City with "four big American mules and a riding plow." By spring, the firm had 16 teams engaged in grading, disking, and planting. Their need for mules and horses was so high that it outstripped local supply, so animals from other regions were freighted to Wharton or Pierce's Station and driven south some 25 miles. That fall, "long strings of rice wagons" headed east of Bay City to gather MCR&IC's first harvest, eventually filling two rail cars destined for the Hinz rice milling company in Beaumont.[13]

The economics of William Dunovant's first crop benefited from the Cane Belt Railroad that passed through Eagle Lake, and he was one of its owners. But in 1900 the nearest shipping point to MCR&IC's crop was over 20 miles to the north. Matagorda's nascent rice industry celebrated the arrival of its first rail transportation link when the Cane Belt Railroad was extended south, reaching Bay City in 1901. The rail line not only reduced shipping costs but saved the rice men and their wagon teams days of travel over alternately muddy or dusty tracks through the prairie.

Matagorda County in 1900 had about 600 acres in rice. Planning for the 1901 season, A.P. Borden enthusiastically announced that "I shall put every acre in rice next year," and added another 2,500 acres to his interests. MCR&IC's acreage east of Bay City grew to 10,000 acres. That year the newly chartered W.C. Moore-Cortes Canal Company (M-CCC) of Houston acquired 20,000 acres on the west side of the Colorado River, and Bay City entrepreneur Victor LeTulle and others formed the Bay Prairie Company in Lane City that planted another 23,000 acres.[14]

In 1902, the *Galveston Daily News* espoused that Matagorda County's rice industry was "on the eve of a great development." The article wasn't exaggerating. That year the massive Matagorda County Rice Mill, the first in the region, was constructed in Bay City adjacent to the Cane Belt Railroad. In addition to new infrastructure development, the volume of rice acres exploded, growing from those first 600 acres to 35,460 in Matagorda County and another 23,600 acres in Wharton. During those two years eleven irrigation companies were chartered, their teams of mules, wagons, and giant machines littering the landscape as they transformed native prairie lands – called "unbroken sod" – into a new economic force.[15]

The outlay of venture capital was initially local, but by 1902 there was an influx of investment dollars from throughout the United States. The business impact of the industry on rural towns in the rice-growing region was incalculable (Figs. 2, 3, & 4). Of 14 businesses listed in Bay City in 1903, for example, six were irrigation companies and three were milling companies. The combined assets of rice-related businesses were over $500,000 compared to $78,000 for all other Bay City companies.[16]

Early Texas Rice Farming Practices. Bay Prairie rice irrigation water was sourced by the Colorado River and supplied by a network of large canals shaped by man and beast using ditchers. Initially pulled by single or paired oxen, it wasn't long before more horsepower was added in the way of "six-up" or "eight-up" teams, defined as pairs of 12 or 16 draft animals.[17] As early as 1902, the larger irrigation interests formed their canals using cable-driven bucket dredges mounted to a barge (Fig. 4). Matagorda and Wharton counties were dissected by over 300 miles of irrigation canals and laterals by the 1920s, a remarkable feat given the industry's initially unsophisticated tools and the challenging terrain.

Moving water from its source to destination relied on a combination of both passive and mechanized processes. The least costly were gravity canals, in which surveyors laid out waterways with a gradual downslope grade to minimize the number of pumping plants and re-lift pumps, the water volume and timing controlled by sluice gates, flumes, and checks. Although the engine-driven pumping plant mechanized – and modernized – water control, it was still an arduous process for draft animals to maneuver the steep banks of the Colorado River to lower centrifugal pumps and steam boilers onto wooden decks, heave irrigation pipes, then hoist one or more tall smokestacks.

The switch from steam to petroleum-driven pumping plants coincided with another industry new in Texas – oil and gas. When A.P. Borden purchased what may have been the first gasoline-powered engine used for a Texas pumping station, the nearest source for refined petroleum products was the East Texas Corsicana Field, its gasoline-grade and heavier lubricating components shipped by rail across the state by 1899. In 1901, gasoline fueled many Texas pumping plants, the bulk of it "Beaumont oil" originating from the giant Spindletop field discovered that year on McFaddin Ranch near Beaumont.

Bay City's Doug Huebner described the planting process. In preparation for a rice crop the land had to be turned over, or "broken," to a depth of about four to six inches, he says. In the early years, the work was done with horses or mules pulling moldboard plows, either "walk-behind" or "ride-on" sulky plows. The term "slip" was commonly used for the simplest type of walk-behind plow, consisting of single handle and a pair of overlapping blades pulled by a mule with a worker tethered to the other end.[18]

Next the soil was worked into a seedbed with a rice harrow, usually a wooden float with iron pegs in it. After seeding, another trip with a harrow was needed to cover it.[19] The first seeds planted in lower Colorado River Valley were Japanese and Honduran. To hedge their bets on weather during growing and harvest season, rice farmers began to try other varieties such as Blue Rose, Early Prolific, Lady Wright, and Louisiana Pearl.[20]

Levees allowed for control of the depth of irrigation water and were integral to rice cultivation. They were built by plowing toward the center line with a moldboard plow, then formed into a dike by pulling a wooden blade, much like a grader (Fig. 5). The blades were called different names, and most rice farmers could tell where you were from by what you called it. In Texas they were called a "push," and in other places were known as a "pull" or a "squeeze."

Binders and threshers were the backbone of the harvest. Initially called self-binders, Bay Prairie's rice binders (Fig. 6) were shipped by rail via the Cane Belt to either Bay City

Hardware or LeTulle Mercantile and assembled in the early years by a man known only as "one-arm Pool." Two men handled the rice binder in the field – a "gang skinner" or "bull whacker," who drove a team of six to ten mules, and another person that operated the machinery.[21]

The working parts of a binder included a cutting mechanism propelled by a chain-driven bull wheel and a canvas tarp strapped around rollers to catch the cut crop. From there it was lifted by a system of levers to the knotter, which bound or tied the rice in a bundle and moved it to the bundle carrier rack where hands collected the bundles and stacked them in the field to dry.[22] It would be many more years before the laborious process of stacking and moving the shocks to bundle wagons was mechanized.

The thresher, or separator, was another rice field adaptation from the Midwestern grain belt. It eliminated a step in the milling process by separating raw seed from the chaff while in the field. Dried shocks were unloaded from the rice wagon with pitchforks and fed into the apparatus (Figs. 7 & 8). Air blowers pushed the lighter weight straw and chafe up to a stack where it was ejected while the separated seed dropped to the bottom through a series of sieves, then driven out through another opening where it was manually sacked in 100-pound burlap "toe sacks" (Figs. 9 & 10). Job titles in the threshing operation included "shockers" who distributed bundles of rice for drying, "spike pitchers" who tossed bundles into the thresher, and the worker who filled the rice sacks was called a "jigger."[23]

As time went by, tractors began to do more of the work done by animals. On Taylor Huebner's Bay City farm, steam tractors were not a big improvement over mules and slips in preparing the soil (Fig. 10). It was labor intensive to provide fuel, requiring many men and mules to deliver water and wood need to keep the tractor "steamed up." They were, however, useful in powering stationary threshers. Doug says the thresher was separated from its power source by about a hundred feet to prevent igniting wooden-framed threshers and combustible rice straw. By about 1912, steel-framed threshers made their appearance.[24]

It wasn't until about 1920 that gasoline tractors were in common use, and even then, they were often cranked over with gasoline but ran on kerosene sourced from a separate tank.[25] Petroleum also fueled threshers, and they evolved into a self-propelled "traction tractor" when a drive chain was attached from a crankshaft to its rear axle.[26]

The fall rice harvest was a community event. Some workers left their homes well before daylight and didn't return home until after dark, while others set up large camps in the rice fields. Bill Blair, of Colorado County, remembers that "the rice workers had a sleep shack, and usually there was a cook shack." Bill added that "there were a lot of mouths to feed, and the foreman charged boys with netting fish from canals and shooting ducks that swarmed the rice fields by the light of the moon." The sound of the popping of guns lasted for hours, although one observer noted that the effect was usually "a few dead ducks, a large number of crippled birds, and now and again a badly injured cow or horse."[27]

Bend in the River Rice. The Bend in the River was at the heart of the turn of the century Texas rice boom, its pioneers A.P. Borden and Manley Sexton. Borden was quick to foresee the importance of irrigation, and even before he harvested his first crop from Long Point Creek, leased a 150-foot-wide irrigation easement in April 1900 from Mary E. Braman. Extending several miles through Cayce and League tracts, he sold the easement to the W.C. Moore-Cortes Canal Company in 1901 after he moved his farming venture to Wharton County.

Bay City's Manly Sexton had a colorful resume. He ran for county assessor, was a farmer and cattleman, and owned a barbershop. Sexton was named a director of the Houston-based Sexton Rice and Irrigation Company (SRIC) in 1901, the company lasting just four years before filing for bankruptcy, its assets purchased by Security Rice and Irrigation Company.[28]

Entrepreneur Sexton saw the future of rice and irrigation about the same time as Borden, approaching Mary E. Braman with an ambitious proposal for her grazing lands. Sexton and Braman signed a five-year farming lease encompassing 800 acres of the Hurd Survey adjacent to the Crier tract, 3,115 acres on the Crier Survey, another 2,952 acres of the League Survey, and 2,569 on Cayce's Survey (Fig. 11). Lease terms stipulated that he could, for a one-dollar payment, select an easement anywhere on the lease to situate pumping plants and canals for "the growing and cultivating of any crop except Johnson grass."[29]

Like Borden, Sexton's timing was faultless, positioning himself just before irrigation and rice producing companies converged on Matagorda County. A year after he negotiated the Braman lease, he sublet much of his holdings to newcomers such as the Prairie Bluff Rice Company, Planters Irrigation Company, and the W.C. Moore-Cortes Canal Company.[30] The Prairie Bluff Rice Company (PBRC), organized by George J. Schieicher and Fred C. Proctor at Pierce Station in 1901, was the first rice planter on the Crier tract. The company contracted for the excavation of a canal about three miles long from Blue Creek in 1901 to irrigate 350 acres of prairie on the Hurd Survey, Pierce Ranch and other Pierce holdings, and Texas Land and Cattle Company lands. After just a year, PBRC sold its interests to another rice newcomer, the Northern Irrigation Company.[31]

Planters Irrigation Company (PIC) and W.C. Moore-Cortes Canal Company (M-CCC) were both Houston syndicates that farmed the League and Cayce surveys. In 1901, PIC dug a massive canal that was one and a half miles long, 40-feet wide, and seven-feet-deep. Its "headgate situated on a lake fed or supplied by the Colorado River" referred to improvement of Jennings Creek near its Colorado River terminus. That year PIC succeeded in irrigating 1,000 acres. The company sold its interests after two years.[32]

The largest venture with Bend in the River holdings was the M-CCC. Most of its over 20,000 Matagorda County acres were purchased from the A.H. Pierce Estate but included 5,000-acres leased from Manly Sexton on Mary E. Braman's "Braman pasture" south of Jennings Creek. Included in its holdings was Borden's Braman easement, which the company used to situate its main canal and headgate "at a point on Jennings Creek and Lake." Available maps suggest that the company utilized and extended the original PIC canal.[33]

The M-CCC lengthened their 1901 canal a total of seven miles to the east and installed a pumping plant on the Colorado River near Borden's Long Point rice crop. Irrigation water was transported by three smaller pumps to another 10 miles of 40-foot-wide laterals. The M-CCC cultivated about 5,500 acres in 1901 and 10,000 acres in 1902. Its rice venture grew so quickly that M-CCC built a company town named Cortes north of their new canal intake on the Cayce tract that, at its peak, boasted a two-story hotel, post office, 15 to 20 tenant houses, a 50,000-sack warehouse, a Southern Pacific Railroad depot, and a boat landing on the river to load and unload supplies.[34]

Two other rice ventures opened at the Bend in the River between 1902 and 1905. Northern Irrigation Company (NIC) was chartered in 1902 by North Dakota investors with a capital stock of $250,000. NIC was the entity that purchased PBRC's assets, and in its first year amassed 17,000 acres of prairie lands, its properties including what would become the town of Markham. To secure its main water source to the north, NIC purchased 221 acres on Blue Creek from the Texas Land and Cattle Company, installing a new pumping station and improving the original PBRC canal.[35]

NIC hired Louisianian Albert M. Anderson as company president and opened offices in Houston and Bay City. Advertisements were posted in city newspapers tendering bids for such things as "rice irrigation machinery" and the contracting of six miles of rice canals. Specifications included a main canal that had to overlap the M-CCC canal by way of an elevated flume and a pumping plant designed to deliver an 80,000 gallon per minute capacity "with a minimum lift of 15 feet and a maximum lift of 20 feet." In its first year, NIC completed half of its goal – three miles of main canals and laterals – but managed to plant 7,000 acres despite mud and water that was "waist-deep in places."[36]

According to rancher Tommy LeTulle, Stephen Samuel Perry farmed rice on the banks of the northern portion of Jennings Creek. Perry was 27 in 1904 when he moved from Brazoria County to the new town of Markham where he ran a general store, raised stock, and planted rice. Perry farmed the Jennings Creek area between 1909 and 1917, then left the rice fields for Freeport. The location of his rice crop is thought to have been on the upper portion of the League Survey on the Olcese tract and Braman pasture to the south and west.[37]

Perry built a small pumping plant on the lake consisting of a boiler and a single pump. Cypress stumps that remain in the lake channel today were probably the source for a cypress wood flume constructed 12-feet above the water level. A mule-dredged canal crossed the oak mottes to his crops. The exact location of his Jennings Creek and Lake canals in not known, but of the three relict rice canals leading from Jennings Lake that remain on Spread Oaks Ranch today, the one that most resembles LeTulle's Perry description is on the southwest side (Fig. 12).[38]

First Failings. If there was any one thing to cause early Matagorda rice farmers unease, it was the inconvenient fact that the combined draw of pumping stations along the lower Colorado River exceeded the capacity of the low river flow. But the reality was tempered by a massive reservoir created by a dam in the river – the great Colorado River log raft – which, by 1902, extended upriver to Bay City. In years with normal rainfall, the dam impounded water above the raft and filled every river tributary and topographic low along the floodplain that, between 1900 and 1910, could be diverted for growing rice. The first day of reckoning came during the drought of 1910.[39]

Matagorda County's 52,000-acre crop in 1909 was a record harvest. Then came the drought of 1910. During the peak of the growing season, the county went three months without rain. The Colorado River was so parched that people walked from one side to the other. That year, with only 12,000 total acres successfully harvested, the financial impact was immediate. Dozens of area farmers failed, along with seven irrigation companies. At the Bend in the River, the financial casualties included M-CCC and NIC.[40]

The M-CCC, unable to pay its creditors, was restructured in 1911. Its new stakeholders included J.M. Moore of First National Bank in Bay City, W.M. Furber of the Markham State Bank, Bay City irrigation man A.J. Harty, and several "capitalists of Houston," the latter likely including Ross Sterling. The new board was able to keep the firm solvent by selling 16,000 acres of its landholdings and putting most of its pumping plant, canals, and warehouses on the market.[41]

Low river levels forced Northern Irrigation Company to shut down its Colorado River and Blue Creek pumping plants, the company filing for bankruptcy in 1910. (Figs. 13 & 14) That year, it advertised "50 head [of] extra good heavy rice mules, saddle horses," and "all kinds of rice machinery" for sale. Within two years the firm liquidated 15,000 acres of its 17,000-acre holdings. The reorganized NIC remained afloat, but its peak had passed. In 1914, A.J. Harty announced that the newly minted Markham Irrigation Company would take control of irrigating the remaining NIC-owned and leased lands.[42]

Northern Irrigation's inability to deliver water had a domino effect – its losses also impacted farmers with NIC lease agreements. The list included Evan and Sam Watkins Jr. on the Bend in the River. The Watkins brothers, who watched their 409-acre crop wither in the summer sun, filed suit to recover losses of $9,000. But NIC's legal advisors had included a limiting clause of $4 per acre in their lease agreement, and the court allowed them just $1,636. It broke Evan and Sam Jr.[43]

The Green & Sawyer Company of Bay City was another casualty in 1910. A year earlier, they signed a lease with Californian Margaret Olcese to construct "ditches, or canals, fluses [sic], laterals, reservoirs, dams and leveis [sic]," along the south shoreline of Jennings Lake. As soon as the ink was dry on their lease, and after only two years in business, the company folded. It is believed that the Green & Sawyer land is where Stephen Perry farmed between 1909 and 1917.[44]

Water issue skirmishes caused by the drought weren't just fought in the courtroom – they were fought in the field. It was not uncommon, for example, for drought-stricken rice farmers to steal water from more fortunate canal owners. Second generation irrigation man Earl Eidebach remembered "they would come at night," either taking "all the boards out of the checks" or they detonated dynamite to destroy irrigation infrastructure. As an unlucky planter was "shut down to repair [their] canal system" the perpetrator often seized the opportunity to "get their acreage watered up." Occasionally there was violence, such as the stabbing of M-CCC canal foreman Walter Jesse in a dispute over "watering rice." Rice farmers nearly always "carried a Winchester" to "threaten one another, but they always hoped that neither one used the gun."[45]

Filling the Void. Not every rice farming region suffered from the 1910 drought to the extent of the lower Colorado River. The industry still had momentum, and several new companies were chartered after the drought, eager to fill the void left by those that collapsed. Rice and irrigation newcomers to the Bend in the River included the Northern Canal Company, "Wilson on Blue Creek," and the Markham Irrigation Company.

The Northern Canal Company (NCC) was based in Jennings, Louisiana and its president, Albert M. Anderson, was also head of Northern Irrigation. The company in its first four years purchased one of NIC's main canals, a 24-acre right of way to its Colorado River pumping plant on the Cayce Survey and filed a permit for a second pumping station at Blue Creek. As for J.F. Wilson and his Blue Creek venture, little is known, only that his holdings were under 500 acres.[46]

Markham Irrigation Company (MIC) was chartered with $50,000 capital in 1912 by a board that included former M-CCC stakeholders J.M. Moore and W.M. Furber. In its first year, they acquired most of M-CCC's holdings on the Crier and League surveys, as well as a barge dredge "for the purpose of extending canals into several thousand acres of sod land." MIC's honeymoon was short. In its first growing season, MCR&IC charged the company with violating its prior and superior water rights, then filed an injunction to prevent the new company from pumping any water. The suit was one of the first concerning water rights among the lower Colorado River rice interests, and it foretold the future.[47]

Governing Water. Although an 1895 statute permitted appropriation of upstream water from Texas rivers for irrigation without regard to downstream users, it wasn't until the 1910s that industrial-scale water issues moved to the forefront of Texas politics. The state's first comprehensive irrigation bill came with the passage of the Burgess-Glasscock Act in 1913. Chief among its statutes was a law declaring that certain waters were the property of the state, which had the authority not only to appropriate these waters but to limit the take to specific uses. Further, water rights would be governed by the newly sanctioned State Board of Water Engineers, and county commissioner courts would be authorized to establish irrigation districts, raise money for the construction of reservoirs, and levy taxes for irrigation projects.[48]

Matagorda County would have a prominent role in Texas water law. Immediately after the Burgess-Glasscock Act was passed, county canal companies and rice growers hired Bay City lawyer John W. Gaines to clarify and revise portions of its passages. Gaines and his backers were the authors of language strengthening the controversial clause that prioritized water rights of early claimants over later ones, and initiated water conservation use. His most important contribution, however, was as an architect to obtain water from sources far removed from Matagorda County – dam water from Austin.[49]

Dam Water. As one of the state's leading rice producers, Matagorda planters were anxious to avoid a repeat of the impact from the devastating 1910 drought. Rice interests took the bold step of buying water from upriver, casting their eye towards faraway Austin. The city of Austin constructed the first dam on the Colorado River in 1893, and after the 2,000-acre reservoir behind the dam failed spectacularly in 1900, private interests began construction of another in 1911. When Matagorda's rice crop was threatened by drought in 1915, some of its principals paid a visit to the contractors repairing the dam's floodgates. Although the city of Austin legally owned the water, it was the dam workers – who had no authority – that released its impounded water. Although the side deal salvaged the downstream rice harvest, not everyone was pleased.[50]

The State Board of Water Engineers took control of the Lake Austin irrigation allocations volumes from the next year, but this time it was Wharton and Matagorda County rice growers that were unsatisfied. The allotments were too low, they chafed, and after a dry spring in 1917, a proactive John W. Gaines negotiated use of "all the water behind the dam down to the normal flow of the Colorado" for a price of $10,000. Although the sale was approved by a federal judge, Austinites opposed the move despite Gaines' promise that the lower Colorado River rice farmers would take only "enough to meet the crop necessities."

The Lake Austin dam gates were opened for successive years between 1915 and 1919. On the one hand, it saved Matagorda's crop during dry spells. But it also set in motion a storm of controversy, bad blood, and lawsuits. At the center of it was Markham Irrigation Company (MIC), reorganized in 1917 with Victor LeTulle as president and A.J. Harty its general manager. MIC, through its purchase of all M-CCC's and most of NIC's assets, now had a monopoly on the west side of the river. Its next move would be to secure the means to irrigate its vast holdings.[51]

Wharton County interests at the Lane City pumping plant negotiated rights to Austin dam water in 1917, then resold the unused volume to downstream planters. But after A.J. Harty fired up MIC's pumping plants, rice men from two counties filed an injunction preventing MIC's access to the Lane City release. The courts sided with MIC, ruling that once the water was returned to the main river channel, it was unallocated public property that "belonged to whoever could get it." The 1917 water rights controversy started a flood of legal actions that went to the Texas Board of Water Engineers for arbitration. Colorado, Wharton, and Matagorda County rice concerns dominated some 25 irrigation contests on the docket. What the Board of Engineers couldn't determine remained in district courts for two more years. The most named defendant was MIC and its manager, A.J. Harty.[52]

Rice farmers lined the riverbanks on a hot 1918 July day, their eyes on the river. Victor LeTulle and A.J. Harty had paid $20,000 – twice the price of any previous year – for release of Austin dam water, and the downstream rise was expected that day. Approved by the Board of Water Engineers, the surprise action allowed for discharge of 1,300 acre-feet per day, and a volume sufficient to water crops for a month – but only for Matagorda County farmers. "Canal riders" were hired to ensure that every irrigation gate upriver between Colorado and Wharton counties was closed.[53]

MIC's unexpected control of Austin dam water alarmed Colorado River Valley rice interests. As one of the furthest of the downstream users, the company should have been at the mercy of upriver irrigators and, as a relative newcomer, the last in line as a water rights claimant. That was certainly the case between 1912 and 1917, when MIC seemed always to be on the losing side of the irrigation contest. The firm, however, was ending the decade by dominating it, the outcome largely due to the shrewdness of its principals, Victor LeTulle and A.J. Harty.[54]

Convinced they were the only source for Matagorda County irrigation water, the next year, 1919, MIC cautioned Colorado River Valley rice growers to notify them far in advance of their irrigation needs to "avoid misunderstandings and disappointments." The challenge, MIC advised, was the "impossibility of buying water impounded at Austin, which had been done for the past two or three years." In part, that was true. But MIC's arrogance suggested they had an alternative watering strategy, and they were about to show their hand.[55]

Reservoir Water. A year earlier, MIC began designing a series of massive irrigation reservoirs, the scale of which had never been attempted in the rice industry. The plan was to impound an area of 3,500 acres with a nine-foot high "earthen levee" to enclose and "submerge" adjacent lowlands. Much of this land was located on the Bend in the River, and what MIC didn't already own or lease, A.J. Harty would buy, his purchases including the Olcese tract, Watkins family land, and the adjacent Harriet Parker-Poole Cattle Company interests. In the spring of 1919, MIC applied to the Board of Water Engineers for an appropriation of Colorado River water to fill their new reservoirs.[56]

Markham's giant earth-moving project would alter the landscape of the Bend in the River forever. First, tributaries that flowed into the Colorado from Dry Creek downriver to Cortes were dammed. Blue Creek, which formed the development's northern boundary, was renamed Blue Creek Lake and its reservoir filled by three canals sourced at the river. A new waterway was dug from Blue Creek Lake to the south and parallel to the river, cutting through and incorporating what was Watkins Lake. From there the channel was connected to the original Jennings Creek, which was dammed across its middle to form

Jennings Lake to the northwest and North Cortes Lake, named for H.W. Cortes of the M-CCC, to the south. The remainder of Jennings Creek was diverted from its earlier river outflow and dammed to shape Harty Lake, named for A. J. Harty (Fig. 15).

MIC's new rice reservoirs needed one of two things to justify the gamble – a year of normal precipitation or a release of water from Lake Austin. Nature eliminated the first option, the region experiencing below-average rainfall between 1917 and 1920. The second was thwarted by man – the Austin City Council – that flexed its political muscle in 1921 by declining any release of water from Lake Travis to Colorado River rice men. After 1921, Matagorda County's rice production declined. Farmers were wisely beginning to avoid the financial risk of uncertain irrigation volumes and diversifying into dry land crops.[57]

LeTulle and Harty changed their strategy. With waters impounded behind the Colorado River log jam now reaching upstream to Dry Creek, Harty designed a river by-pass canal that would extend some 4.5 miles to Jennings Lake, digging laterals to fill each of MIC's five reservoirs along the river (see Fig. 15). The only challenge was a length of 7,040 feet still part of the Braman Estate. MIC principals delivered the Braman heirs an ultimatum – either grant them a right of way or the courts would condemn their land. The Braman's chose the former, and in 1921, sold MIC an easement for $500 to construct, maintain, and operate "a certain canal intake for irrigation purposes." The Braman's used the deed instrument to express their displeasure, their attorney's inserting the sentence: "MIC proposed to resort to eminent domain proceedings in the event of our refusal to convey this strip of land."[58]

The River Rises. The expanse of water that often covered the Colorado River floodplain behind the log raft during high river events was good for rice interests, but bad for towns along its banks. Bay City, for example, began building a protection levee built in 1901 that, by 1913, covered some 12 miles. As a solution to Colorado River flooding, the levee was "protection" in name only – Bay City was inundated four times in the 14 years between 1908 and 1922. The first flood, in 1908, caused only minor damage when a portion of the levee broke, pouring water into the north part of town. Bay City was less fortunate in 1913.[59]

All eyes were on the river as it spilled over its banks in early December 1913 (Figs. 16 & 17). The *Bay City Tribune* assured townspeople that the flood risk was low and that the town "would be able to cope with the rise satisfactorily" on "account of the protection levee." Residents were further counseled that county drainage committee members V.L. LeTulle, D.P. Moore, and A.J. Harty had organized some 500 men who, armed with spades and shovels, were laboring day and night "building [the levee] up at the low places."[60]

Two days later, floodwaters advanced to near the top of the levee, but Bay City remained dry. Then, on December 9, the north levee collapsed. Waters rose to three feet in parts of town. Residents fled their homes, taking refuge in the courthouse, city hall, or any building with a second story. The next day there were 2,000 homeless, destitute people in Bay City.[61]

Relief efforts were organized from across Texas. The chairman of the Bay City Relief Committee was, ironically, V.L. LeTulle, who during the disaster remained in constant "telephonic communication" with the governor. Other flooded Texas cities may have been begging for government assistance, V.L. advised, but not Bay City. The town, he said, needed no outside support and its citizens had ample food and water. Within hours V.L.'s voice was silenced. The new city spokesman, County Judge W.S. Holman, telegrammed

Austin that the initial reports were in error. Bay City had "an urgent need for aid and provisions."[62]

Townspeople from across the region offered aid, their relief efforts hampered by the merging of the Colorado and Brazos rivers to create a 36-mile-long inland sea south of Bay City. Galveston dispatched the relief launch *Wave II* to Matagorda town, transferring its cargo of relief supplies to the Gulf, Colorado & Santa Fe train. With the tracks underwater two miles from Bay City, the convoy was met by an "armada of small boats" to ferry the supplies the remainder of the distance. The boats were donated and delivered by Matagorda and Palacios fishermen only hours earlier, freighted to Bay City on five rail cars of the New York, Texas & Mexican Railway.[63]

The 1913 flood cost Texas up to $15 million and took the lives of nearly 180 people. Six died in Wharton, but none in Bay City. As the Colorado returned to its banks, the "protection levee" was dynamited to allow the water to pass from the stricken town.[64]

Water Bureaucrats. One of the responses to the 1913 flood was the organization of the Colorado River Improvement Association (CRIA) by Matagorda, Wharton, and Colorado county businessmen, the list soon expanding to include Bastrop, Travis, Fayette, and Austin counties. With the notable exception of A.P. Borden, few in the organization were rice men. Although they did not promulgate it, their agenda was largely at odds with lower Colorado River Valley rice concerns. Among CRIA's propositions were deepening of the river channel, connecting the navigable channel to the intercoastal canal system, development of hydroelectricity, and conservation of water. The most controversial proposal was removal of the river raft.[65]

CRIA's initial charter was a study in political mastery. Because the US government would not fund drainage and levee projects – flood control – the founders wisely titled it a navigation project. An important tactic was shifting river governance from local control to federal by using the Rivers and Harbors Act of 1899. It was a move that, if successful, would effectively end the reign of rice men who controlled the river water with seeming impunity.[66]

At a 1916 Army Corps of Engineers hearing in Wharton, CRIA surveyors reported that, in just one year, the raft (Fig. 18) had grown half a mile upriver and was now adjacent to Blue Creek, while silt deposits were filling the river between Columbus and Eagle Lake. River overflows threatened not just urban interests, but thousands of acres of agricultural lands. A.P. Borden testified that floods reduced the value of his Pierce Estate rice crop by about half, citing that of his 23,000 rice acres he was losing $10 an acre – about $230,000 a year.[67]

CRIA requested funding of $8 million for the proposed state and federal joint venture. Congress, however, did not act on the appropriation, and local supporters gave up the fight. Bay City responded by improving its protection levee.

The River Rises, Again. After Bay City was underwater again in 1914, the county raised funds to repair, improve and extend its levee system to 22 miles. Few were willing to publicly discuss the obvious – that the work, under commissioners V.L. LeTulle, D.P. Moore, and A.J. Harty of Matagorda County Drainage District No.1 – was in the hands of rice men who had a vested interest in preventing removal of the river raft. Then, in 1919, the county drainage commissioners reported that their levee improvements were woefully behind schedule. Money was short, they stated, ominously adding that we "will not be responsible, should anything happen to the protection levee."[68]

River waters spread across the prairie three years later, inundating Wharton on May 2, 1922. Bay City, however, was unperturbed. State Reclamation Engineer Arthur A. Stiles had recently inspected the work, and under the newspaper heading "Protection of Bay City Assured By Excellent Levees," Stiles confidently conveyed to Texas Governor Neff that the town's protection levee would withstand the coming rise. A 100-foot section of levee collapsed four days later.[69]

As Bay City filled with water, engineer Stiles reinspected the levees. Reluctant to retract his earlier statements, he advised that the failure was not structural, and that it must have been caused by "animals or varmints burrowing into the levees." Stiles further alienated himself with his remarks that "the water was only three feet deep," and that townspeople seemed to be enjoying themselves by "rowing about in boats" and "playing in the water." In an interview with the *Bay City Daily Tribune*, he added that "I am not concerned in your drainage problems" as "there will be no more floods."[70] Two days later, the town flooded a second time (Fig. 19).

Townspeople anxiously watched the contest between the second river rise and A.J. Harty's scheme to repair a growing 300-foot levee gap with "the big dredge." V.L. LeTulle donated the dredge from the MIC inventory, his altruism tempered by his request for a $10,000 public subscription to pay wages for the "force of men" he rallied to the effort.[71] A.J. Harty, however, arrived a day late. As the big dredge moved into the breach, the river rose another three feet. Water filled the streets of Bay City. Finally, on May 29 – after three weeks – floodwaters receded from the beleaguered town. Within weeks Harty was back at work repairing the damage with his "levee machine."[72]

A New Round of Water Bureaucrats. As in 1913, the 1922 flood prompted renewed flood control efforts. The first formal hearing was a conference of the Colorado River Flood Control Association that summer. Bay City principals openly admitted they didn't know what to do – some wanted flood control, but others were unwilling to sacrifice a 60,000-acre rice industry. A decade had passed since Wharton and Matagorda county businessmen founded CRIA to control urban flooding. Now, with CRIA moribund in the lower Colorado River Valley, they turned to a program introduced by Congressman Joseph J. Mansfield, which allowed counties to finance flood control through a 25-year state tax exemption. The vehicle – the formation of conservation and reclamation districts – was immediately embraced by civic leaders.[73]

The Matagorda County Conservation and Reclamation District (MCRD) and Wharton County Conservation and Reclamation District (WCRD) were founded in 1923 and 1924, respectively. Like the original CRIA, they had responsibility for drainage and improvement to flood protection levees. But it also mandated the clearing of "logs, trees, and other drift" in the river – removal of the log jam – and it immediately divided Colorado River communities. On one side were businessmen and politicians. The former understood the economic importance of flood control and the latter knew the power of the vote. On the other side were rice interests (Fig. 20).[74]

Previously, the need to remove the raft was a topic mostly whispered. But the MCRD and WCRD proposals emboldened area business leaders. At hearings, meetings, and in newspaper editorials, they willingly and loudly vocalized sentiments such as "levees are futile," and "the only way to cure the overflow habitat of the Colorado River" is to "dredge a new channel around the raft that causes all the trouble."[75]

Rice was a multi-million-dollar industry, and to its principals, its value was too important to destroy over the occasional flood. But their position was an oversimplification. The river dam was merely increasing their profits. Water above the raft was ponded at a higher elevation than adjacent agriculture, and it allowed them to rely on gravity flow irrigation instead of bearing the cost of building and operating steam or gasoline pumping plants. As well, the 'they' in the fight were no longer a dozen or so local irrigation companies, but a single conglomerate – Markham Irrigation and its partnership with V.L. LeTulle and wealthy Houston oilman, banker, newspaperman, and future governor Ross S. Sterling. Together, they owned every irrigation canal in the county.[76]

Rice and its proponents R.S. Sterling, A.E. Kerr, and V.L. LeTulle squared off against MCRD and WCRD in 1925. The MCRD immediately surrendered (Fig. 21). Under the newspaper heading "Gravity Interests Show Hand in Colorado River Matter and Propose to Fight to Prevent the Removal of the Raft," the MCRD Board of Commissioners, who had to this point been aligned with the WCRD, succumbed to demands from rice interests and withdrew their support, revoking WCRD's permit to remove the raft in Matagorda county.[77]

A.P. Borden, a vocal backer of the Wharton side, pressured his former MCRD allies to reconsider their position. The response came not from the MCRD, but from their new spokesperson, MIC's president A.E. Kerr. Kerr proclaimed there would be no compromise – removal of the dam would "sacrifice the Matagorda people in a questionable attempt to favor the citizens of Wharton County," and would "certainly destroy the Matagorda gravity irrigation system."[78]

Then the MIC counsel played hardball, advising WCRD that its client had a vested right to a certain volume of river water, a right to maintain the raft in its current location, and most importantly, was entitled to payment for any damages sustained by lowering the water level behind the raft. The last threat raised the stakes – that year, 1925, the value of the Matagorda County rice crop was estimated at $3 million.[79]

Wharton County stood alone but didn't blink. That winter, the WCRD signed a three-year contract with Howard Kenyon Dredging Company. Threats would not prevent them from opening a channel through the log jam.[80]

The River Runneth. Matagorda's rice growers faced another water shortage in 1927 and 1928, but this time the contest wasn't at faraway Austin. It was much closer to home, and its main protagonists were Howard Kenyon of Kenyon Dredging Company and WCRD consulting engineer J.P. Markham. Kenyon and Markham settled 160 workers at three camps (Figs. 22 & 23) along the river and had begun dredging and dynamiting the channel. Using a fleet of "motor-tractors" and stores of "blasting powder," the work was considered "one of the greatest reclamation projects ever undertaken in Texas."[81] Just six months after signing the WCRD contract, the company succeeded in cutting a channel through the raft, a distance of nearly 45 miles.

Wharton, "free from the menace of floods" was in a "joyous, celebratory" mood. Not so Matagorda County, its rice men expressing "doubts and fears" and predicting "certain ruin, utter and complete." What was good for the townspeople was devastating to rice interests. As water poured downstream from behind the raft, the giant impellers of the water intake at MIC's massive Dry Creek gravity canal began to spin slowly, reversed, then shot the remaining irrigation water back into the river, leaving the rice fields high and dry.

Gravity irrigation was over, and no one was confident that companies would be willing to install pumping plants again.[82]

By 1927, the river was passable from Wharton to the Gulf. The WCRD received more good news that year when the federal government approved its request to reclassify the river as a navigable stream. One of the 1899 Rivers and Harbors Act regulations made it a criminal offense to construct any structure that would impede navigation. Local newspapers gushed that the designation "removed beyond the shadow of a doubt" that any parties would attempt to dam the stream or prevent contractors from finishing the raft removal. With that, they grossly underestimated their adversary.[83]

Ross S. Sterling abandoned the fight in 1926, leaving the future of lower Colorado River Valley irrigation to Victor L. LeTulle. LeTulle resorted to desperate efforts to save MIC's 1927 crop – he decided to build his own dam. The structure was uncovered and immediately dynamited by Kenyon's work crews.[84]

The following summer, MIC advised they would call a truce if WCRD and Howard Kenyon would pay to install pumping plants as a compromise. When neither obliged, V.L. responded by building another dam. This time, he authorized his employees to sacrifice an old M-CCC's steel dredge boat, 100 feet long and 50 feet wide. Navigating it from North Cortes Lake through the 1921 Braman Canal and into the river channel at Dry Creek, its hull was dynamited and sunk in the channel. There was no shortage of able-bodied volunteers to drive pilings and fill concrete sacks. Work on the makeshift dam spanned days, then weeks.[85]

WCRD filed an injunction to remove it. When V.L. ignored it, Texas Rangers were called in. The outlaw dam builders managed to evade them for days, disappearing into the river bottom each time the law arrived. When the Rangers learned their approach was monitored by a field phone line, they changed their tactics and at last outwitted the dam builders. Although 31 warrants were issued, they could only capture eight, who were hauled off to the Wharton County jail. After V.L. posted their bond, one of those arrested relates that, as Matagorda Sherriff Joe Mangum was returning them to Bay City, the lawman told them: "y'all go on back and go to work and complete your dam." They did, "and every day the Texas Rangers would come down and they would arrest the farmers and foreman." But other crews were hidden in the river bottom, "and when they would arrest one crew, the others would come out and keep building the dam."[86]

The Texas Rangers finally gained control of the river. V.L. sent the "insurgents" home, and he extricated the remaining structure. Then he filed a lawsuit, naming Kenyon Dredging, the WCRD, and a litany of county officials –including commissioners, A.P. Borden, a judge, sheriff, and constable. The WCRD replied with their own lawsuit, listing MIC and 20 other Matagorda County rice farmers.[87]

A day later V.L. dropped the complaints, telling the court that "the farmers are installing pumps." WCRD then agreed to drop theirs and extended an olive branch, permitting MIC to locate a dredge at Dry Creek and pump sufficient water to salvage their crops. But in August, river "freshets" delivered a new round of logs and debris that lodged against Markham's floating dredge. Kenyon Dredging foreman J.O. Brown and MIC laborers worked side by side for three days, their "heroic efforts" successfully sending the debris downstream.[88]

Victor LeTulle was wise enough to hedge his bets. Although he was publicly battling to maintain the raft and its inexpensive gravity flow irrigation system, he contracted for a $100,000 pumping plant in 1927. It would be the first to run on electricity and the only one of its kind in Texas. The Central Power & Light Company was commissioned to "furnish the power over a specially constructed highline from the city to the plant." V.L. might lose the battle, but he had no intention of losing the war.[89]

The remainder of the drift was largely removed in 1928 and given a hand by nature when, in 1929, floodwaters poured through the channel. The Colorado River, free from a hundred years of obstruction, ran deep and fast, sweeping tons of silt and mud into Matagorda Bay. While viewing the raging torrent as it made its final passage to the sea, WCRD engineer J.P. Markham suffered a heart attack and died.[90] There was no rice crop on the Colorado River near Bay City in 1928, and the 7,500 acres watered in 1929 was just a fraction of the 1913 peak of 60,000 acres.[91]

Controversy and Consolidation. The combination of ruthless business practices and the uncertainty of rice irrigation water drove nearly all its players from the industry in the early 1920s. Where once there were many, by 1923 only two, and then just one. Future Texas governor Ross S. Sterling became a majority stockholder in LeTulle's Markham Irrigation Company in 1923, and that year V.L. LeTulle bought the last of the large independent entities, A.J. Harty's Gulf Coast Irrigation Company (GCIC), mostly as a holding company for MIC. Sterling's private secretary, A.E. Kerr, was named president and treasurer of both entities, and from the LeTulle camp, A.J. Harty was designated vice president and general manager.[92] Between investments and consolidations, MIC in 1925 was the largest privately held irrigation company in North America, with 405 miles of canals that supplied water to 55,000 acres and valued at $3.5 million. (Fig. 24).[93]

With little fanfare, Ross Sterling sold his MIC interests back to Victor L. LeTulle in January 1927. Other owners named on the sale instrument were A.J. Harty and LeTulle family members Louis and Sam LeTulle. Former GCIC and MIC president A.E. Kerr was replaced by V.L. LeTulle, and Louis LeTulle became president of MIC. Two years later, in October 1929, V.L. filed suit against his own company. When the Matagorda County District Court found in his favor, Sherriff Joe Mangum was directed to seize MIC's holdings and liquidate its assets at auction. The company that was worth $3.5 million just four years earlier sold to the highest bidder for $40,000. The winner was V.L. LeTulle.[94]

LeTulle's windfall gave him most of MIC's holdings for pennies on the dollar. It was a mammoth list of possessions, comprised of land, easements and right of ways, canals, laterals, pumping plants, and boilers, dredges, buildings, and equipment, representing MIC's history of purchases from the W.C. Moore-Cortes Canal Company, Northern Canal Company, A.J. Harty's original Gulf Coast Irrigation Company, Texas Irrigation Company, and the Colorado Canal Company. Rolling his windfall into his Gulf Coast Irrigation Company, the MIC company name was erased from the irrigation landscape.

The Gulf Coast Irrigation Company moniker disappeared as well when, in 1931, it was "transferred" by V.L. LeTulle to the Interstate Public Services Company and renamed the Gulf Coast Water Company (GCWC). V.L. maintained it was not a sale, but a reorganization. When the IRS piled up penalties and interest on the unpaid taxes of his "reorganization," V.L. reluctantly paid out $110,234, then sued the government for a refund. He lost, the US Supreme Court unanimously disagreeing with his interpretation. The name V.L. LeTulle's was never again linked to irrigation or the new company, GCWC.

Ironically, GCWC's Matagorda County headquarters remained in Victor LeTulle's Bay City office building.[95]

More Dam Water, Again. Before he sold GCIC, V.L. LeTulle reconfigured three Colorado River plants from Lane City to Jennings Lake with massive electric pumps, impellers, and pipes. The new owners, GCWC, were as anxious to keep them running as their predecessors, and once more the attention shifted to securing water rights from upriver. This time, there were alternatives to Austin dam water – the Board of Water Engineers granted permits to Brownwood for power projects along the upper Colorado River, and the reorganized CRIA had partnered with Chicago-based Insull Interests to construct Hamilton Dam and other major projects. The developments would become the Highland Lakes in Burnet, Llano, and Travis Counties (Fig. 25).[96]

The Brownwood Water and Improvement District (BWID) was first, announcing intentions to divert water from the Colorado's upper tributaries in 1926. There was an immediate backlash. A long list of stakeholders were at odds with the proposal: West Texas concerns, anxious that their water was being "stolen;" power companies – in this instance Syndicate Power – always thirsty for water to produce hydroelectricity; the urban needs of the Brownwood municipality, and finally, the rice growers of coastal Texas – now a powerful lobby that included counties outside of Matagorda, and a coalition that had learned its lesson about water appropriation. Added to the mix was Syndicate Power's partner, the reorganized Colorado River Improvement Association – CRIA – a sometimes foe and sometimes ally of rice interests.[97]

Each party fought vigorously for its position. Spokesmen for the CRIA and Syndicate Power Company partnership – who were planning their own river dams – tried to eliminate the competition. In their attacks, they accused Brownwood dam backers with "political mob tactics" to defend "false and absurd" assertions by the "babbling of ignorant demagogues who aspire to be political leaders." Clarence R. Wharton, representing the South Texas Rice Growers Association in the feud, fired his first salvo in 1927. The "Brownwood boys," he said, were putting a million dollars of private capital invested in rice infrastructure at risk, and he would see to it that the matter "would be decided in a Matagorda district court."[98] Despite the hyperbola, a compromise was reached. On the rice side, the South Texas Rice Growers agreed to waive their water rights above the proposed CRIA and Syndicate dam in Burnet-Llano counties. The Brownwood dam was completed in 1932.[99]

Brownwood changed from villain to hero in 1934. Drought that year had turned Wharton and Matagorda's rice from green to brown, and the Gulf Coast Water Company (GCWC) requested purchase of 14,000 acre-feet of water for $10,000 from their former nemesis.[100] Brownwood's BWID obliged, its impounded water rescuing Wharton and Matagorda's 62,000-acre rice crop that summer. Dubbed "relief water" and "long-range irrigation," Brownwood dam water reached the Wharton County Lane City pumping plant and Matagorda twelve days after the flood gates were opened. The water's 480-mile journey was unprecedented, the feat carried in newsprint across the world as "one of the most unusual undertakings in irrigation ever known."[101]

The buyers, however, made a better deal than they expected. One of the dam's 16-ton flood gates jammed, the "unfortunate mishap" resulting in the release of another 40,000 gallons, nearly the entire capacity of the reservoir. GCWC was applauded for keeping an accurate check of the water used, writing BWID a $2,141 check for the volume that exceeded the agreement.[102]

The CRIA and Syndicate Power Company partnership to construct Hamilton Dam, later renamed Buchanan, was as acrimonious as the BWID project. Located along the upper reaches of the Colorado River in Llano County, surveying was completed in 1926 on a massive structure that, with a nearly two-mile concrete wall, would create the largest body of fresh water south of the Great Lakes. Having learned their lessons from the BWID feud, water allocation between the competing users was agreed upon and signed before the first concrete was poured. Major objections came mostly from the West Texas Chamber of Commerce, but its intransigence was not to be the project's greatest challenge.[103]

The Hamilton Dam project was shaky from the start. First, West Texas interests successfully stalled the project for two years. Then its financing, arranged by the Martin J. Insull-owned Middle West Utilities, was withdrawn. New funding was arranged with two other Insull interests, the Central Texas Hydro-Electric Company, and a bond subscription of $3,750,000 held by Insull's Mississippi Valley Utilities. Construction commenced, but in the spring of 1932, contractor Fegles Construction stopped the job and laid off most of his workmen. Its financiers, Martin and Samuel Insull, were bankrupt and had been indicted by a federal grand jury for mail fraud.[104]

Some $3.5 million had already been expended, but another $4.5 million was needed. Construction was abandoned for two years, the partially built dam held in receivership by attorney Alvin J. Wirtz. A private company called the Colorado River Company (CRC) attempted to attract funding to resurrect the moribund project, but failed in the private sector and was also declined by the federal government and the Public Works Administration (PWA). New Deal government funds might be available for public works projects, but not to private business ventures.[105]

It took some fancy political footwork to turn the private Hamilton dam venture into a public one. The solution was the creation of a state government agency, the new entity titled the Lower Colorado River Authority (LCRA). Funded by emergency state measures that authorized the LCRA to issue $20 million in bonds, the LCRA, as a public authority, was eligible for federal resources. "Widespread and general rejoicing" accompanied Secretary of the Interior Harold Ickes' June 1934 announcement of the PWA loan. The LCRA bought CRC's Hamilton Dam holdings the next year for $1.65 million.[106]

The renamed Buchanan Dam was completed in 1938, the first of a series of dams under the auspices of the LCRA that became known as the Highland Lakes. Rice interests along the lower Colorado River Valley were an enthusiastic backer of the LCRA's new role in flood control, hydroelectric power, and water conservation. More importantly, one of LCRA's charters was to provide reliable downstream irrigation water. That, the rice growers believed, would guarantee them water in perpetuity. For a long time, they were right.

Irrigators thought the battle was over by a 1937 court decision and compromise between Gulf Coast Water Company (GCWC) and LCRA attorney Alvin Wirtz. That year, the GCWC obtained a court order requiring the LCRA to release 1,500 cubic feet per second from the Buchanan reservoir for two weeks, the volume estimated to supply its 90 downstream rice contracts with sufficient water to irrigate 30,000 acres. Wirtz, a skillful opponent, travelled the Texas countryside until he found a sympathetic court willing to reverse the order. In a compromise with far reaching implications, rice interests below the

Highland Dams agreed to limit their future annual allocations to the average amount of water they used for irrigation between 1930 and 1936. Further, they were forced to recognize they had no other rights to Colorado River water other than the number stipulated in the agreement.[107] It was a short-term loss but, they believed, a long-term guarantee. They were wrong.

Epilogue. For the lower Colorado River Valley rice industry, the decade between 1900 and 1910 was one of learning, growth, and profitability. The 1910s to the early 1920s, in contrast, was a period of discipline and consolidation resulting from the reality of water limitations. The 1930s were ushered in by the Great Depression that crippled rice prices. It was followed by a New Deal "government farm program" that provided crop insurance but carried the baggage of federally mandated rice acreage allotments. During that decade came a logical, but previously unachievable, alliance between upstream and downstream power, municipality, flood control, and irrigation interests that precipitated creation of the LCRA.

The 1940s brought several tropical storms and hurricanes that caused more anxiety than they did crop damage. World War II created labor shortages, innovatively resolved by using a labor pool of German POWs. After the War, hooves, steam, and back-breaking manual labor in planting and harvesting were superseded by technology advancements – tractors, combines, and trucks. Rice was still not easy, but it was less hard.

The 1950s are remembered for a pervasive drought that tested the LCRA's ability to supply its users. Between 1952 and 1957, water levels in the newly completed string of Highland Dams dropped as much as 15 feet a year.[108] LCRA administrators, however, were able to allocate sufficient volumes for its downstream legacy rice customers. Had demand from its other users been higher, they would have failed. But that day didn't come for another 50 years.

What had united Colorado River suppliers and users after the 1930s was the same issue that divided them in the 21st century – water allocation. Between 2007 and 2014, the Colorado River Basin experienced the most severe drought ever recorded in the Lone Star State. It would nucleate a repeat of the battles from 75 years earlier, this time pitting upriver urban interests against rice growers.

Matagorda County rice farmers planted 21,500 acres in 2011. That year, the LCRA requested an emergency order from the Texas Commission of Environmental Quality mandating a total Highland Lakes water cut-off for agricultural uses. It was the first time in its history. Only federal crop insurance eased the pain of a 1,562-acre harvest that fall, and those acres succeeded mainly because of well water. The LCRA continued to withhold water for another four years. By 2013 Matagorda rice production plummeted by 94%, while municipal users increased their volume by 21%.[109]

In 2020, Matagorda rice growers planted 12,200 acres, the volume dropping to 10,500 acres in 2022 before history repeated itself – the LCRA announced another moratorium on water for downstream agricultural irrigation.[110] No more Victor LeTulle's, it seems, were left in the arena to fight for Matagorda County rice growers.

The face of modern Spread Oaks Ranch reflects the hand of the rice men. Traces of the Prairie Bluff Rice Company and Northern Irrigation Company irrigation canal remain after nearly 125 years. The road to the ranch parallels, then crosses, the original Planters Irrigation Company and W.C. Moore-Cortes Canal Company canal. A.J. Harty's hand is evident in the shape of Jennings Lake, which now occupies only about a third of its original extent.

Portions of Markham Irrigation's early 1920s reservoirs are evident from Dry Creek to lower Jennings Lake, as well as the narrow, parallel canal of the 1921 MIC-Braman easement. What was probably Markham Irrigation's last Colorado River irrigation well, on the border between the Crier and League surveys, wasn't dismantled until 2020.

Two linear canals, their morphology dulled by time, lead from the east side of upper Jennings Lake and one from the west. Their history will probably never be known. They aren't on any maps but were almost certainly dug between 1900 and 1920. At least one was likely dredged by Stephen Perry, probably the one on the west side.

Today, the canals of Spread Oaks Ranch don't lead anywhere. There is no rice grown on the Bend in the River.

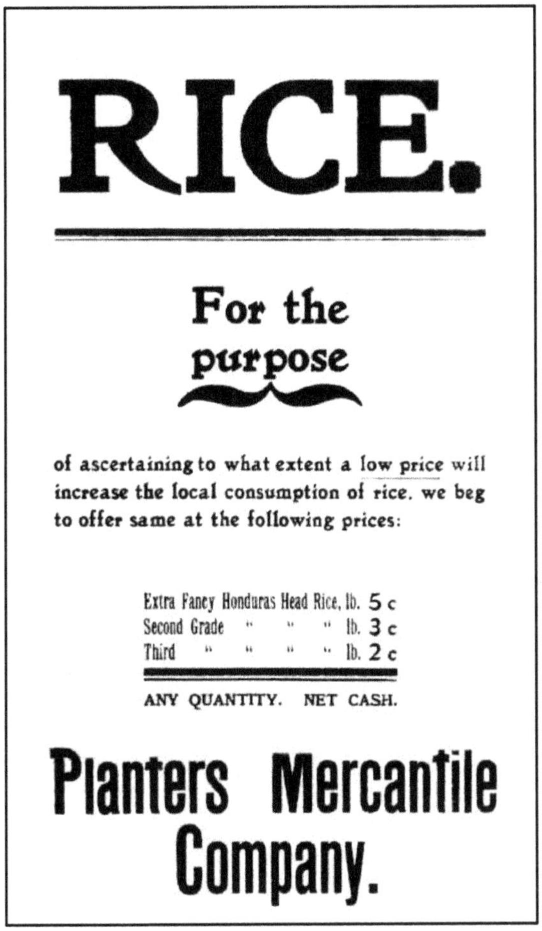

Rough Rice Sacks

and Sewing Twine

We all make mistakes but the worst mistake you can make is to buy a poor sack. Our quality gives us no trouble, and you know our price is right, too.

Korn Wagon & Imp. Company,

EAST SIDE OF SQUARE

BAY CITY TEXAS.

Anticipate your wants and place an order with us for

Rice Bags

We will receive a consignment of nine ounce bags on or about the 25th.

Our price will be net cash on delivery, from which we cannot vary.

PLANTERS' MERCANTILE CO.

RICE.

For the purpose

of ascertaining to what extent a low price will increase the local consumption of rice. we beg to offer same at the following prices:

Extra Fancy Honduras Head Rice, lb. 5 c
Second Grade   "   "   " lb. 3 c
Third   "   "   "   " lb. 2 c

ANY QUANTITY.   NET CASH.

Planters Mercantile Company.

Figs. 1 to 3. The explosion in the Texas Gulf Coast rice industry provided new business opportunities – from seeds to farming implements, rice sacks to warehouses, and initiated a large shipping market. References clockwise from upper left: *Matagorda County Tribune*, Oct. 28, 1904; *Daily Tribune*, Aug. 9, 1905; *Daily Tribune*, June 15, 1904.

Fig. 4. A barge dredge digging one of Northern Headquarters rice canals in 1903, near today's Spread Oaks Ranch. Matagorda Museum, no. 1989.09.326.7.

Fig. 5. Shaping a levee with an early wooden grader (left) powered by men and mules. Matagorda County Museum, no. 2010.02.105B1.26.

Fig. 6. A 1908 image of a mule-drawn self-binder. Rice shocks are in the foreground. Matagorda County Museum, no. 1969. 65. 225C.18.

Fig. 7. A stationary steam tractor with firewood stacked for fuel and a water wagon (right). In center, a rice wagon filled with shocks being pitched into the thresher. The ejected straw (left) is above the seed sacks. Matagorda County Museum, no. 1989.09.105B1.11.

Fig. 8. Another view of a thresher. Rice wagon and shocks (left), toe sacks filled with seed (center) and the ejected straw (right). Nesbitt Memorial Library, no. 04058.

Fig. 9. A line of rice wagons leaving the field at Huebner rice farm south of Bay City. Courtesy Doug Huebner.

Fig. 10. A steam tractor at Huebner rice farm, circa 1918. Steam tractors that replaced pack animals were later replaced by gasoline-driven tractors. Doug Huebner's father Marion Tolivar "Top" Huebner is on left and his uncle Bob to right. Courtesy Doug Huebner.

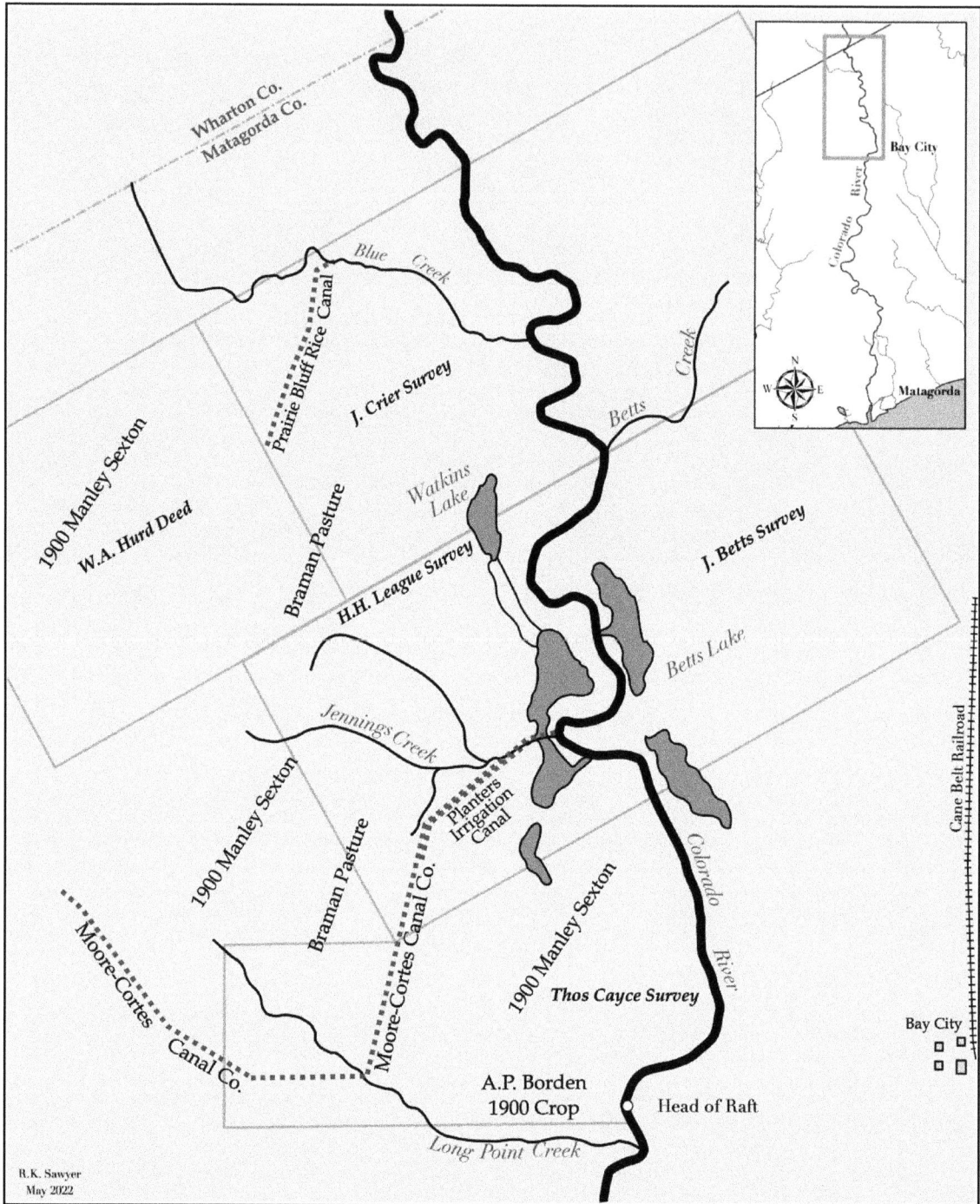

Fig. 11. Interpretation of the earliest Bend in the River rice canals, land leases, and crops circa 1900 to 1902. The basis for the river, lakes, and streams was a 1908 General Land Office (GLO) map. On the original map, the location of both Watkins and Betts lakes are consistent, but the morphology of Jennings Creek is questionable, as are several mapped lakes adjacent to the river which do not appear on earlier or later maps. The log jam by 1902 was parallel to Bay City. Reference: The Texas General Land Office, Matagorda County Rolled Sketch 11, ca 1908 to 1912, no. 8348.

256

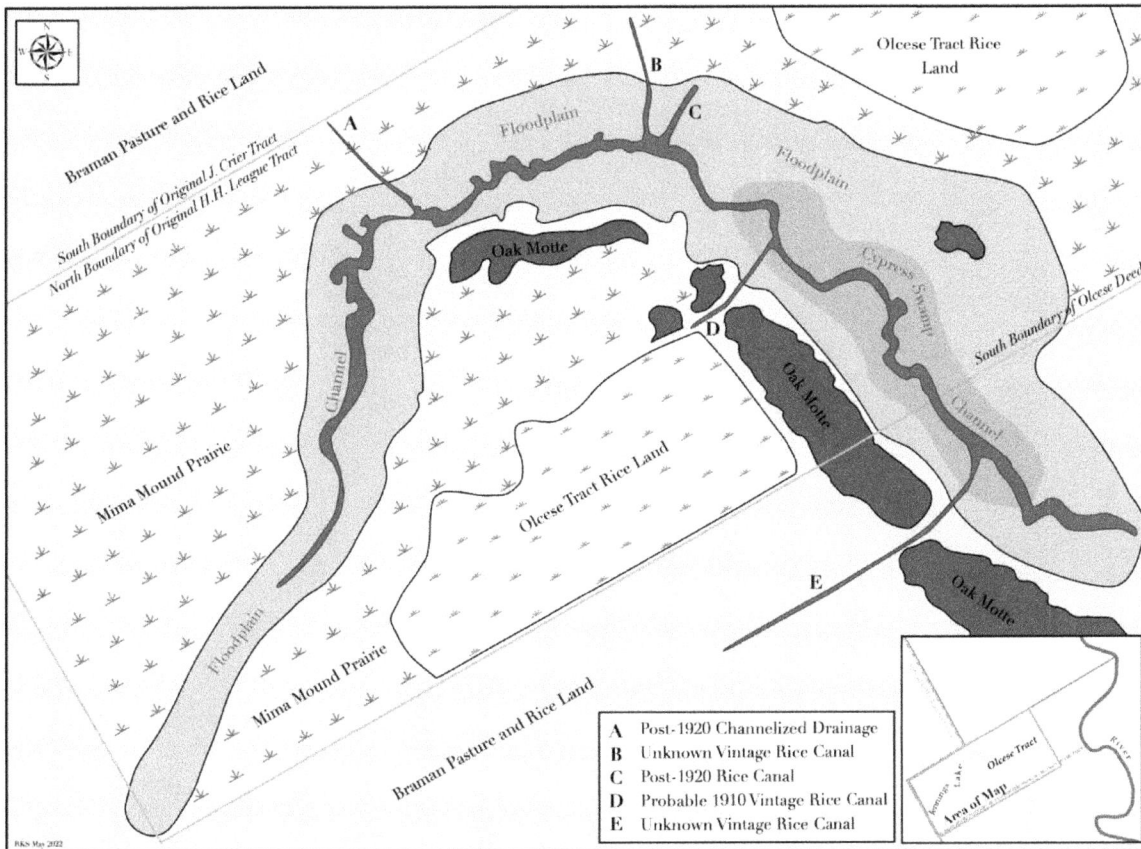

Fig. 12. On area maps, Jennings Creek is labelled both a creek and lake, and either term is correct. During periods of low rainfall, Jennings is confined to its once cypress-covered main creek channel. During periods of high water the level covers its natural floodplain, creating a quarter mile-wide lake at its broadest point. After rice interests dammed the creek in the 1920s, the name used most often has been Jennings Lake. The hand of the irrigators is still visible today – lake edges show a lateral canal dug for drainage (A) and the remnants of four rice irrigation canals (B through E). Lateral D from Jennings Creek to the Olcese rice land was leased by Green & Sawyer in 1909 and was probably part of Stephen Perry's rice operation between 1910 and 1917. Base for drawing is A.P. Borden's hand drawn 1909 map. Modified from Matagorda County Deed no. 23484, Exhibit C.

Fig. 13. The Northern Irrigation Company (NIC) nearly collapsed in 1904 but survived until the 1910 drought forced the company to file for bankruptcy. *Houston Post*, Oct. 1, 1904.

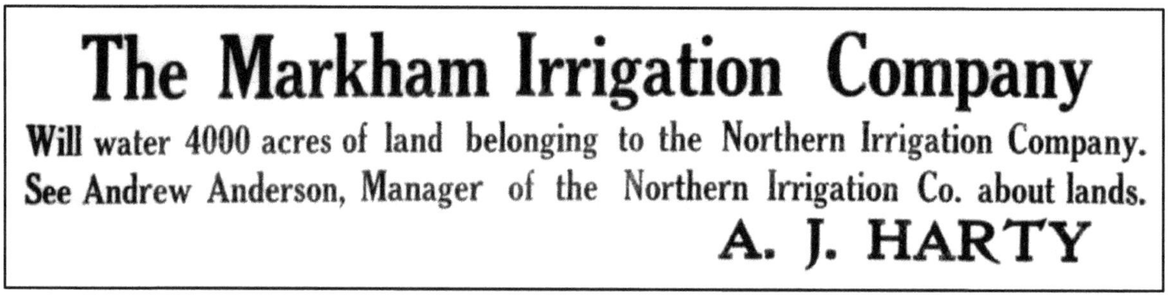

Fig. 14. After NIC collapsed in 1910, Markham Irrigation took control of irrigating its contract rice lands. *Matagorda County Tribune*, Nov. 14, 1914.

Fig. 15 (next page). The base for this compilation of Bend in the River irrigation infrastructure between 1921 and 1928 is a 1921 Markham Irrigation Company (MIC) map. By the early 1920s, MIC acquired the W.C. Moore-Cortes Canal Company (M-CCC) and Northern Irrigation Company (NIC) holdings. Also depicted are the reservoirs created by MIC's A.J. Harty and V.L. LeTulle from the original Jennings Creek and its natural floodplain by levees and water control structures, creating North Cortes and Harty Lake. They have since been drained, leaving only the north Jennings Lake section. Remnants of the 1921 MIC canal on the Braman easement can be seen today. Reference: Markham Irrigation Company, Irrigation Developments Adjacent to West Side of Colorado River, Dec. 31, 1921, courtesy Bruce Herlin.

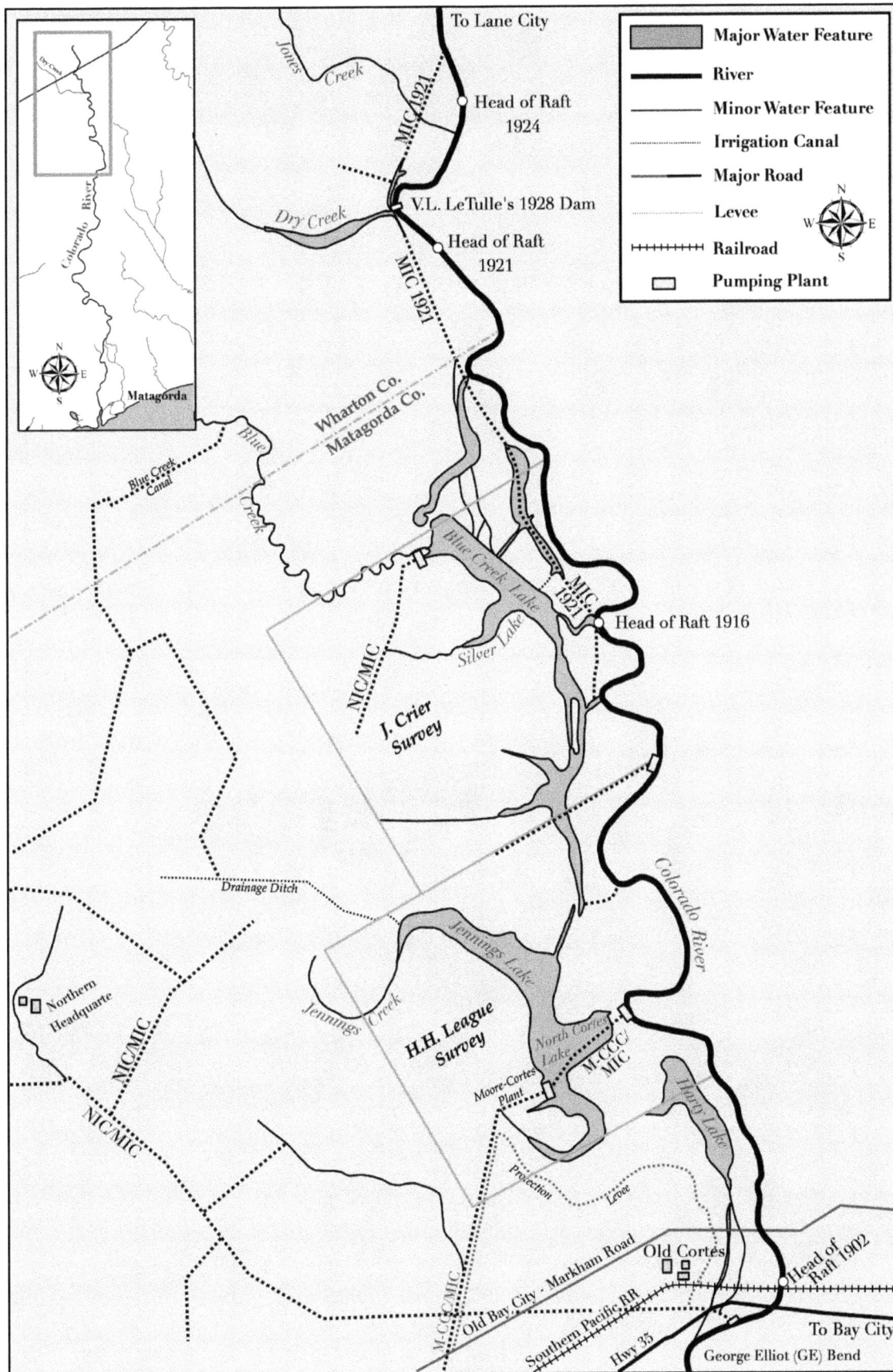

To Lane City

MIC 1924

Head of Raft
1924

Jones Creek

Dry Creek

V.L. LeTulle's 1928 Dam

Head of Raft
1921

MIC 1921

Major Water Feature
River
Minor Water Feature
Irrigation Canal
Major Road
Levee
Railroad
Pumping Plant

N
W E
S

Colorado River

Matagorda

N
W E
S

Wharton Co.
Matagorda Co.

Blue Creek
Canal

Blue Creek

NIC/MIC

MIC 1921

Blue Creek Lake

Silver Lake

Head of Raft 1916

J. Crier
Survey

Colorado River

Drainage Ditch

Jennings Lake

Jennings Creek

H.H. League
Survey

North Cortes
Lake

M-CCC/
MIC

Moore-Cortes
Plant

Harp Lake

Northern
Headquarte

NIC/MIC

NIC/MIC

M-CCC/MIC

Protection Levee

Old Bay City - Markham Road

Old Cortes

Head of
Raft 1902

Southern Pacific RR

Hwy 35

To Bay City

George Elliot (GE) Bend

259

Fig. 16. The Wells Fargo office, downtown Bay City, during the 1913 flood. Matagorda County Museum no.1990.07.15BA1.6.

Fig. 17. Bay City's Stockton House and Jolly's Ice Cream during the 1913 flood. Matagorda County Museum no.1990.07.15BA1.15.

Fig. 18. The raft before the 1920s. Matagorda County Museum no. 1989.09.120.27.

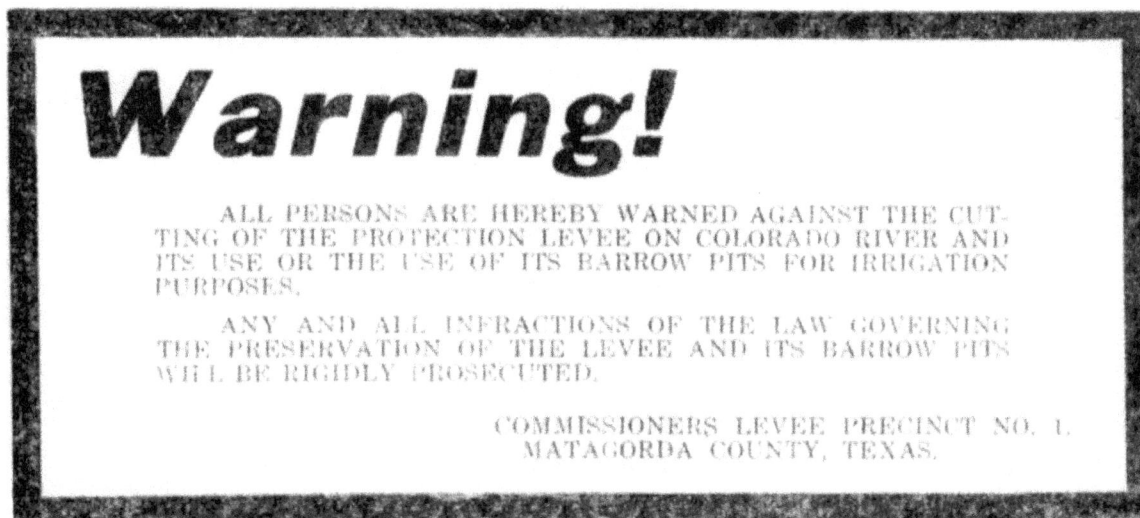

Warning!

ALL PERSONS ARE HEREBY WARNED AGAINST THE CUT-
TING OF THE PROTECTION LEVEE ON COLORADO RIVER AND
ITS USE OR THE USE OF ITS BARROW PITS FOR IRRIGATION
PURPOSES.

ANY AND ALL INFRACTIONS OF THE LAW GOVERNING
THE PRESERVATION OF THE LEVEE AND ITS BARROW PITS
WILL BE RIGIDLY PROSECUTED.

COMMISSIONERS LEVEE PRECINCT NO. 1.
MATAGORDA COUNTY, TEXAS.

Fig. 19. Maintaining the integrity of the Bay City protection levee to prevent town flooding was good business for Matagorda County's rice men, who were well represented in the venture by Matagorda County Drainage District No.1 commissioners V.L. LeTulle, D.P. Moore, and A.J. Harty. *Daily Tribune*, Aug. 22, 1921.

Irrigation Co. Makes Protest

Calls Attention of Commissioners of Reclamation District to Damaging Work Being Done by Dredging Co.

The Markham Irrigation Company hereby issues a protest to the commissioners of the Matagorda County Conservation and Reclamation District No. 1, the protest being in written form and published.

The letter:

Houston, Texas, May 19, 1926.

Hon. Board of Commissioners of Matagorda County Conservation and Reclamation District No. 1,

Bay City, Texas.

Gentlemen:

On Saturday, May 8, and on Monday, May 10, this Company, through its general manager lodged with your body verbal protest against any further work being done this summer in the bed of the Colorado River north of the Bay City-Markham county road bridge. We wish now to file this more formal written protest and to most earnestly request that you take all necessary steps to protect the rice farms against the serious loss which is sure to result if this work on the river bed is not discontinued immediately.

We hardly deem is necessary to call your attention to the fact that under the expressed provisions of the contract with Howard-Kenyon Dredging Company, such company has no legal right to proceed with the work on the river at this time. Paragraph 14 of said contract provides as follows:

"And, Whereas, Geo. Geo. W. Goethals, consulting engineer of Matagorda County Conservation and Reclamation District, has advised the said district not to permit the Wharton County Conservation and Reclamation District and its contractor, Howard Kenyon Dredging Company, party of the second part herein, to dig the pilot ditch, or any part thereof, provided for in its contract with the said Wharton County Conservation and Reclamation District until the lower section in the Colorado River has been cleared out, it is agreed between the parties hereto that the said Howard Kenyon Dredging Company obligates itself not to dig said pilot ditch, or any part thereof, described in said contract with the Wharton County Conservation and Reclamation District, until the Gulf Coast Dredging Company has fully completed its contract with the Matagorda County Conservation and Reclamation District No. 1, and cleared out the lower part of the said river according to its contract with the said Conservation District, and said work has been finally accepted by said Matagorda County Conservation and Reclamation District No. 1."

In view of the above provisions of the contract, there can be no doubt that any work now attempted by the dredging company in the bed of the river is in direct violation of the agreement and that the pilot ditch has been and is now being dug in utter disregard of the contract and in breach of its express provisions.

After a careful investigation of the whole situation, we wish to advise you that any further work on the river at this time will seriously endanger the water supply and most probably result in a total loss of the 1926 rice crop to all farmers in your district. Markham Irrigation Company will, of course, do its best to meet the situation, but from the present outlook we will be unable to protect the rice growers if your board fails to exercise your legal rights and stop the work now being attempted by the dredging company. For and on behalf of the rice farmers, we request that your board give this matter immediate and earnest consideration and that you take such steps in accordance with your contract with the Howard Kenyon Dredging Company as will fully protect the interests of the farmers until the 1926 rice crop is made. Failure on your part to meet the situation promptly will have most serious consequences.

We write you this letter to call the gravity of the situation to your special attention and advise you, and through you the rice farmers, that unless something is done immediately Markham Irrigation Company can not assume responsibility for the loss which the rice growers will suffer on account of water shortage during the summer months.

Yours truly,

MARKHAM IRRIGATION CO.

By B. K. Patton.

Fig. 20. Markham Irrigation Company attorney B.K. Patton brought the fight against removal of the log raft to the public through the local press in 1926. *Matagorda County Tribune,* June 4, 1926.

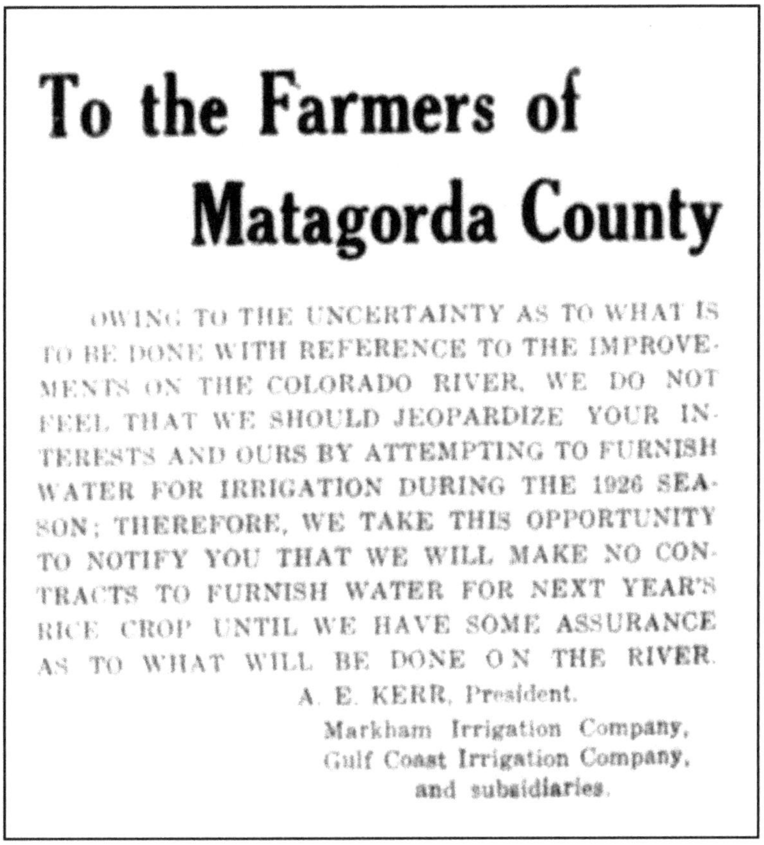

To the Farmers of
Matagorda County

OWING TO THE UNCERTAINTY AS TO WHAT IS
TO BE DONE WITH REFERENCE TO THE IMPROVE-
MENTS ON THE COLORADO RIVER, WE DO NOT
FEEL THAT WE SHOULD JEOPARDIZE YOUR IN-
TERESTS AND OURS BY ATTEMPTING TO FURNISH
WATER FOR IRRIGATION DURING THE 1926 SEA-
SON; THEREFORE, WE TAKE THIS OPPORTUNITY
TO NOTIFY YOU THAT WE WILL MAKE NO CON-
TRACTS TO FURNISH WATER FOR NEXT YEAR'S
RICE CROP UNTIL WE HAVE SOME ASSURANCE
AS TO WHAT WILL BE DONE ON THE RIVER.

A. E. KERR, President.

Markham Irrigation Company,
Gulf Coast Irrigation Company,
and subsidiaries.

Fig. 21. Markham Irrigation Company advised area rice farmers that they would cutoff irrigation water during the standoff between the Matagorda (MCRD) and Wharton County (WCRD) Conservation and Reclamation Districts. The tactic was effective – the MCRD changed sides and withheld their support for removal of the river log raft. *Daily Tribune*, July 31, 1925.

Fig. 22. WCRD engineer J.P. Markham in one of the field offices along the Colorado River, 1927. Matagorda County Museum no. AG.89.D9.120.33.

Fig. 23. Engineer J.P. Markham, standing right, with observers during raft removal. Matagorda County Museum no. 1989.09.120.32.

The Markham Irrigation Company and The Gulf Coast Irrigation Co.
Will water a limited acreage this year
All land must be inspected before a water contract will be issued

CONSULT THE MANAGER IN REGARD TO YOUR LAND. ALL SEED RICE MUST BE INSPECTED BEFORE PLANTING.

THIS COMPANY HAS A FULL LINE OF EAST TEXAS SEED RICE AND WILL BE SOLD TO FARMERS AT COST.

SEED RICE CONTAINING INDIGO, TURTLE BACK OR AS MUCH AS 1 PER CENT OR MORE OF RED WILL BE OBJECTED TO BY THIS COMPANY

WATER CONTRACTS WILL NOT BE ISSUED IF TENANT INSISTS ON AND DOES PLANT SEED CONTAINING THE ABOVE MENTIONED FOREIGN MATTER

Markham Irrigation Co.
Gulf Coast Irrigation Co.

Fig. 24. Crop success or failure for rice interests on along the Colorado River was entirely in the hands of Markham Irrigation between the late 1910s and 1920s. *Daily Tribune*, May 5, 1924.

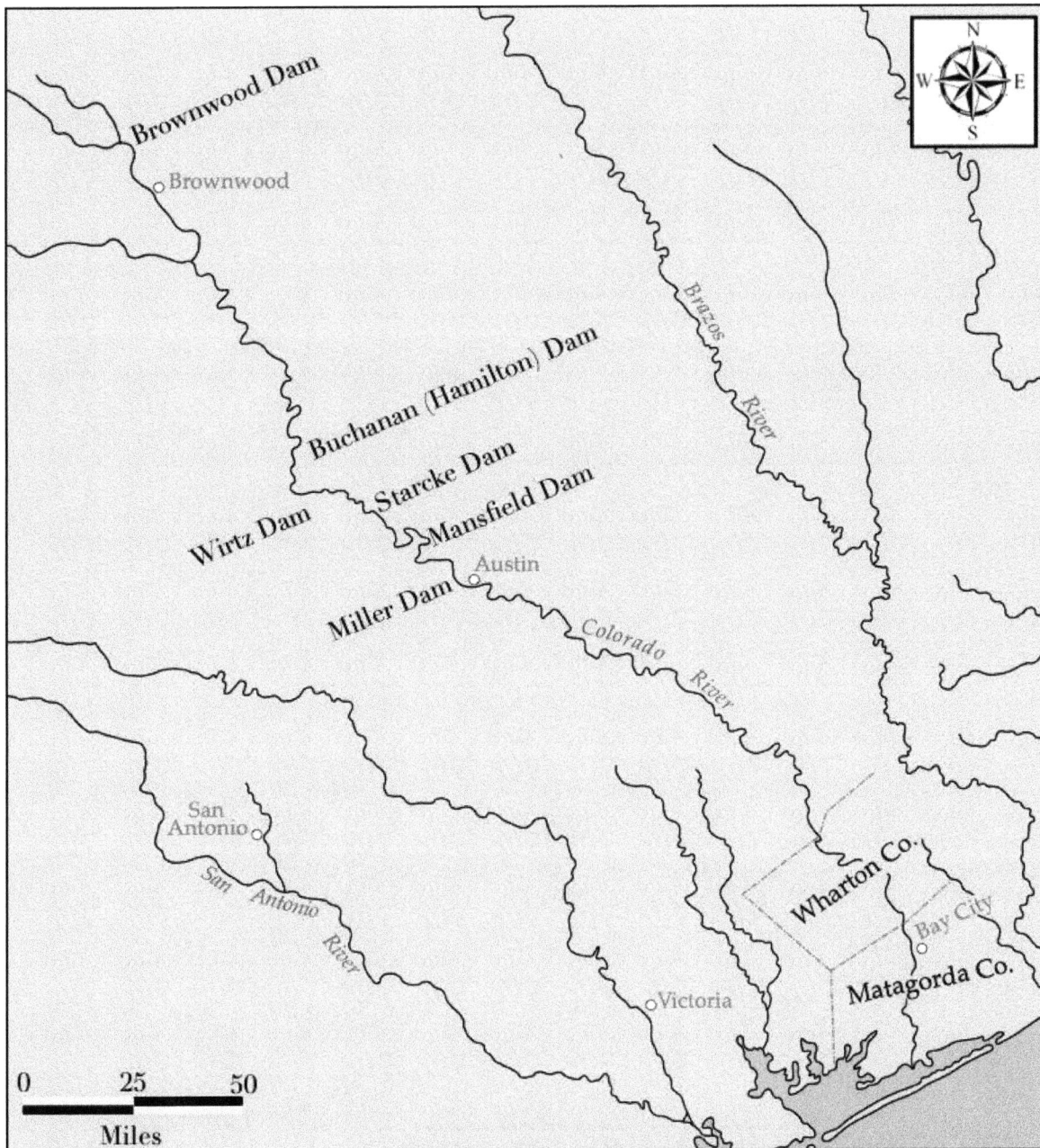

Fig. 25. Water from the Brownwood Dam 480-miles upriver saved Bay Prairie rice crops in 1934. Hamilton Dam, renamed the Buchanan Dam, was completed in 1938 and was the first of a series of dams under the auspices of the LCRA that became known as the Highland Lakes.

REFERENCES CHAPTER 1

[1] Henderson, Mary V., *Minor Empresario Contracts For the Colonization of Texas, 1825-1834*. The Southwest Quarterly, v. 31, no. 4, April 1928, p. 300, https://texashistory.unt.edu/ark:/67531/metapth101088/m1/324/, The Portal to Texas History.

[2] Stephen F. Austin to James Breedlove, Nov. 12, 1829, The Digital Austin Papers, http://digitalaustinpapers.org/document?id=APB1770; Texas General Land Office, https://www.glo.texas.gov/history/archives/forms/files/appendices-history-of-texas-public-lands.pdf.

[3] Ibid.

[4] Cantrell, Gregg. *A Matter of Character: Stephen F. Austin and the Papers Concerning Robertson's Colony in Texas*, The Southwestern Historical Quarterly, V. 104, July 2000 – April 2001, Austin, Texas, p. 240, https://texashistory.unt.edu/ark:/67531/metapth101221/m1/292/.

[5] Campbell, Camilla, Flores de Abrego Jose Gaspar Maria, *Handbook of Texas Online*, http://www.tshaonline.org/handbook/online/articles/ffl26; Oak Leaves Master Index, http://www.usgenweb sites.org/TX Matagorda/ol_index_fam_d-h.htm.

[6] Lewis, W.S., *The Adventures of the "Lively" Immigrants*. The Quarterly of the Texas State Historical Association, July 1989, v. III, no. 1, p. 1-32 and 81-107, https://texashistory.unt.edu/ark:/67531/metapth101015/.

[7] *London Statesman*, Oct. 30, 1821.

[8] Lewis, W.S., p. 1-32.

[9] Stein, Bill. Nesbitt Memorial Library. Nesbitt Memorial Library Journal, v. 6, no, 1, January 1996, p. 1-30. https://texashistory.unt.edu/ark:/67531/metapth151396/, University of North Texas Libraries, The Portal to Texas History; Dewees, William B., *Letters from Texas, Colorado River, Coahuila and Texas, March 15, 1823* (Louisville: Hull & Brothers, 1854), p. 31.

[10] Lamar, M.B., 183?, unpublished. *Difficulties with the Karankawa Indians*, no. 2447, Texas State Archives, courtesy Michael Bailey; Baldwin, A.C., Lamar, M.B., *The Papers of Mirabeau Buonaparte Lamar*, Texas State Library v. 4, part 1, 1924, p. 255,: Bugbee, L. G., *What Became of the Lively?*, The Quarterly of the Texas State Historical Association, v. 3, July 1899 - April, 1900, Texas State Historical Association, The Portal to Texas History, https://texashistory.unt.edu/ark:/67531/metapth101015/; Wortham, Louis L., *A History of Texas: From Wilderness to Commonwealth*, v. 1 (Fort Worth:Wortham-Molyneaux Co., 1924) p. 125-7.

[11] Kuykendal, J.H., *Remininsences of Early Texas*, II. The Quarterly of the Texas State Historical Association, v. 6, July 1902 – April 1903, Texas State Historical Association; Austin, p. 236-253, https://texashistory.unt.edu/ark:/67531/metapth101028/, Texas State Historical Association, The Portal to Texas History.

[12] Bugbee, p. 141-148.

[13] Eugene Barker, ed., *Annual Report of the American Historical Association for the Year 1919: The Austin Papers*, (Washington, D.C.: Government Printing Office, 1924), v. 1, part 1, p. 917-922; 632, 639.

[14] Ibid.

[15] DeShields, James T., *Border Wars of Texas: Being an Authentic and Popular Account, in Chronological Order, of the Long and Bitter Conflict Waged Between Savage Indian Tribes and the Pioneer Settlers of Texas* (Tioga TX Herald Co., 1912); Kuykendal, p. 236-253; Stein, p. 1-30.

[16] Matagorda County Deed v. 162, p. 567-8, dated May 25, 1827.

[17] McLean, Malcolm D., *Papers Concerning Robertson's Colony in Texas*, v. 2, 1975; Fort Worth, Texas, p. 645, https://texashistory.unt.edu/ark:/67531/metapth130183/m1/, Texas State Historical Association, Portal to Texas History.

[18] Matagorda County Deed v. 162, p. 567-8, dated May 25, 1827.

[19] Malcolm D. McLean, *League, Hosea H., Handbook of Texas Online*, http://www.tshaonline.org/handbook/online/articles/fle05.

[20] Cantrell, Gregg. *A Matter of Character: Stephen F. Austin and the Papers Concerning Robertson's Colony in Texas*, The Southwestern Historical Quarterly, v. 104, July 2000 – April 2001, Austin, Texas, p. 232-3, https://texashistory.unt.edu/ark:/67531/metapth101221/m1/.

[21] Felix Robertson to Stephen F. Austin, Nov. 5, 1826, The Digital Austin Letters, http://digitalaustin papers.org/document?id=APB1317.

[22] McLean, p. 652.

[23] H.H. League to Stephen F. Austin, April 11, 1827, The Digital Austin Letters, http://digitalaustinpapers. org/document?id=APB1360; McLean, p. 631.

[24] Cantrell, p. 246.

[25] Brown, John H., *A History of Texas From 1685 to 1892* (St. Louis: L.E. Daniel, 1892), p. 227-9.

[26] H.H. League to Stephen F. Austin, Jan. 2, 1830, The Digital Austin Letters, http://digitalaustinpapers.org /document?id=APB1827.

[27] Stephen F. Austin to Josiah H. Bell, April 4, 1829, The Digital Austin Letters, http://digitalaustinpapers .org/document?id=APB1692.

[28] H.H. League to Stephen F. Austin, Dec. 19, 1829, The Digital Austin Letters, http://digitalaustinpapers .org/document?id=APB1812.

[29] Barker, Eugene. *Minutes of the Ayuntamiento of San Felipe de Austin, 1828-1832*, Southwest Historical Quarterly, v. 22, July 1918-April 1919, Austin, p. 91, https://texashistory.unt.edu/ark:/67531/metapth117156/.

[30] Ibid., p. 86: *Seth Ingram*, Historic Matagorda County, Matagorda County Historical Association, (Houston: D. Armstrong Co., 1986), v. 1, p. 73.

[31] McLean, p. 233-4.

[32] Frank, W., *A History of Texas and Texans*, v. 1, 1914, p. 161, https://texashistory.unt.edu/ark:/67531/metapth760581/m1/; Barker, Eugene. *Minutes of the Ayuntamiento of San Felipe de Austin, 1828-1832*, Southwest Historical Quarterly, v. 22, July 1918-April 1919, Austin, p. 354, https://texashistory.unt.edu/ark:/67531/metapth117156/.

[33] *Seth Ingram*, Historic Matagorda County, Matagorda County Historical Association, (Houston: D. Armstrong Co., 1986), v. 1, p. 73.

[34] Stephen F. Austin to James F. Perry, Sept. 22, 1830, The Digital Austin Letters, http://digitalaustin papers.org/document?id=APB4031.

[35] H.H. League to Stephen F. Austin, Oct. 10, 1830, Eugene Barker, ed., *Annual Report of the American Historical Association for the Year 1919: The Austin Papers*, (Washington, D.C.: Government Printing Office, 1924), v. 1, Part 2, p. 505.

[36] Matagorda County Deed, v. l. A, p. 7.

[37] Historic Matagorda County, p. NA.

[38] Cantrell, p. 247.

[39] Ibid., p. 235.

[40] Stephen F. Austin to Samuel M. Williams, May 31, 1833, The Digital Austin Letters, http://digital austinpapers.org/document?id=APB4579.

[41] *Regimental Histories of Tennessee Units During the War of 1812*, https://www.sos.tn.gov/products/tsla/ regimental-histories-tennessee-units-during-war-1812.

[42] *Brief History of Tennessee Militia in the War of 1812*, http://tennesseestatemilitia.com/brief-history-of-tennessee-militia-in-the-war-of-1812.

[43] Sistler, Byron and Samuel, *Tennesseans in the War of 1812* (Nashville: Sistler & Assoc., 1992; *Regimental Histories of Tennessee Units During the War of 1812*, https://www.sos.tn.gov/products/tsla/ regimental-histories-tennessee-units-during-war-1812.

[44] Eugene Barker, ed., *Minutes of the Ayuntamiento of San Felipe de Austin*, The Southwestern Historical Quarterly, v. 23, July 1919 – April 1920, p. 151.

[45] *Texas Republican*, Dec. 13, 1834.

[46] Dimmick, Gregg J., *Sea of Mud* (College Station: A&M University Press, 2006), p. 340.

[47] Ibid., p. 63, 131.

[48] Undated newspaper clipping, in Levy, Doris Rae. *Texas Centennial Scrapbook*, 1936; https://texas history.unt.edu/ark:/67531/metapth1091118/m1/846/, University of North Texas Libraries, The Portal to Texas History.

[49] *Index to Military Rolls of the Republic of Texas 1835-1845*, https://tshaonline.org/supsites/military/ rep_name.htm.

[50] Harriet Smither, ed., *Journals of the Congress of the Republic of Texas, 1839-1840*, v. 2, Texas Library and Historical Commission State Library, p. 70, Hathi Trust Digital Library https://hdl.handle.net/2027/ uc1.c109597907?urlappend=%3Bseq=78.

[51] Undated newspaper clipping, in Levy, Doris Rae. *Texas Centennial Scrapbook*, 1936; https://texas history.unt.edu/ark:/67531/metapth1091118/m1/846/, University of North Texas Libraries, The Portal to Texas History.

[52] Matagorda County Deed C-157.

[53] *Matagorda Bulletin*, Feb. 7, 1839.

[54] Matagorda County Deed C-421.

[55] Ibid., F-157; McCormick, Andrew Phelps, *Scotch-Irish in Ireland and In America* (New Orleans: NA, 1897).

[56] *San Luis Advocate*, Oct. 13, 1840.

[57] *Democratic Telegraph and Texas Register*, Oct. 7, 1847.

[58] John S. Royall versus Thomas Cayce, Matagorda County Deed, v. 162, June 7, 1845, p. 569-70.

[59] *Wharton County Spectator*, Mar 9, 2009.

[60] Laws Passed at the 2nd Session of the 2nd Congress of the Republic of Texas, April and May 1838, p. 18, Hathi Trust Digital Library https://hdl.handle.net/2027/uc1.a0001789403?urlappend=%3Bseq=18.

[61] Ibid.; Laws of the Republic of Texas, V. 3, 1838, https://texashistory.unt.edu/ark:/67531/metapth45354/m1/9/, University of North Texas Libraries, The Portal to Texas History.

[62] *Old Columbia Cemetery*, https://www.facebook.com/permalink.php?story_fbid.

[63] Rena Maverick Green, ed., *Samuel Maverick, Texan:1803-1870: A Collection of Letters, Journals and Memoirs* (San Antonio, 1952).

[64] McCormick, Andrew Phelps, *Scotch-Irish in Ireland and In America* (New Orleans, 1897).

[65] *Telegraph and Texas Register*, Sept. 28, 1842; E.W. Winkler, ed., *The Bexar and Dawson Prisoners*, p. 292-324, Texas State Historical Association. The Quarterly of the Texas State Historical Association, v. 13, no. 4, July 1909 - April 1910, https://texashistory.unt.edu/ark:/67531/metapth101051/m1/342/, Texas State Historical Association, The Portal to Texas History.

[66] Wooten, Dudley G. *A Comprehensive History of Texas 1685 to 1897*, v. 2, (Dallas, 1898), p. 630, https://texashistory.unt.edu/ark:/67531/metapth587006/m1/665/.

[67] *Tri-Weekly Telegraph*, Dec. 27, 1865.

[68] Young, Barbara L., *Cayce, Henry Petty*, Handbook of Texas Online, http://www.tshaonline.org/handbook/online/articles/fcamj.

[69] *Stephen F. Austin to the People, Sept. 21, 1835, The Digital Austin Papers,* http://digitalaustinpapers.org/document?id=APB4880.

[70] R.R. Royall to Stephen F, Austin, Dec. 28, 1824, The Digital Austin Papers, http://digitalaustinpapers.org/document?id=APB0955.

[71] Charles Douglas to Stephen F, Austin, Jan. 15, 1825, http://digitalaustinpapers.org/document?id=APB1045; R.R. Royall to Stephen F, Austin, Dec. 28, 1828, http://digitalaustinpapers.org/document?id=APB0955.

[72] Pinnell, R. E., 1961, *The Royall Family of America*, Internet Archive, p. 62, https://archive.org/details/royallfamilyroya00pin.

[73] Stephen F, Austin to Samuel M. Williams, March 21, 1832, The Digital Austin Papers, http://digitalaustinpapers.org/document?id=APB4335.

[74] Brown, John Henry, 1820-1895, *History of Texas from 1685 to 1892*, v. 1 (St. Louis, 1892), p.169, https://texashistory.unt.edu/ark:/67531/metapth91045/m1/174/, University of North Texas Libraries, The Portal to Texas History.

[75] Johnson, Frank W., *A History of Texas and Texans*, V. 1, (Chicago, 1914), p. 284, https://texashistory.unt.edu/ark:/67531/metapth760581/m1/331/; Cutrer, Thomas W., *Richard Royster Royall*, Texas State Historical Association, Handbook of Texas, https://www.tshaonline.org/handbook /entries/royall-richard-royster.

[76] Gammel, Hans Peter Mareus Neilsen. The Laws of Texas, 1822-1897, v. 1 (Austin, 1898), https://texashistory.unt.edu/ark:/67531/metapth5872/m1/850/, p. 842; The Southwestern Historical Quarterly, v. 65, July 1961 - April 1962, Austin, https://texashistory.unt.edu/ark:/67531/metapth101195/m1/504/ Texas State Historical Association, p. 446.

[77] Matagorda County Oak Leaves, http://www.usgenwebsites.org/TXMatagorda/hm_ma_royall.htm.

[78] *McKinney Daily Courier*, Jan. 27, 1920.

[79] *1850 Federal Census, Matagorda, Texas*; Roll: 912; Oak Leaves, Matagorda County Genealogy Society, v. V, no. 5, 1986, p. 385b.

[80] Matagorda Co. Deed v. 162, p. 569-70, June 7, 1845.

[81] Various Brazoria County District court documents compiled in Supplemental Order 5206, Sun Oil, Houston Tx, not dated.

[82] Matagorda County Deed v. 55, p. 355-6, March 2, 1853.

[83] *Daily National Democrat,* June 2, 1859.

[84] *Placer Herald,* June 1867; Ninth Census of the U.S., 1870. National Archives and Administration, Washington D.C. M593, RG29.

[85] Pinnell, R. E., 1961, *The Royall Family of America*, Internet Archive, p. 44, https://archive.org/details/royallfamilyroya00pin.

[86] Ancestry.com, https://www.ancestry.com/mediaui-viewer/tree/8406859/person/6134735385/media/d31a65b2-2a8f-4adb-ae34-99b63c5fd8f9?phsrc=oEj41&_phstart=successSource

[87] Matagorda County Deed, v. Q., p. 413, Nov. 20, 1877.

[88] Revolutionary War Pension and Bounty-Land Warrant Application Files, 1800-1900, https://www.ancestry.com/family-tree/person/tree/5823384/person/-1388719579/facts; US Compiled Service Records, Post-Revolutionary War Volunteer Soldiers, 1784-1811, https://www.ancestry.com/family-tree/person/tree/5823384/person/-1388719579/facts.

[89] Matagorda deed DR F-456; Lotto, F., 1902, *Fayette County, Her History and Her People*, in http://www.fayettecountyhistory.org/fayetteville.htm.

[90] *Austin American Statesman*, March 28, 1874; Inventory of the County Archives of Texas: Fayette County, no. 75, June 1940, San Antonio, https://texashistory.unt.edu/ark:/67531/metapth25251/m1/10/, University of North Texas Libraries, The Portal to Texas History; Largest Slave Owners by Year According to Tax Rolls and Censuses, p. 30, Nesbitt Memorial Library Journal, v. 3, No. 1, January 1993, Columbus, Texas, https://texashistory.unt.edu/ark:/67531/metapth151387/m1/30/, University of North Texas Libraries, The Portal to Texas History; Index to District Court Criminal Cause Files, 1837-1875, p. 89, Nesbitt Memorial Library Journal, v. 4, no. 2, May 1994, Columbus, Texas, https://texashistory.unt.edu/ark:/67531/metapth151391/m1/41/, University of North Texas Libraries, The Portal to Texas History.

[91] Noah Smithwick, *The Evolution of a State or Recollections of Old Texas Days* (Austin: Gammel Book Co.: Austin, 1900), p. 42-45.

[92] DR 130-24 No. 5222; Abstract of Land Claims. United States: Civilian book office, 1852), p. 519; Bugbee, Lester G., *The Old Three Hundred*, The Quarterly of the Texas State Historical Association, July 1897-April 1898, v. l, No. 1, p. 110; Matagorda County Deed v. A, p. 549; Matagorda County Deed v. 130, p. 24.

[93] Ibid., DR E-373.

[94] Ibid., I, p 298, no. 4097.

[95] Ibid., no. 3966, Book 1, p. 195-6, 1855.

[96] Stein, Bill, *Consider the Lily: The Ungilded History of Colorado County*, Nesbitt Memorial Library Journal, part 2: 1828-1836, 1996, Nesbitt Memorial Library; https://www.columbustexaslibrary.net/local-history-and-genealogy-material/history-of-colorado-county/consider-the-lily-the-ungilded-history-of-colorado-county/part-2-1828-1836.

[97] Weyland, L.R. and Wade, H., *An Early History of Fayette County, LaGrange Journal*, Jan. 10, 1935, p. 344.

[98] Ibid., p. 114.

[99] Stein, p. 115.

[100] Barker, Eugene C., ed., *Annual Report of the American Historical Association for The Year 1919*, v. II, Washington Govt Printing Office, 1924, p. 1358-9. Hathi Trust Digital Library, https://hdl.handle.net/2027/uc1.b3282140; Harrison, William H. *Alleyton, Texas: Back Door to the Confederacy,* 1993, p.19; The Portal to Texas History https://texashistory.unt.edu/ark:/67531/metapth151411/m1/25/.

[101] Mary Ruth Schack's Family History, Ancestry.com, https://www.ancestry.com/family-tree/person/tree/162714521/; 1837 Taxable Property Assessed in the County of Jackson, Republic of Texas, http://usgenwebsites.org/TXJackson/tax_roll_1837.htm; *Galveston Daily News,* March 30, 1870.

[102] Abstract of Land Claims, United States: Printed at the Civilian book office, 1852. p. 519; Bugbee, Lester G., *The Old Three Hundred*, The Quarterly of the Texas State Historical Association, July 1897-April 1898, v. l, No. 1, p. 110, Hathi Trust Digital Library, https://hdl.handle.net/2027/coo.31924061962191.

[103] The Southwestern Historical Quarterly, v. 21, July 1917 - April 1918, Austin, Texas, 1918, p. 408. https://texashistory.unt.edu/ark:/67531/metapth101073/m1/414/, University of North Texas Libraries, The Portal to Texas History.

[104] Brown, John Henry, *History of Texas: From 1686-1892*, v. 1, p. 297-9.

[105] Transcript of military roster of officers and privates serving under Captain Thomas Alley, October 19, 1835, https://texashistory.unt.edu/ark:/67531/; Smithwick, Noah, *Evolution of a State or Recollections of Old Texas Days*, (Austin: Gammel, 1900), p. 101-4; Wharton, Clarence, *The Republic of Texas* (Houston: Young Printing Co., 1922) p. 119-22, Hathi Trust Digital Library, https://hdl.handle.net/2027/yale.390-02002379031; Hunt, Lenoir, *Bluebonnets and Blood: The Romance of Tejas* (Houston: Texas Books, 1938), p.130.

[106] Paddock, B.B., *History of Texas; Fort Worth and the Texas Northwest Addition*, v. 1 (Chicago: Lewis Pub., 1922), Hathi Trust Digital Library, https://hdl.handle.net/2027/wu.89065939522.

[107] Transcript of Roster of Volunteers who Remain Before Bexar, November 24, 1835, Austin Papers: Series III, 1835, p. 7, https://texashistory.unt.edu/ark:/67531/metapth216940/m1/7/, Portal to Texas History; McLean, Malcolm Dallas, *Biography of William Isbell*, in Papers concerning Robertson's Colony in Texas, v. 10, p. 506, https://texashistory.unt.edu/ark:/67531/metapth28587/m1/507/, The Portal to Texas History.

[108] Hardin, Stephen L., *Alley, John*, Texas State Historical Association, Handbook of Texas, https://www.tshaonline.org/handbook/entries/alley-john; Mary Ruth Schack's Family History, Ancestry.com, https://www.ancestry.com/family-tree/person/tree/162714521/; *Telegraph and Texas Register*, Sept. 29, 1838.

[109] 1860 Jackson County Census, http://usgenwebsites.org/TXJackson/census_1860_pp_25-36.htm; 1870 Jackson County Census, http://usgenwebsites.org/TXJackson/census_1870_pp_1-12.htm.

[110] Wheelock, E.M., McGahan v. Baylor, in *Cases Argued and Decided in the Supreme Court of The State of Texas*, V. 32 (St Louis: Gilbert Book Co., 1882), p. 761, Hathi Trust Digital Library, https://hdl.handle.net/2027/mdp.35112102771849.

[111] Gifford White, ed., *An Abstract of the Original Titles of Record in the General Land Office* (United States: Pemberton Press, 1964); Historic Matagorda County, Matagorda County Historical Association, (Houston: D. Armstrong Co., 1986), v.1, p. 78.

[112] Flack probate records, courtesy Michael Bailey, Brazoria County Museum.

[113] Ibid.

[114] Matagorda County Deed v. A, p. 46.

[115] The Southwest Reporter, *Supreme and Appellate Courts of Arkansas, Kentucky, Missouri, Tennessee, Texas, and Indian Territory*, v. 1. May 8-June 5 (St. Paul: West Pub., 1907).

[116] Matagorda Land Abstracts, No. 2102, Book F, p. 456; The Southwest Reporter.

[117] Ibid.; Robert Riddle, pers. com.

[118] Brown, p.169.

[119] Thrall, Homer S., *History of Methodism in Texas* (Houston, 1872), p. 33-6, https://texashistory.unt.edu/ark:/67531/metapth29782/m1/36/, University of North Texas Libraries, The Portal to Texas History.

[120] Smith, James, *Isaac T. Tinley-William B. Aldridge-Dr. Anthony T. Morris Plantation*, Brazosport Archeological Society, lifeonthebrazosriver.com.

[121] *Matagorda Bulletin*, June 28, 1838.

[122] Gammel, Hans Peter Mareus Neilsen, *The Laws of Texas, 1822-1897*, v. 2 (Austin, 1898), p. 274.

[123] Republic of Texas, County of Matagorda Land Records, June 3, 1839; Republic of Texas Deed No. 812, Book D, p. 144-6, 1839.

[124] Historic Matagorda County, p. 153.

[125] Register of the Parish of Christ Church, 1839-1875, Internments, http://www.usgenwebsites.org/TXMatagorda/ma_cc_interments2.htm.

[126] Probate Records, 1837-1895; Texas, County Court (Matagorda County), Oct. 14, 1840, p. 138-9, Ancestry.com, https://www.ancestry.com/imageviewer/collections/2115/images/007574093_00264/.

[127] Matagorda County Deed No. 1331, v. E, p. 373-4.

[128] *Texas Monument*, Feb. 12, 1851.

[129] Historic Matagorda County, p. 61, 658; James Denison Family Tree, Ancestry.com, https://www.ancestry.com/family-tree/person/tree/110952976/person/382020538259/facts.

[130] The Southwest Reporter, *Supreme and Appellate Courts of Arkansas, Kentucky, Missouri, Tennessee, Texas, and Indian Territory*, v. 1. May 8-June 5 (St. Paul: West Pub., 1907).

[131] Matagorda County deed v. F, p. 456.

[132] Ibid., p. 486.

[133] *1850 Federal Census, Matagorda, Texas*; Roll: 912; Oak Leaves, Matagorda County Genealogy Society, v. V, No. 5, 1986, pp.42; https://www.ancestry.com/imageviewer/collections/ 8054/ images/ 4206179_00349.

[134] *Texas Democrat*, April 10, 1847.

[135] *Texas State Gazette*, Aug. 4, 1855.

[136] Denison vs. League, *Reports of cases argued and decided in the Supreme Court of the State of Texas, during Galveston session, and part of Tyler session, 1856*, v. 16, (St. Louis, Mo., 1881), p. 401-10, https://texashistory.unt.edu/ark:/67531/metapth28558/m1/374 University of North Texas Libraries, The Portal to Texas History.

[137] Civil War Index: Abstract to Muster Roles, p. 1301.

[138] *San Antonio Express*, Dec. 14, 1865.

[139] Texas Bonds and Oath Office Files, Texas State Library and Archives Commission, p. 184.

[140] Davenport, J.H.B, *The History of the Supreme Court of the State of Texas with Biographies of the Chief and Associate Judges* (Austin, 1917).

[141] Haley, James L. *The Texas Supreme Court: A Narrative History, 1836–1986* (University of Texas Press, 2013), 350 pp.

[142] Davenport, J.H.B, *The History of the Supreme Court of the State of Texas with Biographies of the Chief and Associate Judges* (Austin, 1917), p. 82-7; Haley, James L. *The Texas Supreme Court: A Narrative History, 1836–1986* (University of Texas Press, 2013), 350 pp.

[143] Ibid.

[144] *State Rights Democrat*, Nov. 19, 1869.

[145] Haley, p. 9.

[146] Raines, C.W., *Year Book For Texas, 1901* (Austin: Gammell, 1902), Hathi Trust, https://hdl.handle.net/ 2027/hvd.hn4h1h; Davenport, J.H.B, *The History of the Supreme Court of the State of Texas with Biographies of the Chief and Associate Judges* (Austin, 1917), p. 82-7; Haley, James L. *The Texas Supreme Court: A Narrative History, 1836–1986* (University of Texas Press, 2013), 350 pp.

[147] Fretwells: Genealogy and Family History Website, *The Story of Juliet Constance Fretwell*, http://thefretwells.com/research/jcewing.aspx.

[148] *Telegraph and Texas Register*, Sept. 2, 1840.

[149] Linn, John J., *Reminiscences of Fifty Years in Texas* (Austin: Streck Co.,1935), p.10-26.

[150] *Telegraph and Texas Register*, Sept. 2, 1840.

[151] Linnville Raid of 1840 – Stories, https://www.fold3.com/page/1172/linnville-raid-of-1840/stories.

[152] Guthrie, Keith, *Texas Forgotten Ports* (Austin: Eakin Press, 1988), p.152; Fretwells: Genealogy and Family History Website, *The Story of Juliet Constance Fretwell*, http://thefretwells.com/ research/ jcewing.aspx.

[153] Jenkins, John Holland, *A Texan from Bastrop, Describing the Penatekas Fighting Under Chief Buffalo Hump at the Battle of Plum Creek, August 12, 1840*, in Penateka Comanches, Steve Ellis, http://westtexasscoutinghistory.net/oa_penatekahistory_a.html; Owens, Elizabeth McAnulty, *Elizabeth McAnulty Owens* (San Antonio, 1936), p. 22-3, https://texashistory.unt.edu/ark:/67531/metapth1013803/,University of North Texas Libraries, The Portal to Texas History.

[154] Judge Paul Boethel in *A History of Lavaca County* from Capt. "Black" Adam Zumwalt, the Comanche Attack on Linnville and the Battle of Plum Creek, https://www.fold3.com/page/1172/linnville-raid-of-1840/stories.

[155] Ibid.

[156] Linn, p. NA.

[157] Judge Paul Boethel in *A History of Lavaca County*.

[158] *Brazos Courier*, Aug. 11, 1840.

[159] *Telegraph and Texas Register*, Sept. 2, 1840.

[160] Texas Wills and Probate Records, 1833-1974, p. 16 of 723, Ancestry.com, https://www.ancestry .com/imageviewer/collections/2115/images/007574088_00016?pId=2002675; Matagorda County Deed v. I, p. 38.

[161] Heather Frey Blanton, *Never Take A Whale Bone Corset to Indian Fight*, Blog Archives, Dec. 28, 2020, https://ladiesindefiance.com/tag/juliet-constance-ewing-watts-stanton-fretwell/; https://www.ancestry.com/mediaui-viewer/tree/18560634/person/677813558/media/cd6c170a-daf0-4fd1-a883-aaba94ff4790.

[162] Matagorda County Deed No. 3966, Book 1, p. 195-6, 1855.

[163] Mary Engisch Family Tree, *Jacob L. Briggs*, https://www.ancestry.com/family-tree/person/tree/157674278/person/362095204479/facts; 1870 United States Federal Census, https://www.ancestry.com/imageviewer/collections/7163/images/4267853_00449?pId=5151622.

[164] *Civilian and Gazette Weekly*, Oct. 15, 1861.

[165] *Galveston Daily News*, Oct. 18, 1888.

[166] *Galveston Flakes Daily Bulletin*, April 21, 1867; Constitution and By-Laws of Galveston Hook & Ladder Co., No. 1, (Galveston, 1869), p. 4, https://texashistory.unt.edu/ark:/67531/metapth744177/m1/8/, Univ. of North Texas Libraries, The Portal to Texas History.

[167] *Weekly Journal*, Oct. 1, 1852.

[168] Reference NA.

[169] Galveston City Directory, 1866-1867 (Galveston: W. Richardson & Co.), p. 101-2, https://texashistory.unt.edu/ark:/67531/metapth636852/m1/106/, University of North Texas Libraries, The Portal to Texas History.

[170] *Galveston Flakes Bulletin*, Oct. 1, 1870.

[171] *New York Herald*, Nov. 4, 1870.

[172] Ibid.

[173] *Galveston Daily News*, Nov. 14, 1874

[174] Matagorda County Deed DR Q-194.

[175] *Galveston Tribune*, May 6, 1897; Amelia W. Williams, *Jones, William Jefferson*, Handbook of Texas Online, https://www.tshaonline.org/handbook/entries/jones-william-jefferson, Texas State Historical Association.

[176] *Telegraph and Texas Register*, Jan. 16, 1839; *Galveston Tribune*, May 6, 1897.

[177] Brown, John Henry, *Indian Wars and Pioneers of Texas*, Austin, 1880, p.67-8, https://texashistory.unt.edu /ark:/67531/metapth6725/m1/76/, University of North Texas Libraries, The Portal to Texas History.

[178] Ibid.

[179] Gray, S. A & Moore, W. D., *Mercantile and General City Directory of Austin, Texas, 1872-1873* (Austin, 1872), p.11, https://texashistory.unt.edu/ark:/67531/metapth38126/m1/13/ University of North Texas Libraries, The Portal to Texas History; US County Marriage Records, 1817-1965.

[180] Nesbitt Memorial Library Journal, v. 6, No. 3, September 1996, Columbus, Texas, p. 132, https://texashistory.unt.edu/ark:/67531/metapth151398/m1/20/, University of North Texas Libraries, The Portal to Texas History.

[181] The War of the Rebellion: A Compilation of the Official Records of the Union And Confederate Armies. Series 1, v. 15, (Washington D.C.: United States War Department, 1886), p. 151, https://texashistory.unt.edu/ark:/67531/metapth154623/m1/405/, University of North Texas Libraries, The Portal to Texas History.

[182] *Galveston Daily News*, Aug. 11, 1880.

[183] Jones, William J., Sea Island Cotton, in *The Texas Almanac for 1869 and Emigrant's Guide to Texas*, p.116, https://texashistory.unt.edu/ark:/67531/metapth123774/m1/108/, University of North Texas Libraries, The Portal to Texas History.

[184] *Galveston Daily News*, Sept. 9. 1879; *Galveston Daily News*, June 24, 1880.

[185] *Denison Daily News*, July 27, 1878.

[186] *Galveston Daily News*, Jan. 20, 1881.

[187] Ibid., Jan. 30, 1885.

[188] *Bay City Breeze*, May 20, 1897.

[189] *Galveston Tribune*, April 10, 1903.

[190] *Historic Matagorda County*, Matagorda County Historical Association, (Houston: D. Armstrong Co., 1986), v.1., p. 10-3.

[191] Brown, Woodlief, *A Long Narrow Strip of Land*, (Abilene: H.V. Chapman & Sons, 1989), p.46-8.

[192] Wilbarger, J.W., *Indian Depredations* in Texas (Austin: Hutchins Printing, 1889), 691 pp; *Historic Matagorda County*, v. 1, p.42.

[193] Ibid.; Steve Hathcock, *Rio History: The Matagorda Massacre*, https://www.portisabelsouthpadre.com/2016/11/11/rio-history-the-matagorda-massacre/.

[194] Ethel Z., *DeWitt's Colony*, The Quarterly of the Texas State Historical Association, v. 8, no. 2, July 1904 – April 1905, p. 135, https://texashistory.unt.edu/ark:/67531/metapth101033/m1/137/.

[195] Winkler, Earnest W, *The Seat of Government in Texas*, The Southwest Historical Quarterly, v. 10, no. 3 Jan. 1907, p.187; *Epidemic Cholera in Texas*, 1833-1834, The Southwest Historical Quarterly, v. 40, July 1936 to April 1937, p.216-30; Matagorda County Genealogical Society, v. XVII, no. 1, Feb. 1999, p.43; Register of the Parish of Christ Church, 1839-1875, Internments, http://www.usgenwebsites.org/TX Matagorda/ma_cc_interments2.htm.

[196] Miller, Zia, *The Yellow Fever Epidemic of 1862*, http://www.usgenwebsites.org/TX Matagorda/matagorda_yellow_fever.htm.

[197] *Historic Matagorda County*, v.1.

[198] *Tri Weekly Telegraph*, Nov. 3, 1862.

[199] Wreck of the New York Steam-Packet Home: Ninety-Five Lives Lost, *New York Herald*, Oct. 21, 1837; Price, W. Armstrong, *Hurricanes Affecting the Coast of Texas from Galveston to Rio Grande*, Technical Memorandum no. 78, U.S. Dept. of the Army Corps of Engineers, March 1956, 17pp.; Ludlum, D. M., 1963: *Early American Hurricanes, 1492-1870* (Boston: Amer. Meteor. Soc., 1963), 198pp.; Glass, Jim, Racer's Storm: *The Benchmark Hurricane of 1837*, Houston History, v. 5, no. 3, 2008, p.21-7.

[200] Armstrong; Ludlum.

[201] Davant, Robert, and Herskowitz, Mickey, *Mystic Sails, Texas Trails* (Huntsville: Texas Review Press, 2016), p.22-9.

[202] *The Standard*, Oct. 21, 1854; Matagorda County 1854 Hurricane, http://www.usgenwebsites.org/TXMatagorda/hurricane_1854_1875_1886.htm.

[203] Ludlum, p.199; Kincheloe, Castleman Green, unpublished manuscript, no.29, courtesy Brazoria County Historical Museum, p.3-4; Roth, David, *Texas Hurricane History* (Camp Springs, Md.: National Weather Service), p.17; Matagorda County 1854 Hurricane, http://www.usgenwebsites.org/TXMatagorda/hurricane_1854_1875_1886.htm.

[204] *The (Brazoria) Planter*, Sept. 20, 1854; *The (Brazoria) Planter*, Sept. 27, 1854; J. Lancaster, ed., *The Texas Ranger*, Washington, Texas, Oct. 5, 1854, v. 6, no. 8.

REFERENCES CHAPTER 2

[1] *Colorado Tribune* in 1849.

[2] Karen Gerhardt Britton, Fred C. Elliott, and E. A. Miller, "Cotton Culture," *Handbook of Texas Online*, https://www.tshaonline.org/handbook/entries/cotton-culture; Cotton Production in Texas, Texas A&M University, http://cotton.tamu.edu/General%20Production/texascottonproduction/pdf/chapter1.pdf; The Economics of Cotton. ER Services, US History, https://courses.lumenlearning.com/suny-ushistory1os 2xmaster/chapter/the-economics-of-cotton/.

[3] *Handbook of Texas Online*, Rachel Jenkins, Elliott, Tx (Matagorda County), http://www.tshaonline.org/handbook/online/articles/hre65; *Telegraph and Texas Register*, March 6, 1844.

[4] *Weekly Visitor*, Jan. 5, 1900.

[5] Matagorda County Deed No. 7767, Q-413, p. 413.

[6] *Oakland Tribune*, Nov. 20, 1897; *Bakersfield Californian*, Sept. 3, 1927.

[7] Matagorda County Deed DR Q-689; DR S-80; DR U-388.

[8] Ibid., DR Q-637; DR S-258.

[9] Ibid., DR X-48 No. 9898; DR X-144 no. 9970.

[10] Ibid.; Emmet, Chris. p. 100.

[11] *Galveston Daily News*, Nov. 3, 1890; Matagorda County Deed DR Z-283 no. 12569; DR Z-285 no. 12570; DR Z-317 No. 12586; DR 2-172.

[12] *Wichita Daily Eagle*, March 27, 1898.

[13] Emmett, Chris, *Shanghai Pierce, A Fair Likeness* (University of Oklahoma Press, 1953), p. 22-6.

[14] Williams, Annie Lee, *The History of Wharton County* (Austin: Von Boeckmann-Jones Co., 1964), p. 154-5.

[15] Williams, p. 155.

[16] Davant, Robert, and Herskowitz, Mickey, *Mystic Sails, Texas Trails* (Huntsville: Texas Review Press, 2016), p. 123; Emmett, p. 30.

[17] Ibid., p. 30-7.

[18] Ibid., p. 38.

[19] Davant, p. 116, 122-23, 146.

[20] Emmett, p. 40.

[21] Ibid., p. 47; Douglas, C.L., *Cattle Kings of Texas* (Austin: Statehouse Press, 1989), p. 46-7.

[22] Ibid., p. 44; Siringo, Charles A., *A Lone Star Cowboy*, Southwest Heritage Series (Sante Fe: Sunstone Press, 2006), p.18; *Wiley Martin Kuykendall*, in Kuykendall Family, https://www.usgenwebsites.org/TX Matagorda/family_kuykendall.htm.

[23] Ibid., p. 47.

[24] Ibid.

[25] Ibid., p. 45; Wiley Martin Kuykendall, in Kuykendall Family.

[26] Ibid., p. 40-51; Williams, p. Douglas, p. 40.

[27] *Galveston Tribune*, Nov. 6, 1897; *Fort Wayne Sentinel*, Nov. 20, 1897; Emmett, p. 40-51; Douglas, p. 42; *Historic Matagorda County*, Matagorda County Historical Association, (Houston: D. Armstrong Co., 1986), v. 1, p.178.

[28] Williams, p. 156.

[29] Emmet p. 52-3, 74.

[30] Ibid., p. 138.

[31] *Cincinnati Commercial Tribune*, Dec. 30, 1900. Ibid, p. 96, 188.

[32] Siringo, p. 55-63.

[33] Davant, p. 201-2.

[34] Emmet p. 69.

[35] Williams, p. 113.

[36] Ibid., p. 58-9; Thomas, Henry Calhoun, *A Sketch of My Life*, Nesbitt Memorial Library Journal, v. 1, no. 3, February 1990; Columbus, Texas, p. 79.

[37] Ibid., p. 59.

[38] Siringo, p. 53-59.

[39] Ibid., p. 56.

[40] Davant, p. 233.

[41] Emmet, p. 88-92; Davant, p. 227-8.

[42] Thomas, p. 79.

[43] Emmet p. 95.

[44] Ibid., 97-99.

[45] *Galveston Tribune*, Dec. 27, 1898; *Galveston Daily News*, Dec. 28, 1898; p.204.

[46] Emmett, p.105-7.

[47] Ibid., p. 193-4.

[48] LeTulle, Tommy, *The Memoirs of Tommy Beach LeTulle* (Houston: Kemp & Co., 2019), p. 123.

[49] Emmett, p. 139.

[50] *Galveston Daily News*, Sept. 11, 1883.

[51] *Victoria Advocate*, Dec. 11, 1880; *Galveston Daily News*, April 21, 1885; Emmett, p. 95-6.

[52] *Bloomington Weekly Pantograph*, Feb. 28, 1890; *San Antonio Light*, April 16, 1890.

[53] *Austin Weekly Statesman*, May 13, 1886; *Phillipsburg Herald*, Feb. 22, 1889.

[54] *Galveston Daily News*, Jan. 25, 1881; *Dallas Daily Herald*, June 21, 1883.; p. 113-4.

[55] Emmett, p. 114-6.

[56] Ibid., p. 218; Map of the Cherokee Strip Indian Territory (Caldwell: Burgess & Walton Pub., 1884), https://kchistory.org/image/map-cherokee-strip-indian-territory.

[57] *Galveston Daily News*, June 22, 1884; Emmett, p. 220.

[58] Emmett p. 221-3.

[59] Ibid., p. 224.

[60] Ibid., p. 228.

[61] *Ft. Worth Daily Gazette*, March 30, 1888; Emmett, p.1 69.

[62] Ibid.; Ibid., p. 185-91, 196-7.

[63] *Galveston Daily News*, Nov. 28, 1894; *Bay City Breeze*, July 9, 1898.

[64] *Galveston Tribune*, Nov. 6, 1897.

[65] *Saint John's Herald*, April 2, 1891.

[66] *Lawrence Weekly World*, Sept. 12, 1895.

[67] *Galveston Daily News*, March 30, 1897; *Victoria Advocate*, April 9, 1897.

[68] *Colorado Citizen*, Oct. 22, 1889; *Galveston Daily News*, July 9, 1890; Emmett, p. 191.

[69] Emmett, p.1 91.

[70] Ibid., p. 230-1.

[71] Ibid., p. 233-5.

[72] Ibid.

[73] *Lawrence Weekly World*, Sept. 12, 1895. p. 236.

[74] Emmett, p. 238

[75] Ibid., p. 253.

[76] Ibid., p. 57-8.

[77] Ibid., p. 260-1.

[78] *Galveston Tribune*, Dec. 27, 1898; Emmet, p. 261 and 268.

[79] Emmett, p. 270-1.

[80] Ibid., p. 216, 270-1.

[81] *Galveston Daily News*, Jan. 20, 1900; *Houston Daily Post*, April 25, 1901; *Galveston Daily News*, Feb. 1, 1904.

[82] *Galveston Daily News*, Oct. 3, 1894; *Times Picayune*, Sept. 1, 1899; Emmett, p. 274-5.

[83] *Bay City Tribune*, Jan. 20, 1900; Emmett p. 283-4.

[84] Emmett p. 283-4; Laurence Armour III at Pierce Ranch, Texas Rice, Texas A&M University Agricultural Center, Vol. III No. 9, 2003.

[85] *Brownsville Daily Herald*, May 25, 1897; Emmet, p. 287.

[86] *Galveston Daily News*, Jan. 1, 1900; Emmet, p.287.

[87] *Brenham Weekly Banner*, Nov. 25, 1897; Emmett, p. 288.

[88] Emmett, p. 289-90.

[89] Ibid., p. 292-3.

[90] The Southwestern Historical Quarterly, v. 101, July 1997 - April 1998, Texas, https://texashistory.unt.edu/ark:/67531/metapth117155/, Texas State Historical Association, University of North Texas Libraries, The Portal to Texas History.

[91] Williams, p. 251.

[92] *Fort Worth Weekly Gazette*, Jan. 21. 1897.

[93] Emmett, p. 244-5.

[94] *Daily Tribune*, Aug. 18, 1905. Douglas, C. L., p. 41.

[95] *Francitas Bee*, Dec. 29, 1910; Blessing State Bank Historical Marker Application, p.1, Portal to Texas History, https://texashistory.unt.edu/ark:/67531/metapth477611/m1/.

[96] *Boston Daily Globe*, Jan. 11, 1898.

[97] Matagorda County DR U-388 No. 9261.

[98] Brast, Monty, 1985. Lookin' Back, *Wharton Journal-Spectator*, September 11, 1985.

[99] Watkins Family Tree, https://www.ancestry.com/family tree/person/tree/111331089/person/370086504154/facts.

[100] 1860 Federal Census, https://www.ancestry.com/imageviewer/collections/7667/images/4297434_00088?pId=34979164; Watkins Family Tree, https://www.ancestry.com/family-tree/person/tree/111331089/person/370086504154/facts.

[101] US Confederate Pensions, 1884-1895, https://www.ancestry.com/imageviewer/collections/1677/images/32241_1020703347_1325-00135?pId=215831; Watkins Family History, unpub.

[102] 1880 Federal Census, https://www.ancestry.com/imageviewer/collections/6742/images/4244741-00260?pId=40572156.

[103] No. 81553, proof of occupancy, DR 56-56; Matagorda Deed DR U-388; Obituaries of Matagorda County, Matagorda County Genealogical Society, No. 10, Bay City: 2002. Evan Watkins, pers comm., July 24, 2022.

[104] *Weekly Visitor*, June 9, 1899.

[105] Matagorda County DR S-200, No. 8410; DR T-276, No. 8827; DR S-630; DR T-267 No. 8820; DR T-278, No. 8829; DR U-30 No. 9053; DR U-76 No. 9070; *Matagorda Tribune*, April 29, 1900.

[106] *Galveston Daily News*, Sept. 28, 1895; Mary Elizabeth Braman Crouch, Don Egbert Erastus Braman Family, http://www.usgenwebsites.org/TXMatagorda/family_braman.htm.

[107] Braman, D.E.E., Information About Texas, B.B. Lippincott & Co., Philadelphia, 1857.

[108] 1873 Phillips Academy Class Pg.16, no ref available, courtesy Michael Bailey, Brazoria County Historical Museum; *Bay City Breeze*, Feb. 19, 1898.

[109] Matagorda County DRQ-194, no. 7622; The Southwestern Historical Quarterly, v. 57, July 1953 – April 1954, https://texashistory.unt.edu/ ark:/67531/metapth101152/, The Portal to Texas History, Texas State Historical Association, p. 266; Biennial Report of Report of Secretary of State (Austin: State Printing Office, 1889), p. 242.

[110] *Bay City Breeze*, Feb. 19, 1898; Obituaries of Matagorda County, Matagorda County Genealogical Society, no. 10, Bay City: 2002.

[111] *Weekly Visitor*, April 27, 1900.

[112] Abstract of Land Claims (United States: Civilian Book Office, 1852), p. 582; Texas General Land Office, 5-111 HBP; Austin's Register of Families, v.2, date unknown.

[113] Certified Copy of Will and Probate, No. 472, *Texas, Matagorda County, Probate Minutes, 1889-1939; Index to Probate Minutes, 1913-1950; Texas Probate Court (Matagorda County)*.

[114] Matagorda County DR O-472.

[115] *The Southwest Reporter*, The Supreme and Appellate Courts of Arkansas, Kentucky, Missouri, Tennessee, Texas, and Indian Territory, v. 101, May 8-June 5, (St. Paul: West Pub. Co., 1907) p. 538.

[116] Ibid., p. 539.

[117] Ibid., p. 540.

[118] 1910 Federal Census, Ancestry.com, https://www.ancestry.com/imageviewer/collections/7884/images/; *Matagorda County Tribune*, Oct. 8, 1915; Texas Wills and Probate Records, 1833-1974, Wharton County, Probate Minutes, v. J, 1902-1938; Williams, p. 332.

[119] *Wooster, Ralph A., Civil War, Handbook of Texas Online*, http://www.tshaonline.org/handbook/online/ articles/qdc02.

[120] Fitzhugh, Lester N., Saluria, *Fort Esperanza, and Military Operations on the Texas Coast*, 1861-1864. The Southwest Historical Quarterly, v. 61, July 1957 to April 1958, p. 65-100.

[121] *Historic Matagorda County*, v. 1, p. 89, 357.

[122] *Becker, Jack, and Hamilton, M.K., Wartime Cotton Trade, Handbook of Texas Online*, http://www.tsha online.org/ handbook/online/articles/drw01.

[123] Moneyhon, Carl H., Reconstruction, *Handbook of Texas Online*, http://www.tshaonline.org/handbook/ online/articles/mzr01; Civil War and Reconstruction, Katie Whitehurst. https://texasourtexas. texaspbs.org/the-eras-of-texas/civil-war-reconstruction/.

[124] Wooster, Ralph A., *Wealthy Texans, 1870*, The Southwest Historical Quarterly, Vol. 74, July 1970 to April 1971, p. 24-35; *Historic Matagorda County*, v. 1.

[125] *Colorado Citizen*, Sept. 22, 1898.

[126] Fowler, Gene, *Texas Storms: Stories of Raging Weather in the Lone Star State* (Mankato, Minnesota: Capstone Press, 2011), pp. 112.
Block, W.T., *Texas Hurricanes of the 19th Century: Killer Storms Devastated Texas Coastline*, http://www.wtblock.com/wtblockjr/texas2.htm.

[127] *Galveston Daily News*, Sept. 22, 1875; *Victoria Advocate*, Sept. 24, 1875; *San Antonio Express*, Sept. 30, 1875; *Galveston Daily News*, Nov. 14, 1875.

[128] Ibid.

[129] Nichols, Pat, *The Decrows of Decrows Point and Matagorda County*, http://www.rootsweb. ancestry.com/~txmatago/family_decrow_thomas.htm.

[130] Ibid., *Historic Matagorda County*, v. 1.

[131] *Historic Matagorda County*, v. 1, p. 357.

[132] Historic Matagorda County, v. 1, p. 568-71; Oak Leaves, Matagorda County Genealogy Society, v. II, no. 1, 1982, pp. 43.

[133] Moore, Eudora, *Some Memories of Brother Dolph*, in Recollections of Eudora I. Moore, 1852-1882.

[134] Ibid.

[135] *Historic Matagorda County*, v. 1, p. 212.

[136] *Bay City Breeze*, Sept. 13, 1894; Ibid., p. 212, 357.

[137] Ibid., p. 357.

[138] Patent no. 2,481,215, Index of Patents Issued from the United States Patents Office (Washington: US Govt. Printing Office, 1920).

[139] *Daily Express*, Dec. 27, 1910; Northern Irrigation Co. vs. Watkins, 183 S.W. 431, Docket No. 7056, Court of Appeals of Texas, Feb. 11, 1916, Court Listener, https://www.courtlistener.com/opinion/ 4178919/northern-irr-co-v-watkins/.

[140] *American Elevator and Grain Trade*, v.29, no. 6, Dec. 15, 1910, US Dept. of Ag., p.329.

[141] *Matagorda County Tribune*, Nov. 22, 1918; *Matagorda County Tribune*, Feb. 4, 1927.

[142] Second Report of the Board of Water Engineers, v.2 1914/1916 (Austin: Von Boeckmann-Jones, 1917); *Galveston Daily News*, May 4, 1917.

[143] *Matagorda County Tribune*, Dec. 5, 1913; *Atlanta Constitution*, Dec. 7, 1913; *Galveston Daily News*, Dec. 10, 1913; *Daily Tribune*, May 10, 1913; *Galveston Daily News*, May 4, 1917; *Daily Tribune*, April 3, 1920; *Daily Tribune*, Fed. 23, 1923; *Matagorda County Tribune*, Oct. 9, 1925; *Matagorda Daily Tribune*, Feb. 6, 1925; *Matagorda County Tribune*, April 23, 1926; *Historic Matagorda County*, Matagorda County Historical Association, (Houston: D. Armstrong Co., 1986), v. 1, p. 489.

[144] *Matagorda County Tribune*, Jan. 27, 1927; *Matagorda Daily Tribune*, March 4, 1927; DR 8-457.

[145] *Daily Tribune*, May 31, 1932; LeTulle, Tommy, *The Memoirs of Tommy Beach LeTulle* (Houston: Kemp & Co., 2019), p. 34.

[146] LeTulle, p.10; Unnamed newspaper clipping dated Oct. 29, 2015, Matagorda County Museum files.

[147] *Galveston Daily News*, Aug. 5, 1896; *Weekly Visitor*, May 12, 1900; *Bay City Breeze*, Jan. 23, 1896; *Matagorda County Tribune*, June 3, 1899.

[148] *El Paso Daily Herald*, March 15, 1901; *Texas Rice Book*, Southern Pacific, 1901; Taylor, Thomas U., *Rice Irrigation in Texas*, Bulletin of the University of Texas, No. 16, (Austin: Van Boeckmann, Schultze & Co, 1902); *Historic Matagorda County*, p.168.

[149] Matagorda County Deed DR 8-457; DR 95-553; LeTulle, p.14.

[150] *Palacios Beacon*, Nov. 26, 1931; *Morning Avalanche*, Jan. 3, 1940.

[151] *Bay City Breeze*, Nov. 5, 1898; *Weekly Visitor*, June 9, 1899; *Matagorda County Tribune*, June 17, 1899.

[152] *Palacios Beacon*, May 4, 1944, *Palacios Beacon*, Dec. 12, 1946; LeTulle, p.12.

[153] *Matagorda County Tribune*, Aug. 27, 1926; Great Citizens: Governor Ross Shaw Sterling, Houston History, http://02db39d.netsolhost.com/citizens/houstonians/history8r.htm.

[154] Sterling, Ross S., and Kilman, *Ed, Ross Sterling, Texan* (Austin: Univ. Texas Press, 2007); Archeological & Historical Commission City of Houston Planning and Development Department, https://www.houston tx.gov/planning/HistoricPres/landmarks/15L309_3311_Del_Monte.pdf.

[155] Ross Sterling to J.W. Blake, July 1928, *From Pioneer Paths to Superhighways*, Texas State Library and Archives Commission, https://www.tsl.texas.gov/exhibits/highways/creation/ross_sterling_jul11_1928.

[156] *Brownsville Herald*, Sept. 14, 1932; *Texas Governor Ross S. Sterling*, Texas State Library and Archives Commission, https://legacy.lib.utexas.edu/taro/tslac/40032/tsl-40032.html.

[157] *Amarillo Daily News*, Nov. 10, 1931; *Corsicana Semi-Weekly Light*, Nov. 10, 1931.

[158] *San Antonio Light*, April 26, 1932; *Morning Avalanche*, Oct. 5, 1932; *The Daily Court Review*, Sept. 2, 1933; Matagorda County DR 96-154; Archeological & Historical Commission City of Houston Planning and Development Department.

[159] *The Texas Politics Project: Governors of Texas*, https://texaspolitics.utexas.edu/archive/html/exec/ governors/17.html.

[160] Matagorda County Deed No. 23484.

[161] Ibid., Exhibit B, Deed No. 23484.

[162] *Houston Daily Post*, Jan. 14, 1910.

[163] State of California Superior Court, Alameda County, Dept. 4, Case No. 16883, 1917; Clare Family Tree, https://www.ancestry.com/family-tree/person/tree/19719396/person/843231176/facts?_phsrc=oEj17 &_phstart=success; Matagorda County Deed No. 807766, 54-424, 1918.

[164] Matagorda County Deed DR 60-209 No.83748.

[165] *The Herald*, July 30, 1942.

[166] Matagorda County Deed DR 60-209 No.83748; DR D-75.

[167] Northern Irrigation Co. versus Watkins, Court of Appeals of Texas Filing February 11th, 1916, Citation 183 S.W. 431, Docket No. 7056, https://www.courtlistener.com/opinion/4178919/northern-irr-co-v-watkins/.

[168] Ibid.

[169] LeTulle, p. 121-3.

[170] *Matagorda County Tribune*, Aug. 18, 1916; Obituaries of Matagorda County, Matagorda County Genealogical Society, no. 10, 2002.

[171] 1900 Federal Census, https://www.ancestry.com/imageviewer/collections/7602/images/4118578_00752? usePUB=true&_phsrc=dXx1&usePUBJs=true&pId=44532933; *Matagorda County Tribune*, March 24, 1900; https://www.ancestry.com/family-tree/person/tree/111331089/person/370086510923/facts; Watkins family, pers. com.

[172] Watkins Family, http://www.usgenwebsites.org/TXMatagorda/family_watkins.htm.

[173] LeTulle, p. 121, 162.

[174] Ibid.

[175] Matagorda County Deed DR 68/588; DR 56/381; DR 63/245.

[176] Ibid., DR 60/207; DR 56/283; DR 63/245.

[177] Ibid., DR 63/245.

[178] Davant, Robert, and Herskowitz, Mickey, *Mystic Sails, Texas Trails* (Huntsville: Texas Review Press, 2016), p. 229-30.

[179] Davis, Jessie Poole, and Poole, Mark K., *Thomas Jefferson Poole Jr.*, Historic Matagorda County, v. II, 1984, p. 410 – 412.

[180] Davant, p. 230.

[181] Davant, p. 234.

[182] Davis, p. 410 – 412.

[183] Davant, p. 261-71; *Houston Post*, Feb. 1, 1904; *Daily Tribune*, Aug. 19, 1905.

[184] *Bastrop Advertiser*, Aug. 7, 1952; Williams, Annie Lee, *The History of Wharton County* (Austin: Von Boeckmann-Jones Co., 1964), p. http://www.usgenwebsites.org/TXMatagorda/grimes_obits.htm.

[185] *Daily Tribune*, March 15, 1932; *The Daily Tribune*, September 3, 1969; *The Houston Post*, September 4, 1969.

[186] Matagorda County Deed DR 63/245; DR 80-200.

[187] Ibid., DR 80-196.

[188] Matagorda County Trustee's Deed and Warranty DR 96-154; Deed DR 8-457; DR 95-553.

[189] Ibid., DR 73-398; OGML 9-173.

[190] Ibid., DR 6/543; DR 2-172.

[191] Ibid., DR v. 43, p. 302-5; DR132-467.

[192] *Daily Tribune*, Jan. 6, 1927.

[193] *Galveston Daily News*, Nov. 1, 1900.

[194] *Historic Matagorda County*, v.1, p. 346-350.

[195] Ibid.

[196] Davant, p. 261-71; *Houston Post*, Feb. 1, 1904; *Daily Tribune*, Aug. 19, 1905.

[197] History of Oil Discoveries, Texas Almanac, https://texasalmanac.com/topics/business/history-oil-discoveries-texas.

[198] *Historic Matagorda County*, p. 245-6, 340.

[199] *Galveston Daily News*, July 4, 1904; *Victoria Advocate*, April 16, 1904; *Galveston Daily News*, Feb. 18, 1905; *Historic Matagorda County*, p. 245-6, 340.

REFERENCES CHAPTER 4

[1] DR 60-209 No.83748.

[2] *Bay City Breeze*, Feb. 19, 1898.

[3] *Matagorda County Tribune*, Dec. 23, 1899; LeTulle, Tommy, *The Memoirs of Tommy Beach LeTulle* (Houston: Kemp & Co., 2019).

[4] Danny Hemphill, May 6, 2023.

[5] LeTulle, Tommy, *The Memoirs of Tommy Beach LeTulle* (Houston: Kemp & Co., 2019); Matagorda County Deed 94, no. 881582, p.256.

[6] LeTulle, Tommy; Danny Hemphill, May 6, 2023.

[7] Danny and Jimmie Stephens, March 29, 2023; Ibid., June 14, 2023.

[8] LeTulle, Tommy.

[9] Ibid.

[10] *Daily Tribune*, March 3, 1986.

[11] Frazier, Chet, 1961, *The Intellectual Mule*, The Cattleman, v. 48, 1961, p. 49.

[12] Danny and Jimmie Stephens.

[13] *Daily Tribune*, March 3, 1986.

[14] Danny Savage, May 26, 2023.

[15] Anonymous, 2023.

[16] LeTulle, Tommy.

[17] Danny Savage, June 10, 2023.

[18] Matagorda County Deed no. 32590.

[19] Danny and Jimmie Stephens.

[20] Ibid.

[21] Ibid.

[22] Ibid.

[23] Matagorda County Trustee's Deed and Warranty DR 96-154; Deed DR 8-457; DR 95-553.

[24] Dermont, H. Hardy and Ingham S. Roberts, eds., *James M. West*, The Historical Review of Southeast Texas (Chicago: Lewis Pub. Co., 1910), v. II, p. 1009-11.

[25] Burrough, Bryan, *The Big Rich: The Rise and Fall of the Greatest Texas Oil Fortunes* (N.Y.: Penguin Press, 2009); Houston History, Great Citizens – *James Marion West, Jr.*, http://02db39d.netsolhost.com/citizens/houstonians/history8bb.htm.

[26] Ibid.

[27] *Levelland Daily News*, Dec. 18, 1957.

[28] Cartwheeler-Dealer, *Time Magazine*, June 9, 1958.

[29] Wesley West, *Wikipedia*.

[30] Matagorda County Deed DR 118-513 and DR 118-519.

[31] Ibid.; Matagorda County OGML 117-311.

[32] Allen, Arda T., *Twenty-One Sons for Texas* (San Antonio: Naylor Co.,1959), p. 84; Furse, Margaret L., *The Hawkins Ranch in Texas* (College Station: A&M Univ. Press, 2014), p. 96, 121. 121.Furse, Margaret L., p. 96.

[33] Ibid., p. 190.

[34] Probate v. 62, p. 813-42.

[35] Last Will and Testament of Esker L. McDonald, PM 57-881.

[36] 1930 and 1940 Federal Census; *Bay City News*, Aug. 16, 1956; *Palacios Beacon*, Feb. 23, 1961; Danny Savage, June 10, 2023.

[37] *Palacios Beacon*, July 31, 1975.

[38] *Bay City News*, Aug. 23, 1956; *Bay City News*, Dec. 27, 1956.

[39] *Edna Herald*, Jan. 14, 1963.

[40] *Bay City News*, Dec. 27, 1956.

[41] *Texas Mohair Weekly*, Dec. 6, 1957; *Texas Mohair Weekly*, Jan. 1, 1958

[42] Danny Savage, June 10, 2023.

[43] Danny Savage, May 26, 2023.

[44] Matagorda County Genealogical Society, v. XVII, no. 1, Feb. 1999, pp. 83.

[45] Ibid., Matagorda County Deed DR 73-398; OGML 9-173.

[46] *Palacios Beacon*, Aug. 6, 1959.

[47] Danny Hemphill, May 6, 2023.

[48] Manuel Briones May 26, 2023.

[49] Danny Hemphill, May 6, 2023.

[50] *Austin American*, Oct. 12, 1997.

[51] Matagorda County Instrument no. 60929.

[52] Matagorda County Deed DR 132/294.

[53] Ibid., 199/253.

[54] Ibid., 326/341.

[55] Ibid., 577/333; 578/297.

[56] *El Campo Citizen*, Jan. 8, 1915; *Eagle Lake Headlight*, June. 10, 1922; *Victoria Advocate*, June 8, 1959; *Palacios Beacon*, April 16, 1959; *Palacios Beacon*, Jan. 26, 1961; *Colorado Citizen*, Jan. 25, 1973.

[57] Matagorda County Deeds 577/333 and 578/297.

[58] *Victoria Advocate*, Dec. 31, 1943.

[59] *Fort Worth Star Telegram*, Dec. 18, 1957.

[60] *Fort Worth Star Telegram*, June 19, 1962.

[61] *Orange Leader*, May 25, 1962; Sort Worth TV Station WBAP-T New Script dated May 30, 1962, UNT Special Collections, Portal to Texas History, https://texashistory.unt.edu/ark:/67531/metadc946826/manifest/.

[62] *The Odessa American*, July 8, 1962.

[63] *Orange Leader*, May 25, 1962; *Taylor Daily Press*, May 29, 1962.

[64] *Fort Worth Star Telegram*, June 19, 1962.

[65] *Baytown Sun*, Dec. 28, 1969; *Baytown Sun*, April 14, 1986.

[66] *Orange Leader*, May 25, 1962; *Taylor Daily Press*, May 29, 1962.

[67] *Fort Worth Star Telegram*, March 31, 1961.

[68] *Palacios Beacon*, May 9, 1963; *Cuero Record*, Oct. 1, 1964; *El Paso Herald Post*, Feb. 8, 1965; *Time Record News*, Aug. 23, 1968; *Sealy News*, Oct. 26, 1978; Frank Lovic Ramsey, Ancestry.com, https://www.ancestry.com/family-tree/person/tree/106010188/person/342391126913/. *Abilene Reporter News*, July 2, 1961; *Victoria Advocate*, July 23, 1973.

[69] *Historic Matagorda County* (Houston: D. Armstrong Co., 1986), v. 1, p. 267.

[70] *Amarillo Globe*, Aug. 21, 1942; *Big Spring Daily Herald*, Aug. 31, 1942; *Wichita Daily Times*, Sept. 3, 1942; *Historic Matagorda County*, v. 1.

[71] *Palacios Beacon*, Sept. 4, 1991, *The Cuero Record*, Sept. 12, 1961; *Palacios Beacon*, Sept. 14, 1961; *Remembering Carla: 50th Anniversary*, srh.noaa.gov.

REFERENCES CHAPTER 6

[1] Young, J.R., 1835 Map of Texas (Philadelphia: Augustus Mitchell, 1835); Lee, E.F., 1836 Map of Texas (Cincinnati: J.A. James & Co., 1836).

[2] Hard Road to Texas: Texas Annexation 1836-1845, Texas State Library and Archives Commission, https://www.tsl.texas.gov/exhibits/annexation/part1/page1.html.

[3] Richard W. Moore, *Baron de Bastrop*, Texas State Historical Association, https://www.tshaonline.org/handbook/entries/bastrop-baron-de.

[4] Gittinger, Eugene A., *The Colonization of Texas*: 1820-1830. Loyola University Master Thesis, 1940, p. 24, https://ecommons.luc.edu/cgi/viewcontent.cgi?article=1190&context=luc_theses.

[5] Austin, Stephen F., *Journal of Stephen F. Austin on his First Trip to Texas, 1821*, Texas Historical Quarterly, p. 286-307. JSTOR Digital Library, https://ia801701.us.archive.org/33/items/jstor-27784975/27784975.pdf.

[6] Stephen F. Austin, *Plan for the Organization of Congress for the Empire of Mexico, April 8, 1823*, Mirabeau B. Lamar Papers no. 47, Archives and Information Services Division, Texas State Library and Archives Commission.

[7] Ibid.; Gittinger, Eugene A., The Colonization of Texas: 1820-1830. Loyola University Master Thesis, 1940, p. 33.

[8] Eugene Barker, ed., *Annual Report of the American Historical Association for the Year 1919: The Austin Papers*, (Washington, D.C.: Government Printing Office, 1924), v. 1, Part 1, p. 504-5, The Digital Austin Papers, http://digitalaustinpapers.org/document?id=APB0505.

[9] Ibid., p. 517-8.

[10] Ibid., p. 504-5.

[11] Ibid., p. 554-5, 586-9.

[12] Carolyn Hyman, *Iturbide, Agustin de, Handbook of Texas Online*, http://www.tshaonline.org/handbook/online/articles/fit01.

[13] Federal Constitution of the United Mexican States of 1824, World Heritage Encyclopedia, http://self.gutenberg.org/articles/federal_constitution_of_the_united_mexican_states_of_1824.

[14] Eugene Barker, ed., *Annual Report of the American Historical Association for the Year 1919: The Austin Papers*, (Washington, D.C.: Government Printing Office, 1924), v. 1, Part 1, p. 560-2.

[15] Austin, Stephen F., *A Project of a Constitution for the Republic of Texas formed by Stephen F. Austin – City of Mexico, March 1823* in Eugene Barker, ed., *Annual Report of the American Historical Association for the Year 1919: The Austin Papers*, (Washington, D.C.: Government Printing Office, 1924), v. 1, Part 1, p. 601-27.

[16] Mexican Constitution of 1824, Sons of DeWitt Colony Texas, Coahuila y Tejas, http://www.sonsof dewittcolony.org/constit1824.htm.

[17] Smith, Roy W., *The Quarrel Between Governor Smith and the Council of the Provisional Government of the Republic*, Texas Historical Association Quarterly, v. 5, July 1901 – April 1902, p. 272-3, https://texashistory.unt.edu/ark:/67531/metapth101021/m1/343/; Jesús F. de la Teja, *Coahuila and Texas*, Handbook of Texas Online, http://www.tshaonline.org/handbook/online/articles/usc01; Texas General Land Office, https://www.glo.texas.gov/history/archives/forms/files/appendices-history-of-texas-public-lands.pdf.

[18] Mexico – The Federalist Republic, 1824-36, US Library of Congress, http://www.baja.org/muchobueno/mexico/mexico_the_federalist_republic.htm.

[19] 1829 Andrew Jackson-Santa Anna of Mexico, State of the Union History, http://www.stateofthe union history.com/2018/08/1829-andrew-jackson-santa-anna-of.html.

[20] Flores, Manuel, Presidents of Mexican Texas, 1824-1836, *Corpus Christi Caller-Times*, July 31, 2017.

[21] Kilmeade, Brian, *Sam Houston and the Alamo Avengers* (Sentinel Press, 2019), p. 16.

[22] Gittinger, Eugene A., *The Colonization of Texas*: 1820-1830. Loyola University Master Thesis, 1940, p. 95.

[23] Sánchez, José María, *A Trip to Texas in 1828*, Southwestern Historical Quarterly, v. 29, 1926, p. 260-61, 271; Gittinger, Eugene A., p. 95.

[24] *Texas Gazette*, July 3, 1830; Mexico – The Federalist Republic, 1824-36, US Library of Congress, http://www.baja.org/muchobueno/mexico/mexico_the_federalist_republic.htm.

[25] Howren, Alleine, *Causes and Origin of the Decree of April 6, 1830*, The Southwestern Historical Quarterly, v. 16, July 1912 - April 1913, Austin, p. 403, https://texashistory.unt.edu/ark:/67531/metapth101058/m1/411/, Portal to Texas History.

[26] Margaret S. Henson, *Anahuac Disturbances, Handbook of Texas Online*, http://www.tshaonline.org/handbook/online/articles/jca01.

[27] Ibid., p. 275.

[28] Rowe, Edna, *The Disturbances at Anahuac in 1832*, The Quarterly of the Texas State Historical Association v. 6, July 1902 - April 1903, Austin, p. 272, https://texashistory.unt.edu/ark:/67531/metapth101028/m1/273/, Portal to Texas History.

[29] Smith, Henry, *Reminiscences of Henry Smith, 1836*, The Quarterly of the Texas State Historical Association, v.14, July 1910 – April 1911, Austin, p. 37, https://texashistory.unt.edu/ark:/67531/metapth101054/m1/38/, Portal to Texas History.

[30] Ibid., p. 38.

[31] Rowe, Edna, p. 287-8; No Author, *History of Texas, Together with a Biographical History of Milam, Williamson, Bastrop, Travis, Lee, and Burleson Counties* (Chicago: Lewis Pub. Co., 1893), https://texas history.unt.edu/ark:/67531/metapth29785/m1/44/, Portal to Texas History.

[32] Rowe, Edna, p. 277; The Battle of Velasco, Chronological and Archaeological History of the Forts Velasco, https://velascohistoryarchaeology.weebly.com/the-battle-of-velasco.html.

[33] The Battle of Velasco.

[34] Smith, Henry, *Reminiscences of Henry Smith, 1836*. The Quarterly of the Texas State Historical Association, v. 14, July 1910 – April 1911, Austin, 1911, p. 45.

[35] Ibid., p. 41-2.

[36] Ibid., p. 44.

[37] The Battle of Velasco.

[38] *Texas Gazette*, July 23, 1832.

[39] Ibid.

⁴⁰ Kingston, Mike and Plocheck, Robert, *Revolution and the Republic*, Texas Almanac, https://texas almanac. com/topics/history/timeline/revolution-and-republic.

⁴¹ Ralph W. Steen, *Smith, Henry*, Handbook of Texas Online, https://www.tshaonline.org/handbook /entries/smith-henry.

⁴² Smith, Henry, *Reminiscences of Henry Smith, 1836*. The Quarterly of the Texas State Historical Association, v. 14, July 1910 – April 1911, Austin, 1911, p. 42-3.

⁴³ Independence Resolutions & Consultations, Sons of DeWitt's Colony, Texas, http://www.sonsof dewittcolony.org/consultations1.htm.

⁴⁴ Eugene Barker, ed., Stephen F. Austin to General William H. Ashley, October 10, 1832, The Digital Austin Papers, *Annual Report of the American Historical Association for the Year 1919: The Austin Papers*, (Washington, D.C.: Government Printing Office, 1924), v. 1, Part 2, p. 871-87, http://digital austinpapers.org/document?id=APB4446.

⁴⁵ Texas Consultation at San Felipe. Sons of DeWitt Colony, Texas, http://www.sonsofdewittcolony.org/ consultations2.htm.

⁴⁶ Eugene Barker, ed., Stephen F Austin to Ramon Musquiz, Nov. 15, 1832, The Digital Austin Papers, *Annual Report of the American Historical Association for the Year 1919: The Austin Papers*, (Washington, D.C.: Government Printing Office, 1924), v. 1, Part 2, p. 888-89, http://digitalaustin papers.org/document?id=APB4475.

⁴⁷ Eugene Barker, ed., Stephen F Austin to Samuel M Williams, Dec. 6, 1832, *Annual Report of the American Historical Association for the Year 1919: The Austin Papers*, (Washington, D.C.: Government Printing Office, 1924), v. 1, Part 2, pp. 897-9. http://digitalaustinpapers.org/document?id=APB4491.

⁴⁸ Eugene Barker, ed., John A. Williams to Stephen F Austin, Dec. 28, 1832, *Annual Report of the American Historical Association for the Year 1919: The Austin Papers*, (Washington, D.C.: Government Printing Office, 1924), v. 1, Part 2, p. 903-6, http://digitalaustinpapers.org/document?id=APB4496.

⁴⁹ Eugene Barker, ed., Stephen F. Austin to Conventional Committee, 1833, *Annual Report of the American Historical Association for the Year 1919: The Austin Papers*, (Washington, D.C.: Government Printing Office, 1924), v. 1, Part 2, p. 934-40, http://digitalaustinpapers.org/document?id=APB4542.

⁵⁰ Ibid.

⁵¹ Flores, Manuel, Presidents of Mexican Texas, 1824-1836, *Corpus Christi Caller-Times*, July 31, 2017.

⁵² Eugene Barker, ed., Stephen F. Austin to Conventional Committee, 1833, *Annual Report of the American Historical Association for the Year 1919: The Austin Papers*, (Washington, D.C.: Government Printing Office, 1924), v. 1, Part 2, p. 988-9, http://digitalaustinpapers.org/document?id=APB4585.

⁵³ Eugene Barker, ed., Stephen F Austin to Samuel M Williams, Nov. 5, 1833, *Annual Report of the American Historical Association for the Year 1919: The Austin Papers*, (Washington, D.C.: Government Printing Office, 1924), v 1, Part 2, p. 1013-15, http://digitalaustinpapers.org/document?id=APB4607.

⁵⁴ Eugene Barker, ed., Stephen F Austin to Central Committee, July 24, 1833, *Annual Report of the American Historical Association for the Year 1919: The Austin Papers*, (Washington, D.C.: Government Printing Office, 1924), v. 1, Part 2, p. 988-91, http://digitalaustinpapers.org/document?id=APB4585.

⁵⁵ Eugene Barker, ed., Ayuntamiento of Bexar to Stephen F. Austin, Oct. 31, 1833, *Annual Report of the American Historical Association for the Year 1919: The Austin Papers*, (Washington, D.C.: Government Printing Office, 1924), v. 1, Part 2, p. 1012-13, http://digitalaustinpapers.org/document?id=APB4606.

⁵⁶ Letter from Stephen F. Austin, August 25, 1834, republished in *Texas Republican*, Nov. 8, 1834; Clavey, Bruce, *The Inquisition Dungeon of Stephen F. Austin*, Texas General Land Office, https://medium.com/save-texas-history/the-inquisition-dungeon-of-stephen-f-austin-ef258d1c73be.

⁵⁷ Letter from Stephen F. Austin, August 25, 1834, republished in *Texas Republican*, Nov. 8, 1834.

⁵⁸ S. S. McKay, *Constitution of 1824*, *Handbook of Texas Online*, http://www.tshaonline.org/handbook /online/articles/ngc02; Jesús F. de la Teja, *Coahuila and Texas*, Handbook of Texas Online, http://www. tshaonline.org/handbook/online/articles/usc01; Flores, Manuel, Presidents of Mexican Texas, 1824-1836, *Corpus Christi Caller-Times*, July 31, 2017, http://www.tshaonline.org/handbook/online/articles/usc01.

⁵⁹ Jesús F. de la Teja, *Coahuila and Texas*, Handbook of Texas Online, http://www.tshaonline.org /handbook/online/articles/usc01.

⁶⁰ Letter from Stephen F. Austin. August 25, 1834, republished in *Texas Republican*, Nov. 8, 1834.

⁶¹ Frank W. Johnson to Gail Borden Jr., April 15, 1835. The Austin Papers, http://digitalaustinpapers.org/ document?id=APB4765.

[62] Transcript of letter from the Ayuntamiento of Matagorda to the Mexican Congress, July 28, 1834, Portal to Texas History, https://texashistory.unt.edu/ark:/67531/metapth216844/m1/1/.

[63] Letter from Stephen F. Austin. August 25, 1834, republished in *Texas Republican*, Nov. 8, 1834.

[64] Letter from Juan N. Almonte to Samuel M. Williams, Dec. 20, 1834, in Jackson, Jack, and Almonte, Juan Nepomuceno, *Almonte's Texas: Juan N. Almonte's 1834 Inspection, Secret Report & Role in the 1836 Campaign*, Austin, 2003, https://texashistory.unt.edu/ark:/67531/metapth296837/m1/313/.

[65] González Pedrero, Enrique, *País de un solo hombre: el México de Santa Anna, Volumen II, La sociedad de fuego cruzado 1829-1836, México:* Fondo de Cultura Económica, 2004, ISBN 968-16-6377-2.

[66] *Telegraph and Texas Register*, Oct. 17, 1835; The 1857 Texas Almanac, with Statistics, Historical and Biographical Sketches, &c., Relating to Texas, p. 15, https://texashistory.unt.edu/ark:/67531/metapth 123763/ m1/18/, Portal to Texas History.

[67] Flores, Manuel, Presidents of Mexican Texas, 1824-1836, *Corpus Christi Caller-Times*, July 31, 2017.

[68] Henderson, Mary V., *Minor Empresario Contracts For the Colonization of Texas, 1825-1834*, The Southwest Quarterly, v. 31, no. 4, April 1928, p. 300, https://texashistory.unt.edu/ark:/67531/metapth 101088/m1/324/, Portal to Texas History.

[69] Garver, Lois, *Benjamin Rush Milam*, SW Historical Quarterly, v. 28, July 1834 - April 1935, p. 178-81, https://texashistory.unt.edu/ark:/67531/metapth117143/m1/196/.

[70] Barker, Eugene C., *Land Speculation as a Cause of the Texas Revolution*, The Quarterly of the State Historical Association, Texas State Historical Association, v. 10, no. 1, July 1906, p. 76 - 82, JSTOR, https://www.jstor.org/stable/30242911.

[71] Ibid., p. 84.

[72] Ibid., p. 879-85.

[73] Garver, Lois, *Benjamin Rush Milam*, SW Historical Quarterly, v. 28, July 1834 - April 1935, p. 178-81, https://texashistory.unt.edu/ark:/67531/metapth117143/m1/196/, p.183; Jackson, Jack, and Almonte, Juan Nepomuceno, *Almonte's Texas: Juan N. Almonte's 1834 Inspection, Secret Report & Role in the 1836 Campaign*, Austin, 2003, p. 294, https://texashistory.unt.edu/ark:/67531/metapth296837/m1/313/; Kingston, Mike and Plocheck, Robert, *Revolution and the Republic*, Texas Almanac, https://texas almanac.com/topics/history/timeline/revolution-and-republic.

[74] Johnson, Frank W., *A History of Texas and Texans*, v. 1, (Chicago, 1914), p. 179, https://texashistory .unt.edu/ark:/67531/metapth760581/m1/226/; Holley, Mary Austin, *Texas*, The Texas State Historical Association, Austin, 1990, p. 328; https://texashistory.unt.edu/ark:/67531/ metapth296847/m1/366/.

[75] Jackson, Jack, and Almonte, Juan Nepomuceno, *Almonte's Texas: Juan N. Almonte's 1834 Inspection, Secret Report & Role in the 1836 Campaign*, Austin, 2003, p. 295-7.

[76] Ibid., p. 299.

[77] Transcript of the Address to the People of Texas by the Central Committee, Oct. 28, 1834, San Felipe Texas, https://texashistory.unt.edu/ark:/67531/metapth217630/m1/1/, Portal to Texas History.

[78] Ibid.

[79] Jackson, Jack, 1941-2006 & Almonte, Juan Nepomuceno, 1803-1869. Almonte's Texas: Juan N. Almonte's 1834 Inspection, Secret Report & Role in the 1836 Campaign, page 299.

[80] Ibid., p. 299.

[81] Ibid., p. 330.

[82] *Telegraph and Texas Register*, Oct. 17, 1835; The 1857 Texas Almanac, with Statistics, Historical and Biographical Sketches, &c., Relating to Texas, p. 15, https://texashistory.unt.edu/ark:/67531/metapth 123763/m1/18/ Portal to Texas History; *Corpus Christi Caller-Times*, July 26, 2016.

[83] Barker, Eugene, *Difficulties of a Mexican Revenue Officer in Texas*, Reprint from the Texas State Historical Association, January 1901, p 1-3, https://texashistory.unt.edu/ark:/67531/metapth29769/m1/14/.

[84] Ibid., p. 3-7; Margaret S. Henson, *Anahuac Disturbances, Handbook of Texas Online,* http://www.tsha online.org/handbook/online/articles/jca01.

[85] Barker, Eugene, *Difficulties of a Mexican Revenue Officer in Texas*, Reprint from the Texas State Historical Association, January 1901, p. 8-9, https://texashistory.unt.edu/ark:/67531/metapth29769/m1/14/.

[86] Ibid., p. 9-10.

[87] Ibid., p. 12.

[88] Kite, Jodella, D., *The War and Peace Parties of Pre-Revolutionary Texas, 1835-1836*, East Texas Historical Journal, v. 29, 1, p. 13.

[89] Transcript of Letter from Martin Perfecto de Cos to the Ayuntamiento of Columbia, July 12, 1835, 3pp., https://texashistory.unt.edu/ark:/67531/metapth218168/m1/1/, Portal to Texas History.

[90] Kite, Jodella, D., *The War and Peace Parties of Pre-Revolutionary Texas, 1835-1836*, East Texas Historical Journal, v. 29, 1, p. 13.

[91] McLean, Malcolm D., *Papers Concerning Robertsons Colony*, v. 10, 1983, p. 67, https://texas history.unt.edu/ark:/67531/metapth28587/m1/74/.

[92] Johnson, Frank W., *A History of Texas and Texans*, v. 1, (Chicago, 1914), p. 239, https://texas history.unt.edu/ark:/67531/metapth760581/m1/226/.

[93] Barker, Eugene C., *Land Speculation as a Cause of the Texas Revolution*, The Quarterly of the State Historical Association, Texas State Historical Association, v. 10, no. 1, July 1906, p. 88-9, JSTOR, https://www.jstor.org/stable/30242911.

[94] General Cos's Warning to Texans, July 1835, *Inside the Gate*, https:\\drtlibrary.worpress.com/2009/07/16/general-coss-warning-to-texans-july-1835/.

[95] Barker, Eugene C., *Land Speculation as a Cause of the Texas Revolution*, The Quarterly of the State Historical Association, Texas State Historical Association, v. 10, no. 1, July 1906, p. 90.

[96] Ibid.

[97] Dienst, Alex., *The Navy of the Republic of Texas*, The Quarterly of the Texas State Historical Association, v. 12, July 1908-April 1909, p. 166-170, Austin, https://texashistory.unt.edu/ark:/67531/metapth101048/m1/193/; Wooten, Dudley G., ed., *A Comprehensive History of Texas 1685 to 1897*, v. 1 (Dallas: Scarff Publishing, 1898; p. 176, https://texashistory.unt .edu/ark:/67531/metapth587009/m1/207/.

[98] Stephen F. Austin to Mary Austin Holley, August 21, 1835, The Digital Austin Papers, http://digital austinpapers.org/document?id=APB4851.

[99] Dienst, Alex., p. 166-70.

[100] Richardson, Rupert N., *Texas: The Lone Star State* (New York: Prentice-Hall, 1943), p. 91-2.

[101] Stephen F. Austin to the People of Texas, Sept.9. 1835, The Digital Austin Papers, http://digital austinpapers.org/document?id=APB4866.

[102] *Stephen F. Austin to the People, Sept. 21, 1835,* The Digital Austin Papers, http://digitalaustinpapers. org/document?id=APB4880.

[103] Brown, John Henry, *History of Texas: From 1686-1892*, v. 1, p. 297-9.

[104] Smithwick, Noah, *Evolution of a State or Recollections of Old Texas Days* (Austin: Gammel, 1900), p. 101-4.

[105] Smith, Ruby C., *James W. Fannin Jr. in the Texas Revolution*, The Quarterly of the Texas Historical Association, v. 23, no. 2, October 1919, p. 83-4, JSTOR Digital Library, https://www.jstor.org/stable/27794555.

[106] Kingston, Mike and Plocheck, Robert, *Revolution and the Republic*, Texas Almanac, https://texasalmanac.com/topics/history/timeline/revolution-and-republic; Rather, Ethel Z., *DeWitt's Colony*, The Quarterly of the Texas Historical Association, v. 8, no. 2, July 1904 - April 1905, Austin, p. 151, https://texashistory.unt.edu/ark:/67531/metapth101033/m1/151/.

[107] Rather, Ethel Z., *DeWitt's Colony*, The Quarterly of the Texas Historical Association, v. 8, no. 2, July 1904 - April 1905, Austin, p. 153, https://texashistory.unt.edu/ark:/67531/metapth101033/m1/153/.

[108] Smithwick, Noah, *Evolution of a State or Recollections of Old Texas Days* (Austin: Gammel, 1900), p. 101-104; *General Austin's Book for Campaign of 1835*, Texas State Historical Association, The Quarterly of the Texas State Historical Association, v. 11, July 1907 – April Austin, 1908, p. 3, https://texashistory .unt.edu/ark:/67531/metapth101045/; Hunt, Lenoir, *Bluebonnets and Blood: The Romance of Tejas*, (Houston: Texas Books, 1938), p. 130.

[109] Bennet, Miles S., *The Battle of Gonzales, the "Lexington" of the Texas Revolution*, The Quarterly of the Texas Historical Association, v. 2, no. 4, April 1899, JSTOR Digital Library, https://www.jstor.org/stable/30242776; Smithwick, Noah, *Evolution of a State or Recollections of Old Texas Days* (Austin: Gammel, 1900), p. 101-104.

[110] Wharton, Clarence, R., *The Republic of Texas* (Houston: Young Printing Co, 1922), p. 119-122, Hathi Trust Digital Library, https://hdl.handle.net/2027/yale.39002002379031.

[111] Bennet, Miles S., *The Battle of Gonzales, the "Lexington" of the Texas Revolution*, The Quarterly of the Texas Historical Association, v. 2, no. 4, April 1899, JSTOR Digital Library, https://www.jstor.org/stable/30242776; Come and Take It – The Battle of Gonzales, Texas General Land Office, https://medium.com/save-texas-history/come-and-take-it-the-battle-of-gonzales-4bc0862b846a.

[112] Stephen F. Austin to the Harrisburg Committee of Safety and Correspondence, Oct. 5, 1835, The Digital Austin Papers, http://digitalaustinpapers.org/document?id=APB4911.

[113] Stephen F. Austin to David G. Burnet, Oct. 5, 1835, The Digital Austin Papers, http://digitalaustin papers.org/document?id=APB4914.

[114] Domingo de Ugartechea to Stephen F Austin, Oct. 4, 1835, http://digitalaustinpapers.org/document ?id=APB4907.

[115] Smith, Ruby C., *James W. Fannin Jr. in the Texas Revolution*, The Quarterly of the Texas Historical Association, v. 23, no. 2, October 1919, p. 84, JSTOR Digital Library, https://www.jstor.org/stable/27794555.

[116] George M. Collinsworth to *Stephen F. Austin, Oct. 8, 1835, The Digital Austin Papers,* http://digital *austinpapers.org/document?id=APB4922.*

[117] *General Austin's Book for Campaign of 1835*, Texas State Historical Association, The Quarterly of the Texas State Historical Association, v. 11, July 1907 – April Austin, 1908, p. 3, https://texashistory.unt.edu/ark:/67531/metapth101045/.

[118] Craig H. Roell, *Goliad Campaign of 1835, Handbook of Texas Online,* http://www.tshaonline.org/handbook/online/articles/qdg01.

[119] Huson, Hobart, *Captain Phillip Dimmitt's Commandancy of Goliad, 1835–1836: An Episode of the Mexican Federalist War in Texas, Usually Referred to as the Texian Revolution* (Austin: Von Boeckmann-Jones Co., 1974), p. 103; Hardin, Stephen L., *Texian Iliad – A Military History of the Texas Revolution* (Austin: University of Texas Press, 1994), p. 46-7; Craig H. Roell, *Goliad Campaign of 1835, Handbook of Texas Online,* http://www.tshaonline.org/handbook/online/articles/qdg01.

[120] Raymond Estep, *José Antonio Mexía*, Handbook of Texas, https://www.tshaonline.org/handbook/entries/mexia-jose-antonio.

[121] Claudia Hazelwood, *George Fisher*, Handbook of Texas, https://www.tshaonline.org/handbook/entries/fisher-george.

[122] Barker, Eugene C., *The Tampico Expedition,* The Quarterly of the Texas State Historical Association, v. 6, no. 3, 1903, p. 171-2, http://www.jstor.org/stable/30242681.

[123] Ibid., p. 174-6.

[124] Smith, Roy W., *The Quarrel Between Governor Smith and the Council of the Provisional Government of the Republic*, Texas Historical Association Quarterly, v. 5, July 1901 – April 1902, p. 277-8, https://texashistory.unt.edu/ark:/67531/metapth101021/m1/; Barker, Eugene C., *The Tampico Expedition,* The Quarterly of the Texas State Historical Association, v. 6, no. 3, 1903, p. 173-7, http://www.jstor.org/stable/30242681; Bruce, Henry, *Life of General Houston, 1793-1863* (N.Y.: Dodd, Mead & Co.).

[125] Stephen F. Austin to the Committee of Safety at San Felipe, Oct. 11, 1835, The Digital Austin Papers, http://digitalaustinpapers.org/document?id=APB4937.

[126] Smith, Roy W., p. 299.

[127] Barker, Eugene C., *The Texas Revolutionary Army*, Texas State Historical Association, The Quarterly of the Texas State Historical Association, v. 9, no. 4, July 1905 – April 1906, https://texashistory.unt.edu.ark:/67531/metapth101036/m1/5/, p. 236.

[128] Ibid., p. 249-50.

[129] Phillip Dimmitt to Stephen F. Austin, Oct. 20, 1835, The Digital Austin Papers, http://digitalaustin papers.org/document?id=APB4968; James Bowie and James Fannin to Stephen F. Austin, Oct. 22, 1835, The Digital Austin Papers, http://digitalaustinpapers.org/document?id=APB4977.

[130] Kilmeade, Brian, *Sam Houston and the Alamo Avengers* (Sentinel Press, 2019), p. 69.

[131] James Bowie and James Fannin to Stephen F. Austin, Oct. 24, 1835, The Digital Austin Papers, http://digitalaustinpapers.org/document?id=APB4981.

[132] Garver, Lois, *Benjamin Rush Milam*, SW Historical Quarterly, v. 28, July 1834 - April 1935, p. 178-81, https://texashistory.unt.edu/ark:/67531/metapth117143/m1/196/, p.193.

[133] Alwyn Barr, *Siege of Bexar*, Handbook of Texas, https://www.tshaonline.org/handbook/entries/bexar-siege-of

[134] Barr, Alwyn, *Texians in Revolt: the Battle for San Antonio, 1835* (Austin: University of Texas Press, 1990), p. 57.

[135] Richardson, Rupert N., *Texas: The Lone Star State* (New York: Prentice-Hall, 1943), p. 100.

[136] Smith, Roy W., *The Quarrel Between Governor Smith and the Council of the Provisional Government of the Republic*, Texas Historical Association Quarterly, v. 5, July 1901 – April 1902, p. 279; Paul D. Lack, *Consultation*, Handbook of Texas, https://www.tshaonline.org/handbook/entries/consultation.

[137] Ibid., p. 100-102.

[138] Paul D. Lack, *Consultation*, Handbook of Texas, https://www.tshaonline.org/handbook/entries/consultation.

[139] Smith, Roy W., *The Quarrel Between Governor Smith and the Council of the Provisional Government of the Republic*, Texas Historical Association Quarterly, v. 5, July 1901 – April 1902, p. 285-7.

[140] Ibid.

[141] Stephen F. Austin to the Provisional Government, Dec. 14, 1835, The Digital Austin Papers, http://digitalaustinpapers.org/document?id=APB5075.

[142] Stephen F. Austin to R.R. Royall, Dec. 25, 1835, The Digital Austin Papers, http://digitalaustinpapers.org/document?id=APB5090.

[143] Huson Hobart, *Goliad Declaration of Independence*, Handbook of Texas, https://www.tshaonline.org/handbook/entries/goliad-declaration-of-independence.

[144] Smith, Roy W., p. 283-92.

[145] Ibid. p. 298.

[146] Ibid., p. 306-7.

[147] Ibid., p. 323-4.

[148] Ibid., p. 327.

[149] Ibid., p. 334-5.

[150] Ibid., p. 337.

[151] Brown, John H., *A History of Texas From 1685 to 1892* (St. Louis: L.E. Daniel, 1892), p. 315.

[152] Cantrell, Gregg, *A Matter of Character: Stephen F. Austin and the Papers Concerning Robertson's Colony in Texas*, The Southwestern Historical Quarterly, v. 104, July 2000 - April 2001, Austin, p. 248-9, https://texashistory.unt.edu/ark:/67531/metapth101221/m1/.

[153] Sterling C. Robertson to Stephen F. Austin, June 7, 1831, The Digital Austin Letters, http://digitalaustinpapers.org/document?id=APB1360.

[154] McLean, Malcolm D., *Papers Concerning Robertson's Colony in Texas*, v. 9, 1982; p. 50, https://texashistory.unt.edu/ark:/67531/metapth91050/m1/, Portal to Texas History.

[155] Cantrell, Gregg, *A Matter of Character: Stephen F. Austin and the Papers Concerning Robertson's Colony in Texas*, The Southwestern Historical Quarterly, v. 104, July 2000 - April 2001, Austin, p. 235.

[156] Stephen F. Austin to Samuel M. Williams, May 31, 1833, The Digital Austin Letters, http://digitalaustinpapers.org/document?id=APB4579.

[157] Oliver Jones to James F. Perry, June 10, 1834, The Digital Austin Letters, http://digitalaustinpapers.org/document?id=APB4648; Cantrell, Gregg, *A Matter of Character: Stephen F. Austin and the Papers Concerning Robertson's Colony in Texas*, The Southwestern Historical Quarterly, v. 104, July 2000 - April 2001, Austin, p. 257.

[158] Cantrell, Gregg, *A Matter of Character: Stephen F. Austin and the Papers Concerning Robertson's Colony in Texas*, The Southwestern Historical Quarterly, v. 104, July 2000 - April 2001, Austin, p. 51.

REFERENCES CHAPTER 7

[1] Harbert Davenport and Craig H. Roell, *Goliad Campaign of 1836*, TSHA Handbook of Texas, https://www.tshaonline.org/handbook/entries/goliad-campaign-of-1836.

[2] Smith, Roy W., *The Quarrel Between Governor Smith and the Council of the Provisional Government of the Republic*, Texas Historical Association Quarterly, v. 5, July 1901 – April 1902, p. 299-301, https://texashistory.unt.edu/ark:/67531/metapth101021/m1/.

[3] Yoakum, Henderson, *History of Texas: From Its First Settlement in 1685 to Its Annexation to the United States in 1846* (Redfield, N.Y.: 1855) v. 2, p. 58, ark:/67531/metapth2386.

[4] Smith, p.312-3.

[5] Yoakum, p. 57.

[6] Smith, p.316-22.

[7] Ibid., p.341.

[8] Ibid., p.342.

[9] Yoakum, p. 58.

[10] Jenkins, John, *James Bowie to Gov. Henry Smith on 2 Feb. 1836*, Papers of the Texas Revolution, v. 4 (Austin: Presidia Press, 1973).

[11] Smith, p.339; Kingston, Mike, and Plocheck, Robert, *Revolution and the Republic*, Texas Almanac, https://texasalmanac.com/topics/history/timeline/revolution-and-republic; Stephen L. Hardin, *Battle of the Alamo*, Texas State Historical Association, https://www.tshaonline.org/handbook/entries/alamo-battle-of.

[12] William R. Williamson, *James Bowie*, Texas State Historical Association, Handbook of Texas, https://www.tshaonline.org/handbook/entries/bowie-james.

[13] Foote, Henry Stuart, *Texas and the Texans*, vol. II (Philadelphia: Thomas, Cowperthwait & Co., 1841), p.222, https://texashistory.unt.edu/ark:/67531/metapth33002/m1.

[14] Brown, John Henry, *History of Texas, from 1685 to 1892*, v. 1., St. Louis, 1893, p.436.

[15] Foote, p.225-6.

[16] Harbert Davenport and Craig H. Roell, *Goliad Campaign of 1836*, TSHA Handbook of Texas, https://www.tshaonline.org/handbook/entries/goliad-campaign-of-1836.

[17] Foote, p.229; Smith, p. 34.

[18] Ibid., p.343.

[19] Newell, C., *History of the Revolution in Texas, Names of the Persons Who Fell at the Alamo*, a.7 (N.Y.: Wiley & Putnam, 1838), p. 211-2, https://texashistory.unt.edu/ark:/67531/metapth6109/m1/223/ the Portal to Texas History.

[20] Santa Anna to McArdle, March 16, 1874, Texas State Library and Archives Commission, https://www.tsl.texas.gov/treasures/republic/alamo/santa-anna-letter-01.html.

[21] Shuffler, R. Henderson, *The Signing of Texas' Declaration of Independence: Myth and Record*, Southwest Historical Quarterly, v. 65, July 1961 to April 1962, Austin, p.327, https://texashistory.unt.edu/ark:/67531/metapth101195/m1/, The Portal to Texas History.

[22] Greer, J.K., *The Committee on the Texas Declaration of Independence*, Southwest Quarterly, v. 30, no. 4, April 1927, p. 246, https://texashistory.unt.edu/ark:/67531/metapth117142/, The Portal to Texas History.

[23] Ibid., p.134-5.

[24] Blount, Lois F., *A Brief Study of Thomas J. Rusk Based on his Letters to his Brother David, 1835-1836*. Southwest Historical Quarterly, v. 34, no. 4, April 1932, p.273, https://texashistory.unt.edu/ark:/67531/metapth101091/, The Portal to Texas History.

[25] Kingston, Mike, and Plocheck, Robert, *Revolution and the Republic*, Texas Almanac, https://texasalmanac.com/topics/history/timeline/revolution-and-republic.

[26] Ibid.

[27] Stein, Bill, *Consider the Lily: The Ungilded History of Colorado County*, part 2: 1828-1836, Nesbitt Memorial Library; 1996, https://www.columbustexaslibrary.net/local-history-and-genealogy-material/history-of-colorado-county/consider-the-lily-the-ungilded-history-of-colorado-county/part-2-1828-1836.

[28] Harbert Davenport and Craig H. Roell, *Goliad Campaign of 1836*, TSHA Handbook of Texas.

[29] Dimmick, Gregg J., *Sea of Mud* (Austin: TSAHA, 2004), p. 340; Harbert Davenport and Craig H. Roell, *Goliad Campaign of 1836*, TSHA Handbook of Texas, https://www.tshaonline.org/handbook/entries/goliad-campaign-of-1836.

[30] Kilmeade, Brian, *Sam Houston and the Alamo Avengers* (Sentinel Press, 2019), p.176.

[31] Blount, p.274.

[32] The Quarterly of the Texas State Historical Association, v. 4, July 1900 - April 1901, Austin, Texas. p.249, https://texashistory.unt.edu/ark:/67531/metapth101018/m1/281/, Portal to Texas History.

[33] Kilmeade, p.177.

[34] Blount, p.274-5.

[35] Kilmeade, p.178.

[36] Ibid., p.180.

[37] Dimmick, p.29.

[38] Henderson, Mary V., *Minor Empresario Contracts For the Colonization of Texas, 1825-1834*. The Southwest Quarterly, v. 31, no. 4, April 1928, p.303-4, https://texashistory.unt.edu/ark:/67531/metapth101088/m1/324/, Portal to Texas History.

[39] Transcript of Petition from Sub-contractors of Galveston Bay and Texas Land Company to Santa Anna, July 25, 1835, https://texashistory.unt.edu/ark:/67531/metapth217708/m1/, Portal to Texas History.

[40] Jackson, Jack, and Almonte, Juan Nepomuceno, *Almonte's Texas: Juan N. Almonte's 1834 Inspection, Secret Report & Role in the 1836 Campaign*, Austin, 2003, p.75, https://texashistory.unt.edu/ark:/67531/metapth296837/m1/313/.

[41] Ibid., p.403.

[42] Yoakum, p.137; Jackson, Jack, and Almonte, Juan Nepomuceno, *Almonte's Texas: Juan N. Almonte's 1834 Inspection, Secret Report & Role in the 1836 Campaign*, Austin, 2003, p. 403, https://texashistory. unt.edu/ark:/67531/metapth296837/m1/313/; Kilmeade, p.190.

[43] Jackson, p.404.

[44] Ibid.

[45] Kennedy, William, Texas: the rise, progress, and prospects of the Republic of Texas, v. 2 (London, 1841), p.221, https://texashistory.unt.edu.ark:/ 67531/metapth2392/m1/227/, Portal to Texas History.

[46] Jackson, p.406.

[47] J.D. Winters, ed., *True veterans of Texas: An authentic account of the Battle of San Jacinto*, (Pearsall Leader Print, 1890), p.2, https://texashistory.unt.edu/ark:/67531/metapth27718/m1/, Portal to Texas History.

[48] Ibid.

[49] Yoakum, p.206-7.

[50] Jackson, p.407, https://texashistory.unt.edu/ark:/67531/metapth296837/m1/313/, Portal to Texas History.

[51] Dimmick, p.27.

[52] J.D. Winters, p. 3.

[53] Dimmick, p.113.

[54] Robert T. Shelby, *Powell, Elizabeth*, Handbook of Texas Online, https://www.tshaonline.org.hanbook. entries/powell-elizabeth; Harbert Davenport and Craig H. Roell, *Goliad Campaign of 1836*, TSHA Handbook of Texas.

[55] Blount, p. 276-77; Henson, Margaret Swett, *Politics and the Treatment of the Mexican Prisoners after the Battle of San Jacinto*, The Southwestern Historical Quarterly v. 94, no. 2, 1990, p.195-6, JSTOR, http://www.jstor.org/stable/30241360.

[56] Dimmick, p.92.

[57] Ibid., p.123-130.

[58] Ibid., p.153.

[59] Henson, p.195.

[60] *Telegraph and Texas Register*, Sept. 6, 1836

[61] Estep, Raymond, *Lorenzo de Zavala and the Texas Revolution*, The Southwest Historical Quarterly, v. 57, no, 3, Austin, 1954, p. 332.

[62] J.D. Winters, p. 3.

[63] Binkley, William C., *The Activities of the Texan Revolutionary Army after San Jacinto*, The Journal of Southern History 6, no. 3, 1940, p. 333, https://doi.org/10.2307/2192140; Henson, p.197; Jackson, p.413.

[64] Henson, p. 198-9.

[65] The Treaty of Velasco (Public), May 14, 1836. The State Library and Archives Commission, https://www.tsl.texas.gov/treasures/republic/velasco-public-1.html.

[66] The Austin Papers, Series III, 1836. Transcript of file of documents concerning Santa Anna and issues relating to Texas's independence, November 25, 1836, https://texashistory.unt.edu/ark:/67531/metapth 217007/, University of North Texas Libraries, The Portal to Texas History.

[67] *Telegraph and Texas Register*, Sept. 20, 1836; Estep, p. 333.

[68] Foote, p.335-9.

[69] *Telegraph and Texas Register*, Sept. 21, 1836.

[70] Foote, p.339-44; Henson, p.201.

[71] Resignation of Lorenzo de Zavala, Texas State Library and Archives Commission, https://www.tsl. texas.gov/treasures/giants/zav-resign.html.

[72] *Telegraph and Texas Register*, Oct. 4, 1836.

[73] *Telegraph and Texas Register*, Sept. 13, 1836.

[74] Binkley, p. 334-41; Henson, p.209-11.

[75] Dimmick, p.295-7.

[76] *Telegraph and Texas Register*, Aug. 23, 1836.

[77] Ibid.

[78] Binkley, p.333.

[79] *Telegraph and Texas Register*, Oct. 4, 1836.

[80] Henson, p.202.

[81] Jackson, p.411-2.

[82] *Telegraph and Texas Register*, Aug. 23, 1836.

[83] Nielsen, George R., *Lydia Ann McHenry and Revolutionary Texas*, *The Southwestern Historical Quarterly* v. 74, no. 3, 1971, p.402, JSTOR, http://www.jstor.org/stable/30236655.

[84] Henson, p.202.

[85] The Austin Papers, Series III, 1836. Transcript of table of contents from Stephen F. Austin's letter and memorandum album, and a letter from Stephen F. Austin to President Andrew Jackson, July 4, 1836, https://texashistory.unt.edu/ark:/67531/metapth217056/, University of North Texas Libraries, The Portal to Texas History,

[86] *Evening Telegraph*, July 14, 1870, Binkley, p.344.

[87] Boethel, Paul, *Colonel Amasa Turner: The Gentlemen from Lavaca and Other Captains at San Jacinto* (Austin: Von Boeckmann-Jones Co., 1963), 168 pp; David G. Burnett 1788-1870, Sons of DeWitt Colony Texas, http://www.sonsofdewittcolony.org/burnetdg.htm.

[88] Binkley, p.331-46; Boethel, 168pp; David G. Burnett 1788-1870, Sons of DeWitt Colony Texas, http://www.sonsofdewittcolony.org/burnetdg.htm.

[89] Binkley, p.331-46.

[90] Henson, p.202-3; Brazosport Archaeological Society, Orozimbo Plantation, http://bmns.org/wp-content/uploads/2021/05/Orozimbo-Plantation-Part1.pdf.

[91] *Telegraph and Texas Register*, Aug. 23, 1836; *Telegraph and Texas Register*, Sept. 13, 1836.

[92] *Kentucky Gazette*, Feb. 16, 1837.

[93] *Telegraph and Texas Register*, Oct. 4, 1835.

[94] Joe E. Erikson, *Collinsworth, James*, Handbook of Texas Online, https://www.tsahonline.org/handbook/entries/collinsorth-james.

[95] Priscilla M. Benham, *Rusk, Thomas Jefferson*, Handbook of Texas Online, https://www.tshaonline.org/handbook/entries/rusk-thomas-jefferson.

[96] Binkley, p.331-46.

[97] Captain Amasa Turner Biography, http://www.sonsofdewittcolony.org/dewitt.htm.

[98] Brown, John Henry, *History of Texas, from 1685 to 1892*, v. 2., St. Louis, 1893; E.W. Winkler, E., *The Bexar and Dawson Prisoners*, The Quarterly of the Texas State Historical Association, v. 13, no. 4, July 1909 - April,1910, p. 292-324.

REFERENCES CHAPTER 8

[1] Comer, Clay, *The Colorado River Raft*, Southwestern Historical Quarterly, v. 52, July 1949-April 1949, Texas State Historical Association, p. 410-426, https://texashistory.unt.edu/ark:/67531/metapth101121/m1.

[2] *Matagorda Bulletin*, April 14, 1838.

[3] *Ibid.*; Laws of the Republic of Texas, v. 2 (Houston,1838) p. 29-33, Portal to Texas History, https://texashistory.unt.edu/ark:/67531/metapth45355/m1/; *Matagorda Bulletin*, Jan. 10, 1838.

[4] *Texas State Gazette*, Dec. 7, 1850.

[5] Laws Passed by the Eighth Congress of the Republic of Texas (Houston, 1844), p.23-28, Portal to Texas History, https://texashistory.unt.edu/ark:/67531/metapth45348/m1/.

[6] *Telegraph and Texas Register* March 6, 1844.

[7] *Colorado Gazette and Advertiser*, Nov. 9, 1839; *Telegraph and Texas Register*, June 22, 1842; *Historic Matagorda County* (Houston: D. Armstrong Co., 1986), v. 1, p. 132.

[8] *Texas Democrat*, March 31, 1849.

[9] Stein, Bill. Consider the Lily: The Ungilded History of Colorado County, Nesbitt Memorial Library Journal, v. 6, no. 3, September 1996, p.125. https://texashistory.unt.edu/ark:/67531/metapth151398/m1/13/

[10] *Texas National Register*, July 10, 1845; *Telegraph and Texas Register*, July 16, 1845; *Tri-Weekly Herald*, May 31, 1884.

[11] *Times Picayune*, July 16, 1845.

[12] Reports of Cases Argued and Decided in the Supreme Court of the State of Texas, v.18 (1856/1857) Ward v. Wheeler, p. 249-267, Hathi Trust Digital Library, https://hdl.handle.net/2027/hvd.32044078585627.

[13] *Texas Democrat*, March 11, 1846; *Hartford Daily Courant*, April 1, 1846.

[14] *Ibid.; Ibid.*

[15] *Daily Picayune*, April 4, 1846.

[16] *Texas Democrat*, March 11, 1846.

[17] *Houston Telegraph*, March 17, 1870.

[18] *Texas Democrat*, March 11, 1846.

[19] *Democratic Telegraph and Texas Register*, Dec. 21, 1846; Stein, Bill, p.125.

[20] *Ibid.*, May 10, 1847.

[21] *Ibid.*, July 5, 1847.

[22] *Ibid.*, Sept. 23, 1847.

[23] *Ibid.*, June 14, 1847.

[24] *Ibid.*, May 4, 1848; *Democratic Telegraph and Texas Register*, June 15, 1848.

[25] Stein, Bill, p.126.

[26] Ibid.

[27] *Democratic Telegraph and Texas Register*, Nov. 15, 1849

[28] *Texas Democrat*, July 7, 1849.

[29] Comer, Clay, p. 410-426.

[30] *Texas Democrat*, July 7, 1849.

[31] *Ibid.*

[32] *Texas State Gazette*, Dec. 28, 1850; *Texas State Gazette*, Jan. 4, 1851.

[33] *Colorado Tribune* April 17, 1848; Feb. 2, 1854 Lease Agreement, Document 418, courtesy Matagorda County Museum; Transcribed Will Record, 1837-1895; Administrators Bonds, Sales, and Letters, 1837-1880 in: Texas, US Wills and Probate Records, 1833-1974.

[34] *Texas Monument*, Dec. 25, 1850.

[35] *Colorado Tribune*, July 12, 1852

[36] *Texas State Gazette*, Jan. 4, 1851.

[37] Annual Report of the Secretary of War, 33rd Congress, 1st Session, Sen. Doc. (1853/54), II, p. 569, Hathi Trust Digital Library, https://hdl.handle.net/2027/hvd.hnwti3; Comer, Clay. p. 410-426.

[38] *Ibid.; Ibid.*

[39] Comer, Clay. p. 410-426.

[40] *Ibid.*

[41] *Texas Monument*, April 5, 1854.

[42] *Augusta Daily Constitution and Republic*, Dec. 29, 1853.

[43] Annual Report of the Secretary of War, 33rd Congress, p. 571.

[44] *Texas Monument*, April 5, 1854; Comer, Clay, p. 410-426.

[45] *Galveston Weekly News*, July 11, 1854.

[46] *Democratic Telegraph and Texas Register*, Nov. 13, 1850.

[47] *Texas Monument*, April 5, 1854.

[48] *Ibid.*, Aug. 29, 1854.

[49] *Matagorda County 1854 Hurricane*, Letter written by F. W. Robbins to his brother, Chester Hamlin in Petersburg, Va., http://www.usgenwebsites.org/TXMatagorda/hurricanes.htm#1854.

[50] *The Standard*, Oct. 21, 1854.

[51] Davant, Robert, and Herskowitz, Mickey, *Mystic Sails, Texas Trails* (Huntsville: Texas Review Press, 2016), p. 73.

[52] *Matagorda County Tribune*, June 26, 1914.

[53] *Tri-Weekly State Times*, Jan. 17, 1854; *Matagorda County Tribune*, June 26, 1914.

REFERENCES CHAPTER 9

[1] *Historic Matagorda County*, Matagorda County Historical Association, (Houston: D. Armstrong Co., 1986), v.1, p. 176.

[2] Douglas, C. L. Cattle Kings of Texas (Dallas: Cecil Baugh, 1939), p. 40.

[3] Davant, Robert, and Herskowitz, Mickey, *Mystic Sails, Texas Trails* (Huntsville: Texas Review Press, 2016), p. 209-1.

[4] Siringo, Charles A., *A Lone Star Cowboy*, Southwest Heritage Series (Sante Fe: Sunstone Press, 2006), p.181-3; Emmett, p. 50-1, 66; Davant, Robert, and Herskowitz, Mickey, p.222.

[5] Emmett, p. 58-9, 79; Thomas, Henry Calhoun, *A Sketch of My Life*, Nesbitt Memorial Library Journal, v. 1, no. 3, February 1990; Columbus, Texas, p.79; Davant, Robert, and Herskowitz, Mickey, p. 58.

[6] Siringo p.30-31; Emmet p. 54-57.

[7] Ibid., p. 22.

[8] Ibid., p. 26.

[9] Ibid., p.12, 40; *Historic Matagorda County*, v.1, p. 181.

[10] Ibid., p.22.

[11] *Phillipsburg Herald*, Feb. 22, 1889; Douglas, C.L., *Cattle Kings of Texas* (Austin: Statehouse Press, 1989), p. 47.

[12] *Savanna Morning News*, April 12, 1884; *Daily Democrat,* April 30, 1883; The Chisolm Trail, Texas Historical Commission, no date.

[13] Jimmy M. Skaggs, *Cattle Trailing*, Handbook of Texas History Online, www.tshaonline.org/handbook /entries/cattle-trailing.

[14] Emmett, p. 165-6.

[15] Ibid., p. 166-7.

[16] Siringo, p. 256-8; Roland, Paul, *Home on the Range: The Impact of the Cattle Trails on Indian Territory*, Armstrong Undergraduate Journal of History, v. 8 no. 2 (Norman: University of Oklahoma, 2018).

[17] Jimmy M. Skaggs, *Cattle Trailing*, Handbook of Texas History Online.

[18] Siringo p. 44-7.

[19] Ibid., p. 259.

[20] Ibid., p. 12-3.

[21] *Phillipsburg Herald*, Feb. 22, 1889; *Historic Matagorda County*, p. 181; The Chisolm Trail, Texas Historical Commission; Jimmy M. Skaggs, *Cattle Trailing*, Handbook of Texas History Online.

[22] Block, W.T., Chapter VII: *A History of Jefferson County, Texas - Early Transportation and Commerce*, http://hans.wtblock.com/wtblockjr/History%20of%20Jefferson%20County/chapter%207.htm.

[23] Siringo, p. 44, 49.

[24] Ibid., p. 40.

[25] Ibid., p.38-9, 41.

[26] Ibid., p. 44, 128.

[27] Ibid., p. 43.

[28] Ibid., p. 245.; H. Allen Anderson, *Amarillo TX,* Handbook of Texas Online, https://www.tshaonline.org/ handbook/entries/amarillo-tx.

[29] Siringo, p. 47.

[30] The Red River War of 1874, Texas Beyond History, https://www.texasbeyondhistory.net/redriver/.

[31] Michael D. Pierce, *Red River War (1874–1875)*, Oklahoma Historical Society, *The Encyclopedia of Oklahoma History and Culture,* https://www.okhistory.org/publications/enc/entry.php?entry=RE010.

[32] Red River Historian, https://www.redriverhistorian.com/red-river-wars.

[33] Map of the Cherokee Strip Indian Territory (Caldwell: Burgess & Walton Pub., 1884), https://kchistory .org/image/map-cherokee-strip-indian-territory; http://www.usgennet.org/usa/ok/state/ outlet/strip.html.

[34] *Fort Worth Daily Gazette*, Sept. 7, 1890.

[35] *Galveston Daily News*, June 22, 1884; Emmet, p.2 20; Roland, Paul, *Home on the Range: The Impact of the Cattle Trails on Indian Territory*.

[36] Ibid., Ibid.

[37] *Daily State Journal*, May 3, 1871.

[38] Emmett, p. 217.

[39] *Galveston Daily News*, Sept. 19, 1888; *Gainesville Daily Hesperian*, Nov. 24, 1888; *Galveston Daily News*, Dec. 24, 1890.

[40] *Fort Worth Daily Gazette*, May 27, 1890; *Galveston Daily News*, Dec. 24, 1890; Emmett, p. 228.

[41] Kansas Historical Society, *Cowtowns*, July 2010, https://www.kshs.org/kansapedia/cowtowns/15598.

[42] Davant, Robert, and Herskowitz, Mickey, p. 225-6.

[43] Siringo, p. 53; Kansas Historical Society, *Cowtowns*, July 2010.

[44] Ibid., p.63-5; Ibid.

[45] Ibid.; Ibid.

[46] Ibid., p. 181-3, 205-8; Kathy Alexander, *Henry Newton Brown, Outlaw Marshal of Kansas*, Legends of America, https://www.legendsofamerica.com/we-henrynewtonbrown/.

[47] *San Antonio Light*, Jan. 7, 1884; Emmet, p. 143, 174.

[48] *Savanna Morning News*, April 12, 1884.

[49] Brown, Woodlief, *A Long Narrow Strip of Land*, (Abilene: H.V. Chapman & Sons, 1989), p. 77.

[50] *Memories of Mary A. Maverick* (Alacrity Press, 2018), p. 106-7.

[51] R. Bruce Winders, *Samuel A. Maverick, Texas Legend, The Alamo*, https://www.thealamo.org/remember/military-occupation/samuel-a-maverick.

[52] *Memories of Mary A. Maverick*, p. 40, 71.

[53] Ibid., p. 26, 38.

[54] Ibid., p. 55.

[55] Ibid., p. 75.

[56] Ibid., p. 99.

[57] *The (Brazoria) Planter*, Sept. 20, 1854; *The (Brazoria) Planter*, Sept. 27, 1854; J. Lancaster, ed., *The Texas Ranger*, Washington, Texas, Oct. 5, 1854, Vol 6-No. 8; Ludlum, David. M., 1963. *Early American Hurricanes: 1492-1870* (Boston: American Meteorology Society, 1963), p.199; Kincheloe, Castleman Green, Unpublished manuscript, no.29, courtesy Brazoria County Historical Museum, p. 3-4; Roth, David, Texas Hurricane History (Camp Springs, Md.: National Weather Service), p. 17; Matagorda County 1854 Hurricane, http://www.usgenwebsites.org/TXMatagorda/ hurricane_1854_1875 _1886.htm.

[58] *Telegraph and Texas Register*, Sept. 28, 1842; E.W. Winkler, ed., *The Bexar and Dawson Prisoners*, The Quarterly of the Texas State Historical Association, v. 13, no. 4, July 1909 - April 1910, p. 292-324, https://texashistory.unt.edu/ark:/67531/metapth101051/m1/342/, Texas State Historical Association, The Portal to Texas History.

[59] *Memories of Mary A. Maverick*, p. 26, 69, 78.

[60] Ibid., p. 92, 96.

[61] Siringo, p. 1-2.

[62] Ibid., p. 10-17.

[63] Emmett, Pg. 55-6. Siringo, p. 19-20.

[64] Siringo, p. 23-9.

[65] Ibid., p. 30-31.

[66] Ibid., p. 33-7; 53.

[67] Ibid., p. 226-7, 274.

[68] Ibid., p. 246-8.

[69] *Daily Tribune*, May 29, 1913.

[70] Siringo, p. 227.

[71] Art Leatherwood, *Brahman Cattle, Handbook of Texas Online,* http://www.tshaonline.org/handbook/online/articles/atb01.

[72] Borden, A.P., *India Cattle In the United States*, American Breeders Magazine, American Breeders Association, v.1, no.1, 1910, p. 91.

[73] Sellon, Debra C., and Long, Maureen T., *Equine Infectious Diseases* (Elsevier, 2014), 650 pp.

[74] Schreiner, Charles III, *The Background and Development of Brahman Cattle in Texas*, The Southwest Historical Quarterly, v.52, July 1949-April 1949, Texas State Historical Association, p. 433, JSTOR, https://www.jstor.org/stable/30237547/; Williams, p. 157.

[75] Borden, p. 93; Schreiner, p. 434.

[76] Ibid., p. 94.

[77] Williams, p. 330.

REFERENCES CHAPTER 10

[1] *Saint Landry Clarion*, Feb. 21, 1891.

[2] *San Antonio Daily Light*, May 14, 1901; *Galveston Daily News*, Dec. 15, 1901; *Texas Rice Book*, Southern Pacific, 1901.

[3] Bennet, Maes W., An Analysis of Beef Cattle Prices (1955), LSU Historical Dissertations and Thesis, https://digitalcommons.lsu.edu/gradschool_disstheses/102; *Early Matagorda County Rice Production*, Earl Eidebach interview, Matagorda County Museum, http://www.usgenwebsites.org/TXMatagorda/rice_eidlebach_interview.htm.

[4] Jim Bradshaw, The Pump That Transformed the Prairie, in *Eunice News*, March 16, 2019, https://www.eunicetoday.com /news/pump-transformed-prairie.

[5] Ibid.

[6] *Saint Landry Clarion*, Feb. 21, 1891.

[7] Hobaugh, William C., Stutzenbaker, Charles D., Flickinger, Edward L., "The Rice Prairies," in: *Habitat Management for Migrating and Wintering Waterfowl in North America* (Lubbock: Texas Tech University Press, 1989), p. 368; Gerry Doyle, *Joseph Eloi Broussard*, https://www.tshaonline.org/handbook/entries/broussard-joseph-eloi.

[8] *Halletsville Herald*, Nov. 2, 1899.; *Weekly Visitor*, Dec. 15, 1899; *Bryan Eagle*, Oct. 25, 1900; *Victoria Daily Advocate*, Oct. 26, 1900; Osborn, William S., *A History of the Cane Belt Branch of the Gulf, Dolorado & Sante Fe Railway Company*, https://texassantafehistory.com/q%20cane%20belt.pdf.

[9] *Matagorda County Tribune*, Dec. 9, 1899; *Weekly Visitor*, Dec. 15, 1899; *Bryan Eagle*, Oct. 25, 1900; *Victoria Daily Advocate*, Oct. 26, 1900; *Liberty Vindicator*, Nov. 9, 1900.

[10] Brown, Woodlief, *A Long Narrow Strip of Land*, (Abilene: H.V. Chapman & Sons, 1989), p. 32.

[11] Allen, Arda T., *Twenty-One Sons for Texas* (San Antonio: Naylor Co.,1959), p. 82.

[12] *Weekly Visitor*, Jan. 26, 1900; *Updated History of the Rice Industry in Matagorda County*, Presented at the Rice Producers Luncheon on September 20, 2012, http://www.usgenwebsites.org/TXMatagorda/rice industry.htm.

[13] *Weekly Visitor*, Jan. 26, 1900; *Moulton Eagle*, June 16, 1900; *Galveston Daily News*, Nov. 26, 1900; *Brownsville Daily Herald*, Oct. 15, 1900.

[14] *The Messenger*, Jan. 18, 1900; *Weekly Visitor*, April 17, 1900; *Liberty Vindicator*, Nov. 9, 1900; *Liberty Vindicator*, Dec. 14, 1900; *Texas Rice Book*, Southern Pacific, 1901; Taylor, Thomas U., *Rice Irrigation in Texas*, Bulletin of the University of Texas, No. 16, (Austin: Von Boeckmann, Schultze & Co, 1902).

[15] Taylor, Thomas U.

[16] Walton & Walton, *Directory of Texas Industries from Official Sources* (Austin: Gamel-Statesman Publishing, 1903), p. 296.

[17] LeTulle, Tommy, *The Memoirs of Tommy Beach LeTulle* (Houston: Kemp & Co., 2019).

[18] Doug Huebner, pers. com., May 21, 2023.

[19] Ibid., April 24, 2023.

[20] *Galveston Daily News*, Oct. 1, 1924; Mary Herring, *Harvest Equipment: A Brief History of the Combine*, in *Farm Equipment Value Guide*, May 24, 2020, https://ironsolutions.com/a-brief-history-of-the-combine/

[21] LeTulle, Tommy.

[22] LeTulle, Tommy; Doug Huebner, pers. com., May 1, 2023.

[23] Ibid.; *A Rich History of Rice Farming in Richvale*, North State Public Radio, https://www.mynspr.org/agriculture/ 2015-10-21/a-rich-history-of-rice-farming-in-richvale.

[24] Doug Huebner, pers. com., May 1, 2023.

[25] Ibid., May 21, 2023.

[26] *Water Supply and Irrigation Papers*, USGS, no. 70 (Washington: Govt. Printing Office, 1902), p. 121-2.

[27] *Galveston Daily News*, Nov. 20, 1896; Bill Blair interview by R.K. Sawyer, May 9, 2009.

[28] *Houston Daily Post*, Nov. 9, 1901; *Houston Daily Post*, Jan 12, 1905; *Matagorda County Tribune*, July 12, 1918.

[29] Matagorda County Deed DR 7-15.

[30] *Houston Daily Post*, Nov. 9, 1901; *Houston Daily Post*, Jan 12, 1905.

[31] Taylor, Thomas U., p. 331; *Manufacturers Record*, v. 40 no. 24, Jan. 1, 1902.

[32] Ibid.; *Water Supply and Irrigation Papers*, USGS, no. 70 (Washington: Govt Printing Office, 1902), p. 121-2; April 4, 1902, Routing Statement, Document 955, courtesy Matagorda County Museum.

[33] Taylor, Thomas U.

[34] *Hallettsville Herald*, July 2, 1903; Taylor, Thomas U.; Memoirs of Tommy LeTulle, p. 36; *Historic Matagorda County*, Matagorda County Historical Association, (Houston: D. Armstrong Co., 1986), v. 1.

[35] *Houston Daily Post*, Jan. 27, 1902; *Austin Daily Statesman*, July 4, 1902; *Houston Post*, Feb. 5, 1912; Matagorda Deed Records, Abstract 28/186,

[36] *Houston Daily Post*, Aug. 8, 1902; *Cuero Daily Record*, Nov. 10, 1902; *Weekly Visitor*, July 17, 1903; *Sunday Gazetteer*, July 19, 1903; *Brownsville Daily Herald*, Oct. 20, 1903; *Houston Daily Post*, Aug. 27, 1904.

[37] *Historic Matagorda County*, v. 1, p. 348; 1910 to 1930 US Federal Census, Ancestry.com.

[38] LeTulle, Tommy, p. 157-8.

[39] Taylor, Thomas U.

[40] *Bellville Times*, Aug. 11, 1910.

[41] *Palacios Beacon*, Oct. 20, 1911; *Houston Post*, April 1, 1912.

[42] *Houston Post*, Sept. 26, 1910; *Houston Post*, Feb. 5, 1912; *Fayette County Record*, April 17, 1912; *Matagorda County Tribune*, Nov. 14, 1914.

[43] Northern Irrigation Co. versus Watkins, Court of Appeals of Texas Filing Feb. 11, 1916, Citation 183, SW 431, Docket no. 7056, https://www.courtlistener.com/opinion/4178919/northern-irr-co-v-watkins/.

[44] *Houston Daily Post*, Jan. 14, 1910; Matagorda County Deed No. 23484.

[45] *Galveston Daily News*, June 12, 1912; *Matagorda County Tribune*, July 23, 1915; Earl Eidebach interview, Matagorda County Museum.

[46] *Houston Daily Post*, Jan. 11, 1902; *Houston Post*, Nov. 8, 1914; *San Antonio Light*, Jan. 6, 1915; *Matagorda County Tribune*, Oct. 20, 1916.

[47] *Bryan Daily Eagle*, March 13, 1912; *Houston Post*, April 1, 1912; *Fayette County Record*, April 17, 1912; Matagorda Canal Co. v. Markham Irr. Co., 154 SW 1176, Texas Court of Appeals, Feb. 26, 1913, *in* Court Listener, https://www.courtlistener.com/opinion/4191883/matagorda-canal-co-v-markham-irr-co.

[48] *Galveston Tribune*, April 9, 1913; Mead, Daniel W., Dam and Water Power Development, Nov., 1917.

[49] *Daily Tribune*, Dec. 22, 1915; Matagorda Tribune, March 23, 1917.

[50] *San Antonio Light*, July 24, 1915; *Galveston Daily News*, Nov. 5, 1915; *Galveston Daily News*, May 4, 1917; Dowell, C.L., *Dams and Reservoirs in Texas*, Texas Water Comm. Bull. 6408 (Austin: Texas Water Comm., 1964).

[51] Second Report of the Board of Water Engineers, v.2 1914/1916 (Austin: Von-Boeckmann-Jones, 1917); *Galveston Daily News*, May 4, 1917.

[52] News Notes From Irrigation Projects of the Country, *The Irrigation Age*, (Chicago: Anderson Pub.,1916), p. 172, https://archive.org/details/irrigationage32federich/page/174/; *Matagorda County Tribune*, Feb. 2, 1917; *Matagorda County Tribune*, Aug. 24, 1917; *Austin Statesman*, Dec. 5, 1918; *Galveston Daily News*, Dec. 12, 1918.

[53] Untitled newspaper clipping, July 6, 1918; *Daily Tribune*, July 9, 1918; *Shiner Gazette*, July 25, 1918.

[54] *Austin Statesman*, Dec. 5, 1918; *Galveston Daily News*, Dec. 12, 1918.

[55] *Matagorda County Tribune*, Jan. 10, 1919.

[56] *Daily Tribune*, May 30, 1919; Miscellaneous Matagorda County Deeds, 1919-1921.

[57] Baker, O.E., and Genung, A. B., A Graphic Summary of Farm Crops (Washington: US Dept. of Agriculture, 1938).

[58] Matagorda County Deed DR 65-86, no. 86109.

[59] *Matagorda County Tribune*, June 12, 1914; *Houston Post*, May 1, 1908.

[60] *Daily Tribune*, May 10, 1913; *Matagorda County Tribune*, Dec. 5, 1913; *Atlanta Constitution*, Dec. 7, 1913; *Galveston Daily News*, Dec. 10, 1913.

[61] *Galveston Daily News*, Dec. 10, 1913; *Galveston Daily News*, Dec. 12, 1913; *Matagorda County Tribune*, Dec. 19, 1913.

[62] Ibid.

[63] Ibid.; *Galveston Daily News*, Dec. 13, 1913.

[64] Ibid.; Ibid., Dec. 12, 1913.

[65] *Weimer Mercury*, May 28, 1915. *San Antonio Express*, Nov. 30, 1913.

[66] *Galveston Daily News*, Nov.19, 1913.

[67] *Matagorda County Tribune*, June 9, 1916.

[68] Ibid., Jan. 3, 1919.

[69] *Austin Statesman*, May 16, 1922.

[70] *Daily Tribune*, May 17, 1922.

[71] Ibid., May 15, 1922, Ibid., May17, 1922

[72] *San Antonio Express*, May 25, 1922; *Victoria Advocate*, May 29, 1922.

[73] *Galveston Daily News*, Sept. 8, 1922.

[74] *Matagorda County Tribune*, Nov. 30, 1923; *Galveston Daily News*, July 16, 1928.

75 *Daily Tribune*, May 27, 1922.

76 *Matagorda County Tribune*, Sept. 10, 1926; *Matagorda County Tribune*, Sept. 17, 1926.

77 Ibid., Aug. 14, 1925; *Matagorda County Tribune*, Aug. 21, 1925.

78 *Matagorda County Tribune*, Ibid., Sept. 18, 1925.

79 Ibid., Oct. 2, 1925.

80 Ibid., Feb. 5, 1926.

81 *Eagle Lake Headlight*, May 9, 1925; *Matagorda County Tribune*, Sept. 17, 1926.

82 *Matagorda County Tribune*, Sept. 10, 1926.

83 *Matagorda Daily Tribune*, March 4, 1927.

84 *Galveston Daily News*, Oct. 20, 1927.

85 Ibid., July 16, 1928; Memoirs of Tommy LeTulle, p. 33-4.

86 Ibid.; *Taylor Daily Press*, July 16, 1928; Earl Eidebach interview, Matagorda County Museum.

87 *Taylor Daily Press*, July 16, 1928; *Brownwood Bulletin*, July 18, 1928; *Galveston Daily News*, July 20, 1928.

88 *Corsicana Daily Sun*, July 21, 1928; *Galveston Daily News*, July 21, 1928; *Weimer Mercury*, Aug. 7, 1928; *Palacios Beacon*, Aug. 9, 1928.

89 *Matagorda Daily Tribune*, May 6, 1927.

90 *Victoria Advocate*, June 3, 1929.

91 *Historic Matagorda County*, v. 1, p.139, 189, 224.

92 *Daily Tribune*, Fed. 23, 1923.

93 *Matagorda Daily Tribune*, Feb. 6, 1925; *Matagorda County Tribune*, Oct. 9, 1925.

94 Ibid., Jan. 27, 1927; *Matagorda Daily Tribune*, March 4, 1927; DR 8-457.

95 *Palacios Beacon*, Nov. 26, 1931; *Morning Avalanche*, Jan. 3, 1940.

96 *Abilene Morning News*, Aug. 3, 1927; *Wichita Daily Times*, Oct. 16, 1927.

97 *San Antonio Express*, Nov. 30, 1913.

98 *Brownwood Bulletin*, Aug. 24, 1927; *Matagorda County* Tribune, Sept. 2, 1927; *Matagorda County* Tribune, Sept. 23, 1927.

99 *Abilene Morning News*, Feb. 15, 1927; *Abilene Morning News*, March 23, 1932.

100 *Shiner Gazette*, July 12, 1934.

101 *Abilene Daily Reporter*, Aug. 8, 1934.

102 *Brownwood Bulletin*, Aug. 8, 1934; Earl Eidebach interview, Matagorda County Museum.

103 *Abilene Daily Reporter*, Feb. 15, 1928; *Abilene Morning News*, Sept. 25, 1928; *Lampasas Daily Leader*, Oct. 16, 1931; Dowell, C.L., *Dams and Reservoirs in Texas*, Texas Water Comm. Bull. 6408 (Austin: Texas Water Comm., 1964).

104 *Abilene Morning News*, Feb. 15, 1927; *Burnet Bulletin*, Jan. 8, 1931; *Abilene Morning News*, Feb. 5, 1931; *San Antonio Express*, April 23, 1932; *Wichita Daily Times*, April 23, 1932; *Valley Morning Star*, May 20, 1932; *San Antonio Express*, July 6, 1934.

105 Journal of the House of Representatives of the Third and Fourth Called Sessions of the Forty-Third Legislature of the State of Texas, 1934; Austin, Texas, p. 302, https://texashistory.unt.edu/ark:/67531/ metapth193850/m1/808/; *Lampasas Leader*, Feb. 16, 1934; *Llano News*, Oct. 22, 1987; Adams, John A. Jr, *Damming the Colorado* (College Station: A&M Univ. Press, 1990), p. 20.

106 *Burnet Bulletin*, July 5, 1934; *Llano News*, Sept. 13, 1934; Henry Gammel, *The Laws of Texas*, Supplemental Volume to the Original Ten Volumes 1822-1897 (Austin: Gammels Book Store, 1934), General and Special Laws passed by the 44th Legislature, p. 283; *Bastrop Advertiser*, Feb. 14, 1935; *Shamrock Texan*, Aug. 10, 1935.

107 Texas Attorney General Opinion, 0-2313, June 15, 1940; Banks, Jimmy, and Babcock, John E., *Corralling the Colorado* (Austin: Eakin Press, 1988), p. 102-3.

108 Banks and Babcock, p. 186.

109 TPW Magazine, v. 72 no. 6, July 2014, p. 44-7; Mathew Tresaugue, Drought Threatens Texas Rice Farmers' Future, *Albuquerque Journal*, April 7, 2014, https://www.abqjournal.com/380240/drought-threatens-texas-rice-farmers-futures.html; Logan Hawkes, LCRA Seeks Approval to Cut Irrigation Water for Fourth Straight Year, *Farm Progress*, Nov. 20, 2014. https://mobile.farmprogress.com/water-shortage/lcra-seeks-approval-cut-irrigation-water-fourth-straight-year; TPW Magazine, v. 72 no. 6, July 2014, p. 44-7.

110 Matagorda County Statistics, USDA-NASS Southern Plains Div., https://www.nass.usda.gov/Statistics_by_State /Texas/Publications/County_Estimates/ce_pdf/ce_321.pdf.

Index

BOOKS BY R.K. SAWYER

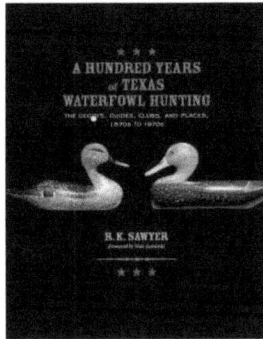

A Hundred Years of Texas Waterfowl Hunting:
The Decoys, Guides, Clubs, and Places, 1870s to 1970s

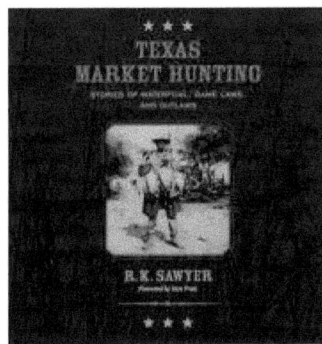

Texas Market Hunting:
Stories of Waterfowl, Game Laws, and Outlaws

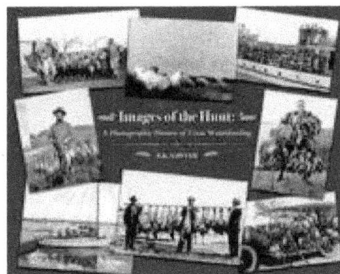

Images of the Hunt:
A Photographic History of Texas

Copies are available from https://robertksawyer.com

OTHER BOOKS AVAILABLE FROM NUECES PRESS

1919 – The Storm

Corpus Christi – A History

A Soldier's Life

Great Tales from the History of South Texas

Recollections of Other Days

Perilous Trails of Texas

Columns   2009 – 2011

Columns 2 2012 – 2013

Columns 3 2014 – 2015

Columns 4 2016 – 2018

Streets of Corpus Christi Texas

Thomas Noakes Diary of War & Drought

100 Tales of Old Texas

Water Woes

Zachary Taylor's Army in Texas

The Tarpon Club of Texas

Copies and more information are available from

www.nuecespress.com

www.ingramcontent.com/pod-product-compliance
Lightning Source LLC
Chambersburg PA
CBHW061231150426
42812CB00054BA/2561